Penguin Modern Economics

Regional Analysis

Penguin Modern Economics Readings

General Editor
B. J. McCormick

Advisory Board
K. J. W. Alexander
R. W. Clower
J. Spraos
H. Townsend

Regional Analysis

Selected Readings

Edited by L. Needleman

Penguin Books

Penguin Books Ltd, Harmondsworth,
Middlesex, England
Penguin Books Inc., 7110 Ambassador Court,
Baltimore, Maryland 21207, U.S.A.
Penguin Books Australia Ltd, Ringwood,
Victoria, Australia

First published 1968
This selection © L. Needleman, 1968
Introduction and notes © L. Needleman, 1968

Printed in the United States of America
Set in Monotype Times

Contents

Part Five Location Theory

Part Six Some Statistical Techniques

Introduction

Regional analysis as a specialist study has existed for barely twenty years. But in that period there has been such a proliferation of articles of such diversity of subject matter and treatment that survey articles and books of readings have become not only possible but necessary, if students are to find their way through the dense, inter-disciplinary thicket of the subject. The major textbook in the field, *Methods of regional analysis*, by the doyen of regional scientists, Walter Isard, contains about one thousand bibliographical references, and that list was compiled as long ago as 1960. By now, the bibliography of relevant works must have increased by many hundreds of items, even allowing for a merciful obsolescence among earlier studies. The fecundity and heterogeneity of the subject has always encouraged the production of survey articles, and many of the papers reprinted in this anthology are of this type. More recently, collections of readings have begun to be published, the most comprehensive being *Regional development and planning: a reader* edited by John Friedmann and William Alonso. The present selection differs from those previously published in that it is concerned specifically with the economic aspects of regional science and especially with the techniques of regional economic analysis. Apart from the broad survey of the whole of the subject given in the first article, the papers in this selection present some of the concepts and tools of regional analysis, describe regional data and outline, and occasionally test, regional economic models of trade and development.

The first article in this anthology, 'Regional economics: a survey', by John Meyer, describes the development and present status of regional economics, introduces and assesses most of the major pieces of research in the field, and finally suggests lines along which the subject might develop. Professor Meyer's survey is the standard introduction to the subject and it is unnecessary to attempt to cover the same ground in an introduction to this book of readings. But like most of the other articles in this selection, Meyer's article is largely concerned with regional analysis rather

7

than with regional economic policy and there may be some value in having a brief discussion here of the relationship between the two.

Almost all countries, even very small ones like Belgium, have a regional problem, in the sense that there are great and lasting differences in prosperity between different areas within each country. The problem is not a new one, but it is only in the last thirty years or so that national governments have become willing, and have considered themselves able, to influence the distribution of regional prosperity, and it is only since 1945 that integrated regional policies have been developed and resulted in legislation.[1]

There are many indices that can be used to measure regional prosperity. An obvious one is income per head of the population, and this tends to be the favoured measure of regional well-being in studies of regional differences within the United States and within many of the underdeveloped countries also. In more homogeneous, industrialized countries such as Britain and Holland where inter-regional differences in real income per head are small by the standards of, say Brazil or other developing countries,[2] the emphasis is more on differences in unemployment between regions. The percentage of unemployment in the labour force measures only part of the potential output forgone. A supplementary measure, which may be even more important in some instances is the activity-rate, that is, the percentage of the population of working age who are actually in the labour force. Two further measures that are sometimes used are the rate of growth of income per head and the rate of net emigration of population out of the region.

Given the existence of inter-regional differences in prosperity, the broad policy problems for the government are, first, whether or not to intervene in an attempt to reduce these differences, and second, if intervention is considered appropriate, how to intervene most effectively? In principle, the government could decide

1. See *Area redevelopment policies in Britain and the countries of the common market*, Area Redevelopment Administration, U.S. Department of Commerce, January 1965, for accounts of the development of regional policy in Western Europe.

2. See J. G. Williamson, 'Regional inequality and the process of national development: a description of the patterns', Table 1, reprinted in this volume, p. 112.

these questions using the standard cost–benefit framework[3] by first deciding what its objectives were and the relative weights it attached to each of its objectives. The function so obtained is the government's objective function. The government could then attempt to forecast how its objectives would be affected in the absence of government intervention, and also what would be the effect of specific intervention policies. The government would choose the policy (which might be non-intervention) which resulted in the highest value of the government's objective function.

In order to have any idea at all about what would happen in the absence of, or as a result of, government intervention, it is necessary to have theories of regional development and trade, and, if detailed forecasts are to be made, models of development, specified in detail and using accurate regional statistics will be required. Unfortunately, we rarely know enough about the workings of regional economies for us to be able to construct detailed models that have any chance of giving good predictions – thus our ignorance of the size and composition of inter-regional trade is profound. But we are sometimes in a position to fill the empty economic boxes of less ambitious, more aggregative models and a large part of the literature of regional economics is concerned with attempts to construct fairly simple models of this sort. Examples of such work can be found in the articles by Borts and Stein, by Engerman and by Chenery reprinted in this volume.

Critics of government intervention in regional matters sometimes argue that such intervention is unnecessary, since free market forces are capable of restoring equilibrium on their own and also that intervention is likely to be harmful, since giving aid to depressed regions and restraining growth in prosperous regions is to reward failure and to penalize success. In answer to these criticisms, it may be said, to take the second point first, that whether helping depressed regions rewards failure or not depends on the sort of help given. Encouraging expanding firms located in

3. See O. Eckstein, 'A survey of the theory of public expenditure criteria', in J. M. Buchanan (ed.), *Public finances: needs, sources and utilization*, Princeton University Press, 1961; O. Eckstein, 'Benefit–cost analysis and regional development', in W. Isard and J. H. Cumberland (eds.), *Regional economic planning*, Organization for European Economic Co-operation, 1960, and A. R. Prest, and R. Turvey, 'Cost–benefit analysis: a survey', *Economic Journal*, vol. 75, 1965, pp. 683–735.

prosperous areas to set up branches in depressed areas by offering them substantial cash grants, is neither to reward failure nor to discourage enterprise. As for the belief that market forces if left alone will restore equilibrium, for some countries at least the evidence suggests that as far as regional unemployment is concerned, either there is no net movement towards equilibrium or that such movement is very slow indeed. Inter-regional differences in unemployment tend to persist for long periods even when, as in the United Kingdom, the government operate policies specifically designed to reduce those differences.[4]

Even if it were the case that free market forces were rapidly effective in achieving equilibrium in, say, regional labour markets, the regional and national governments may prefer other situations to the equilibrium state. The free market equilibrium will be affected by the existing distribution of income between regions, which the national government may wish to alter, and, more important, it will reflect private costs and benefits and not social costs and benefits.[5]

The net private benefit to an employer in a depressed region from employing an extra man may be taken to be the increase in net profit as a result of having one extra worker. This amount might be quite small, of the order of a few hundred pounds a year at most. But the net social benefit to the community of obtaining employment for a hitherto unemployed man is likely to be much greater than this, as it will include, roughly, not only the increase in the profit of the employer but also the wage of the newly employed man less, of course, any reductions in the profits or wages of the rest of the community. In this case, the net social benefit may easily be several hundreds pounds in excess of the net private benefit.

The high unemployment and low activity rates that characterize the regions that remain depressed are evidence of reserves of

4. See L. Needleman, and B. Scott, 'Regional problems and location of industry policy in Britain', *Urban studies*, vol. 1, 1964, p. 163.

5. The private benefits of an activity are the benefits accruing to the person or firm responsible for that activity: the social benefits are the benefits to the whole of the community arising from the activity. Private and social costs are defined in a similar way. Private costs and benefits are usually very much easier to identify, measure, and understand, than social costs and benefits and, as a consequence, are frequently appealed to in deciding policy.

unused labour resources, which, if employed could raise national output substantially. In the United Kingdom it has been suggested that if the unemployment and activity rates in the less prosperous regions could be brought into line with those in the more prosperous south of the country, the national labour force might be increased by perhaps 2 or 3 per cent.[6] Advocates of public intervention argue that the value of the increased output so obtained would far outweigh the costs of intervention. Such an argument may satisfy a national government, one of whose objectives it is to increase national output per head. But it may be less appealing to an inhabitant of a prosperous region who accepts that national income per head is increased, but who believes that there is a redistribution of income from the prosperous to the less prosperous regions. He may point out that he pays part of the cost of governmental intervention in higher taxation, but that the benefit from increasing employment in the depressed region accrues very largely to the inhabitants of that region. In fact, however, for every person that remains unemployed in the country the national revenue loses not only the unemployment benefit and other public relief paid to the unemployed man, but also the taxes that that man would have paid if he were employed. Ignoring non-fiscal effects, employed taxpayers, even those in prosperous regions, will obtain a net benefit from government intervention as long as the costs of such intervention to reduce unemployment are less than the loss in revenue through letting that unemployment remain. For Britain, in the early 1960s this loss in revenue was estimated to be of the order of £290 per man for each year the man remained unemployed. If as a result of government intervention, unemployment were reduced even for only five years, then in these circumstances intervention would reduce the national tax bill as long as the costs of such a once-for-all intervention were less than the present value of £290 a year for five years discounted at, say, 6 per cent interest, that is, about £1,220.[7]

Another argument for public intervention, which may appear even more cogent to an elected government, is that electors in

6. National Economic Development Council, *Conditions favourable to faster growth*, H.M.S.O., 1963, pp. 15–17.

7. See L. Needleman, 'What are we to do about the regional problem?', *Lloyds Bank Review*, January 1965, pp. 54–5.

depressed regions where unemployment is high and mounting tend to vote for opposition party candidates. The government may well be encouraged to spend considerable sums of money in promoting increased employment when to do so produces such net social benefits to the community and such net private benefits to the government.

Given that the government feel justified in intervening, the question then arises – how can the government intervene most effectively? The answer depends partly on what the government want to achieve in their regional policy and partly on the nature of the regional problem in each particular case. Clearly if the government's major objective in regional policy is to reduce unemployment in less prosperous regions, the appropriate combination of measures may well be different from that which will most effectively raise the average income level in those regions. Indeed in some circumstances, measures which raise the average income in a region could lead to increases in unemployment.[8]

Again, for any given set of regional policy objectives, the measures which will be most effective in helping impoverished regions are likely to be very different in countries like those in Western Europe, where the depressed regions have already been industrialized, from those in countries where the poor regions are still predominantly agricultural, as is the case in most underdeveloped countries. In western countries, the existence of an industrial infra-structure and a skilled labour force often make it possible to restore prosperity by relatively minor adjustments to regional demand and to the regional structure of industry. But in countries

8. Assume that the government attempt to raise average incomes in a region by both increasing public investment and by raising the legal minimum wage rates in that region. The net effect could be that though the real output of the region rises, thus providing an increase in income per head, employment may fall as capital is substituted for the now more expensive labour. In this case the average level of income would be higher than before but it would be more unequally distributed between the employed and the unemployed. Whether this result would actually happen in any particular circumstances would depend on the precise nature of a large number of behavioural relationships within the economy, including the demand and supply functions for labour and capital within the region and the demand and supply functions for regional imports and exports. For a discussion of some of the issues raised above, see the paper by Engerman in this volume, pp. 277–334.

where the less prosperous regions have never been industrialized, it may not be possible to raise average incomes to anywhere near the level of the industrial regions without a massive increase in investment in the region, and often also, a programme for transferring labour from agriculture to industry.[9]

Where the regional problem is largely a matter of an uneven dispersion of unemployment between regions, there are broadly two types of policy that can be followed: either work opportunities can be expanded in the depressed areas or the workers in the depressed areas can be encouraged to move to the prosperous areas. The first policy will usually though not always involve persuading firms outside the impoverished region to move to, or set up branches within, the region. Another possibility is to make industrial conditions within the region so favourable by tax incentives or by a regional devaluation[10] that the existing firms within the region expand so as to absorb all the surplus labour. The second policy relies unequivocally on encouraging more labour mobility.

Which policy is emphasized in the government's overall strategy for dealing with regional unemployment depends very much on the traditions, institutions and economic circumstances of the country concerned. Thus, in some countries, the United States for example, there is a tradition of high labour mobility between different areas, whereas in Britain people change their job and their house less frequently and more reluctantly. It seems likely that it would be less difficult to run a policy of encouraging emigration out of depressed areas in the United States than in Britain. There may be powerful reasons other than conservatism for the reluctance of people in some countries to move to another region. To do so may involve having to learn an unfamiliar language and immersion, if not absorption, in an alien culture. Even in more homogeneous countries, such as Britain, there may be institutional

9. For a discussion of some of the problems involved in attempting to raise the rate of growth of output in a region that has never been industrialized, see the article by Chenery reprinted in this volume, pp. 198–233.

10. For a discussion of some of the regional tax incentives and their effects in the United Kingdom, see T. Wilson, *Policies for regional development*, Oliver and Boyd, 1964; and, A. J. Brown, H. Lind, and J. Bowers, 'The "Green Paper" on the development areas', *National Institute Economic Review*, May 1967, pp. 26–33.

barriers to movement. Thus, many of the unemployed in the depressed areas of Britain enjoy subsidized housing which they would almost certainly not obtain if they moved to the areas of full employment.

Where the slump is so deep that even the more prosperous regions have substantial unemployment a policy of encouraging labour mobility is unlikely to be effective. For an unemployed man in a depressed area to move at all he must have reasonable hopes of finding a job. If the chances of gaining employment by moving, though greater than if there were no move, are still small, then the worker will often prefer to remain where he is and be un-employed among friends rather than among strangers.

This suggests that policies which rely on persuading labour to move in order to cure regional inequalities in unemployment are unlikely to work in times of national depression. At such times, attempts to coax firms to move are also likely to be ineffective (see page 16 below). A prerequisite for achieving a substantially more even distribution of unemployment between regions seems to be that there should be at least one region in which firms are expand-ing and in which there is near full employment. But even where encouraging labour mobility is a feasible policy, it will frequently be a less effective one than attempting to persuade firms to move. The people who migrate most readily in search of work are the young and the enterprising, the adaptable and the skilled, and it is not among these but among the older workers that persistent un-employment tends to be concentrated. Those who are most likely to take advantage of subsidies to move are likely to be those least in need of such assistance.

Further, emigration from the more prosperous to the less pros-perous regions reduces aggregate demand within the depressed region and tends to increase it within the prosperous region. The unemployed in the depressed area spend even though they are un-employed, so that when they emigrate, aggregate demand within the region falls by an amount equal to the expenditure of the emi-grants plus any multiplier effects generated. The higher the level of public assistance to the unemployed, the greater the depressing effect of emigration. On the other hand, the immigration of previ-ously unemployed workers into the fully employed prosperous areas will, in the first few years at least, add to the inflationary pressure of such regions rather than reduce it. The output of the newly employed immigrant increases aggregate supply, but the consumption of the immigrant and his family, and much more important, the social and industrial investment done by him or on his behalf in the first few years after the move adds much more to aggregate demand and so produces a net effect that is inflationary for a number of years.[11] The more that social capital, such as housing, schools, and hospitals is provided by the public authorities, other things being equal, the greater will be the inflationary effect of immigration into a region at full employment.

As against this, encouraging firms, or branches of firms, to settle in areas of high unemployment increases demand within such areas and helps to reduce the increase in demand in the prosperous areas. Such 'encouragement' can take two forms: the pull of bribes to firms who move to less prosperous regions and the push of preventing firms from expanding at the existing sites within the prosperous regions. In most fields of industrial policy, governments prefer measures which rely on rewards rather than on punishments to bring private costs and benefits in line with social costs and benefits and location of industry policy is no exception. Industrialists whose activities are restricted coalesce into vocal and well-organized pressure groups, whereas policies which reward industrialists from general taxation seldom provoke any corresponding protest from the mute and scattered ranks of the taxpayers.

The arguments against the 'push' policy is that if firms are not allowed to expand where they want to expand, at their existing sites or elsewhere within the prosperous region, then rather than setting up branches in the less prosperous region, they may expand by going abroad or they may decide not to expand at all. These are, of course, possibilities, but whether a government is wise to embark on a 'push' policy or not depends on the *degree* to which firms respond to the push by moving to the areas of high unemployment. As very little research appears to have been done on the reactions of firms to restrictive measures of this sort it is difficult to say how successful a 'push' policy on its own is likely to be. It is obvious, however, that in a free enterprise economy no government can channel industry from the prosperous areas into

11. See E. J. Misham, and L. Needleman, 'Immigration, excess aggregate demand and the balance of payments', *Economica*, vol. 33, 1966, especially Table 2, pp. 144 and 145–6.

the depressed areas unless the firms in the prosperous areas wish to expand in the first place.

Against the 'pull' policy, it is argued that even if firms could be persuaded to move to areas which are not their first choice, the average costs of production in the new location would be very much higher than in the old. The advocates of the 'pull' policy counter by, first, querying the truth of this contention and secondly, by arguing that even if the contention were true it would not necessarily be a valid objection to the 'pull' policy.

Clearly some types of industry are tied to their particular location by the nature of their operations, and it would be expensive, and foolish, for any government to attempt to persuade industries of this sort to move to areas of high unemployment. But it appears that the costs of production of a substantial proportion of manufacturing and service industries are, within wide limits, not sensitive to the precise choice of location,[12] and 'foot-loose' industries of this sort might be more amenable to government inducements.

But even if it were true that a policy of regional dispersion of industry did result in higher average costs of production than a policy of non-intervention this is not a conclusive objection to the 'pull' policy. Minimizing average costs of production, *per se* is not the only objective of policy and it may conflict with other objectives, such as increasing the national standard of living. It may well be that total national output will be higher when the formerly unemployed workers in the depressed regions are employed by migrating firms than when they remain unemployed under the non-interference policy. If this is the case, then average real income per head will be greater when the 'pull' policy is implemented than when there is no governmental interference and this may be considered to outweigh the disadvantage of higher unit costs at the higher output.

References

ISARD, W., *et al.* (1960) *Methods of regional analysis: an introduction to regional science*, M.I.T. Press.

FRIEDMANN, J., and ALONSO, W. (eds.) (1964) *Regional development and planning: a reader*, M.I.T. Press.

12. See, for example, W. F. Luttrell, *Factory location and industrial movement*, National Institute of Economic and Social Research, 1962, vol. 1, pp. 175–9 and 319–22.

Part One Introductory Surveys

Of the three surveys in this section, the first, by Meyer is a guide, probably *the* guide, to regional economics as a whole. The topics covered by the remaining two papers, regional accounts and regional input–output analysis, have had much written about them, most of it complex and technical. The surveys by Leven and Tiebout are clear, brief, and controversial. Leven emphasizes the conceptual issues in regional accounts. A complementary survey, more concerned with techniques of regional accounting is R. Stone, 'Social accounts at the regional level: a survey', reprinted in R. Stone, *Mathematics in the social sciences and other essays*, Chapman and Hall, 1966, pp. 118–51.

Tiebout's appraisal of regional input–output models was written in the infancy of the subject it examines. His warnings of the difficulties involved in constructing and interpreting regional input–output tables have not been challenged, but neither have they prevented a proliferation of such studies since he wrote.

1 J. R. Meyer

Regional Economics: A Survey

J. R. Meyer, 'Regional economics: a survey', *American Economic Review*, vol. 53 (1963), pp. 19–54.

The creation of a new area of specialization is always a matter of interest in any academic field and the phenomenal rise of what has come to be known as 'regional analysis' in economics is no exception.

The manifestations of this emergence are many. Within the last decade both a new professional association and a journal dealing with problems of regional development have come into being. This new journal, published by the Regional Science Association, has moreover all the hallmarks of academic success; it has consistently grown in size, scope, number of contributors, and even in quality of typography. Also within the last decade, a fully-fledged and highly successful research institution, Resources for the Future, has been created which is greatly concerned with problems that conventionally are described as falling within the province of the new field. This organization reported in 1957 [102], furthermore, that no less than about 140 U.S. universities had serious research or education programs underway in regional studies and there are substantial reasons for believing that the extent of these activities has probably enlarged rather than contracted since that time. Similarly, conferences, almost innumerable, have been organized to discuss, evaluate, and promote regional science studies both here and abroad. Indeed, perhaps one of the most impressive testimonials to the appeal of the new field is that it has enlisted the official or semi-official interest of such diverse governments, among others, as those of Italy, France, Spain, Greece, Argentina, Turkey, Venezuela, India, Colombia, and Pakistan.

Economists and economics have long had, of course, special surges of interest or, less euphemistically, fads and fashions in their studies and research. Furthermore, if we construe economics as an applied science and argue, at least within limits, that most of the great steps forward in economic understanding and theory have come in response to specific policy challenges, this tendency toward temporarily pursuing certain lines of research with seemingly exaggerated zeal is not necessarily unfortunate. It may be, rather, the very substance and requisite accompaniment of intellectual progress in a field where progress often is concerned with generating principles or concepts for the understanding and solution of practical problems. Understanding such research and its conceptual results or creations normally requires, in turn, an appreciation of the policy problems that have provided the stimuli.

It would be wrong, though, to infer that identification of these stimuli would fully explain the rise and recent popularity of regional economics. Nor would these alone provide an adequate basis for understanding recent developments in the field. Regional economics has very obvious and important intellectual forebears, and indeed it seems highly probable that certain theoretical developments in general economics, particularly having to do with general interdependence systems provided the conceptual basis without which regional economics could not have flourished. One very straightforward explanation of the surge in regional economics, in fact, is to say that it resulted from a fortuitous blending of many economists' desires to apply certain recently honed conceptual tools and policy makers' desires to seek more adequate and analytical answers to complex problems related to regional and urban growth.

Sensible discussion of either the stimuli or the conceptual precursors of regional economics requires, moreover, a definition of just exactly what constitutes this new field. Special semantic problems, unique to the new field, are also quickly encountered, not the least of which is simply defining a region. The definitional problems will be considered, therefore, in section I. As will become clear there, definitions of, and in regional economics are not always easily come by, a difficulty probably shared in common with almost all new fields of specialization. Following these definitional exercises, a more thorough consideration of the policy-problem stimuli will be undertaken in section II. Then, in section

III, the theoretical foundations of regional economics, as borrowed from general economics, will be treated. This will be followed in section IV by a discussion of the different approaches to regional economics that have emerged in actual regional studies. Finally, section V attempts to summarize and provide some evaluation of all that precedes.

I. Definitional Problems

An almost unavoidable temptation when first coming to grips with the problem of defining regional economics is to assert that it is simply *all* of economics scaled to whatever level is required to adequately measure or forecast economic activity for a specific geographic area. There would be considerable truth moreover in such a characterization, for regional economics has been, if anything, ambitious in its selection of objectives. Also implicit in such a definition is a strong urge to define regional economics in terms of particular study and policy objectives, thus emphasizing its pragmatic origins.

Difficulty in giving regional economics a distinct character in terms of conventional economic disciplines also partially explains and is explained by the tendency to place regional economic studies in a broader, interdisciplinary framework. Almost from the beginning, the convention, at least in formal discourse, has been to speak of 'regional analysis' and 'regional science' rather than 'regional economics'. Included and welcomed have been such diverse fields as sociology, demography, geography, and history. Indeed, at times, *the* distinguishing characteristic of regional analysis has almost seemed to be its interdisciplinary aspect. This diversity combined with definitional uncertainty was very well expressed by Harvey Perloff in the introduction to the Resources of the Future survey already cited [102, p. v]:

No fully satisfactory way of classifying regional studies was found – not unexpectedly. Regional studies tend to deal with many features and often involve the use of several academic disciplines. Thus, no general system of classification can be expected to provide self-contained categories; there is inevitable spill-over. The subject classification employed in this report sets up categories whose cores, if not boundaries, are identifiable and whose titles are widely used, with popular and technical meanings that are not too far apart. The topical categories employed are: (1) Physical elements and natural resources; (2) Population and human ecology; (3) Regional economic development; (4) Metropolitan studies and metropolitan planning, and (5) Regional history, literature, and socio-cultural elements. Two other categories were found necessary: (6) Methods and techniques of regional analysis, and (7) Comprehensive regional studies.

A somewhat narrower (but still staggeringly broad!) definition of regional analysis specifically in terms of its objectives has been provided by Walter Isard [70, p. 413]:[1]

An analyst is perplexed with many problems when he looks at a region. One problem may be to identify specific industries which can individually or in groups operate efficiently and with profit in the region. Another related problem may be to improve the welfare of the people of the region, that is, to raise *per capita* incomes and perhaps achieve a more equitable distribution of income; the auxiliary problem of measurement of income and of the performance of a society is also present. Still another problem may be to avoid an industrial mix which is too sensitive to the ups and downs of national and world business, and which is composed too heavily of old, slow-growing, or declining industries; this is the problem of diversification. Finally, a fourth problem which can be mentioned is to plan industrial development for a region, as part of a system of regions, in an internally consistent manner.... [Another] pressing problem ... and which for many regions is the most critical, is the problem of how to put to best use a limited, if not a niggardly, endowment of resources.

A distinctive aspect of Isard's definition is its exclusive emphasis on what economists would normally construe or recognize as economic problems. This also gives it an immediate advantage as a definitional point of departure for organizing a survey article of this kind.

Still, it is much too broad – at least if the survey is to be short of monograph length and a complete tour of modern economics! Two simplifications, though, suggest themselves: these are to limit attention to problems of regional analysis with unique conceptual characteristics, and specific areas of particularly heavy inter-

1. Isard's textbook [70], from which this quotation is taken, constitutes a good single-volume introduction to regional economics and contains excellent bibliographies arranged by subject.

change between conventional economic theory and regional economics.

The conceptually unique problems appear to be mainly empirical in character and center around the difficulties encountered in defining a 'region'. Traditionally three different approaches have been used in defining regions [21, 22, 34, 102, and 119]. The first stresses *homogeneity* with respect to some one or combination of physical economic, social or other characteristics; the second emphasizes so-called *nodality* or *polarization*, usually around some central urban place; and the third is *programming-* or *policy-oriented*, concerned mainly with administrative coherence or identity between the area being studied and available political institutions for effectuating policy decisions. Naturally enough, regional definitions as established in practice often represent a compromise between these different pure types. In particular, availability and limitations of data can and do dictate departures from 'ideal type' definitions in many situations.

Strictly speaking, moreover, the three traditional definitions of regional type are not mutually exclusive. In fact, all regional classification schemes are simply variations on the homogeneity criterion and it is somewhat misleading to suggest otherwise. The only real question is what kind of homogeneity is sought. Thus, a so-called program or policy region is essentially homogeneous in being entirely under the jurisdiction of some one or a few specific government or administrative agencies. A nodal region is homogeneous in that it combines areas dependent in some trade or functional sense on a specific center. Some so-called homogenous regions are homogenous with respect to physical characteristics, like geography or natural resource endowment, while others are defined to be similar in their economic or social characteristics. Finally, homogeneity with respect to statistical compilations, as noted before, may often be the real determinant of regional boundaries for practical purposes.

Some of the most interesting work in regional economics in a purely theoretical or conceptual sense has been concerned with the definition of indexes for measuring homogeneity when more than one dimension or measures of such qualities exist. M. J. Hagood [42 and 43], for example, has performed some highly suggestive experiments with the use of statistical factor or component

23

analyses as a means of defining homogeneous regional groupings for the United States in terms of agricultural and demographic variables. In the process, incidentally, she developed some interesting contributions to the clarification of factor analysis procedures and to the development of objective methods for stratifying a statistical sample [44]. Some interesting extensions of this work have also been made by V. V. Almendinger in connection with defining politically and socially homogeneous communities for the New York metropolitan region and Penn–Jersey transportation studies [1 and 123].

As interesting as these statistical procedures might be to the applied statistician, econometrician, or psychometrician, however, it seems rather doubtful that they are of much tangible value to the regional analyst actually confronted with a problem of defining a geographic area for study. Given the pragmatic, problem-solving orientation of regional economics it would seem that Joseph Fisher of Resources for the Future was probably understating the case when he said [34, p. W-6]:[2]

I should like to suggest that the most helpful region in many instances is what might be called the *economic development region* . . . [where] . . . the emphasis is on the development of policies, programs and actions to move the region from where it is economically toward pre-determined economic objectives.

The same view is echoed at length in the writings of the most extensive contributor to the regional definition problem, Jacques R. Boudeville [21 and 22], although Boudeville also seems to be arguing at times that only a nodal region is useful for policy purposes. Most major exceptions to a policy approach to the regional definition problem will occur, moreover, for the exclusively pragmatic reason of having to make adjustments to data availability.

The problem of regional definition becomes crucial whenever attempts are made to obtain estimates of regional income and product accounts.[3] Such estimates are often essential because

2. A very forceful endorsement of this pragmatic approach to regional definition can also be found in the writings of several others and particularly by E. M. Hoover [64].

3. An excellent recent survey of the problems of regional social accounting can be found in R. N. Stone [112]. Somewhat earlier but still very useful discussions can be found in [130], particularly W. Hochwald's paper on con-

policy objectives are commonly set in terms of achieving a stipulated *per capita* income or production level for a region. The income estimation problem at the regional level, unfortunately, clearly involves more than simply scaling down national income and product accounts. Indeed, many regional analysts would argue that the only way to properly estimate regional income categories would be to adopt a completely fresh approach, developed on the basis of entirely new regional or local sources of information [61, 103, and 104]. Among other justifications, a fresh approach is urged on the grounds that the objectives of regional policy planning are so very different from those encountered at the national level that different concepts are immediately needed in the measurement of regional income and product. Some regional economists, moreover, would rather see national income accounts built up progressively from regional accounts than vice versa. At the minimum a very compelling case can be made for keeping reasonably detailed and unaggregated records of local economic activity in order to create data at whatever level of aggregation is required for policy or research purposes [64]. In reality, though, practical considerations such as limitations on available research resources, usually dictate that regional income estimates be derived from more readily available national income figures.

The special problems of regional income estimation mainly derive from the simple fact that regional economies are almost invariably more open, in the sense of being more reliant on external trade and institutions, than national economies. The type of problem that bedevils the estimator of regional income is aptly illustrated by both the commuter, who lives in one region and works in another, and the large multiplant national corporation. Not only will large corporations typically have installations in different areas but ownership is likely to be dispersed in an unknown fashion over several regions. Government activities, particularly at the federal level, are also difficult to distribute on a regional basis. In general, regional income accounting is complicated by the fact that much needed data are often compiled only on a national basis, and by the conceptual problems associated

ceptual issues [62]. For a discussion of some of the same issues but in a 'dynamic context', see Isard and G. Freutel [72].

with defining a resident, the commuter and large corporation being merely two of the more common examples of these difficulties. These difficulties, though, are not insurmountable since regional, state or other local income accounts suitable for many purposes have been or are in the process of being constructed [13, 14, 36, 46, 47, 60, 105, and 107].

While regional definition problems do possess several reasonably unique elements not encountered in conventional economic analyses, they hardly would appear substantial enough to give regional economics a thoroughly distinct identity. If the search for that identity is directed to locating points of particular conceptual emphasis within regional economics, without much question regional economics, especially as it has evolved and developed within the last decade, uses both location theory and international trade theory more than any of the other conventional economic disciplines.[4] This is hardly surprising, of course, since both location theory and international trade theory emphasize economic relations between geographical areas. It is significant, moreover, that Walter Isard who has fathered much of modern regional economics, spent a great deal of his time in the late 1940s and early 1950s, when the recent surge of interest in regional economic analysis first began, on the problem of integrating or synthesizing location theory and international trade theory [68 and 73]. His particular objective was to correct what he considered to be an intrinsic failing in traditional international trade theory, its failure to pay attention to the cost of overcoming spatial separation.

One common alternative approach to defining regional economics is, in fact, to allude to it as the economics of spatial separation. This, however, would seem to be unduly confining since the policy problems considered by regional economists have been considerably wider in scope than the location problems emphasized by such a definition. Indeed, in actual regional analyses spatial separation as such hasn't been so much the policy concern as the fact that resources, particularly labor, are not completely mobile between regions. The 'economics of resource immobility'

4. In light of what has just been said about the difficulties of finding a unique identity for regional analysis, it is perhaps significant that international trade theory shares with regional economics a tendency to synthesize elements from almost all other phases of economic analysis.

therefore might be a reasonably accurate, though still less than fully comprehensive, description of regional economics.

Before 1950, which would also be before the phrase 'regional analysis' came into common professional usage, what generally was regarded as regional economics was heavily involved in business cycle theory and analysis. Indeed, in the forties studies relating to the inter-regional propagation and transfer of business cycles, those by R. Vining [116–18] and P. Neff [97 and 98] being particularly important, were the dominant concern in regional economic studies. A discussion of this work will be omitted from this paper, however, on the simple grounds that this aspect of regional economics has been rather neglected in recent years.[5] The current emphasis, for better or worse, is on maximization under static conditions, a change almost inherent in the heavy introduction of international trade and location theory concepts into regional economics.[6]

II. Problems of Regional Economic Policy

Modern regional analysis, as reconstituted with a major emphasis on static maximization problems rather than the dynamics of the business cycle, has apparently met a number of desperately felt policy needs. Among other sources, the apparent success in the thirties and forties of the Tennessee Valley Authority has been a major encouragement and inspiration, both domestically and abroad, to those who would undertake to improve the status of economically backward or handicapped areas by government action, a task to which much of the recent applied work in regional economics has been devoted. In the United States a special interest in regional economics in the older South [63] and New England [53, 54, 89, and 23] has been very much motivated by

5. Symptomatic of the trend is the omission of cycle studies from Perloff's categorization scheme quoted above.

6. Also eliminated from consideration here is the extensive work done in recent years on the development of benefit–cost ratios and similar measures of capital-investment effectiveness for water resource development. While this work has been of considerable interest to regional economists and closely related to certain aspects of their work, these contributions to capital budgeting procedures would appear to belong more to the realm of general capital theory since they possess no particularly unique regional characteristics.

such considerations. To a lesser extent, and with a greater emphasis on growth possibilities not realized rather than on immediate economic difficulties as such, the same is true of some of the interest in regional problems evidenced in the Rocky Mountain area [40]. Similarly, the Upper Midwest Economic Study, recently inaugurated at the University of Minnesota and already reporting research results [58, 77, 79, and 110], has as one of its avowed aims formulating an 'action program' to raise the region's rate of economic progress to at least parity with the rest of the country.

Interest in regional economic problems long has had a special source of stimulation in the United States because of the deliberately (and perhaps artificially) regionalized organization of the Federal Reserve System. Thus it is not surprising that much, perhaps even a preponderance, of the domestic empirical work in regional economics has been sponsored at least partially by Federal Reserve Banks. The already mentioned Upper Midwest Project and G. Freutel's work on interregional payment balances [36] are just two of the more important examples.

Much of the foreign interest in regional economic growth has had a similar source but with a special emphasis on a variation of the balanced growth problem. In many countries experiencing rapid economic development a not uncommon circumstance is the existence of a sharp disparity of fortunes between newly industrialized urban areas and the rest of the country. An attempt is often made to ameliorate the political strains created by this so-called 'economic dualism' by initiating special regional development programs. The efforts in Italy to expedite development of the Mezzogiorno, in Venezuela of the Guayana, in Brazil of the Amazonian North, in Argentina of Patagonia, in Chile of Aisen Province, are just a few examples of efforts to meet such political problems by either opening up new territory to settlement by economically oppressed groups or directly transferring more economic opportunity to such groups. Of course this same problem of balanced growth and attempts to effectuate income transfers to unfortunate areas are not unknown in the industralized parts of the world either;[7] the U.S. government worries about West Vir-

7. A good summary of the sources of this problem and possible policy solutions can be found in A. H. Conrad [31].

ginia, the French about Brittany, and the English about Glasgow. In fact, one of the postwar period's earliest and most ambitious schemes to geographically redistribute economic opportunity was undertaken by the British with their 'New Towns Plan', the evaluation of which provides some of the better reading on problems of economic policy formation in regional economics [108].

Actually, urban problems and analyses have assumed an increasingly dominant role in empirical research in regional analysis in the United States. To a certain degree this has been a function of simple financial support since the interstate highway program made substantial funds available for research activities associated with the highway construction. The nature of this support has had, moreover, some interesting effects on the direction of regional research efforts.

Many early research expenditures made under the interstate highway program were primarily concerned with making urban traffic forecasts and estimates. Two techniques usually were employed for this purpose. The first was the highly expensive one of making origination and destination counts by going to homes or stopping automobiles on the highways and performing interviews, and by making controlled cordon counts of the number of vehicles and persons passing certain points in the city. When interviews were performed, information was sought not only on origins and destinations but also on trip purpose (e.g. whether for work, recreation or shopping) and a record was kept of the mode of transportation employed. The main objective was to estimate the level of demand for highway capacity at different points within urban areas so as to determine the needs for new capacity and to locate the capacity with, it was hoped, maximum effectiveness.

Design of these origin and destination interviews obviously poses few conceptual or empirical problems of interest to economists, though many possibilities for improvement do lie in the province of statistical sampling procedures. Origin and destination studies by interview tend, however, to be highly expensive and a full census of originations and destinations almost invariably was impossible. To fill the gaps a second estimation technique, known as gravity model analysis, normally was employed. Gravity models are based on simple sorts of analogues to physical models and they have had a long and controversial history in sociological analyses of regional characteristics [26, 113, 121, and 124]. For gravity models in urban transportation analyses the traffic between two points is hypothesized to be positively related to the 'mass' at each point and negatively to the 'friction' operating on travel between the points. Friction can be measured in terms of distance, time, cost, and various other factors. Similarly, mass has been variously defined as population, the number of automobile owners and, in some more sophisticated models, as purchasing power or effective demand or even 'potential' commercial or industrial 'drawing power' (as reflected in retail and industrial employment or other measures of such activities).

When broadened in this fashion these models pose economic questions of some empirical interest and significance; without such broadening, of course, the models are rather puerile and mechanistic and devoid of behavioral content. It is not surprising, therefore, that much of the effort to broaden and improve gravity model applications to urban traffic analyses is traceable to the influence of economists who have worked on various urban transportation studies. Particularly pathbreaking in this respect were the transportation studies directed by J. D. Carroll for Detroit and Chicago and various papers that developed from those studies [24, 25, 125, and 126]. An effort to incorporate economic and other behavioral information into the making of traffic projections also has been made as part of the Pittsburgh area transportation study [129] and the concurrent economic study of the Pittsburgh region conducted by the Pittsburgh Regional Planning Association; particularly interesting in this regard is a paper by I. S. Lowry containing a number of suggestions for improving gravity models [87].

Considerably more revolutionary and experimental have been the efforts made in the Penn–Jersey transportation study to project future population distributions and thereby transportation demands by assuming that residential choices are made on the basis of certain rational economic considerations as embodied in a linear programming model [48 to 52, and 59]. As will be explained in greater detail later, some critics would argue that with this linear programming model the pendulum has swung too far in the direction of letting economic considerations determine the projections. Be that as it may, it is clear that economists and regional economics are now thoroughly involved in urban transportation planning.

The interest of economists and regional analysts in urban problems has not been limited, of course, to transportation planning. The interdependence between urban transportation, land use, population growth patterns, and industrial development generally is considered to be so close that more purely economic studies of urban trends and patterns have become increasingly prevalent. Besides the already cited Pittsburgh Regional Planning Association effort, there was at an earlier date the New York metropolitan region study (which also included historical and political studies). Indeed, the reports growing out of this study form an excellent introduction to an understanding of urban economic problems [19, 28, 45, 55, 65, 81, 106, 109, 115, and 123]. Similarly, the Upper Midwest study includes a special inquiry into the problems of the Twin Cities' metropolitan area. The new professional interest of economists in urban problems is, of course, symptomatic of a great expansion of concern about urban problems in general in U.S. society.

Transportation problems have also supplied a policy impetus to regional analysis in a larger geographic context than the urban area. Private intercity railroads, trucking lines, and local service airlines in the United States happen, for a number of historical and other reasons, to be regionally structured. To a lesser extent the same is true of the large commercial trunk airlines. Furthermore, recent 'crises' in U.S. transportation have been positively correlated with railroad passenger volumes, short hauls (of both passengers and freight), and small volume shipments. These characteristics vary sharply from region to region with New England clearly being the most disadvantaged.

In general, regional analysis apparently has filled a void by developing tools applicable to economic planning problems at a time when economic planning has been increasingly in favor in many circles and governments. Thus, the great strength of appeal of regional analysis would appear to be its essentially pragmatic character and, in particular, its willingness to integrate theory and data and to undertake empirically difficult analyses.

III. Theoretical Foundations

This emphasis on integration of theory and empiricism also shows itself in modern regional analysis' theoretical roots. These, in large part are 'borrowings' of developments in general economics that occurred during the 1940s and can be listed under four headings: (a) a revitalization of location theory, particularly as contained in Lösch's work, published in English in 1953 [83] but available in German in the forties; (b) international and interregional multiplier theory as illustrated by the work of Metzler [88], Goodwin [41], Chipman [30], and others; (c) Leontief interindustry input–output analysis [83 and 84]; and (d) mathematical programming.[8]

(a) Location theory

With the possible exception of Löschian location theory, these theoretical developments all share the important quality of having obvious empirical possibilities. Indeed, one could say that they almost beg for empirical implementation. By contrast, Lösch's theory not only is highly idealized and stylized but has few immediate or obvious empirical possibilities and has thus far been devoid of any important empirical implementation. One plausible (but not necessarily correct!) explanation of its appeal in regional analysis is that it partially satisfies the search for an identity in the new field. Location theory had, and has, been generally overlooked in general economic studies and by giving it special prominence, regional analysts partially distinguished their activities from the rest of economics. Furthermore, Lösch's theory still may prove to have empirical possibilities, as M. Beckman has forecast [16]. At present, however, the more eclectic and general, though less logically elegant, revisions of Weberian location theory developed by Isard [69] and largely anticipated by E. M. Hoover [64] would seem to have more practical utility.

(b) Multiplier theory

Interregional multiplier analysis, as an empirical device, is closely bound up in regional economics with the concept of an economic

8. For bibliography and discussion of the literature on mathematical programming see [15, 32, and 33].

base. Furthermore, regional economists deserve at least some credit for pioneering the application of multiplier concepts. Homer Hoyt, a pioneer of urban economic studies, employed the concept of an economic base with its implicit multiplier concept as early as 1937 [127]. Revisions and improvements of the base concept have been stimulated, of course, by subsequent development of multiplier concepts in general business cycle theory.

The essential notions of the economic base-multiplier concept as applied in regional studies are the same as similar concepts used elsewhere in economics and are quite clear and simple, though subject to a number of modifications, qualifications or adjustments to provide greater meaningfulness or sophistication in actual application.[9] The first step is to define certain activities as being exogenous or determined outside of the economy under analysis. Translating conventional international trade theory into regional terms, the 'economic base' of a region is that group of industries primarily engaged in exporting from the region under analysis to other regions. An empirical multiplier is determined by observing the historical relationship between this export activity in the region. This empirical multiplier is then applied to estimates of economic base to forecast total economic activity.

A crucial aspect of the procedure is, of course, estimating the size of the economic base. In particular applications where the concern is so often with trying to improve the economic status of a specific region, attempts often are made to estimate the extent of new export activities that might have a chance of economic survival, thus creating a base for expansion in the general economy of the region under analysis. The usual procedure for defining new export possibilities is to make some sort of interregional production cost comparisons, and a common technique of doing this in regional analysis is to perform a so-called 'comparative cost analysis' [70, pp. 233–44].

While based on ideas akin to those found in international trade theory, comparative cost analyses as applied in regional economics are different in that the cost comparisons usually are made directly and in absolute terms without reference to calculations

9. A comprehensive survey of the history, applications and concepts of economic base studies will be found in R. B. Andrews [3–12]. Other useful discussions of the base concept can be found in [66 and 114].

of internal comparative advantage. Specifically, the comparisons normally are made strictly between regions on the apparent assumption of some sort of interregional market equilibrium existing in factor prices. Thus the procedure usually devolves to doing a set of cost comparisons for supplying certain products to specified markets from the given region as compared with alternative sources of supply for these same markets. The first step in the analysis is to look at factor or input costs that are particularly important or almost necessarily different between regions; thus transport costs are almost always analyzed and usually labor costs or costs of a peculiarly important input (e.g. power for aluminium, oil or gas for petrol-chemicals) are also analyzed.

The great virtue of comparative cost analysis is that of all partial analyses, empirical simplicity. It also suffers from the usual disabilities of partial analyses in that the needed preliminary simplifications may not be obvious or easily ascertainable in complex interdependent situations. Particularly likely to be ignored are such considerations as economies of scale, factor price changes induced by inelastic supply functions, and external economies attributable to urbanization or similar influences.

An attempt to correct many of these deficiencies in comparative cost analysis has been made by Isard, E. W. Schooler, and T. Victoriez with what they call 'industrial complex analysis' [70, ch. 9, and 74]. The basic innovation of industrial complex analysis is a somewhat more sophisticated attempt to define meaningful industrial groupings or complexes for cost comparison by using input–output matrices. Also involved is a broadening of the considerations permitted to influence the cost comparisons, with particular emphasis on tests for the existence of scale economies.

The strongest objections usually made to economic base or multiplier analyses in regional economics are not concerned, however, with the legitimacy or illegitimacy of the cost comparisons by which the base is estimated. Some of the most vehement opposition to base analyses has been concerned with the question of simply finding a suitable definition of what is exogenous. Base analysis implies that a gap or discontinuity would be found if industries were arranged hierarchically according to the level of their export activity. However, in many cases where such an analysis has been undertaken, the ordering has been found to be essentially continuous.

Furthermore, even if a group of export industries can be identified readily, there are often reasons for denying that the multiplier coefficients will be stable over time. In fact, a very common objection made to base analysis is that regional studies usually are concerned with economic development of an area and one of the main objectives of that development is to change the relationship between export and import activities. It is quite obvious, moreover, that an economy can exist without exports and can grow without a growth of its exports, as must be true for the world economy taken as a whole. Quibbles also have been entered, sometimes quite legitimately, about the reliability of multiplier coefficients estimated from historical data.

While the economic base concept is thus subject to many serious reservations and objections, it still has had a most remarkable vitality. Indeed, some kind of economic base notion is to be found in almost all regional projection exercises, at least implicitly.[10] The substantive issue is really not whether a base of exogeneity concept is to be employed but how much openness or interdependence will be tolerated. Unquestionably, the remarkable durability of the underlying idea of exogeneity embodied in the base concept is simply that no other empirically implementable alternative now exists.

(c) Input–output analysis

This is even true of the second applied technique of great importance in regional economics, input–output analysis and its closely associated matrix multiplier concepts. Even in these more sophisticated and interdependent models some choice usually must be made of an exogenous bill of goods to be entered as 'final demand'. In broad, idealized outline, the objective of an interregional interindustry input–output analysis is a matrix of input–output coefficients identified not only by industry but also by geographic areas or regions [67, 70, ch. 8, and 92]. Thus, if there were 50 industries and 5 regions, the ideal matrix would contain 62,500 coefficients decomposable into 25 submatrices of 2500 (50 × 50)

10. A persuasive argument has been advanced by D. C. North [100], in fact, for defining regions, at least for purposes of historical analysis, so that they have homogeneous export bases.

entries each; for each region there would be 5 matrices, one of which defined its own interindustry relationships and 4 relating to trade relationships by industry with the other regions. Such an idealized table, however, is usually impossible to realize because of data insufficiencies. A central preoccupation of regional input–output analysis has therefore been the making of adaptations to overcome these data difficulties, and most of these adaptations involve aggregation aimed at eliminating some of the empirical detail needed to estimate the idealized table.

One obvious simplification is to treat each region as if it were an *almost* autonomous economic unit and proceed as with the estimation of an input–output table for a national economy by consolidating all inflows and outflows to other regions into an import–export sector. What this essentially amounts to is an aggregation over all rows and columns in the idealized matrix outside of the particular region of study, a record being retained mainly of the interindustry relationships within the region under study. This is probably the most common approach now taken to the estimation of regional input–output relations; two good illustrative examples of such tables can be found in the work of W. Z. Hirsch [60] and R. Artle [13].

A second approach, rather opposite in its aggregation procedure, is to completely forget about interindustry relations and concentrate on interregional trade patterns. This essentially amounts to aggregating over industries but not over regions. An illustrative example of such an approach is contained in the procedures proposed for the Upper Middle West study [58]. This procedure has the great advantage that interindustry coefficients for individual regions are usually very hard to come by, not uncommonly being estimated by simply assuming that the national coefficients apply within a region. Furthermore, an inter-regional trade-flow approach retains the emphasis where it usually is needed for policy purposes.

A third simplification is to define interregional trade coefficients for each commodity as an input, forgetting about inter-industry differences in import patterns within each region. Thus, instead of having separate import input coefficients for each region and industry, a trade coefficient is constructed for each region by a particular type of input. This essentially reduces all the interindustry trade relationship submatrices between the specific region and regions other than itself in the idealized model to a single vector for each region. For example, if there were 50 industries in the model, instead of having 50 × 50 matrix of coefficients to define trade relationships between one region and another, there would be instead only a fifty-element vector. The essential assumption lying behind this procedure is that if imports of a commodity are needed as inputs by industries of a given region, exactly the same relative imports of the commodity will be needed for all industries in the region. The aggregation is essentially over trade input coefficients since industry destination of imported inputs is ignored. One great advantage of this scheme is that it is empirically implementable with available Interstate Commerce Commission data on commodity flows. Illustrative examples of this approach can be found in the work of H. Chenery [27] and L. Moses [93].

A fourth approach to data simplification for interregional input–output models is the balanced regional growth model developed by Leontief and Isard [84, chs. 4 and 5]. It is based on the notion that a hierarchical arrangement or definition of industries is possible in which certain industries can be described as basically catering to national markets, and others to regional or local markets. The input–output analysis then proceeds according to this hierarchical ordering with activity levels for the national industries being estimated first. These national industry outputs are then allocated to the different regions according to regional participation coefficients to form part of the final demand for each region, the remainder being regionally produced commodities. Following this, the regional composition of interindustry activity can be estimated by conventional input–output methods; in fact, national interindustry relationships have usually been suggested for this exercise. The process can be carried down, of course, to as low a level of geographic disaggregation as data permit and objectives might require. As for applications, the New York metropolitan region study used a rather heuristic variation of this balanced growth approach in arriving at its projections [19 and 115].

A fifth and most ingenious approach to data simplification in regional input–output analysis has very recently been advanced by Leontief and A. Strout [85]. The essence of the method is to use gravity-type structural equations to explain or estimate the magnitude of interregional flow. Specifically, the flow of a commodity from one region to another is assumed to be directly proportional to the product of its total output in a shipping region by its total input in a receiving region divided by the aggregate amount of the commodity produced and consumed in the entire economy, all multiplied by an empirical constant. (Leontief also permits every region to be both a shipper and receiver of a commodity which at the level of aggregation now employed in input–output he properly argues is a more realistic assumption than hypothesizing the economically rational solution of only one-way flows.) The constants can be statistically estimated by various methods or, what is most important from the standpoint of data conservation, by solving the equations of the regional input–output system, including the gravity-flow equations in the system. If this latter direct or 'exact' solution, as Leontief calls it, is obtained, the existence of the balance equations inherent in input–output systems makes it possible to estimate the interregional flows without directly observing them; the only data needed are those on total outputs and inputs for all regions and the use made of each commodity as an input to internal production in each region. The crucial question, of course, is how well the flow estimates generated by use of the hypothesized gravity-flow structure approximate reality. In this regard initial experiments have been most encouraging. In fact, in tests on bituminous coal, cement and steel shapes the 'exact solution' has performed about as well as least squares on projections and in some senses even better.

Input–output techniques are subject, of course, to a number of criticisms since they embody so many important and controversial simplifying assumptions. These are so well known, to users of input–output as well as its critics, and so extensively catalogued elsewhere [91, 93, and 123] that no repetition will be made here. Suffice it to say that regional input–output models tend to have all the problems of national models plus some additional ones of their own. In particular, there is at least some limited evidence that interregional trade coefficients may be even more unstable over time than interindustry coefficients [93]. Such instability almost surely applies as well to the regional participation coefficients used in the balanced regional growth model.

The fact still remains that with all its problems and difficulties input–output does have the great advantage of being an empirically workable model that provides an organizational framework and set of consistency checks that are difficult to achieve with less formal techniques. The danger does exist, though, that preoccupation with the empirical detail involved in establishing these models may lead to an oversight of importance, perhaps of such importance that it leads to grossly inaccurate estimates. Thus, it is often argued that an understanding of basic historical trends and forces is more essential to making good projections than accurate interindustry and interregional trade coefficients. Still this is not an intrinsic shortcoming of the model as such. Rather it is a question of what constitutes a proper allocation of research resources in regional analysis and, as will be observed in the next section, this is a question very much in dispute. Finally, it must be recognized that input–output and economic base analyses, with all their shortcomings and deficiencies, are the tools almost invariably relied upon at the present time when actual empirical work in regional economics must be performed.

(d) *Mathematical programming*

The fourth basic theoretical tool commonly employed in modern regional analysis, mathematical programming, is without question the best from a strictly conceptual point of view if one believes in a reasonably pervasive economic rationality.[11] It suffers, though, from two serious handicaps. The first is that of simple data availability; the data requirements for a good linear programming model are often staggeringly large and even farther beyond what is currently available than the requirements for input–output. The second difficulty is that economic rationality is often either not obviously pervasive or, more accurately, is too

11. The conceptual aspects of applying mathematical programming to location and regional analysis problems are discussed by T. C. Koopmans and M. Beckman [78], Beckman and T. Marschak [16], L. Lefeber [80], B. H. Stevens [111], and L. N. Moses [94]. Actual applications of such techniques are reported by Henderson [56–7], F. T. Moore [90], and K. A. Fox [35].

complex to be readily incorporated into presently operational programming models.

The most ambitious effort to date in the use of linear programming techniques in a regional project has been the Penn–Jersey study's household location model, and their experience illustrate both basic difficulties [48–52, and 59]. They started with the highly appealing and simple notion that different types of households have certain specific amounts that they can budget for 'the bundle of services' associated with a particular type of house. Included in the definition of housing type was the amount of land consumed so that the selection of different housing types gave rise to different land-use patterns. Families differently located in the income scale and with different numbers of children or other characteristics are, moreover, hypothesized to have different willingnesses to pay for specific types of housing as expressed by the size of their budgets available for each housing type. Later the model was modified to make the budgets not only specific to housing types but also to areas on the grounds that it is more realistic to assume that families consider the residential location and its amenities as well as the structure and size of yard when deciding the amount that they are willing to pay for a particular house.

Still another modification, introduced in order to effect a considerable reduction in the computational burden, was simply to preselect the housing type in every geographic area that seemed most suitable for each family type in that area on the grounds that this selection was usually obvious without running the model. After the budgets had been estimated for each family type in each area and for every housing type, all costs for each housing type and location *not* associated with land acquisition were deducted from the budget estimate to determine the net rent-paying ability of each family for each housing type in a specific location. That is, transportation, structure, and amenity (schooling, public services, etc.) costs were subtracted from the total available budget to determine how much was left for land acquisition or rent. Households were then hypothesized to compete with one another for the available land, bidding rents up to a maximum (the objective function) subject to the constraints that all households get located and that total land use does not exceed total land available. One immediate advantage of this research design is that it yields an estimate of the rent surface as an output rather than being required as an input, a considerable gain since urban land values or rents are difficult data to obtain.

The striking thing about this model is the degree to which the important bahavioral considerations are built into the model prior to its actual running. This immediately raises at least a research resource allocation problem of whether it is wise to devote considerable effort to building such a model until the reliability of its inputs has been established. Particularly important among the prior questions are estimating the budgets by household type and location and choosing a particular housing type in each area for each family. Indeed, this choice of particular housing type in each locale is crucial in determining the actual land-use pattern. For example, if in the preselection process, housing types are chosen so as to yield the greatest per-acre rent-paying ability, a bias is built in toward finding high density land-use patterns. The converse is true if the housing yielding the greatest per-family rent-paying ability is preselected. In recognition of these difficulties, the Penn–Jersey group are now considering the preselection of housing types so as to provide the greatest per-family net rent-paying ability as determined by subtracting a prior estimate of the initial rent surface from the budget along with the other cost estimates. They would then proceed as before, maximizing rent-paying on a gross basis. This scheme, of course, immediately loses some of the advantages of not needing a prior rent surface but this deficiency can be at least partially overcome by iterating the model a few times if the rents estimated by the model differ substantially from the rents assumed *a priori*.

Purists, of course, might still raise a number of quibbles about the behavioral assumptions incorporated in this model even as modified. It is, however, a highly imaginative and heroic attempt to apply the techniques of mathematical programming to an actual location problem, and by any standards it is the most ambitious effort of its kind yet undertaken in regional economics. As such, its trials and tribulations are surely suggestive, and it is difficult to escape the conclusion on the basis of that experience that programming may still be beyond available data and research resources, at least given the present paucity of prior or established knowledge about urban economics and location patterns. It is difficult, on the other hand, to conceive how the necessary knowledge and insights needed for adequately implementing these models will ever be acquired without such experimental undertakings.

IV. Types of Approach to Regional Studies

It is probably apparent by this point that if the important issues associated with data collection are put to one side, the basic disagreements arising in the application of regional analyses tend to be as much a matter of viewpoint or philosophical orientation as of technical detail. Specifically, two rather different approaches are discernible. In one the emphasis is on historical and behavioral characteristics; in the other the orientation is more toward quantification, forecasting, and the development of a logically rigorous framework for the analysis. To be sure, these distinctions are at least somewhat arbitrary, as most such classifications usually are. Thus, those with an historical–behavioral inclination also often try to make quantitative forecasts and those with an analytical–quantitative approach normally will try to develop an understanding of underlying behavioral patterns. Furthermore, one of the dominant concerns in the field at the moment is with finding means of fusing or synthesizing the best elements in different approaches into better, more comprehensive procedures [70, ch. 12, and 71].

Still, very important differences in emphasis do exist. For example, those with an historical–behavioral orientation tend to stress the analysis of trends and evolutionary patterns. They try to 'dig beneath' the data to an understanding of motivations, particularly those leading to significant changes in structure and conduct. Thus their concern tends to be more with structural change than with its continuity. They are not too disturbed, moreover, if this structural change makes forecasting hazardous or uncertain or if their forecasts are not formally rigorous and consistent in all details. Their involvement tends to be more with whether what they have said and forecast is plausible in light of current or apparent trends in behavior. In keeping with this, they often will emphasize such considerations as entrepreneurship, market structure, and external economies that normally are not conveniently incorporated into the more formal analytical frameworks.[12] Finally, they are often quite willing to sacrifice a good static analysis even for an admittedly poor dynamic analysis, for as one proponent of this point of view, B. R. Berman, has so eloquently put it [18, p. 300]:

It may be argued that dynamic models are harder to construct than static, or that we cannot begin to fashion dynamic models until we have a static model of some believability. But for practical purposes ... a crude dynamic model may be better than a highly tooled, multi-jeweled static creation.

Two leading prototypes of regional analyses with this emphasis on behavioral considerations are the New York metropolitan region study and, to a lesser extent, the Pittsburgh area economic study.

By contrast, those of the analytical-quantifier persuasion will emphasize formal structure and consistency. Far from being fascinated by structural discontinuities, they often will seek to establish empirically that behavioral instability, at least of sufficient impact to modify their structural parameters, is more the exception than the rule. They will be interested in developing relationships to explain structural change only if confronted with obvious necessity. Similarly, they are usually willing to sacrifice some dynamics to obtain better static models. They are also likely to be much more concerned with problems of regional income and social accounting. A good one-sentence summary of the beliefs held by those adopting this more formal approach was once rendered by Isard in defense of input–output procedures as follows [70, p. 341]: 'When combined with intuition and hunch, input–output projections yield results at least as good as those based on intuition and hunch alone.' Most of the work with regional analysis in Europe and in underdeveloped countries displays these more formalistic tendencies [82 and 70], and the Penn–Jersey study with its emphasis on a linear programming approach is

12. For a further expression of these views, see B. Chinitz's paper [29] on the implications of market structure and industry characteristics for regional development.

surely of this kind. The Upper Midwest study, on the other hand, represents a very interesting compromise or hybrid of the two different basic approaches.

Some of these differences in approach are traceable to and explained by differences in policy orientations. The behaviorist seems to look to the making of piecemeal adjustments in existing institutions and public policy arrangements as the soundest procedure. He tends to formulate less ambitious goals and to think in terms of a series of short-run policy adjustments over time. This results in his emphasizing flexibility and adaptability. As R. Vernon stated when summing up the New York metropolitan study [115, p. 196]:

No projection of the economic and demographic characteristics of a metropolitan area can be free of the risk of error; no public or private planner can afford to assume that the potential error is small. From a policy viewpoint, this may suggest that planners and investors should regard the preservation of flexibility as a virtue in itself, a virtue worth paying for at the seeming sacrifice of other standards of performance.

By contrast, those with the more formal outlook are oriented more toward drawing up comprehensive development plans. This at least partially explains the popularity of this approach in underdeveloped countries confronted with long-range problems of considerable magnitude and often facing a requirement to justify loans for large-scale development investments before world banking and development authorities. Indeed, an emphasis on long-range, comprehensive planning apparently done to the best of current technical capabilities has an almost inherent and undeniable appeal, and perhaps the appearance of indispensability when undertaking capital budgeting decisions. Something of the ambition and confidence in policy matters of those advocating a more formal approach to regional analysis is connoted in the following statement by J. R. Boudeville [22, pp. 11–12]:

Regional Economy is a science of decision. It presupposes the determination of aims, the use of means and the choice of the most effective instruments to achieve those aims. ... The problems of bringing to light the interrelations of the economic trends and the coherence of the means and aims requires the presence of a regional command familiar with the new techniques. ... Admittedly, excellent regional schemes have been carried out without the aid of modern techniques. The Roman aqueducts and Gothic cathedrals did not wait for Strength of Materials calculations to be architectural feats. Similarly, we can admire the work of the pioneers of our time. Nevertheless, the role of the economist is to produce general rules superseding the old empirical approach and piecemeal work, which is always expensive.

The obvious, appropriately evasive comment for any reviewer attempting to maintain at least an appearance of neutrality when confronted with such contrasting viewpoints is, simply, that each approach probably has a role. In this case, moreover, such a statement is not only diplomatic but probably correct. Structural coefficients will be relatively stable in many circumstances while not in others. Even if not stable, moreover, structural estimates often will be required just simply to *begin* a rational analysis. However, if the initial analysis is not followed by studies aimed at understanding the patterns of change, the resulting forecasts and policy decisions are likely to be next to, but not quite, worthless. Furthermore it does seem rational to build flexibility into the decision process *but* in proportion to the degree of uncertainty attached to the crucial structural estimates used in making initial decisions. This degree of uncertainty also may very well vary for different aspects of the decision process and these differences too should be reflected in the degree of flexibility retained. In short, decision-making for economic policy is still a very crude science and it behoves the cautious man to be eclectic.

Whatever the orientation or preferences adopted on these issues, it seems rather difficult to deny that at the moment regional analysis tends to be somewhat stronger in the formulation of analytical frameworks than in fundamental understanding of any behavioral regularities at work shaping regional and metropolitan growth patterns. Particularly notable for their scarcity throughout the fifties were quantitative studies aimed at hypothesis-testing that were so common in most other fields of economics at that time. Indeed, ever since the interest in interregional analysis of business cycles diminished in the late forties, there has even been a relative lack of suggestions on hypotheses to be tested. Rather, the conceptual activity in regional analysis has been concerned mainly with the construction of logically consistent schemes for organizing and presenting data, particularly social accounts, with a secondary emphasis on normative policy prescriptions. Many of the hypotheses that have been developed from the theoretical work, moreover, have either been at a highly aggregative level, like those embodied in many economic base multiplier concepts, or have been such obvious abstractions as to not easily elicit serious statistical study, like Lösch's location theory. Accordingly, the work of those with an historical–behavioral bent at least serves the extremely useful purpose of beginning to fill this hypothesis void. Furthermore, this work illustrates the important point that bringing to bear certain aspects of conventional economic theory and thought now often ignored in regional economics can be highly productive of new insights and hypotheses in this field.

Further verification on this point has been provided recently by three excellent efforts [2, 96, and 122] to develop formal models defining relationships between urban land-use patterns and explanatory economic factors. These models not only give an organization to the discussion that was badly needed but yield eminently testable hypotheses. Indeed, the only criticism that might be made is to regret that the authors have not yet proceeded on to the testing, especially since the process probably would have sharpened the hypotheses. These theories all place almost exclusive emphasis on economic variables, like relevant prices and costs or proxies for costs such as 'elapsed travel time' for access to places of work or other centers. It would seem highly probable that a number of sociological variables, like those commonly encountered in cross-section consumer budget studies, are required for a really adequate empirical explanation of locational choices. Of particular importance would appear to be variables defining family characteristics (e.g. number of children and employed individuals) when seeking explanations of residential choices.

The importance of these family-characteristic variables has been demonstrated, in fact, in results obtained by J. F. Kain [75 and 76] in a study of Detroit residential location patterns based on data collected as part of the Detroit area transportation study. Kain, in collaboration with J. Niedercorn [99] and others, has also been testing other hypotheses about urban location patterns as part of the RAND study of urban transportation and land use. In this study the emphasis is on the relationship of urban transportation to metropolitan growth patterns, although other determinants of urban growth are also being investigated. The studies are, for the most part, formally econometric in character and based as much on intercity as intracity comparisons, thus taking advantage of the fact that the RAND project is liberated from the geographical and policy constraints that often have inhibited effective hypothesis testing in specific regional studies. The plethora of available cross-section data based on intercity samples makes it possible to entertain a considerably widened range of hypotheses and tests with these data.

Of a somewhat similar character are a series of recent studies on urban transportation characteristics recently completed by the North-western University Traffic and Transportation Institute [95, 101, and 120]. These studies, among other contributions, embody the first really substantial attempt to estimate demand and cross-elasticity parameters that are essential to intelligent formulation of urban transportation policies. The evidence produced is not, incidentally, comforting to those who believe that creation of more and better public transit, by government subsidy if necessary, will relieve automobile congestion in urban areas by attracting commuters away from their private automobiles. The cross-elasticity of demand between private auto and public transit commutation would appear to be so low that actual payments might have to be made to transit riders to induce any considerable shift in patronage.

That regional economics will benefit from the confrontation of hypotheses with actual data is also suggested by the results of those few quantitative studies that have been directed to the testing of hypotheses in regional economics. These tests, incidentally, need not be formidable or involve formal econometrics to have a high yield. For example, much of the New York metropolitan region study's activities involved the formulation, reformulation, and testing of hypotheses against available data, though only occasionally with formal statistical procedures. The tests were formal or consistent in an economic sense, however, since they were unified by continual reference to the basic hypothesis that underlaid the entire project, namely that New York is what it is because of its peculiar attraction for 'external economy industries' that 'have a compelling need to be close to other firms in order to make sales or hold down costs' [115, p. 6]. The model is 'closed', moreover, by an ingenious historical explanation of why New

York has developed a particularly advantageous position in these external or agglomeration economies [115, ch. 2].

These same traditions of combining historical and economic explanations and reformulating hypotheses as experience and data accumulate seem to have been perpetuated in the Pittsburgh area economic study, which has some of the same personnel and leadership as the New York study. In this study, though, the emphasis seems to be more on the special role played in regional growth by natural resource endowments; furthermore, the highly interesting hypothesis has been tentatively advanced that these resources, by inducing the growth of heavy, large-scale mass-production industries with a technological bias in their management requirements, have indirectly prevented Pittsburgh from realizing the same agglomeration economies for its size that other cities with more diversified, small-scale industries have experienced [29].

An orientation to hypothesis-testing is also evident in the background studies being prepared as part of the Upper Midwest study. These background studies, incidentally, are justified in the general research design of the main project both for their own sake and as a source of information on changes in coefficients needed to make desired long-range forecasts. The early focus in this study, for quite understandable reasons, has been on the recent technological revolution in agriculture and the implications of this revolution for labor-force migration. For example, L. A. Sjaastad in a highly interesting study of migration patterns in the Upper Midwest tests the hypothesis that since 'a good part of what we consider human capital is an accumulation of skills and experience specific to an occupation ... income differentials could persist over long time periods even in a market system with no lags or imperfections save lack of perfect foresight' [110, p. 45]. His preliminary empirical evidence on migration patterns by age groups and geographic areas within the Upper Midwest lends, moreover, considerable support to the hypothesis.

This very basic question of resource mobility also has been studied empirically by W. H. Miernyck [89] and G. H. Borts [20]. Miernyck, in an interview study of displaced New England textile workers, also finds that the problems of adaptation to technological change tend to weigh most heavily on older workers and are far from being automatically self-correcting, at least in the short run. In fact, Miernyck finds that re-employment in the textile industry is about the only real hope for many older unemployed textile workers in New England because of their high degree of skill specialization; and such re-employment opportunities appear only slowly in a declining industry.

Borts considerably broadens the analysis, explaining the persistence of regional wage differences in terms of regional differences in capital movements, birth rates, the marginal efficiency of new investments, and export industry composition, as well as any residual labor immobility. Borts also presents a more refined analysis of the interrelationships between wage differences and labor and capital movements. He builds a strong case for the hypothesis that capital movements, exogenously induced by an expansion in demand for the particular industries or exports of certain regions, have been the principal factor sustaining interregional wage differences in the United States.

Support for at least part of this hypothesis is also provided by a study of changes since 1929 in the distribution of manufacturing activities in the United States by V. R. Fuchs [37–9]. A major conclusion is [38, p. 177]:

The most important redistributions occurred in labor-oriented industries such as textiles and apparel, or in industries oriented to natural resources such as chemicals, lumber and paper. The single most important locational development since 1929, the growth of the aircraft industry in the Southwest, is probably attributable more to climate than to any other factor.

Accordingly, Fuchs, like Borts, stresses the importance of exogenous factors in shaping regional growth characteristics. Indeed, a prime objective of Fuchs is to reject the hypothesis that locational changes in manufacturing can be explained endogenously by shifts in local market industries following demand into regions with newly expanded populations. In short, Fuchs tends to see changes in manufacturing locations much more as a cause than as an effect of population shifts.

A somewhat different view of these causal relationships is to be found in a study by H. S. Perloff, E. S. Dunn, E. E. Lampard, and R. E. Muth [105] on the relationships between regional growth, incomes, and resources. These authors who have something to say (historically, conceptually, and empirically) on almost every aspect of the regional income differentiation question, guardedly adopt the view that for manufacturing 'the tie to resources has not been dominant' while access to 'terminal markets' deserves heavy emphasis as an explanation of locational shifts [105, p. 394]. The discrepancies between the findings of Perloff and associates and those of Fuchs are at least partly attributable to differences in definitions and choice of analytical procedures. Specifically, Fuchs chose to analyze the location of market-oriented industries directly while Perloff and colleagues put a major emphasis on the direct analysis of natural-resource-using industries; furthermore, they define natural resources in the conventional fashion, thus excluding climate and low-cost labor, two factors which play a very prominent role in Fuch's explanations.

Perloff, Dunn, Lampard, and Muth also argue that capital flows have not been and probably will not be in the future sufficient to quickly eliminate interregional differences in wages for similar skills. Outmigration of labor is therefore seen as required to achieve interregional equilibration of incomes, and this migration has occurred at such 'painfully slow rates' that they favor positive governmental action to alleviate the difficulties. They clearly suggest [pp. 105, 606–7], moreover, that this action should extend beyond policies aimed at improvement of the overall levels of national prosperity to specific regional aid programs. They grant, though, that general prosperity since 1940 has slowly but surely helped with alleviation of regional income imbalances. Furthermore, they associate the worst regional income imbalances with problems created by structural changes in agriculture, the major part of which may now be completed. The question therefore arises, but is left unanswered, of whether regional income imbalances will be as serious a problem in the future as in the recent past.

No short summary can do justice, however, to this complex, thoughtful and important study of regional problems. Among many virtues, it provides a wealth of data on regional changes and characteristics that have not been readily accessible previously. It will unquestionably be a standard reference for future empirical researchers in regional economics. Evaluated together with the other recent efforts to revive hypothesis-testing on regional problems, it leads to the almost incontestable conclusion that regional economics has both the data and hypotheses to become a behavioral as well as a normative science.

V. Conclusions

A basic theme of the preceding discussion is that regional economics has progressed significantly in the last decade and has been concerned, in a generally effective fashion, with contributing to the solution of a number of important policy questions. Some of this progress, however, has been achieved at the neglect of certain important questions and a diversion of effort away from fruitful research channels. In short, regional economics is incomplete in a number of important respects, apart from the mere existence of a number of untouched research questions and problems. Specifically, the suggestion has been advanced that regional economics has reached a stage where it could benefit from some redirection of effort away from the design of broad conceptual frameworks and accumulation of regional income accounts toward the formulation and testing of behavioral hypotheses, with the initial emphasis being placed on hypotheses that could be quite readily developed from the application of general economic concepts already available.

Some redirection of effort along these lines seems justified if for no other reason than that many of the sophisticated research designs now being attempted in regional economics require a considerable input of 'behavioral understanding' to be effective. The Penn–Jersey linear programming model, with its highly complicated structure of behavioral assumptions, is illustrative; in fact, the most immediate contribution of the Penn–Jersey study may be a better understanding of some behavioral characteristics because of research stimulated by the necessity to have reasonable realistic inputs in the model. Similarly, the validity and accuracy of many input–output applications obviously depends on a knowledge of the structural coefficients involved. These, in turn, are often undergoing continual change; and explaining these changes requires more knowledge of behavioral characteristics than is now normally available.

In a pragmatic, decision-oriented field like regional economics some attention also might be given to the highly practical question of when and whether more complex research designs yield sufficiently improved results to justify their costs. Particularly relevant would be some empirical tests of the effects of incorporating greater or less interdependence and aggregation into regional forecasting models. For instance, is a gain in accuracy always obtained from using a matrix multiplier in place of a highly aggregative composite coefficient of the type normally employed in so-called economic base analyses? If not, is there a pattern to the performance comparisons so that this information could be used to improve the allocation of research resources in future undertakings? In general, regional analysis might benefit from an incorporation of some of the ideas found in modern statistical decision theory and particularly the notion that the costs of obtaining better decisions should be compared with the obtainable yield.

The scarcity of hypothesis-testing in regional analysis is all the more regrettable when the availability of much excellent and highly relevant data is noted. Specifically, among other things, the nature of U.S. government census practices, the regionalization of the banking system, and the common requirement by the Bureau of Public Roads that a considerable proportion of any research funds made available under the interstate highway program be spent on local data-gathering and interview studies have resulted in a remarkable collection of cross-section data being available on regional, state, metropolitan, and even intracity characteristics. Indeed, it is hardly any exaggeration to say that regional economics is in many ways one of the most fortunately blessed fields in economics in terms of data availability.

Yet it gives an appearance, as noted previously, of being notably undernourished in data. The paradox is more apparent than real. The data problems in regional economics stem more from a choice of activities and interests by regional economists than from any other factor. With a few notable exceptions, regional economists have shown a great propensity for under-taking the difficult tasks first. For example, estimating input–out-put tables is difficult enough at the national level, even with all the statistics that are only available at that level of aggregation. Mathematical programming often encounters serious data problems when confined to the analysis of a limited optimization problem within an individual firm. Constructing good income accounts has proven a quite formidable task even for well-financed and -staffed national agencies. In fact, it is still true in the United States, where national income accounting has been pioneered, that a number of notable deficiences or guesses exist in the available social accounts. It is at least relevant to ask, therefore, if constructing elaborate regional accounts as advocated by many regional economists, is a justifiable expenditure of limited research resources until the more important limitations in the national accounts are removed.

Regional data problems are not, of course, unimportant or undeserving of attention. Many of them must be solved, in fact, before certain important empirical investigations can be undertaken. Furthermore, there is obviously a considerable demand in some quarters for better regional accounts as an aid to policy-making. Nevertheless, a more nearly optimal allocation of research resources within regional economics would seem to involve less relative effort on income accounting and interregional trade-flow coefficient estimation and more attention to developing and testing hypotheses. In the short run, moreover, a number of interesting and highly pertinent hypotheses could be subjected to at least preliminary testing with data that are already available and of quite respectable accuracy.

In sum, regional economics is very much what it is today because it has stood ready to attempt analytical solutions to difficult policy problems. Its major contributions thus far have been to provide broad measures and frameworks needed to evaluate and organize these activities – and this is without question a considerable contribution. Further implementation or realization on these efforts will require, however, greater knowledge of regional growth processes and related behavioral patterns than is now available. To do this, regional economics almost certainly must become increasingly involved with hypotheses about the behavior and role of financial organizations, market structures, entrepreneurship, private and public investment decisions, taxes, fiscal policies, and all the other subjects normally encompassed in economics but now encountered only occasionally in regional economics. By contrast, relatively less effort is likely to be needed on studies concerned exclusively with constructing research frameworks and studying the effects of spatial separation for its own sake. Since these two latter areas have tended to be the distinctive elements in regional economics in recent years, this suggests that regional economics may increasingly be indistinguishable from the rest of economics. It is not clear, moreover, that such a development should be viewed with great alarm in a world made increasingly smaller and more homogeneous by political and institutional developments and by improvements in transportation, communications, and other technologies, with all that these imply for resource mobility.

References

1. ALMENDINGER, V. V. (1961) *Topics in the regional growth model:* I, Penn–Jersey Study Paper No. 4.
2. ALONSO, W. (1960) 'A theory of the urban land market', *Papers and Proceedings Reg. Sci. Assoc.*, 6, 149–57.
3. ANDREWS, R. B. (May 1953) 'Mechanics of the urban economic base: historical development of the base concept', *Land Economics*, 29, 161–67.
4. ANDREWS, R. B. (August 1953) 'Mechanics of the urban economic base: the problem of terminology', *Land Economics*, 29, 263–8.
5. ANDREWS, R. B. (November 1953) 'Mechanics of the urban economic base: a classification of base types', *Land Economics*, 29, 343–50.
6. ANDREWS, R. B. (February 1954) 'Mechanics of the urban economic base: the problem of base measurement', *Land Economics*, 30, 52–60.
7. ANDREWS, R. B. (May 1954) 'Mechanics of the urban economic base: general problems of identification', *Land Economics*, 30, 164–72.
8. ANDREWS, R. B. (August 1954) 'Mechanics of the urban economic base: special problems of base identification', *Land Economics*, 30, 260–69.
9. ANDREWS, R. B. (November 1954) 'Mechanics of the urban economic base: the problem of base area delimitation', *Land Economics*, 30, 309–19.
10. ANDREWS, R. B. (February 1955) 'Mechanics of the urban economic base: the concept of base ratios', *Land Economics*, 31, 47–53.
11. ANDREWS, R. B. (May, August, November 1955) 'Mechanics of the urban economic base: causes and effects of change in the base ratios and the ratio elements', *Land Economics*, 31, 144–55, 245–56, 351–77.
12. ANDREWS, R. B. (February 1956) 'Mechanics of the urban economic base: the base concept and the planning process', *Land Economics*, 32, 69–84.

13. ARTLE, R. (1959) *Studies in the structure of the Stockholm economy: towards a framework for projecting metropolitan community development.*

14. ASHBY, L. D., and TRUEX, E. P. (1952) *The estimation of income payments to individuals in North Carolina counties.*

15. BAUMOL, W. J. (December 1958) 'Activity analysis in one lesson', *Am. Econ. Rev.*, **48**, 837–73.

16. BECKMAN, M. (1955) 'Some reflections on Lösch's theory of location', *Papers and Proceedings Reg. Sci. Assoc.*, **1**, N1–N9.

17. BECKMAN, M., and MARSCHAK, T. (1955) 'An activity analysis approach to location theory', *Kyklos*, **8**, 125–34.

18. BERMAN, B. (May 1961) 'Analysis of urban problems – Discussion', *Am. Econ. Rev.*, **51**, 299–300.

19. BERMAN, B., CHINITZ, B., and HOOVER, E. M. (1961) *Projection of a metropolis*, Cambridge, Mass.

20. BORTS, G. H. (June 1960) 'The equalization of returns and regional economic growth', *Am. Econ. Rev.*, **50**, 319–47.

21. BOUDEVILLE, J. R. (1960) 'A survey of recent techniques for regional economic analysis', *Regional economic planning: techniques of analysis*, W. Isard, and J. H. Cumberland (eds.), 377–98.

22. BOUDEVILLE, J. R. (August–September 1962) 'Frontiers and interrelations of regional planning', paper given at *International Congress on Economic Development.*

23. BRIGHT, A., and ELLIS, G. (ed.) (1954) *The economic state of New England.*

24. CARROLL, J. D. (1955) 'Spatial interaction and the urban-metropolitan description', *Papers and Proceedings Reg. Sci. Assoc.*, **1**, D1-D14.

25. CARROLL, J. D., and BEVIS, H. W. (1957) 'Predicting local travel in urban regions', *Papers and Proceedings Reg. Sci. Assoc.*, **3**, 183–97.

26. CARROTHERS, G. A. P. (Spring 1956) 'An historical review of the gravity and potential concepts of human interaction', *Jour. Am. Instit. Planners*, **22**, 94–102.

27. CHENERY, H. B., CLARK, P. G., and CAO-PINNA, V. (1953) *The structure and growth of the Italian economy.*

28. CHINITZ, B. (1960) *Freight and the metropolis.*

29. CHINITZ, B. (May 1961) 'Contrasts in agglomeration: New York and Pittsburgh', *Am. Econ. Rev.*, **51**, 279–89.

30. CHIPMAN, J. S. (1950) *The theory of intersectoral money flows and income formation.*

31. CONRAD, A. H. *Unemployment in a growing economy: the U.S. case and a program for balanced regional growth.* Public lecture delivered at the University of Edinburgh 19 April 1962. Published by the Netherlands Econ. Inst. Div. of Balanced International Growth, Mimeographed.

32. DORFMAN, R. (December 1953) 'Mathematical or linear programming: a non-mathematical exposition', *Am. Econ. Rev.*, **43**, 797–825.

33. DORFMAN, R. (September 1960) 'Operations research', *Am. Econ. Rev.*, 50, 580–86.
34. FISHER, J. L. (1955) 'Concepts in regional economic development programs', *Papers and Proceedings Reg. Sci. Assoc.*, 1, W1–W20.
35. FOX, K. A. (October 1953) 'A spatial equilibrium model of the livestock feed economy in the United States', *Econometrica*, 21, 547–66.
36. FREUTEL, G. (June 1952) 'The eighth district balance of trade', *Monthly Review*, Federal Reserve Bank of St Louis, 34, 69–78.
37. FUCHS, V. R. (Spring 1959) 'Changes in the location of U.S. manufacturing since 1929', *Jour. Reg. Sci.*, 1, 1–17.
38. FUCHS, V. R. (May 1962) 'The determinants of the redistribution of manufacturing in the United States since 1929', *Rev. Econ. Stat.*, 44, 167–77.
39. FUCHS, V. R. (1962) *Changes in the location of manufacturing in the United States since 1929.*
40. GARNSEY, M. E. (1950) *America's new frontier, the mountain west.*
41. GOODWIN, R. (December 1949) 'The Multiplier as matrix', *Econ. Jour.*, 59, 537–55.
42. HAGOOD, M. J., DANILEVSKY, N., and BEUM, C. O. (September 1941) 'An examination of the use of factor analysis in the problem of subregional delineation', *Rural Sociology*, 6, 216–33.
43. HAGOOD, M. J. (March 1943) 'Statistical methods for delineation of regions applied to data on agriculture and population', *Social Forces*, 21, 287–97.
44. HAGOOD, M. J., DANILEVSKY, N., BEUM, C. O., and BERNERT, E. H. (September 1945) 'Component indexes as a basis for stratification in sampling', *Jour. Am. Stat. Assoc.*, 40, 330–41.
45. HANDLIN, O. (1959) *The newcomers.*
46. HANNA, F. A. (August 1954) 'Cyclical and secular changes in state per capital incomes, 1929–50', *Rev. Econ. Stat.*, 36, 320–30.
47. HANNA, F. A. (1959) *State income differentials 1919–1954.*
48. HARRIS, BRITTON (November 1960) 'Plan or projection: an examination of the use of models in planring', *Jour. Am. Inst. Planners*, 26, 265–72.
49. HARRIS, BRITTON (September–October 1961) 'Some problems in the theory of intra-urban location', *Op. Res.*, 9, 695–721.
50. HARRIS, BRITTON (1961) *Regional growth model-activity distribution sub-model*, Penn–Jersey Study Paper No. 7.
51. HARRIS, BRITTON (April 1962) 'Experiments in projection of transportation and land use', *Traffic Quarterly*, 16, (2), 305–19.
52. HARRIS, BRITTON (1962) *PJ area systems*, Penn–Jersey Study Paper No. 14.
53. HARRIS, S. (1952) *The economics of New England.*
54. HARRIS, S. and others (1958) *New England textiles and the New England economy: report by the New England Governors' textile committee to the conference of New England Governors.*

55. HELFGOTT, R. B., GUSTAFSON, W. E., and HUND, J. M. (1960) *Made in New York*.

56. HENDERSON, J. M (1957) 'The utilization of agricultural land: a regional approach', *Papers and Proceedings Reg. Sci. Assoc.*, 3, 99–114.

57. HENDERSON, J. M. (1958) *The efficiency of the coal industry: an application of linear programming*.

58. HENDERSON, J. M. (June 1961) 'An economic analysis of the upper midwest region', *Four papers on methodology*, Upper Midwest Economic Study Technical Paper No. 1, 1–22.

59. HERBERT, J. D., and STEVENS, B. H. (Fall 1960) 'A model for the distribution of residential activity in urban areas', *Jour. Reg. Sci.*, 2, 21–36.

60. HIRSCH, W. Z. (August 1959) 'Interindustry relations of a metropolitan area', *Rev. Econ. Stat.*, 41, 360–9.

61. HIRSCH, W. Z. (May 1962) 'Design and use of regional accounts', *Am. Econ. Rev.*, 52, 365–73.

62. HOCHWALD, W. (1957) 'Conceptual issues of regional income estimation', *Regional Income*, Nat. Bur. of Econ. Research Stud. in Income and Wealth, 21, 9–26.

63. HOOVER, C. B., and RATCHFORD, B. U. (1951) *The economic resources and policies of the south*.

64. HOOVER, E. M. (1948) *The location of economic activity*.

65. HOOVER, E. M and VERNON, R. (1959) *Anatomy of a metropolis*.

66. HOYT, H. H. (May 1941) 'Economic background of cities', *Jour. Land and Pub. Util. Econ.*, 17, 188–95.

67. ISARD, W. (November 1951) 'Interregional and regional input–output analysis: a model of a space-economy', *Rev. Econ. Stat.*, 33, 318–28.

68. ISARD, W. (May 1954) 'Location theory and trade theory, short run analysis', *Quart. Jour. Econ.*, 68, 305–20.

69. ISARD, W. (1956) *Location and space economy*.

70. ISARD, W. (1960) *Methods of regional analysis*.

71. ISARD, W., and CUMBERLAND, J. H. (eds.) (1961) *Regional economic Planning: techniques of analysis for less developed areas*, Papers and Proceedings of the First Study Conference on Problems of Economic Development Organized by the European Productivity Agency.

72. ISARD, W., and FREUTEL, G. (1954) 'Regional and national product projection and their inter-relation', *Long Range Economic Projection*, Nat. Bur. of Econ. Research Stud. in Income and Wealth, 16, 427–71.

73. ISARD, W., and PECK, M. J. (February 1954) 'Location theory and international and interregional trade theory', *Quart. Jour. Econ.*, 68, 97–114.

74. ISARD, W., SCHOOLER, E. W., and VIETORISZ, T. (1959) *Industrial complex analysis and regional development*.

75. KAIN, J. F. (1962) 'The journey-to-work as a determinant of residential location', *Papers and Proceedings Reg. Sci. Assoc.*, 9

76. KAIN, J. F. (April 1962) *A multiple equation model of household locational and trip-making behaviour*, The RAND Corp.

77. KNUDTSON, A., and COX, R. (January 1962) *Upper Midwest agriculture: structure and problems*, Upper Midwest Economic Study, Study Paper No. 3.

78. KOOPMANS, T. L., and BECKMAN, M. (January 1957) 'Assignment problems and the location of economic activities', *Econometrica*, **25**, 53-76.

79. KREUGER, A. (June 1961) 'Interrelationships between agricultural income and population', *Four papers on methodology*, Upper Midwest Economic Study Technical Paper No. 1, 70-81.

80. LEFEBER, L. (1959) *Allocation in space.*

81. LICHTENBERG, R. M. *et al* (1960) *One-tenth of a nation.*

82. LISLE, E. A. (August-September 1962) 'Regional planning and urban development'. Paper given at International Congress on Economic Development.

83. LEONTIEF, W. W. (1951) *The structure of American economy 1919-1939*

84. LEONTIEF, W. W., *et al* (1953) *Studies in the structure of the American economy.*

85. LEONTIEF, W. W., and STROUT, A. (September 1961) 'Multiregional input-output analysis', Paper presented at International Conference on Input-Output Techniques.

86. LÖSCH, A. (1953) *The economics of location.*

87. LOWRY, I. S. (September 1960) *Design for an intra-regional locational model*, Pittsburgh Regional Planning Association Economic Study of the Pittsburgh Region, Working Paper No. 6.

88. METZLER, L. A. (October 1950) 'A multiple region theory of income and trade', *Econometrica*, **18**, 329-54.

89. MIERNYK, W. H. (1955) *Inter-industry labor mobility.*

90. MOORE, F. T. (May 1955) 'Regional economic reaction paths', *Am. Econ. Rev.*, **45**, 133-48.

91. MORGENSTERN, O. (ed.) (1954) *Economic activity analysis.*

92. MOSES, L. N. (1955) 'Interregional analysis', *Report on Research for 1954, Harvard Economic Research Project.*

93. MOSES, L. N. (December 1955) 'The stability of interregional trading patterns and input-output analysis', *Am. Econ. Rev.*, **45**, 803-32.

94. MOSES, L. N. (1957) 'An input-output, linear programming approach to interregional analysis', *Report, 1956-57, Harvard Economic Research Project.*

95. MOSES, L. N., and WILLIAMSON, H. W. (October 1962) *Economics of consumer choice in urban transportation.* Paper presented at a Symposium on The Dynamics of Urban Transportation.

96. MUTH, R. F. (January 1961) 'Economic change and rural–urban land conversions', *Econometrica*, **29**, 1–23.

97. NEFF, P. (May 1959) 'Interregional cyclical differentials: causes measurement, and significance', *Am. Econ. Rev.*, **39**, 105–19.

98. NEFF, P., and WERFENBACH, A. (1949) *Business cycles in selected industrial areas.*

99. NIEDERCORN, J. M., and KAIN, J. F. (August 1962) *Changes in the location of food and general merchandise store employment within metropolitan areas, 1948–1958.* Paper presented at the Western Economics Association Meeting.

100. NORTH, D. C. (June 1955) 'Location and regional economic growth', *Jour. Pol. Econ.*, **43**, 243–58.

101. OI, W. Y., and SHULDENER, P. W. (1962) *An analysis of urban travel demands.*

102. PERLOFF, H. S. (1957) *Regional studies at U.S. universities: a survey of regionally oriented research and graduate education activities.*

103. PERLOFF, H. S. (1957) 'Problems of assessing regional economic progress', *Regional Income*, Nat. Bur. of Econ. Research Stud. in Income and Wealth, **21**, 35–62.

104. PERLOFF, H. S. (May 1962) 'A national system of metropolitan information and analysis', *Am. Econ. Rev.*, **52**, 356–64.

105. PERLOFF, H. S., DUNN, E. S., LAMPARD, E. E., and MUTH, J. F. (1960) *Regions, resources and economic growth.*

106. ROBBINS, S. M., and TERLECKYJ, N. E. (1960) *Money metropolis.*

107. RODD, R. S. (June 1961) 'Information for an economic analysis of the upper Midwest region', *Four papers on methodology*, Upper Midwest Economic Study, Technical Paper No. 1, 23–40.

108. RODWIN, L. (1954) 'Planned decentralization and regional development with special reference to the British new towns', *Papers and Proceedings of the Regional Science Association*, **1**, A1–A8.

109. SEGAL, MARTIN (1960) *Wages in the metropolis.*

110. SJAASTAD, L. A. (June 1961) 'Migration in the upper Midwest', *Four papers on methodology*, Upper Midwest Economic Study, Technical Paper No. 1, 41–69.

111. STEVENS, B. H. (Summer 1958) 'An interregional linear programming model', *Jour. Reg. Sci.*, **1**, 60–98.

112. STONE, R. (1960) 'Social accounts at the regional level: a survey', *Regional economic planning: techniques of analysis*, Isard, W., and Cumberland, J. H. (eds.), pp. 263–93.

113. STOUFFER, S. A. (December 1940) 'Intervening opportunities: a theory relating mobility and distance', *Am. Soc. Rev.*, **5**, 845–67.

114. TIEBOUT, C. M. (February 1956) 'The urban economic base reconsidered', *Land Economics*, **32**, 95–9.

115. VERNON, R. (1960) *Metropolis 1985.*

116. VINING, R. (July 1945) 'Regional variation in cyclical fluctuation viewed as a frequency distribution', *Econometrica*, **13**, 183–213.

Introductory Surveys

117. VINING, R. (July 1946) 'The region as a concept in business-cycle analysis', *Econometrica*, 14, 201–18.

118. VINING, R. (May 1949) 'The region as an economic entity and certain variations to be observed in the study of systems of regions', *Am. Econ. Rev.*, 39, 89–104.

119. VINING, R. (January 1953) 'Delimitation of economic areas: statistical conceptions in the study of the spatial structure of an economic system', *Jour. Am. Stat. Assoc.*, 48, 44–64.

120. WARNER, S. L. (1962) *Stochastic choice of mode in urban travel: a study in binary choice.*

121. WARNTZ, W. (1959) *Geography of prices: a study in geo-econometrics.*

122. WINGO, L., JR., (1961) *Transportation and urban land.*

123. WOOD, R. C. with assistance of ALMENDINGER, V. V. (1961) *1400 Governments.*

124. ZIPF, G. K. (1954) *Human behavior and the principle of least effort.*

125. *Chicago area transportation study, final report, Volume II, data projections*, 1960.

126. *Detroit metropolitan area traffic study, Part I, data summary and interpretation*, 1955.

127. Federal Housing Administration, *Basic data on northern New Jersey housing market*, July 1937.

128. *Input–output analysis: an appraisal*, Nat. Bur. of Econ. Research Stud. in Income and Wealth, 16, 1958.

129. *Pittsburgh area transportation study, Vol. I, study findings*, 1961.

130. *Regional income*, Nat. Bur. of Econ. Research Stud. in Income and Wealth, 21, 1957.

2 C. L. Leven

Regional and Interregional Accounts in Perspective

C. L. Leven, 'Regional and interregional accounts in perspective', *Regional Science Association, Papers and Proceedings*, vol. 13 (1964), pp. 127–44.

This paper will attempt to review critically the development of regional accounts, to comment on some misconceptions in the use of such accounts, and to make some suggestions for the direction of subsequent research. The discussion will be divided into four sections. First, there will be a discussion of the development of regional accounts up to this time. Second, some problem of measurement in implementing the accounts will be reviewed and evaluated. The third section will consider some methodological issues, i.e. problems of formulating operational definitions and difficulties encountered in the analytical manipulation of the accounts. Finally, the fourth section will attempt a reconsideration of some of the conceptual issues in regional accounts analysis, with particular reference to the theoretical notions about regional economic growth which underlie the accounts as they typically have been formulated.

Before proceeding to the substance of the discussion it might be well to define rather specifically what is meant by 'accounts' and 'regional'. 'Social accounts' refers to the description of a particular phenomenon as the sum of a set of components, where some of the components are free to vary, and the others will be assumed to bear a fixed relationship to the variant ones. A system of such accounts will be regarded as a description of those aspects of the region's structure that are involved with the phenomena which are being accounted for. Analytically, such a system can be used to determine the effect on the structure, as a whole and in detail, of changes in the independent variables within it. The changes in the independent variables will be regarded as having been generated out of some other analysis, or stipulated as policy alternative, at least in the case of those variables amenable to policy manipulation.

'Region' will mean any continuous area which has either an assignable spatial location or spatially definable boundaries, such that the functional relationships between the defined region and any other region depend upon their defined locations and/or boundaries. Metropolitan areas or nonmetropolitan 'functional economic areas' will be regarded as regions which typically have a high ratio of external to internal trade and a high degree of economic interdependence among their inhabitants.[1]

The Development of Regional Accounts

The description of the development of regional accounts contained in this section must necessarily be brief, so there will be no attempt at presenting a complete bibliographical history, already available elsewhere (Isard, 1957; Perloff, 1957). Also, no attempt will be made to trace the developments in economic base analysis prior to the series of articles by Richard B. Andrews appearing in *Land Economics* about fourteen years ago. There are two reasons for this; first, such developments have been traced rather thoroughly by Professor Andrews in that series, and second, prior to that time the interests of economists in regional analysis were quite limited and there were not any regional scientists, or at most one, to be interested.

Also, the discussion will omit any consideration of the much longer tradition in the estimation of aggregate or *per capita* income payments for small regions like counties.[2] While related to work in regional accounts, such estimates are not directly aimed at the analysis of regional economic structure, but at interregional comparisons of real income and sometimes the distribution of income among major classes of factors of production. Similarly, there will be no direct attempt to cover developments in what

1. 'Functional economic areas' are multicounty regions, generally centered around third-order central places, and have been suggested by Professor Karl A. Fox as logical spatial units for local economic development analysis and policy formation.

2. Copeland (1952) contains descriptions of techniques and an excellent bibliography of work up to that period. Since then there have been few methodological developments, but several in regard to data retrieval.

could be called the analysis of interregional convergence, usually directed at the testing of convergence hypotheses with respect to levels of real *per capita* income, wage rates, or rates of return of capital.[3] Finally, there will be no explicit consideration of intra-metropolitan transportation and land-use models.[4] At least up to this point, most of the work on such models does not really fit the preceding definition of accounts, but rather is more closely related to distributional solutions of sets of spatial equilibrium equations (Herbert and Stevens, 1960; Harris, 1963).

Turning then to the Andrews articles as a starting point, it seems reasonable to inquire as to why they can be so regarded. An obvious point is that they were contemporaneous with the really serious beginnings of regional science as a discipline; but so was a good deal of other work on the economic base by geographers and planners. But the interesting thing about the Andrews articles is that they are frequently quoted in the literature of regional science and regional economics. And this continues to be the case in spite of the fact that besides a very complete review of fairly obscure earlier work (which itself is hardly ever cited) the series contains very little, if any, of what could currently be regarded as useful technique, and no theoretical discussion beyond very elementary economic base ideas.[5]

Actually, the real significance of the Andrews work is that it represents the first attempt to look at economic base studies, not as a mechanical analytical device, but as embodying a conceptual notion worthy of critical evaluation. In most earlier work the economic base was an expedient technique for estimating the future population of a city. It was developed primarily in conjunction with studies done by the Federal Housing Administration during the thirties. Their problem was a simple one; at least simple to

3. For examples and discussion of 'convergence' studies, see R. Easterlin (1960), and Borts and Stein (1961).

4. Note the prominence given to these articles in John Meyer (1963).

5. Interestingly, the item of earlier work which probably most nearly anticipated current work in regional accounts, 'Oskaloosa *vs* the world', *Fortune*, April 1938, is not even referred to in the Andrews work. Another example of earlier work anticipating later developments is variously unpublished manuscripts of Professor David Crane, Department of City Planning at the University of Pennsylvania, in connection with a study of Massachusetts communities which was done in the late forties.

state. In making plans for public housing, they were concerned with the future demand for housing. The notion of the economic base, essentially borrowed from the New York Regional Study of 1928 (Andrews, 1953–6), reduced the problem of estimating total future population to estimating future 'town-building' employment, with an assumed fixed ratio of 'town-filling' to 'town-building' employment and a fixed number of inhabitants per employed worker. True, the economic base idea did rest on certain conceptions of a structural nature, but only in a rather vague way.

In Andrews' articles, however, the economic base for almost the first time is regarded primarily as a vehicle for describing and analyzing a region's economic structure,[6] and the process of regional growth itself. Quite naturally, he considered, among other things, the unit of measurement of the economic base. As long as the base idea was nothing more than a technique for estimating employment this question was meaningless. In a theory descriptive of the process of regional change, however, the question of 'Change in What?' became significant. Andrews considered a variety of alternatives (employment, payrolls, sales, value added, etc.) and came up with the idea that one should use all of these measures simultaneously.

The present author on first looking into Andrews was not convinced. In accordance with good Keynesian theory, it seemed that the lack of precision in Andrews' research recommendations was unnecessary. Income, employment and production were all functionally related and so a plea was made for 'value added' as the appropriate measure; not as conventionally defined, however, but as value added at all stages of production in the region, commodity by commodity – sort of a gross product by industrial origin (Leven, 1954).

Another appeal of the value-added or gross-product concept to those with a background in economics was that it lent itself readily to the making of allowances for charges against a region's trade balance as well as for credits to it. After all, if the planners and geographers felt that it was export trade that determined a region's future, the least the economists could do was to give them a comprehensive measure of it. This led to the notion of an ex-

6. Although not in economic base terms, the *Fortune* article cited above would have to be regarded as an exposition of regional economic structure.

tended rest of the world account as central to the analysis, and this led, rather naturally, to the formulation of a set of double-entry income and product accounts for a regional economy.[7]

To a considerable extent these accounts and regional accounts that have been formulated since that time are step-children of the United States national income accounts. The handling of government requires somewhat special consideration since, for a region, the federal government occupies a super-regional position. The rest of the world account generally has received a more complete statement than in the national accounts; in particular, flows of factor payments over the borders are treated explicitly, instead of being suppressed into the current commodity flow figures as is done for the United States. Exports are regarded as including 'invisibles', as in the case of the United States accounts, but unlike the treatment in conventional economic base studies.

Probably the most important innovation is the addition of *indirect* to *direct* exports, that is the value added in the production of raw materials for export. This innovation was necessary to get to a measure of gross product, rather than income, by industrial origin. The gross-product concept appeared necessary to account for differences in the commodity composition of changes in export demand, and their effect on the final equilibrium level of gross regional product.[8] Finally, Professor Tiebout demonstrated the similarities between the economic base concept, and the more familiar concept of the foreign-trade multiplier (Tiebout, 1957). The regional economists felt quite comfortable.

Contemporaneous with the developments discussed above, a number of specific empirical regional inter-industry studies were made (Hirsch, 1959; Hochwald, Striner and Sonenblum, 1960; Isard and Kuenne, 1953; Moore and Peterson, 1955). These, too, were cast substantially in the image of their ancestors at the national level, usually with even less alteration of their format than in the

7. The first explicit formulation of income and product accounts for a region occurred as part of the background analysis for a series of community studies appearing in the 1954 Annual Report of the Federal Reserve Bank of Chicago. Their formulation was jointly conceived, though perhaps not for the first time, by the present author and Professor Dick Netzer, both then members of the bank's research staff.

8. See Leven (1961) for further discussion of the treatment of indirect exports.

case of regional income accounts.[9] Regional input–output models will be discussed in another paper at these meetings, but one point only might be noted here, namely that it took several years for it to become clear that these two kinds of analyses were much more complementary than competitive (Leven, 1961). The derivation of figures for indirect exports in the accounts does require an inter-industry calculation, and the input–output analyses would seem to require some kind of multiplier analysis to estimate final demand in the household sector.

Another development in regional accounting which deserves at least some mention is a number of brief forays into accounting for moneyflows on a regional basis (Hartland, 1950; Hile, 1955). A major factor underlying these studies is the unsuitability of a conventional savings and investment account, in real terms, as a tool for analyzing the warranted rate of growth of a region. The net foreign investment residual in the income and product accounts simply does not have much significance for an 'open' region where capital movements are not only large, relative to real capital formation, but also frequently contractual on a fairly long-term basis. The moneyflows accounts attempt to trace out some or all of these gross capital flows, but in retrospect it does not seem that the question to which they are directed is a particularly interesting one. Potentially, they might be useful for explaining regional differences in the cost of capital, or other prices for that matter, but this has not been gone into at all thoroughly.[10]

There are a few other developments which should be noted. Accounts have been formulated directly in terms of employment (Tiebout, 1962; Hoover, 1964), and suggestions for formulating them in terms of land use have been made (Leven and Perloff, 1964).

In some accounts studies, the sectors of final demand have been broken down, but only as subcategories of the basic four-section division in the national income accounts (Tiebout, 1962). Finally, suggestions have been made for broadening the scope of phenomena covered, particularly with respect to the social costs and

9. And in some cases, they assumed that the regional coefficients were equal to those for the United States.

10. See Leven and Perloff (1964), footnote 8, for a suggestion on this point that was made by Professor Ruth Mack.

benefits of local government activities (Hirsch, 1964) and to the inclusion of an accounting for stocks of human and nonhuman resources associated with the conventionally accounted for activity flows (Perloff, 1961; Leven and Perloff, 1964).

While considerable interest has been expressed in interregional accounts, the only ones actually implemented empirically have followed a fairly straightforward input–output framework (e.g. Moses, 1955). So far as regional income and product accounts are concerned, no real attempt at implementation has been made, although the definitional compatability between accounts as formulated for a single region and Lloyd Metzler's concept of interregional multipliers has been pointed out (Leven 1961; Metzler, 1950).

The foregoing discussion is intended to describe more or less where we are now with respect to the design and scope of regional accounts systems. The remainder of this paper will be concerned with a critical evaluation of some problems of measurement, methodology, and theoretical concepts. No attempt will be made, however, at a chronology of such developments, but rather, the discussion will be limited to those issues which seem at present to be still unresolved, together with some suggestions for future research directions which might aid in their resolution.

Some Problems of Measurement

This section will not attempt to assess either the emergence of or resolution of data limitations *per se*. Unavailability and unreliability of data needed to implement empirically regional accounts certainly have been and continue to be serious research problems. Most of these problems relate to the lack of co-ordination and sometimes lack of competence of many state and local statistical agencies and to limited access dictated by rules against disclosure.[11]

11. It should be noted that disclosure problems are becoming less serious. The Bureau of the Census will process individual respondent data for non-government researchers where the results, but not the individual respondent data, are sufficient. What still is needed is a way of confidentially processing individual respondent data from the census with individual respondent data from a variety of other sources without disclosure to the researcher or the respective statistical agencies. This is a useful function which might be solved through the establishment of regional data centers.

These kinds of problems, however, extend to all phases of regional analysis and regional science and are not peculiar to regional accounts. Here the discussion will be confined to problems of measurement in principle.

One issue of interest is the question of the extent to which estimates of particular regional parameters can be obtained by disaggregation of national data. In part, this is simply a matter of disclosure, but there are also more basic matters. Most important, there is no way to derive the detailed information on interregional commodity flows (except for I.C.C. waybill data which is of only limited usefulness), labor commutation and capital transfers from present national data sources, as all of these movements sum to zero for the nation as a whole.[12] The possibilities for developing regional measures of input coefficients for individual industries (which might be useful in some contexts, as will be pointed out later) also appear doubtful, at least so far as the author understands the United States Department of Commerce's data collection procedure. It does seem possible to obtain some regional measures of the pattern of consumer spending from survey work done in connection with the Consumer Price Index. Nevertheless, the prospects of deriving regional accounts data primarily from existing federal data collection programs do not appear bright.[13]

A more specific measurement problem which has received considerable discussion is that of determining an efficient and accurate means for estimating the export flows from a region, by commodity. The technique of 'localization coefficients', frequently used in traditional economic base studies was discarded by regional scientists at an early stage. In addition to its inherent assumptions of interregional homogeneity with respect to production functions, consumption patterns, and even product mix, it also measures only 'net' as opposed to 'gross' exports; it is the latter which are relevant for multiplier calculations.[14] Thus, by underestimating exports, it overestimates the size of the foreign-

12. That such information could be collected by a federal agency is, of course, true, but this would represent a new data gathering task.

13. For further comment on this point, see Ruggles and Ruggles (1964).

14. For a fuller discussion of these limitations, see H. Blumenfeld (1955), and Leven (1963).

trade multiplier. And even worse, this technique will produce a consistently more downward biased estimate of exports, the greater the degree of aggregation employed in classifying industries (Leven, 1958).

Thus, except for one possibility, there would seem to be a general consensus that direct commodity flow information is necessary to determine export flows. The possible exception is the 'minimum requirements' technique, which estimates exports as the excess of regional production over the amount indicated by a regression relationship between regional population and the minimum per cent of the labor force employed in each of several regional-size classes, in any particular commodity classification (Ullman and Dacey, 1960). Unpublished calculations, using the minimum requirements technique, which were made by Professor Ullman for Sioux City, show considerable variations from survey-determined data for individual broad industry groupings, but produce a total export estimate practically identical to that determined from the surveys.[15] This suggests the possibility that the minimum requirements technique at least is unbiased and perhaps even better. It would seem useful to engage in some further testing of this hypothesis, particularly in light of the very much lower cost of making these kinds of calculations as opposed to primary data collection. Moreover, even if not generally applicable, they might be fairly reliable estimators for selected commodity classes.

Another measurement problem has concerned the allocation of undistributed corporate profits of multiregional firms. Taking the expedient of assuming that they should be accounted for as accruing all to home offices,[16] there remains the problem of estimating the excess of profits earned in 'foreign' branches of 'domestic' corporations over those earned by 'domestic' branches of 'foreign' ones. In an income accounting system such an estimate is necessary as a component of the term $(F_{zx} - F_{xz})$ in the relationship

$$Y_R = Y_P - (F_{zx} - F_{xz}) - (T_{zz} - T_{xz}) - (U_{zx} - U_{xz}) - W_x - B_{xx}$$

15. The published data based on field survey can be found in Sioux City Planning and Zoning Commission, 'Economic Report, 1959'.

16. For a justification, see Leven (1958), pp. 53-6.

where Y_R is income of the region's residents; Y_P is net product in the area;[17] F_{zx} and F_{xz} are factor payments, T_{zx} and T_{xz} are taxes and government transfer payments, and U_{zx} and U_{xz} are unilateral transfers received from and paid to abroad, respectively; W_x is undistributed profits of domestic corporations; and B_{xx} is business transfer payments from domestic firms to the region's residents.[18] In any accounting system, though, as many items as there are linearly independent relationships in the system can be determined as residuals. Thus, if any of the items so determined in the system containing this relationship can, alternatively, be estimated directly, then the net inflow of undistributed corporate profits component of $(F_{zx} - F_{xz})$ can be determined as a residual. Personal income accruing to the region's residents, Y_R, would seem to be such an item. Moreover, the prospects for obtaining estimates of this item from Bureau of Internal Revenue statistics seem quite good, at least in principle. And, even in the absence of this possibility, estimating county or multicounty regional personal income by applying allocation techniques to state income payments data probably should have appeared more appealing than trying to estimate interregional corporate profits flows all along. This also indicates that the whole discussion of the appropriate regional allocation of such undistributed profits was rather pointless; their only purpose was to get an estimate of Y_R. Interestingly, though, what appeared to be an arbitrary expedient, assigning them to home offices, now appears to be logically consistent with the remainder of the system.

The final measurement problem which will be discussed concerns the appropriate strategy for obtaining the data on interindustry flows needed to determine the amount of production activity going indirectly into exports and other sectors of final demand, respectively. So long as all that is needed is the input purchases of each industry from every other industry *in the region*, as opposed to the total input purchases of each industry, it would seem simpler to design a survey instrument which is aimed at

17. In earlier statements, this term was ambiguously defined simply as 'income produced in the region', with no allowance for subtraction of capital consumption allowances of domestic establishments.

18. For a complete description of the specific system of which this relationship is a part, see Leven (1961).

filling in the rows as opposed to the columns. Generally, a firm produces a smaller number of outputs than it buys inputs, and it is more likely that they will know to whom they sell in the region than from whom they buy. Where it would be necessary to know total inputs including amounts imported, it would, of course, be necessary to fill up the table, column by column, based on either survey data on inputs or production function assumptions. But which kind of interindustry formulation seems most appropriate is really a methodological question, that is, it depends upon the kinds of questions which we want the accounts system to be able to answer. That is the subject of the next section.

Some Matters of Methodology

In this section, the discussion will turn to some matters concerning the way in which particular items in the accounts are to be defined and the way in which certain analytical relationships are to be determined, but all within the context of accounts based on a simple economic base or foreign-trade multiplier theory. Discussion of the viability of such a simple theoretical underpinning will be covered in the next section.

Let us turn first to the question of the appropriate form in which to express interindustry relationships. As has been pointed out earlier, the most useful information would be a complete interindustry account, made up of a matrix of total interindustry inputs *and* a matrix showing the amount of each input obtained as imports. The necessity of obtaining imports by supplying industries (as opposed simply to total imports of each domestic industry) is necessary to allow fully for the effects of the industrial composition of changes in final demand on activity levels. The determination of such an account would require the estimation of two of the following three sets of information: (1) the technologically required total inputs of every domestic industry, (2) the inputs of every domestic industry supplied by other domestic producers, (3) the imports inputs of every domestic industry. Two of the three sets would suffice, since the matrix represented by the first set would be the sum of the other two matrices. A question which has been raised earlier, and which still seems appropriate is, 'Which set of information would be most useful if only one set could be obtained?' (Leven, 1961). Clearly, the import information alone would be of relatively little use. The choice between the other two would seem to depend largely on a judgment as to the relative importance of changes in technology as opposed to changes in trading relationships (the proportion of each input obtained from domestic as opposed to foreign sources) as a determinant of changes in activity levels, give the level of final demand. As pointed out in earlier work, the choice would seem to depend on the size and complexity of the region's economy. Where trade is small relative to total activity, say for the United States, the first set of information, that is, an input–output table seems called for. For even a fairly large metropolitan region, however, changes in trading relationships stemming from changes in relative prices

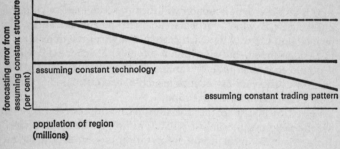

forecasting error from assuming constant structure (per cent)

assuming constant technology

assuming constant trading pattern

population of region (millions)

Figure 1

and from local agglomeration are likely to dominate technological change and so the second set of information seems called for. For want of a better name this has been called a 'from-to' table (Leven, 1961, p. 170).

As indicated in Figure 1 (ignoring the dotted line), the error in projections of activity levels stemming from changes in trading relationships is likely to be quite large for a very small area, falling rather sharply to a quite small amount for the United States, as a whole. Errors due to changes in technological requirements, however, would be likely to be fairly invariant with respect to regional size. Technological change still is likely to be fairly important, even in a very small region. As the figure is drawn, it indicates that 'from-to' tables would dominate up to a region as large as about half the United States' population. But note that there are no scales indicated on the vertical axis. While one can speculate on the relative slopes of these lines, it seems much more difficult to speculate even about their relative, much less absolute, ordinates. Accordingly, their relative positions easily could be as shown by the dotted line, where 'input–output' tables dominate for all except the very smallest regions. Determining the relative slopes and positions of such lines still appears to be a worthwhile research task.

Another methodological matter concerns the definition of the foreign-trade multiplier. In this connection two issues not previously discussed at all will be raised, both relating to misconceptions in the present author's earlier work and previously undetected by the author, or, apparently, by anyone else. In earlier work the foreign-trade multiplier for a single region *vis-à-vis* the rest of the world was determined as

$$(1) \qquad \frac{1}{1 - V_C/Y_P}$$

where V_C is the value added in the region, directly and indirectly, in the production of goods for personal consumption, and Y_P is the total value added or, approximately, the gross product produced in the region.[19] Where investment is regarded as endogenous and V_I is the value added in production of investment goods, the multiplier would have been

$$(2) \qquad \frac{1}{1 - (V_C + V_I)/Y_P}.$$

The ratio of V_C/Y_P is simply an average approximation to the marginal propensity to generate value added domestically in the production of goods for consumption; it is the value added equivalent of the marginal propensity to consume domestically produced goods, which, in turn, is nothing more than the difference between the marginal propensity to consume and the marginal propensity to import.

The multiplier formulation indicated above is seriously in error

19. For derivation of the formula, see Leven (1961) p. 236, and for the reconciliation between the definitions of value added and gross product, see Leven, op. cit., footnote 17.

in two respects. First, it makes no allowance for differences in the size of the multiplier, depending on the industrial composition of a change in some category of final demand, say export demand. It was the possibility of allowing for just such differences which served as much of the rationale for incorporating interindustry calculations into the accounts in the first place. Second, the marginal propensity to consume is related not to the increment to regional disposable personal income, but to regional gross product! This destroys most of the point even of bothering to determine Y_R in the accounts. Accordingly, the multiplier formula should be

$$(3) \qquad \frac{1}{1 - \dfrac{V_C}{Y_R} \cdot \dfrac{Y_R}{Y_P}} \cdot \varDelta V_X (I - T)^{-1} \Bigg/ \varDelta V_X$$

where V_C, Y_P, and Y_R are all scalar quantities, as defined earlier, $\varDelta V_X$ is a $(1 \times n)$ vector, indicating the change in value added by industry resulting directly from a specified change in the export bill of goods,[20] and $(I - T)$ is an $(n \times n)$ matrix, where T is the matrix of from-to coefficients. Both for convenience and for other reasons to be discussed below, the formula is written in terms of average rather than marginal relationships, but it will be simpler for the moment to discuss them as if they were written in marginal terms.

In any event, the product of the first two scalar terms represents the foreign-trade multiplier for a change in export demand which generated *no further interindustry effect at all*. The term V_C/Y_R is the domestic value added, directly and indirectly, out of the propensity to consume out of domestic disposable personal income. There is no necessity to calculate value added indirectly in production for consumption on an interindustry basis as long as we assume unit income elasticity of consumption demand for all commodities. If this were not the case and some other consumption bill of goods were specified, the scalar quantity V_C would be

20. The symbol V_x did not appear in earlier versions of the author's work. It is not to be confused, however, with V_e the value added *directly and indirectly* in production for export. V_x is direct value added only. Its symbolic equivalent in Leven, op. cit., would be

$$v_e^i \ (i = 1, \ \ldots , n).$$

replaced by the scalar $\sum_{i=1}^{m} V_c^l (I - T)^{-1}$. Note that while V_C is a scalar quantity indicating the total value added in consumption in all industry's products, V_c is a vector showing a value added in the production of goods for consumption industry by industry. This vector multiplied by the matrix $(I - T)^{-1}$ and summed over i industries results in a scalar quantity.

The second term is simply the propensity to generate personal disposable income to the region's residents out of an increase in gross product produced in the region. Thus, generalizing with respect to consumption, but continuing to treat investment as exogenous, the foreign-trade multiplier would be

$$(4) \qquad \frac{1}{1 - \dfrac{\sum_i V_c(I - T)^{-1} \; Y_R}{Y_R} \cdot \dfrac{1}{Y_P}} \cdot \Delta V_x(I - T)^{-1} \; \bigg/ \; \Delta V_x.$$

This is the regional accounts equivalent to the nonbasic : basic employment multiplier concept.

The third term in equation (3) is the vector by industry of the change in value added *directly and indirectly* from production to export resulting from a given change in value added *directly* in producing for export (V_x alone is the *direct* value added). To express this in terms of the effect of a change in export sales on value added or employment, substitute $\Delta S_x \cdot V_x/S_x$ for ΔV_x, where ΔS_x is the vector of changes in export sales by industry. Then the foreign-trade multiplier with respect to the effect of change in sales on total value added or employment would be

$$(5) \qquad \frac{1}{1 - \dfrac{\sum_i V_c(I - T)^{-1} \; Y_R}{Y_R} \cdot \dfrac{1}{Y_P}} \cdot \Delta S_x \cdot \frac{V_x}{S_x} (I - T)^{-1} \; \bigg/ \; \Delta S_x.$$

These multipliers naturally would be smaller than the employment or value-added multipliers due to trade leakages from the import of raw materials for the production of exports. In other words, the impact of an extra dollar of export *sales* obviously would be less than of an extra dollar's worth of value added in producing for export.

As seen in Table 1, the reformulation of the multiplier does make a difference in the quantitative results, at least for certain

Table 1
Foreign-trade Employment or Value-added Multipliers, by Industry of Change in Final Demand, Sioux City, 1958*

Industry	Household component	Interindustry = component	Multiplier
Agriculture	1.55	1.04	1.62
Meat packing	1.55	1.21	1.87
Other food processing	1.55	1.10	1.71
Other manufacturing	1.55	1.11	1.72
Transportation and communication	1.55	1.06	1.64
Trade	1.55	1.30	2.01
Finance, insurance and real estate	1.55	1.10	1.70
Services	1.55	1.13	1.74

* Computed from data in 'Sioux City Economic Report, 1959'.
Note: These show the multiplier effect of a unit change in export employment or value added. The effect of a unit change in export sales on export employment or value added would be smaller.

industries, and at least in Sioux City, where revised figures could be derived. The value computed on the basis of equation (1) was 1.64. So far as the household multiplier is concerned, the difference is limited in that where Y_R is less (greater) than Y_P, the first term of equation (3) will be bigger (smaller), but the second term will be smaller (bigger) as compared will the earlier formula, equation (1).

Another problem in deriving multiplier values is deciding whether average or marginal propensities should be used. As a practical matter where data have been collected only for a single time period and no cross-section data are available, the average relationships are all that can be computed anyway. Even so, a rationale for actually preferring average-to-marginal relationships has been constructed (Tiebout, 1962). The essence of the argument is that where growth in regional income takes the form of an increase in the number of employed persons, with average income per worker remaining the same, the region's marginal propensity to consume is actually the average propensity to consume of future residents, who probably can be assumed to have pretty much the same spending habits as the present residents. Implicit in the argument is that where increased income takes the form of increased average income to a fixed labor force, the appropriate measure of the region's marginal propensity to consume is the marginal propensity to consume of these workers. But marginal propensity to consume over what period? For the United States as a whole, the average propensity to consume has remained quite stable over several decades. This suggests a good possibility that in the context of analyzing long-run regional growth, the average propensity to consume might be the appropriate measure, both for determining the impact of increased number of workers and increased earnings per worker even if a measure of the short-run marginal propensity to consume were available.

Taking Y_R/Y_P as an approximation for dY_R/dY_P may be a more serious matter. This assumes a constant proportionality between labor commutation rates, net receipt of property income from abroad, taxes net of transfer payments to nonlocal government, and undistributed profits of domestic corporations, all with respect to gross product originating in the region. In most cases, it would seem prudent, at least, to consider making adjustments for these assumptions, but it is hard to see how they could be made in other than an *ad hoc* manner.

A fine methodological point concerns the explicit definition of direct exports. In regional accounts, as in the national accounts, the definition has been extended to include 'invisibles', including, in addition to services, commodities purchased by nonresidents while in the region. But, to some extent, this begs the question of who is a resident. In particular, it requires some decision with respect to the residence classification of institutional populations, such as students, military personnel, and inmates of prisons and state hospitals. In general, such individuals have been regarded as members of the local community,[21] and their personal outlays regarded as local consumption.[22] While the people involved are transients, they are likely to be replaced by other transients, much like themselves. While satisfactory, this treatment is arbitrary and opens up the whole question of regional definition in a functional context. Some of the major alternatives which seem to exist are to define the region as all of the people working there, or living there, or perhaps buying there.[23] This, however, is more a conceptual than a methodological issue and it will be discussed in the next section.

Some Conceptual Issues

This concluding section primarily will attempt to re-evaluate the concept of 'export or die', inherited from economic base theory and still the fundamental theoretical underpinning of most work in regional accounts. Let me state right at the outset that I think that this concept may be seriously inadequate. While not a convincing counter-argument, it is still somewhat disturbing to note that the economy of the world as a whole does grow without exporting anything (the sending of missiles into space would be a unilateral transfer; not an export).

For metropolitan regions it is probably true that increasing size, almost invariably, is associated with an increasing absolute level of income earned through exporting.[24] But this is hardly a convincing demonstration of a causal relationship. For example, it is also true that a rising level of aggregate income in any economy would virtually always be associated with a rising absolute level of net investment. But even though this is the case, most of us regard businessmen's statements to the effect that the only way

21. Although their support typically would be accounted for as a transfer from abroad.

22. Outlays on local goods of the institutions with which they were associated might, however, be classed as exports if these were instrumentalities of nonlocal government.

23. For a discussion of the problems of asymmetry between alternative definitions, see W. Hochwald (1957).

24. The relationships of size to gross export sales would probably not be so regular due to wide variations in the imported raw material component of different commodities in different places.

to secure economic growth in the American economy is by creating inducements for private business investment as at best misguided, and at worst dangerous half-truths.

At the same time, however, we do not always see the same kind of limited applicability in the export theory of regional growth determination. We have probably paid too little attention to Professor Tiebout's uneasiness on this score several years ago.[25] At that time the answer to the question 'Can a region grow without an increase in exports?' intuitively seemed to be 'Yes'. Unfortunately, this observation was waylaid by the observation that increased regional size was associated with increased export volume. In reconsidering that controversy at this time, it seems appropriate to consider the possibility that, at least in part, increased exports may be a consequence, not a cause of increased growth in increased *per capita* real income.

To illustrate, suppose we have a three-person economy on a remote island, consisting of two barbers and a masseur, who provide each other with personal services, otherwise living on wild nuts and berries. Under such conditions, increased productivity in their primary occupations would lead to increased real income. This greater productivity initially might take the form of increased leisure for all of them. But it also might result in a sufficient increase in the haircut price of musical entertainment, the haircut price of massages remaining the same, to induce one of the barbers to forsake his shears for a fiddle. Or, in the absence of a lack of musical ability on the part of any of the aboriginal inhabitants, they might bid up the price of musical entertainment sufficiently high to persuade a musician to immigrate to their island. Quite clearly growth in *per capita* income could proceed indefinitely without external trade limited only by the productivity of the inhabitants of the island and the possible gains from the division of labor. Accompanying growth in the island's population could also increase indefinitely without external trade, limited only by the foregoing limitations and by a continued differential of *per capita* real

25. See Tiebout's exchange with North some years ago. The real limitation of that discussion was that the only real alternative explanatory variables considered explicitly were autonomous investment or shifts in the consumption function; in short, traditional Keynesian variables, which are most applicable only to problems of change in the short run. See Tiebout and North (1956).

income of the islanders over levels someplace else, including full allowance for detractions to real income stemming from congestion.[26]

But there is something else that is also likely to happen to the island's economy. Specifically, opportunities for the division of labor are not likely to be exhausted within the island. Comparative advantages in production most probably would arise and trade with other regions would occur. Moreover, so long as the possibility of gains from trade is not exhausted, the absolute volume of trade would increase along with the increase in the island's total population.

Basically, then, in this example the driving force behind economic growth is rising productivity. This is hardly a very startling statement. Such increased productivity could stem from increases in the stock of physical capital, but also from increases in the stock of human capital, from resource discovery, from invention, or from a change in tastes. The increase in the volume of trade is simply an expected consequence of market adjustments to higher productivity. It is generated mainly by the proliferation rather than intensification of human wants as real income rises and by secular changes in technology which tend to increase the technological possibilities for exploiting the division of labor.

What the foregoing discussion seems to indicate is the desirability of reconsidering both the delineation of sectors of final demand and the definitional distinction between final and intermediate production. This latter distinction as well as the sector definitions is arbitrary. For example, 'Is the cost of air-conditioning an office an intermediate business input or wages in kind to the employees?'

As noted above, almost all work in regional accounts has proceeded on the basis of a consumption-investment-government-rest of the world sectoring, or some simple variant thereof. In trying to develop a new theoretical conception of regional growth, it might be useful to reconsider the appropriateness of this particular sectoring.

26. Moreover, in a more realistic situation where we assumed some small but not increasable amount of initial trade throughout, the process could be accelerated by induced agglomeration of industries to supply input needs of domestic producers; in this case, exports might actually decrease!

Turning first to exports, the relevant question is whether they really are independent of activity levels within the region. Here it might be useful to distinguish between exports of commodities for which *per capita* demand is a decreasing function of distance, and those for which it is not. The former group would probably be most trade and personal services and some business services. The reason for this distinction, of course, is that exports of the first type are likely to generate feedback effects, while the latter would not. For example, increased exports to the surrounding hinterland would increase income in the region, which would increase imports from the hinterland, which would increase its income and imports, and hence further increase exports of the region. Even where there might be large trade to the hinterland, however, it would not necessarily be important to segregate it into a separate sector unless the region were also significant in the hinterland's export market.[27]

So far as investment is concerned, some revisions also seem to be in order. In the case of residential investment, it would seem to be just as closely related to consumer income as any other category of consumer spending in the long run. Therefore, it might be useful to redefine investment so as to exclude residential construction. In the long run, investment in inventories ought to be very closely related to output levels; hence, they probably could be regarded as intermediate inputs. There would be a statistical problem here, however, in that data for a single year could not necessarily be regarded as reflecting equilibrium inventory-sales ratios.

This would leave only business plant and equipment expenditures left in investment. These could be broken down usefully in two ways. First, plant could be distinguished from equipment; square feet of floor space may vary more directly with output than the amount of equipment. This is, of course, a statement which does require verification. Second, so far as increases in investment are concerned, it might be useful to separate them into

27. This discussion of the export sector really opens up anew the whole question of geographic delimitation of regions. For the most part, metropolitan regions have been defined so as to approximate a closed labor market. A closed retail shopping market also could be used as a definition. In this case, though, we would have to be prepared to find more overlapping of adjacent areas than in the case of labor market areas. In any event, this is outside the scope of this paper.

increased investment expected in establishments already existing in the region from investment in establishments to be started anew. And the latter might be broken down into those expected to go into existing structures and those expected to go into new structures.

Government presents more of a problem.[28] Outlays, both current and capital, of local government which are *of the type that are primarily locally financed* might go back into the interindustry matrix; the hypothesis is that they are close to unit community-income elastic in the long run. Local expenditures of the type ordinarily financed mainly by grants and aids from state or federal government would remain as a separate sector of final demand, with current and capital outlays probably separated.

Sales to agencies of state and federal government totally outside the region can probably be regarded as a single exogenous category of final demand. The only likely problem that might arise would be the necessity of allowing for 'feedbacks'. In this regard, however, exports to government would be no different in principle than exports to private purchasers. Feedbacks might be especially important for a metropolitan area which constituted a large share of a state's, or maybe even the nation's, tax base.

This still leaves sales to agencies of nonlocal government which are located within the region itself. This is probably the most difficult, though certainly not the most critical, part of the government sector to account for. Some sales, like those to a local air base, clearly are exports, and with no more chance of manifesting a feedback relationship than if they were far away. On the other hand, things like postal services, meat inspection, and many judicial functions could be regarded as local activities, either for interindustry uses or final consumption, and could be so accounted for. The cost of providing them would be accounted for as a transfer payment in kind to the region's residents or firms using the services. Also, in this case it might seem well to separate current from capital outlays, if possible.

So far as consumption is concerned, there would seem to be

28. In much of the author's earlier work, the government sector was suppressed into the other sectors, but this was mainly for reasons of expedience of simplicity. It was never argued that these were generally defensible grounds for such treatment.

some sense in trying to separate it into three categories, consumption of goods with known and fairly constant population elasticities of demand, consumption of goods with known and fairly constant income elasticities of demand, and other consumption. The first two categories could be fitted into the interindustry matrix and the last left as a sector of final demand. This and other suggestions made for redefining the sectors of final demand involve putting some parts of final demand into the interindustry matrix. There must also be a consideration of whether anything in the interindustry matrix should be brought out into the final demand sector.

In this regard it should be noted that this is not meant as an attempt to maim or disfigure interindustry or income and product accounts, but rather an attempt to use them more effectively as techniques for structural analysis. It must be recognized that accounts aimed at explaining changes in activity levels should not necessarily be designed in the same way as those geared to measure aggregate income in a welfare context or activity levels in the context of nonviolation of factor input constraints. With this in mind, it would seem advisable to take a much closer look at the distinctions we have made between intermediate and final output. It seems a little foolish, for example, to treat household expenditures on toothpaste as exogenous and business outlays on research and development as endogenous, even in the short, much less the long run. The whole business-services area, including mainly outlays for administrative and auxiliary activities, would appear to include many likely candidates for transfer from the interindustry matrix to final demand.

Obviously, all of these remarks about resectoring are intended neither as firm recommendations nor expressive of an explicit theoretical reformulation, although they do reflect hypotheses about the nature of regional growth. Rather, they are meant mainly as a plea for a more flexible use of social accounts. We should be very careful to remember that there is no logically correct way of setting up regional, or any other accounts, for that matter, independently of a preconceived analytical purpose to which they are to be put. In fact, it was the absence of such a preconceived analytical purpose that gave Professor Andrews so much difficulty in deciding what was the right unit of account for economic base studies. As a consequence, we should not expect that a particular set of definitions necessarily will hold for different questions, or even for the same questions in different kinds of regions or at different stages of a given region's development.

References

ANDREWS, R. B. (May 1953–February 1966) 'Mechanics of the urban economic base', a collection of reprints of articles in *Land Economics*, vols. 29–31.

BLUMENFELD, H. (Fall 1955) 'The economic base of the metropolis', *Journal of the American Institute of Planners*.

BORTS, G., and STEIN, J. (1961) 'Investment return as a measure of comparative regional economic advantage', in W. Hochwald (ed.), *Design of regional accounts*, Johns Hopkins.

COPELAND, L. C. (1952) *Methods for estimating income payments in counties*, University of Virginia, Bureau of Population and Economic Research.

EASTERLIN, R. (1960) 'Interregional differences in *per capita* income, population and total income, 1840–1950', *Studies in income and wealth*, vol. 24, National Bureau of Economic Research.

HARRIS, B. (1963) 'Linear programming and the projection of land use', *Penn–Jersey Paper* no. 20, Penn–Jersey Transportation Study.

HARTLAND, P. (1950) *Balance of interregional payments of New England*, Brown University Studies, no. 14.

HERBERT, J., and STEVENS, B. (Fall 1960) 'A model for the distribution of residential activity in urban areas', *Journal of Regional Science*.

HILE, G. (1955) 'The balance of payments of the southeast in 1950', *Regional Science Association Papers and Proceedings*, I.

HIRSCH, W. (1959) 'Application of area input–output analysis', *Regional Science Association Papers and Proceedings*, no. 5.

HIRSCH, W. (1961) 'A general structure for regional economic analysis', in W. Hochwald (ed.), *Studies in regional accounts*, Johns Hopkins.

HOCHWALD, W. (1957) 'Conceptual issues of regional income estimation', *Studies in Income and Wealth*, no. 21, National Bureau of Economic Research.

HOCHWALD, W., STRINER, H., and SONENBLUM, S. (1960) *Local impact of foreign trade*, National Planning Association.

HOOVER, E. *et al.* (1964) *Region with a future*, University of Pittsburgh Press.

ISARD, W. (1957) *Methods of regional analysis*, M.I.T. Press.

ISARD, W., and KUENNE, R. (November 1953) 'The impact of steel upon the Greater New York–Philadelphia industrial region', *The Review of Economics and Statistics*.

LEVEN, C. L. (November 1954) 'An appropriate unit for measuring the urban economic base', *Land Economics*.

LEVEN, C. L. (1958) 'A theory of regional social accounting', *Regional Science Association Papers and Proceedings*.

LEVEN, C. L. (1961) 'Regional income and product accounts: construction and applications', in W. Hochwald (ed.), *Design of regional accounts*, Johns Hopkins.

LEVEN, C. L. (1963) *Theory and method of income and product accounts for metropolitan areas*, Center for Regional Economic Studies, University of Pittsburgh, reprint.

LEVEN, C. L., and PERLOFF, H. (1964) 'Towards an integrated system of regional accounts: stocks, flows and the analysis of the public sector', in W. Hirsch (ed.), *Studies in regional accounts*, Johns Hopkins.

METZLER, L. (October 1950) 'A multiple region theory of income and trade', *Econometrica*.

MEYER, J. (March 1963) 'Regional economics: a survey', *The American Economic Review*.

MOORE, F., and PETERSON, J. (November 1955), 'Regional analysis: an interindustry model of Utah', *The Review of Economics and Statistics*.

MOSES, L. (December 1955) 'The stability of interregional trading patterns and input–output analysis', *The American Economic Review*.

PERLOFF, H. S. (1957) *Regional studies at U.S. universities*, Resources for the Future Inc.

PERLOFF, H. (1961) 'Relative regional economic growth: an approach to regional accounts', in W. Hochwald (ed.), *Studies in regional accounts*, Johns Hopkins.

RUGGLES, R., and RUGGLES, N. (1961) 'Regional breakdown of national economic accounts', in W. Hochwald (ed.), *Studies in regional accounts*, Johns Hopkins.

TIEBOUT, C. M. (October 1957) 'Regional and interregional input–output models: an appraisal', *The Southern Economic Journal*.

TIEBOUT, C. M. (1962) *Markets for California products*, California Development Agency.

TIEBOUT and NORTH (April 1956) Tiebout, 'Exports and regional economic growth', North, 'A reply', and Tiebout, 'Rejoinder', *Journal of Political Economy*.

ULLMAN, E., and DACEY, M. (1960) 'The minimum requirements approach to the urban economic base', *Regional Science Association Papers and Proceedings*.

3 C. M. Tiebout

Regional and Interregional Input–Output Models: An Appraisal

C. M. Tiebout, 'Regional and interregional input–output models: an appraisal', *Southern Economic Journal*, vol. 24 (1957), pp. 140–47.

It is not too much of an overstatement to say that post-World War II regional research has been almost completely dominated by regional applications of input–output models. Whatever the form of the variations, the basic input–output theme is present. While users of, and writers on, input–output techniques are quite honest in admitting its limitations, one does sense a feeling that this approach is clearly preferable to other frameworks in attacking regional problems. Indeed, one leading writer in the field of regional analysis notes that, 'too many of the (economists) tools represent transfers of concepts and methods traditionally used by the national–international type of economist' (Isard, 1957). It is not the function of this paper to put forth the case for the Keynesian-style 'national–international' framework in regional analysis as an alternative form of or supplement to input–output, This has been done elsewhere (Daly, 1940; Hildebrand and Mace. 1950; Tiebout, 1956). Rather it is the purpose of this paper to re-review the various operational uses of regional input–output analysis. Such a review will not only give the reader some idea of the current uses of input–output in regional analysis, but will also enable him to more adequately judge its possibilities and limitations.

National and Regional Input–Output Models: Summary View

The conceptual framework of an open, static input–output model is given by Leontief (See Leontief, 1953). The accounting balance equation is given as:

$$(1.1) \qquad X_t - \sum_{k=1}^{m} x_{tk} = Y_t.$$

Here X_i represents the total output of industry i. x_{ik} gives the amount of i products absorbed by industry k. Given the number of industries $1, 2, \ldots, m$; equation (1.1) yields the amount of i products going to final demand, that is to Y_i.

The structural equations are given by the production coefficients for each industry.

$$(1.2) \qquad x_{ik} = a_{ik}X_k \qquad i = 1, 2, \ldots, m. \qquad k = 1, 2, \ldots, m.$$

where, a_{ik} is the production coefficient indicating the amount of i needed to produce a unit of k. Substituting (1.2) in (1.1) yields:

$$(1.3) \qquad X_i - \sum_{k=1}^{m} a_{ik}X_k = Y_i.$$

This system of linear equations may be solved for X, if a bill of final demands, $Y_1, Y_2, \ldots, Y_m$, is known.

Regional models have the effect of adding another dimension to national models, namely the religions are identified. X_i become $_rX_i$, which represents the total output X, of industry i, in *region r*. Here $_{rs}x_{ij}$ represents the flow from industry i in region r to industry j in region s. If the number of regions r, $s = 1, 2, \ldots, n$ is known, the interregional model takes the form,

$$(2.1) \qquad _rX_i - \sum_{s=1}^{n} \sum_{j=1}^{m} {_{rs}x_{ij}} = {_rY_i} \qquad i = 1, 2, \ldots, m.$$

In this equation $_rY_i$ represents the final demand for the products of industry i in region r.

Production coefficients are given as,

$$(2.2) \qquad \frac{_{rs}x_{ij}}{_rX_i} = {_{rs}a_{ij}}.$$

(2.2) states that the inputs from industry i in region r to industry j in region s are some proportion of the total production, X, of good j in region s. (Note that the production coefficient now has a spatial as well as technical component.)

Total output for the whole system of regions and industries may be determined by substituting (2.2) in (2.1) and solving for $_rX_i$. This is the same process as used in equations (1.1), (1.2), and (1.3). Four further considerations apply to regional models.

87

(1) Not all of the sub-boxes come into interregional trade, i.e. possibly, $_{rs}x_{ik} = 0$. Such industries as barber shops do not enter interregional trade.

(2) Regional models, like their national counterpart, may be open or closed. Here, however, a greater variety of alternatives exist. Models may be open regionally; for example, households within the region may be part of final demand. Models may also be closed regionally, e.g. households are endogenous. Either of these two possibilities may be combined within a national model which, in turn, may be either open or closed.

(3) Another characteristic of regional models is that they may or may not assume technological equivalence. That is to say, the production of coefficients, equation (2.2), may be assumed the same throughout the nation or they may vary from region to region.

(4) The final point concerning regional models is that the balance of regional payments equilibrium, may be considered. Not all models are concerned with this condition.

Yet the major item to note is that equations (2.1) and (2.2) merely add a spatial component to national models. This is important. National models have limitations of their own which have been discussed elsewhere (Christ, 1955; Dorfman, 1954; Leontief, 1953). Any limitations placed on national models also apply with equal force to regional models. Above and beyond these limitations, regional models have limitations of their own.

Input–Output Models in Regional Analysis

In general there are three frameworks in which the input–output techniques may be used in regional analysis: (1) *local impact studies*; (2) *regional balance of payments studies*; and (3) *interregional flows studies*. Other uses may exist, but they will not be discussed here.

Regional impact analysis poses the following question: if a new industry were to be located in an area, what would be the *total* change in the level of economic activity? (Isard, Kavesh, and Kuenne, 1953; Isard and Kuenne, 1953; Isard and Whitney, 1952). One method of studying the total impact is through the interrelations of an input–output matrix. Using steel as an example, not only is the expansion due to a new steel plant taken into account, but secondary effects are considered as well. Other industries will expand in response to the increase in steel output. Some of these industries will agglomerate at the site of the new steel plant while other inputs will come from outside the region under consideration. Those which do agglomerate, however, are part of the increased activity of the region. Just which industries will agglomerate around the new steel plant can only be decided on the basis of location theory. Of course, the industries which do agglomerate will have input requirements of their own which may be analyzed.

Regional balance of payments studies have been carried out using input–output techniques. (Isard, 1953; Moore and Petersen, 1955). Essentially, these studies seek to show, in a quantified way, the relation of a region to the rest of the nation. Thus, for example, an autonomous change in the level of exports can be shown to have certain implications for the regional economy.

One of the more interesting applications of this technique is the work of Moore and Petersen. Strictly speaking, their study is not merely a balance of payments study, since it contains elements of intraregional analysis. The Moore–Petersen model used regional production coefficients wherever possible. Also, they close the model somewhat at the regional level by placing households within the bill of goods. National figures, however, were used to estimate the consumption aspects of the multiplier.

Their technique in estimating the balance of trade is similar to that used by Isard (Isard, 1953). Total production of the ith commodity in the region was measured against total consumption in both the industrial and household sectors. The difference, by assumption, represents the net imports or exports.

Interregional flows studies attempt to show, again in a quantifiable manner, the structural relationships between regions. The effects of an autonomous shock may be traced to, and through, the n regions under consideration.

The only empirical study of interregional flows is the splendid work of Leon Moses (Moses, 1955). Moses uses the conceptual framework discussed earlier for a three region eleven matrix. Solving this system he shows, for the first time, the interregional flows within the United States. The assumptions of the Moses model, as well as greater details concerning the assumptions of the other models, will be discussed next when we turn to the limitations of regional input–output techniques.

Limitations of Regional Input–Output Models

Two choices are open to us in reviewing these regional uses of input–output techniques. (1) We may take up each type of study in turn; or (2) we may take up the assumptions common to all or most of the studies, and then see what implications this has for the various areas under view. While neither method is completely satisfactory, the second method seems to provide the simplest exposition.

Regional production coefficients

The criticism of regional input–output analysis may well start with the whole issue of production coefficients. If their use at the national level is at all dubious, even more is left to be desired at the regional level. This will be apparent in the discussion of three aspects of regional production coefficients: (1) the use of national coefficients at the regional level; (2) the use of 'average' coefficients; and (3) the implications of the spatial component of the production coefficient.

As an operational necessity, all models discussed (Moore and Petersen excepted) have used national coefficients as regional coefficients. That is to say the production functions for various industries are assumed to be uniform throughout the whole country. Yet a mere examination of Northern versus Southern fuel bills is enough to indicate that this is not the case. Obviously, other instances could be cited.

Production coefficients may be divided into three categories: (1) average coefficients as determined, operationally, by the last Census of Manufactures; (2) best coefficients which represent the coefficients of the newest of 'planning board' plants in the industry; and (3) the worst coefficients which represent the coefficients of the marginal firm. Which coefficient one chooses depends on the assumed capacity of the industry and which firms bear the impact of demand changes. If demand is assumed to increase, best coefficients will apply if the industry was previously operating at capacity; added production will have to come from new plants. If the industry is assumed to be operating at less than capacity, worst coefficients could be the ones to use. Further, with a decrease in demand, worst coefficients will come into play, it is the older marginal firm which is assumed to drop out.

In regional studies, it is important to use the correct coefficients. In regional impact studies, for example, best coefficients are the ones to use. They are not used, however, since they are not known or can only be ascertained at great expense. In balance of payments and in interregional flows studies, the difference between best, worst, and average coefficients is important. The best coefficients are associated with newer or more efficient producers in the industry. Insofar as newer producers are more efficient than older firms, a drop in demand may have relatively less effect on the producers using best coefficients. For example, a general drop in textile demand may have a greater impact on older New England mills than mills in the south. If average production coefficients are used throughout, this result will not be shown in the model.

Regional coefficients have still another serious pitfall. They not only specify the amount of needed inputs per unit of output, but they also specify the regional source. This source is assumed to be a constant proportion of total output, i.e., trading patterns are assumed to be stable. Thus if region h imports half of its coal from region i and the other half from region j, this trade pattern is assumed to hold for *all* levels of output.

Now there is no logical reason to expect trading patterns to exhibit stability. Moses, aware of this, attempts to investigate the stability of trade coefficients for the years 1947, 1948, and 1949, using I.C.C. waybill data (Moses, 1955). His hesitant conclusion is that 'the author believes that they have exhibited sufficient stability to warrant their being subjected to further statistical evaluation on various levels of regional and commodity aggregation' (Moses, 1955, p. 826). Such instability as exists in the data given by Moses *may* be correlated with changes in the demand of the sectors under consideration.[1] The real test which trade

1. Variations in total shipments were checked against the stability of Moses' coefficients. A weighted average of per cent changes in trade coefficient (Moses, 1955, p. 824) with per cent changes in I.C.C. waybill total

coefficients must withstand is stability in the face of changes in final demand.

The case for stable trading coefficients presents an interesting paradox. Moses is quite explicit that 'the assumption of stable trade coefficients is the crucial issue' (Moses, 1955, p. 810). Even for short run predictions, 'the following conditions should be satisfied: (1) There is excess capacity in the transport network between every pair of regions. (2) Each industry in each region has excess capacity. (3) There is a pool of unemployed labor for each region.'[2] These assumptions are necessary to justify constant costs. Constant costs, Moses feels, are needed to justify stable trade patterns.

Now let us go back to the operational method, not that of Moses, by which net imports or exports were determined. In every case it is the residual of regional production measured against regional consumption. Thus it is possible for a region to produce a commodity and import it as well. Indeed, the Moses model contains many examples of such flows. But this is inconsistent (except when spatial extent is considered – a region may import a commodity at one border and export it at another border). Surely, if local producers have excess capacity and constant costs, the region cannot import that commodity. Local producers with lower transport costs would be able to undersell their more distant rivals. Neither the assumption of stable trade patterns nor that of importing and exporting the same commodity makes too much sense alone – granting a case can be made for the latter. Together they clash head on.

Product mix

The residuals method of determining export balances is not only inconsistent with the assumptions of constant cost and excess

tonnage for each of the five commodity classes. (Interstate Commerce Commission, 1949.) Changes in the coefficients and total tonnage were compared for the years 1947–8 and 1948–9. The coefficient of linear correlation = 0.61. With a standard error of 1.83, this correlation could happen by chance about 6.5 per cent of the time. This is certainly not conclusive evidence, but may offer a clue for further testing.

2. See Moses (1955), p. 812. While it will not alter the analysis that follows, Moses may be too severe on this point. If various costs *rise proportionately*, trade patterns will be stable.

capacity, but may not measure imports and exports in any meaningful manner at all. This is an extreme statement; but if excess capacity is assumed for industry i in region r, any imports of i into r may be more indicative of product mix, the degree of heterogeneity of products in an industrial classification, than of an import balance.[3]

The failure to handle product mix adequately can lead to some ridiculous results in determining net exports and imports. In Wisconsin, for example, where the internal production of automobiles just about equals consumption, there would be no imports of automobiles. This implies, in turn, that Wisconsin residents drive only the local product, a Nash or Hudson. Clearly, this is one area where no further research is needed to see if Wisconsinites do actually drive only Nash or Hudson cars. Yet, even a more homogenous product such as premium beer, a major Wisconsin industry, does not eliminate imports. Budweiser from St Louis and Hamms from St Paul are large sellers in Wisconsin.

A moments reflection will point out the general inadequacy of the residuals method of determining the volume of net exports and imports. In an economy where the degree of product variation is as high and the ratio of transport cost to total cost is as low, one might expect a great deal of product mix, even in a 200 industry matrix. The residuals assumption is not a very safe one. Those concerned with export–import balances might do well to try alternative approaches.[4]

3. This point raises an interesting side issue. The usual method by which the various industrial sectors are classified runs in terms of similarity of input requirements. A supplementary method might be to divide the economy into m regions. For any arbitrary inter-industry classification, the degree of product mix is indicated to the extent to which regions import and export the same commodity. The classification which minimizes this simultaneous flow may be considered as containing the least product mix. In some cases the export–import flows are not known. Where excess capacity exists and is known, product mix may be assumed if the same commodity is imported – for reasons shown above. Again, to the extent that this inconsistency is minimized, the product mix is cut. The possibility of simultaneous imports and exports due to spatial extent, as discussed above, is no problem since all we are seeking is a minimum, not a zero.

4. Alternative approaches includes: the use of I.C.C. waybill data, unfortunately given in weights and not values; direct estimates from local producers; and money flow analysis from the Federal Reserve Districts.

The final problem relating to product mix and net exports and imports, comes in determining the regional multipliers. Moore and Petersen have calculated a series of Utah income multipliers which average, unweighted, 3.9. This multiplier should not be confused with the simple Keynesian consumption function multiplier. The Utah multiplier has two components: (1) the intraregional interindustry effect of a change in export demand, and (2) the consumption function multiplier effect via changes in household income. Moore and Petersen note that, 'the multiplier would be different if gross figures (for exports and imports) had been used (Moore and Petersen, 1955, p. 379). In other words, in measuring the imports and exports as net figures instead of gross flows, the sum of the import leakages is understated. It is impossible with the data now available to estimate this error, but it may be substantial.

Regional impact studies and agglomeration

The final operational criticism of input–output models deals with agglomeration considerations in regional impact studies. It is argued that once the new industry is established in a region other industries will agglomerate and they, in turn, will need inputs. Just which industries will agglomerate, it is argued, can be decided on the basis of location theory. This is a bit too glib. It may be stated, without trepidation, that, except for a limited number of industries, location theory is not in a condition to predict at the fine margin this analysis requires.[5] At best, all that can be hoped for is a rough approximation. Moreover, any failure in predicting the production coefficients of the impact industry (steel in our example) will appear in the estimates of agglomeration. Beyond this, nonappearance of an industry which is expected to agglomerate will break the link in the interindustry effect. Alternatively,

5. The shortcomings in location predictions stems in part from the shortcomings in location theory. At present, partial equilibrium analysis in location theory can do no more than specify the conditions for spatial equilibrium. This is not the same as specifying the conditions and showing the operational well behaved conditions of calculus by which this optimum may be reached. This is what Lösch had in mind when he stated, quite bluntly, that, 'there is no scientific solution for the location of the individual firm, but only the practical one: the test of trial and error'. See Lösch (1954).

any industry which unexpectedly does agglomerate will have just the opposite effect.[6]

Regional and interregional input–output models: Summary

The past discussion of input–output techniques as applied to regional analysis has been wholly one-sided. Only the operational limitations have been discussed.[7] No doubt this may appear to be unfair, but for purposes of review and appraisal it was necessary. The empirical results of regional input–output analysis present us with a set of data which is supposed to describe reality. Unfortunately, there is no alternative set of data with which the researchers' results may be compared. Hence, it is vital to scrutinize the method and assumptions to see such limitations as may exist.

It seems fair to state that most operational regional studies have produced only the most tentative results. Basically this stems from two considerations: (1) the lack of adequate data; and (2) the necessity to make certain operational assumptions which depart, in varying degrees, from what we usually assume about reality. It may be that further work in this area will eliminate some of the problems raised above. Note, however, that this is not necessarily a call for further research in this area. Such a call for further research, certainly a common expression in academic circles, implies a judgment as to the allocation of scarce research

6. Isard, Kavesh, and Kuenne feel that input–output techniques are useful in describing the 'economic base' of a city. See Isard, Kavesh, and Kuenne (1953). Again using the steel plant as an example, they construct a city around such a plant. Evidently they assume a closed regional model, since 'households which receive wages, salaries, and other income in the first round . . . also behave like industries' (op. cit., p. 318). Adding to the total of steel and agglomerating export industries the total of local activities, 'yields a meaningful net of economic interrelations which may be viewed as the economic base of the city' (op. cit., p. 319).

Ordinarily the 'economic base' of a community consists of the exogenous activities which, when known, determine the level of income for the whole city. Yet this use of the term implies that the economic base of the city is all of the economic activities within the community. If this is what the authors mean, it is not very useful. If it is not what they mean, they would do well to create an exogenous and endogenous sector. Under their current usage, all activity is export or export linked which, in terms of the usual base analysis, means the whole economy is exogenous.

7. At the *conceptual* level input–output analysis offers many advantages. The reader is reminded that this is not the issue at hand.

resources. Before such a call is put forth on behalf of regional input–output research, alternative methods of attacking similar
issues should be appraised.

References

CHRIST, C. (1955) 'A review of input–output analysis', *Input–output
   analysis: An appraisal, studies in income and wealth*, Princeton
   University Press, pp. 137–69.

DALY, M. C. (June–September 1940) 'An approximation to a geographic
   multiplier', *Economic Journal*, 50, pp. 248–58.

DORFMAN, R. (May 1954) 'The nature and significance of input–output',
   Review of Economics and Statistics, 36, pp. 121–33.

HILDEBRAND, G., and MACE, A. (August 1950) 'The employment
   multiplier in an expanding industrial market: Los Angeles County,
   1940–47', *Review of Economics and Statistics*, 32, pp. 241–9.

INTERSTATE COMMERCE COMMISSION (1949) *Statistics of railways in
   the United States: 1947*, p. 43. Also 1948 and 1949 editions, U.S.
   Government Printing Office.

ISARD, W. (May 1953) 'Regional commodity balances and interregional
   commodity flows', *American Economic Review, Supplement*,
   43, pp. 167–80.

ISARD, W. (1957) 'The value of the regional approach to some basic
   economic problems', *Regional income, studies in income and wealth*,
   2, p. 78, Princeton University Press.

ISARD, W., KAVESH, R., and KUENNE, R. (June 1953) 'The economic
   base and structure of the urban metropolitan region', *American
   Sociological Review*, 17, pp. 317–21.

ISARD, W., and KUENNE, R. (November 1953) 'The impact of steel upon
   the Greater New York–Philadelphia urban industrial region', *Review
   of Economics and Statistics*, 35, pp. 289–301.

ISARD, W., and WHITNEY, V. (April 1952) 'Atomic power and regional
   development', *Bulletin of Atomic Scientists*, 3, pp. 119–24.

LEONTIEF, W. (1953) 'Structure change' and 'Some basic problems
   of empirical input–output analysis', *Studies in the structure of the
   American economy*, Oxford University Press.

LÖSCH, A. (1954) *The economics of location*, transl. by W. Woglom and
   W. Stolper, p. 29, Yale University Press.

MOORE, F., and PETERSEN, J. (November 1955) 'Regional analysis: an
   interindustry model of Utah', *Review of Economics and Statistics*,
   37, pp. 368–80.

MOSES, L. (December 1955) 'Interregional input–output analysis', *American Economic Review*, 45, pp. 803–32.

TIEBOUT, C. M. (April 1956) 'Exports and regional economic growth',
   Journal of Political Economy, 64, pp. 160–65.

Part Two Regional Development in Particular Countries

In the first article in this section, J. G. Williamson examines the problems of regional development across many countries and over long periods of time within individual countries. The great value of this paper is that it brings together from scattered and inaccessible sources a mass of information on comparative regional development and summarizes it in a convenient form.

The next article, by Borts and Stein, presents a number of variations on a neo-classical model of regional development. The predictions of the models are compared with the actual patterns of regional growth in the United States, but the descriptive content of the paper is small, the main emphasis is on the construction of the models. By contrast, Chenery's paper contains much information on the development of Southern Italy and the model he uses is also quite different, being a policy-orientated and highly simplified, regional input–output model.

4 J. G. Williamson

Regional Inequality and the Process of National Development: A Description of the Patterns

J. G. Williamson, 'Regional inequality and the process of national development: a description of the patterns', *Economic Development and Cultural Change*, vol. 13 (1965), pp. 3–45.

Introduction

Economists have long recognized the existence and stubborn persistence of regional dualism at all levels of national development and throughout the historical experience of almost all presently developed countries. Increasingly active theoretical discussions, empirical research, and especially political concern with this aspect of economic growth has given the phenomena of regional imbalance and inequity a popular new term – the 'North–South problem'. In spite of the recent attention which this problem has attracted, very little progress has been made in formulating and testing a general explanation for the occurrence of inequality in the spatial distribution of national income. One only needs to observe that Frenchmen, Italians, Brazilians, and Americans still tend to treat their North–South problems[1] as unique to their own national experience with economic growth. This may be explained by the fact that only a small amount of research effort has been devoted to comparative studies of regional inequality as related to the process of national development.[2] This empirical investigation

1. Throughout this paper we use such terms as 'North–South problem' and 'regional dualism' interchangeably with regional income differentials. They are not to be interpreted literally, since in comparing regions there is a whole spectrum or range of regional differentials – not just a dichotomy. Furthermore, it must be obvious to the reader that North is not equivalent to developed for all nations. These are purely literary simplifications.

2. There are, of course, significant exceptions. Besides the increasing empirical evidence relating to well-known North–South problems in Italy and Brazil, there has been an active interest in regional inequality in American historical development. See, for instance, Easterlin (1960) and Hanna (1959). Furthermore the *Economic survey of Europe in 1954* (Geneva, 1955), ch. 6, pp. 136–71, devoted a good part of that issue to an examination of

into the nature of spatial inequality within national borders and over the development spectrum is an attempt to fill that void. Unfortunately, only a description of the aggregate patterns is presented here. It must be frankly admitted that, to a large extent, the more difficult task of disaggregation and identification of causation is left untouched.

Expectations

There is an abundant accumulation of theoretical writings in which hypotheses about the nature of regional inequality during the development process are implied. Given that significant economic growth first appears in one region of a national state, it should occasion no surprise that the *absolute differential* between rich and poor regions (North and South) should persist or even increase. Even if both regions should grow at the same percentage rate after the fortuitous 'random shock' in the North, the absolute regional differential will not only persist but increase. Regional income differentials are measured in this paper, however, in terms of relatives, not absolutes: the income *per capita* of each region is taken as a percentage of the average national income *per capita*. For example, the Brazilian Northeast in 1959 contained 25 per cent of Brazil's population but only 10 per cent of her income. The Southern states, on the other hand, contained 35 per cent of the population but 50 per cent of the income. In a less awkward fashion, the degree of inequality may be better summarized by indicating that most of the Northeastern states had *per capita* incomes of less than 50 per cent of the Brazilian national average.

An inequality measure of this sort implies a comparison of regional growth rates and is much more informative for our purposes than one which considers absolute differentials.[3] Using this measure as the most appropriate index, what *a priori* notions might we have about the behavior of regional income differentials

---

regional imbalance and inequality within the European nations. For the most recent examples of studies of this sort see Baer (1964), Lasuen (1962) and Tachi (1964).

3. The problem of choice of indices is clearly an important one; we discuss this point at length below.

as national development proceeds? Does our 'historic and current system of social and economic organization [perpetuate] interregional growth and income differentials once they come into existence?' (Hughes, 1961). The answer may be as easy, or as difficult, as explaining why growth tends to be high and self-sustaining in nations which have already experienced it and so difficult to generate in currently underdeveloped Asian and African nations. The increasing divergence in international income *per capita* levels, at least prior to World War II, is well known, and a similar theoretical apparatus may be used to predict increasing divergence among geographic units *within* national borders and perpetuation of *'poles de croissance'*.[4]

But presumably economic interdependence among regional units within nations should be much stronger than between countries themselves. Retaining the most restrictive classical assumptions, internal factor mobility should tend to eliminate interregional income *per capita* differentials, geographic dualism, or spatial polarization. Under conditions of free factor mobility, and abstracting from transportation costs, spatial inequality can persist only via lags in dynamic adjustment. That spatial inequality, depressed areas, and backward regions appear to persist may simply suggest to some that internal factor flows (tending to reduce interregional inequality) do not occur with sufficient speed and quantity to offset the dynamic indigenous conditions which cause relatively faster resource augmentation and technological change in the rich developing regions (tending to increase inequality).

In fact, one could reasonably appeal to the high degree of sectionalism, fragmentation, and general national disintegration in the youthful stage of national development to predict increasing regional inequality during those early decades. Given that young nations historically, as well as those currently, embarking on modern economic development have been typically devoid of national labor, capital, and trade markets approaching even

4. This is a term used often in French literature to describe regional growth differentials. See Perroux (1955) and the use of the derivative 'polarization' in Hirschman (1958). It should be pointed out that the efforts of Perroux and his students have not added much to our knowledge of the *process* of interregional communication of growth. See Kindleberger (1964).

rudimentary degrees of efficiency, this seems the only reasonable prediction. Regions within nations do not typically possess equal capacity for growth, and when development begins in some of these islands, regional barriers may be too great to communicate the growth stimulus to other less fortunate regions. As long as the barriers to trade and factor flows (as well as communication of technological change) persist, regional inequality will clearly increase.

The problem is hardly that simple, however. Myrdal's theorizing about backwash effects, Hirschman's concern with dualism and polarization, and Kuznets' more cautious 'empirical' guesses suggest that even internal factor flows may not always be equilibrating in the classical fashion. On the contrary, in the initial stages of national development regional inequality is likely to increase all the more sharply due to a number of disequilibrating effects.[5]

Labor migration

Interregional labor migration is likely to be extremely selective because of either the prohibitive money costs of migration at low levels of income or traditional inertia in the non-urbanized, non-industrialized poor Southern regions. The migrants may be characterized as the vigorous and entrepreneurial, the educated and skilled, and of productive age. (We are not describing the dominant characteristic of emigrants from the backward South, but suggesting that these characteristics will be more prevalent among the migrants than among the average population of the Southern regions.) Selective migration of this type obviously accentuates the tendency towards regional income divergence: labor participation rates, *ceteris paribus*, will tend to rise in the rich and fall in the poor regions; furthermore, precious human capital will tend to flow out of the South and into the North, making regional resource endowment *per capita* all the more lopsided and geographic imbalances all the more severe.

What has been said above about migration patterns in early development stages is hardly original to this study. It appears as one

5. Disequilibrium here describes an internal factor flow which tends to increase regional inequality. We are not necessarily using it to describe factor movements which do not respond correctly to interregional factor price differentials. The two concepts may or may not coincide.

important theoretical buttress for the operation of both Myrdal's backwash effects (Myrdal, 1957) and Hirschman's polarization effects:

Instead of absorbing the disguised unemployed, Northern progress may denude the South of its key technicians and managers as well as well as of the more enterprising young men. . . . Thus actual pay differentials between North and South are likely to overstate considerably the real productivity differentials in the most productive and skilled grades. In addition, of course, mobility is highest in these same lines so that it becomes almost a certainty that the South will lose to the North first and foremost its more highly qualified people.[6]

To illustrate the potential disequilibrating effects of interregional labor migration, Eckaus has characterized migration patterns during the early stages of Italian industrial development as being precisely of this type, although his contention is not defended empirically:

The nineteenth century was a time of extraordinary emigration, generally heavier in the South, where at some times and places it exceeded the natural increase in population. The concentration of immigrants in the younger, productive ages left the South with a working force of deteriorating quality (Eckaus, 1961).

Dziewonski presents us with a contemporary example of the perverse effects of interregional migration at low levels of national development. He has noted that the Polish government has deliberately minimized interregional labor migration, since central planners are concerned with the past effects it has had in further contributing to regional inequality and dualism via effects upon relative participation rates and labor force quality (Dziewonski, 1962). This, too, appears to be consistent with the notion that in early stages of growth interregional labor flows may generate further spatial inequalities rather than reduce them. This would appear to follow from the fact that Poland has not reached a mature stage of growth.

Capital migration

The interregional flow of private capital may tend to be perverse as well. External economies and general benefits derived from

6. The Canadian province of Nova Scotia was for a long time noted for its major exports of 'brains' and fish. Hirschman (1958).

agglomeration of capital projects in the relatively rich Northern regions may cause capital to emigrate from the South to the North, tending to accelerate interregional inequality and to widen the North–South schism. High apparent risk premiums, lack of entrepreneurial ability, and immature capital markets may further depress investment activity and capital accumulation in the South. The latter, immature development of financial institutions, may prove to be not only important but also the most easily measurable of these factors in explaining perverse capital flows. Spain may serve as our example here:

Capital migrates mainly through the banking system. Spanish banks are of a highly mixed character, being commercial and industrial, and are highly oligopolistic. Seven banks handle more than seventy per cent of the total credit. The result is that the deposits of the backward regions are transformed into credits for the industries in the north, particularly for those industries in which the banks participate. But capital migrates also via the capital market, for benefits are more certain and higher in the developed industrial sectors of the country. Most of the direct investment by entrepreneurs of Southern origin is also made in developed regions. Better infrastructural setting, superior transport and communications facilities, and larger markets all play a role. (Lasuen, 1962, pp. 179–80).

Nor is the evidence of perverse interregional flows of private capital isolated to the underdeveloped nations of Europe. The same pattern appears to exist in Pakistan, with heavy capital flows from East to West Pakistan, and in Indonesia, with similar flows from the outer to the central islands. And, of course, given our accumulated evidence that capital flows are heavily influenced by growth rates (demands for capital), capital 'scarcity' in the South does not always imply high marginal productivity and high price.

Central government policy

The national or federal government's overt or unconscious intention to maximize national development may tend to increase still further the degree of regional inequality if active political expression in the South is lacking (as in the American post-Civil War Reconstruction period) or even in spite of such expression. In an overt fashion, the central government may allocate investment to the North, where 'urgent demands for several types of capital-intensive public investments appear' (Hirschman, 1958, p. 192), which favors the fast-growing industrial regions and helps generate even more rapid growth there, only to create large social overhead capital requirements in the future. This is a common argument in the historical arsenal of Southern apologists in both Italy and the United States to explain relative lags in Southern industrial development.

In a less overt but equally important fashion, the central government may manipulate the external terms of trade in favor of the industrial North. A national tariff policy implemented with the intention of fostering and protecting industrial development, common to most underdeveloped nations past and present, clearly involves a geographic transfer to the rich Northern regions.[7] Southern senators and representatives in the United States were certainly aware of this and attached great importance to its effect during the three or four decades prior to the Civil War when their voice was important in American policy making.

Interregional linkages

More generally, there may be a lack of interregional linkages in the early stages of national growth, so that the spread effects of technological change, social change, and income multipliers are minimized. Part of the national growth process is simply economic unification of regional markets. To the extent that such interregional linkages are slow in developing, national development is all the more likely to be regionalized in the earliest stages of growth. Furthermore, if the North possesses a large and productive agricultural area, 'the South will be largely cut off from beneficial contact with Northern development, while remaining exposed to the adverse polarization effects' (Hirschman, 1958, p. 189; Friedman, 1959, pp. 167–79). This factor should help explain the relatively severe problems of North–South dualism which have persisted, for example, in the histories of Brazil's Nordeste, Colombia's Oriente, Italy's Mezzogiorno, and the U.S. South.

7. Eckaus questions the significance of a protective tariff policy in contributing to nineteenth- and early twentieth-century Italian North–South differentials. Eckaus (1961), pp. 313–14.

The working hypothesis of this study, however, is not that inter-regional divergence of income *per capita* levels will persist indefinitely into the mature stages of national growth. On the contrary, there are a number of reasons why we should expect the elements which tend to cause divergence to diminish over time, allowing the more classical equilibrating effects to make themselves felt.[8]

Labor migration

Migration is likely to become less selective as economic development proceeds. There are a number of justifications for this expectation. Growth will have been occurring in the poor regions, although at a slower rate, and the prohibitive costs of migration may disappear, eliminating the bias against the unskilled and low-income groups in the Southern regions. Traditional rural inhibitions to interregional migration should have been significantly weakened by whatever economic progress has occurred in the South. Occupational wage differentials between the skilled and the unskilled are likely to diminish in the North relative to the South, further causing a change in the composition of internal migration. The South may not only retain its educated and skilled, while losing its unskilled, but may even attract the former type of migrant from the North.[9] At any rate, it certainly seems likely that the rate of internal labor mobility should increase as the integration of regional markets into a truly national economy proceeds. This has been the case historically for most developing nations: even after the Turnerian frontiers were filled in the United States in the 1890s, population mobility refused to decline and even increased in recent decades (Lebergott, 1964); the same appears to

8. Myrdal's analysis strikes me as excessively dismal. In the first place, he fails to recognize that the emergence of growing points and therefore of differences in development between regions . . . is inevitable and is a condition of further growth anywhere. Secondly, his preoccupation with the mechanism of cumulative causation hides from him the emergence of the strong forces making for a turning point once the movement toward North–South polarization within a country has proceeded for some time.' Hirschman (1958), p. 187.

9. What little evidence we do have suggests that this is certainly the case of the American South in the post-World War II period. Just how far back in American economic history this pattern can be traced is uncertain.

have been the case in France, since the degree of population mobility has increased throughout the late nineteenth and early twentieth centuries (Goreux, 1956).

Capital migration and interregional linkages

Not only should the economy tend to develop a national labor market after experiencing continued secular growth, but more efficient national capital markets should evolve apace. If indeed perverse interregional capital flows had been typical of early growth stages, the development of more sophisticated capital markets in the Southern regions themselves should help deter the net outflow of capital. External economies and benefits accruing from agglomeration of capital projects may eventually become exhausted at the margin in the North while they begin to assert themselves in the poorer Southern regions as industrialization proceeds there (albeit, perhaps, at a slower rate). Finally, if growth becomes relatively rapid in the South due to any other factors, the capital flow will most likely undergo a natural reversal.[10] In Myrdal's terminology, the spread effects may begin to assert themselves from those islands of industrial growth as the economy fully integrates itself and commodity and factor markets become more efficient.

Central government policy

Perhaps most important, central governments may allow themselves the luxury of equality in the geographic distribution of income and pursue an active policy of income transfer to the poor regions. This may take the more dramatic form of TVA's, or regional concern may be implemented through highly-publicized institutions like the *Casa per il Mezzogiorno*, or it simply may result from a more general national commitment, not necessarily spatial, to welfare and equity. In the latter case, the appearance of a progressive income tax structure and concomitant welfare payments may be sufficient to create large regional transfers to the

10. We certainly know very little about interregional capital flows, but Professor Lance Davis of Purdue is currently adding a great deal to our knowledge. In his study of American history, he thus far has found significant evidence of sharp reductions in interregional interest rate differentials from 1870 to 1914.

South without the emphasis on federal social overhead investment in the backward regions.

Finally, with regard to the central government's pattern of regional investment, it should be clear that after development has proceeded for some time, the need for public investment relative to private may tend to diminish, and in any case a larger portion of public investment may be financed from earnings of previous investments. This, of course, provides an excellent opportunity to alter the geographic composition of public investment in favor of the less developed areas (Hirschman, 1958, p. 1954).

Any one of these factors, or any combination of them, may be enough to cause regional inequality to diminish. Once the process of regional convergence or depolarization begins, however, it is likely to become cumulative, with the forces tending towards regional equality mutually strengthening each other contributing to a more rapid speed of adjustment.

The initial hypothesis of this study is, therefore, that the early stages of national development generate increasingly large North–South income differentials. Somewhere during the course of development, some or all of the disequilibrating tendencies diminish, causing a reversal in the pattern of interregional inequality. Instead of divergence in interregional levels of development, convergence becomes the rule, with the backward regions closing the development gap between themselves and the already industrialized areas. The expected result is that a statistic describing regional inequality will trace out an inverted 'U' over the national growth path; the historical timing of the peak level of spatial income differentials is left somewhat vague and may vary considerably with the resource endowment and institutional environment of each developing nation.

The rest of this paper summarizes the empirical evidence concerning the relation between levels of development and regional inequality.[11] To achieve this end and to utilize such data as exist,

11. If it has not been made so already, we should make it clear that this study does not concern itself with patterns of regional concentration of income and population over the national development spectrum. Our concern will be with the regional dispersion of *per capita* income and labor force productivity. It should be noted that the two concepts of regional concen-

we have used alternative techniques. First, an international cross-section analysis is pursued for twenty-four countries during the decade of the 1950s. Second, the cross-section approach is applied to the United States census data (1950 and 1960) where counties are treated as the regional unit and the states as nations. Third, national time series analysis is applied to those few countries for which data is available.

Finally, we shall also attempt to shed light on three other related questions: (1) What is the relative importance of income growth versus population redistribution in contributing to the time patterns of regional inequality? (2) What role does the labor participation rate play in producing differences in income *per capita* levels? (3) Does regional inequality differ sharply between industrial sectors?

International Cross-Section Analysis

The ideal measure of regional development in a study of this sort would be real income *per capita* (including income in kind) by geographic units which have maximum regional homogeneity. This ideal statistic is rarely available. First, the regional units are more or less given by the nature of decentralized political administrative units: for the United States the units are states; for Puerto Rico, *municipios;* for Canada, provinces; for Colombia, departments; for Spain, *provincias*. The regional units are not necessarily those which would be chosen by an economist or an economic geographer. Second, proper regional cost of living indices do not exist, and therefore any differential in regional price levels could possibly bias our results, since the data are usually given in the form of income in prices prevailing for the national

tration and regional income *per capita* differentials need not converge. For example, in the case of twentieth-century France, it appears that concentration of industry, income, and population around Metropolitan Paris and surrounding areas has been consistent with *convergence* in regional income *per capita* levels. On the other hand, with the United States, 'it is interesting to observe that the lower rate of spatial redistribution of various country-wide aggregates toward the second half of the period (1900/10–1960) is accompanied by *greater* reduction in inequality of income *per capita* among regions'. See Kuznets (1960). It would be extremely fruitful to examine this aspect of the problem more intensively.

unit. The nature of the regional units is unlikely to impart a systematic bias into the study, but regional price level differentials may be a serious problem, since the cost of living is usually lower in the poor agricultural regions. Furthermore, the divergence between regional price levels is likely to diminish as the nation develops.[12] Third, those regions which are primarily agricultural and which have less developed money economies will absorb a systematic downward bias, since their estimates of income rarely accurately record income in kind. The nature of the bias may vary with the level of national development as the Southern regions also become fully monetized and market oriented. Finally, the income accounting concept (not to mention serious reservations about the reliability of the data themselves!) varies considerably from country to country.[13] Puerto Rican regional development levels are measured by median income per family, Norwegian by assessed income *per capita*, Canadian by personal income *per capita*, German by net national product *per capita*, and so on. It can only be hoped that none of these limitations is serious enough to negate the striking patterns discovered in the data.

Table 1 presents the results of the international cross-section study. Statistics for these twenty-four nations were available to us, and they are grouped according to Kuznets' seven level-of-development classifications. These twenty-four include thirteen European, four 'empty' overseas European, four Latin American, and three Asian nations. Regression analysis was not attempted for this portion of the study because of the difficulty of cardinal ranking of these countries by levels of development or income *per capita*. Column 2 indicates the years from which the measures of inequality were computed. The period covered overall ranges from 1949 to 1961. Where data for a number of years were available (as in the case of Italy, Norway, and the United States, for example), they were utilized to more closely approximate an average decade estimate of regional inequality.

12. It is interesting to note that for one country where allegedly adequate regional cost of living indices are available, Finland (1950), the use of those price indices produced little effect upon our estimates of regional inequality.

13. This criticism does not hold for the United States county–state study or for the time series studies which follow this section. In the case of the time series studies, however, the number and nature of the regional units sometimes vary over time.

Columns 3 and 4 give a measure of the extent of the 'North–South problem' within these nations at widely differing levels of development. Column 3, V_w, is a weighted coefficient of variation which measures the dispersion of the regional income *per capita* levels relative to the national average while each regional deviation is weighted by its share in the national population;[14] the higher the V_w, the greater the size of geographic income differentials. Column 4, V_{uw}, is much less useful for our purposes since it is unweighted and will be determined in part by the somewhat arbitrary political definition of regional units (the number of which varies considerably between countries: see footnote to Table 1). As a final word of caution preparatory to an examination of the results themselves, it should be noted that twenty of the twenty-four observations fall within groups I and IV or between 'middle' and 'high' income levels. This is indeed unfortunate, since it will not allow us to test significantly the hypothesis that V_w should rise, or in other words, that regional inequality should increase, during early stages of development. Furthermore, the sample does not include any of the Communist East European nations, other than Yugoslavia, and this is a lamentable exclusion.

The results are quite striking. Our measure of regional inequality, V_w, ranges widely between a maximum of 0.700 for

14. More precisely,

$$V_w = \frac{\sqrt{\sum_i (y_i - \bar{y})^2 \frac{f_i}{n}}}{\bar{y}}$$

where f_i = population of the ith region,
  n = national population,
  y_i = 'income *per capita*' of the ith region,
  $\bar{y}$ = national income *per capita*,

and $V_{uw} = \dfrac{\sqrt{\dfrac{\sum_i (y_i - \bar{y})^2}{N}}}{\bar{y}}$, where N = number of regions.

As a brief reading of the footnotes to Table 1 will suggest, this study utilizes a more detailed regional breakdown than usually appears in the literature. For example, we computed V_w from nineteen Italian regions rather than unnecessarily limit ourselves to the conventional separation into North, Central, and South.

111

Table 1

International Cross-Section

Country and Kuznets group classification (1)	Years covered (2)	V_w (3)	V_{uw} (4)	M_w (5)	Size (square miles) (6)
Australia	1949/50–1959/60	0.058	0.078	4.77	2,974,581
New Zealand	1955	0.063	0.082	4.93	103,736
Canada	1950–61	0.192	0.259	17.30	3,845,774
United Kingdom	1959/60	0.141	0.156	11.39	94,279
United States	1950–61	0.182	0.189	16.56	3,022,387
Sweden	1950, 1955, 1961	0.200	0.168	15.52	173,378
Group I average		0.139	0.155	11.72	
Finland	1950, 1954, 1958	0.331	0.276	26.64	130,165
France	1954, 1955/6, 1958	0.283	0.215	20.80	212,659
West Germany	1950–55, 1960	0.205	0.205	16.98	94,723
Netherlands	1950, 1955, 1958	0.131	0.128	12.45	12,850
Norway	1952, 1957–60	0.309	0.253	23.84	125,064
Group II average		0.252	0.215	20.14	
Ireland	1960	0.268	0.271	24.20	26,601
Chile	1958	0.327	0.440	30.65	286,397
Austria	1957	0.225	0.201	18.69	32,369
Puerto Rico	1960	0.520	0.378	42.31	3,435
Group III average		0.335	0.323	28.96	
Brazil	1950–59	0.700	0.654	53.78	3,288,050
Italy	1951, 1955, 1960	0.360	0.367	30.94	117,471
Spain	1955, 1957	0.415	0.356	32.32	195,504
Colombia	1953	0.541	0.561	46.70	439,617
Greece	1954	0.302	0.295	26.56	51,246
Group IV average		0.464	0.447	38.06	
Yugoslavia	1956 1959, 1960	0.340	0.444	24.54	95,558
Japan	1951–9	0.244	0.222	19.98	142,644
Group V average		0.292	0.333	22.26	
Philippines	1957	0.556	0.627	29.59	115,600
Group VI average		0.556	0.627	29.59	
India	1950/51, 1955/6	0.275	0.580	19.39	1,221,880
Group VII average		0.275	0.580	19.39	
Total average		0.299	0.309	23.78	

Definitions (see Appendix Tables for source descriptions and for a more extensive description of regional units):

(1) *Australia*, 1949/50–1959/60. Based on personal income *per capita*. Six regions: New South Wales (including Australian Capital Territory), Victoria, Queensland, South Australia (including Northern Territory), Western Australia, and Tasmania.

(2) *New Zealand*, 1955. Based on personal income *per capita*. Ten pro-

vincial districts and sectors: Auckland, Hawkes Bay, Taranaki, Wellington, Marlborough, Nelson, Westland, Canterbury, Otago, and Southland.

(3) *Canada*, 1950–61. Based on personal income *per capita*. Eleven provinces: Newfoundland, Prince Edward Island, Nova Scotia, New Brunswick, Quebec, Ontario, Manitoba, Saskatchewan, Alberta, British Columbia, and Yukon and Northwest Territories.

(4) *United Kingdom*, 1959/60. Based on total net assessed income *per capita*. Fifteen regions: nine English 'Standard Regions', West Central Scotland, East Central Scotland, Highlands, Scottish Border Counties, Northern Ireland, and Wales.

(5) *United States*, 1950/61. Based on personal income *per capita*. 1950–54 V_w estimates are from Hanna (1959), p. 36, and V_{uw} was derived from Hanna's data (T–4, pp. 38–41); 1955–61, income *per capita* estimates are from various issues of the *Survey of current business*, and population estimates are taken from the *Statistical abstract for the United States*. Nine regions based upon Bureau of Census groupings: New England, Middle Atlantic, East North Central, West North Central, South Atlantic, East South Central, West South Central, Mountain, and Pacific.

(6) *Sweden*, 1951, 1955, 1961. Based on assessed income *per capita*. Twenty-four *lans* plus Stockholms *stad*: Stockholms *stad*, *Stockholms lan*, Uppsala, Södermanlands, Östergötlands, Jönköpings, Kronobergs, Kalmar, Gotlands, Blekinge, Kristianstads, Malmöhus, Hallands, Göteborgs o. Boh., Älvsborgs, Skaraborgs, Värmlands, Örebro, Vastmanlands, Kopparbergs, Gävleborgs, Västernorrlands, Jämtlands, Västerbottens, and Norrbottens.

(7) *Finland*, 1950, 1954, 1958. Based on declared income *per capita*. Twenty-three 'economic regions' for 1950. Ten provinces for 1954, 1958: Undenmaan, Turun-Porin, Ahvenanmaa, Hämeen, Kymen, Mikkelin, Kuopion, Vaasan, Oulun, and Lapin.

(8) *France*, 1954, 1955/56, 1958. Based on disposable income *per capita* for 1954 and personal income *per capita* for 1955/56 and 1958. Twenty-one regions: Alsace, Aquitaine, Auvergne, Bourgogne, Bretagne, Centre, Champagne, Franche-Comté, Languedoc, Limousin, Lorraine, Midi-Pyrénées, Nord, Normandie (Basse), Normandie (Haute), Pays de la Loire, Picardie, Poitou-Charentes, Provence, Region parisienne, and Rhône-Alpes.

(9) *West Germany*, 1950–55, 1960. Based on net product at factor cost *per capita*. Nine provinces of West Germany (excluding the Saar and Berlin): Schleswig-Holstein, Hamburg, Niedersachsen, Bremen, North Rhein–Westfalen, Hessen, Rheinland-Pfalz, Baden-Würtemburg, and Bayern.

(10) *Netherlands*, 1950, 1955, 1958. Based on net product at factor cost *per capita*. Eleven provinces: Groningen, Friesland, Drenthe, Overijssel, Gelderland, Utrecht, Noord-Holland, Zuid-Holland, Zeeland, Noord-Brabant, and Limburg.

Regional Development in Particular Countries

(11) *Norway*, 1952, 1957–60. Based on assessed income *per capita*. Twenty counties: Østfold, Akershus, Oslo, Hedmark, Oppland, Buskerud, Vestfold, Telemark, Aust-Agder, Vest-Agder, Rogaland, Hordaland, Bergen, Sogn og Fjordane, Møre og Romsdal, Sør-Trøndelag, Nord-Trøndelag, Nordland, Troms, and Finnmark.

(12) *Ireland*, 1960. Based on earned income *per capita*. Twenty-six counties: Carlow, Dublin, Kildare, Kilkenny, Laoighis, Longford, Louth, Meath, Offaly, Westmeath, Wexford, Wicklow, Clare, Cork, Kerry, Limerick, Tipperary, Waterford, Galway, Leitrim, Mayo, Roscommon, Sligo, Cavan, Donegal, and Monaghan.

(13) *Chile*, 1958. Income concept not given in source. Nine regions: Tarapaca y Antofagasta, Atacama y Coquimbo, Aconcagua y Valparaiso, Santiago y O'Higgins, Colchagua y Curico y Talca y Mank y Linares, Ñuble y Concepcion y Arauco y Bio-Bio, Malleco y Cautin, Valdivia y Osorno y Llanquihue y Chiloé y Aysen, and Magallanes.

(14) *Austria*, 1957. Based on national income *per capita*. Nine provinces: Wien, Niederoesterreich, Oberoesterreich, Steiermark, Tirol, Kärnten, Salzburg, Voralberg, and Burgenland.

(15) *Puerto Rico*, 1960. Based on median family income. Income and population estimates are from the 1960 United States *Census of population*, T–35 and T–37, pp. 116 and 117. Seventy-six *municipios*.

(16) *Brazil*, 1950–59. Based on national income *per capita*. Twenty-one states: Amazonas, Para, Maranhão, Piaui, Ceara, Rio Grande do Norte, Paraiba, Pernambuco, Alagoas, Sergipe, Bahia, Minas Gerais, Espirito Santo, Rio de Janeiro, Est. du Guanabara, São Paulo, Parana, Santa Catarina, Rio Grande do Sul, Mato Grosso, and Goias.

(17) *Italy*, 1951, 1955, 1960. Based on net national product *per capita*. Nineteen regions: Piemonte, Valle d'Aosta, Lombardia, Trentino-Alto Adige, Veneto, Friuli-Venezia G., Liguria, Emilia-Romagna, Toscana, Umbria, Marche, Lazio, Abruzzi e Molise, Campania, Puglia, Basilicata, Calabria, Sicilia, and Sardegna.

(18) *Spain*, 1955, 1957. Based on national income *per capita*. Fifty provinces.

(19) *Colombia*, 1953. Income concept not clear in source: given as 'income' *per capita*. Sixteen departments: Antioquia, Atlantico, Bolivar, Boyaca, Caldas, Cauca, Cordoba, Caudinamarca, Choco, Huila, Magdalena, Nariño, Norte de Santander, Santander, Tolima, and Valle.

(20) *Greece*, 1954. Based on national income *per capita*. Eleven regions: Sterea Hellas and Euboia, Macedonia, Aegean Islands, Pelopennesos, Cyclades, Thessaly, Crete, Dodecanesos, Thrace, Ionian Islands, and Epirus.

(21) *Yugoslavia*, 1956, 1960. Based on national income *per capita*. Six provinces in 1956: Serbia, Croatia, Slovenia, Bosnia and Hercegovina, Macedonia, and Montenegro. Eight provinces in 1960: Serbia is broken down into the sub-regions of Serbia Proper, Voyvodina, and Kosovo and Metohiya.

(22) *Japan*, 1951–9. Based on personal income *per capita*. Forty-six prefectures.

(23) *Philippines*, 1957. Based on personal income per family. Ten regions: Metropolitan Manila, Ilocos and Mt Province, Cagayan Valley and Batanes, Central Luzon, Southern Luzon and Marinduque and Mindoro and Palawan, Bicol Province, Western Visayas, Eastern Visayas, South West Mindanao and Sulu, and North East Mindanao.

(24) *India*, 1950/51, 1955/6. Based on national income *per capita*. Eighteen states: Andhra, Assam, Bihar, Gujärat, Kerela, Madhya Pradesh, Madras, Maharashtra, Mysore, Orissa, Punjab, Rajasthan, Uttar Pradesh, West Bengal, Delhi, Himachal Pradesh, Manipur, and Tripura.

Brazil, a country with the most widely publicized North–South problem, and a minimum of 0.058 for Australia. If we examine the averages for each income class, the relationship between level of development and degree of regional inequality appears to be quite significant. The severity of the North–South problem seems to be quite minor indeed among the mature economies, although for any of these countries it may be politically significant. Group I has an average V_w of 0.139; but the degree of inequality increases sharply as we move from the high income to middle income group where the index of regional inequality measures 0.464, between three or four times that of the high income group. It is interesting to note that the middle income group contains both of those nations which are universally noted for their severe North–South schism, Brazil with its Nordeste, and Italy with its Mezzogiorno. As we move from group IV to VII the evidence becomes thin, but we have only one exception, the Philippines, to the hypothesis that regional inequality should increase in the early stages of growth. Both groups V and VII have average V_w's significantly less than the middle income class, and India appears to have the less serious regional income problem than the average of Yugloslavia and Japan. With one exception, it does appear that the pattern of regional inequality is in the form of an inverted 'U', reaching a peak in the middle income class.[15] However, it should be pointed

15. Using available national income *per capita* estimates (Chenery, 1960), the Spearman rank correlation coefficient is 0.721 for the nineteen nations in groups I–IV. These results are consistent with those of the only other cross-section study dealing with regional inequality with which we are familiar. The *Economic survey of Europe in 1954* revealed an association between high

out that the evidence supporting a tendency towards increasing regional divergence from group VII to group IV is of a much weaker sort than that supporting the convergence stage from group IV to group I. Of the four observations falling between the low and middle income classes, three support the hypothesis, and two of these, Japan and India, *may* be unusually low relative to their income class averages. That is, Kuznets' indices of inequality based on industrial sectors reveal unusually low measures for both those nations relative to their respective income classes (Kuznets, 1963, appendix, Table 1, pp. 70–71).

The variation within each of these income classes is in some cases quite large and extremely interesting as well. Among the most developed nations, Canada, the United States, and Sweden, all have significantly more serious North–South problems than the average for income class I as as a whole. With the exception of Australia, these three nations also have the largest land mass. The suggestion here is that geographic size may secondarily influence the degree of regional inequality; given the level of national development, the larger the geographic size of the national unit, the greater will be the degree of regional inequality. This could be explained by any number of factors that may already appear obvious to the reader; the greater the geographic size, the larger the scope for wide regional variations in natural resource endowment due to increased distance, both economic and cultural; the weaker the linkages between regions and the stronger the incidence of localism. The relatively low V_w's in New Zealand and the United Kingdom are both consistent with this notion, since their national borders encompass small geographic areas. Australia would appear to be an exception to this generalization, but even this conflict, large land mass but a minimum problem with regional inequality, can be explained by the arid nature of most of that continent; only the coastal areas are densely populated.

The same relationship appears to hold for less developed nations as well. In group II, both West Germany and the Netherlands have relatively low degrees of regional inequality for the postwar period, and both are significantly smaller in geographic

national income *per capita* and low degrees of regional inequality (pp. 136–71).

116

size than the rest of the group. In group III, however, tiny Puerto Rico is a glaring exception to this generalization, although again Austria and Ireland with small land areas have low V_w, while Chile reveals a high incidence of regional dualism consistent with its large size. The evidence is equally strong among the middle income nations of group IV: Brazil and Colombia are both large relative to the rest of that group, and both have North South problems more severe than that of the rest of the group. Greece, with a relatively low V_w, is less than half as large as the next biggest nation, Italy. No attempt was made to pursue this relationship further in groups V–VII, since the number of observations is obviously too small.[16]

Although we have no way of evaluating the political importance of regional equality of income distribution to any one nation, it does seem strange that so many of these countries in our sample feel that their North–South problems are especially unique and severe. For instance, the French concern with 'Paris and the French desert'[17] seems somewhat extravagant, given the size and level of development of that nation.[18] For that matter, Italy's highly popularized schism between North and South does not appear to be a severe case of regional dualism at all, given its income level. It should be made clear again, however, that we have

16. It should be clear that our 'size' variable is very crude as a measure of interregional migration barriers and incidence of non-homogeneity within a nation. The Philippines is an excellent example of a country of moderate size but with tremendous natural barriers to migration; the nature of its geography may help explain its apparent high degree of regional inequality. Furthermore, severe regional dualism may in part be explained by historical accident. Yugoslavia's unusual history, which has produced such a high degree of ethnic, religious, and linguistic non-homogeneity, surely explains a large part of their contemporary problems with regional inequality.

17. This is J. F. Gravier's term. See Gravier (1947).

18. It should be emphasized again, however, that we are not referring to *absolute* regional differentials but relatives: sharp declines in percentage regional deviations from the national average may be quite consistent with increasing absolute gaps in regional income levels. Our own feeling is that the latter measure is not very helpful in understanding the inequality process; but, as Professor Benjamin Higgins has pointed out privately, if 'the policy issue is how to reduce the gap in productivity and income between leading and lagging regions, the absolute gap between richest and poorest regions in the country may be more significant than [an] index of dispersion'.

made no attempt to measure regional concentration of population and urbanization, but only have measured regional variation in *per capita* income levels weighted by the distribution of population.

One more comment might be made before examining the *changes* in regional inequality during the postwar era. Recall that our weighted index of regional inequality, V_w, involves the squaring of the *per capita* income differentials. Although this is useful for the analysis of variance which appears in Table 9, nevertheless it is conceivable that by squaring the differences we may be making our index unnecessarily sensitive to a few extreme deviations in regional *per capita* income. In order to check our results, we used an alternative statistic which sums the differentials to the first power signs disregarded.[19] This alternative measure, M_w, appears in column 5: M_w appears to produce significantly different results only in the case of the Philippines, where our alternative index of regional inequality is much more consistent with that country's level of development (see Table 1).

— Table 2 presents us with some more information regarding the problem of regional inequality. There we have summarized the recent *changes* in geographic income differentials for those countries for which such short-term time series are available. Sixteen of the original twenty-four nations are classified according to the direction of change in V_w since the mid-late 1940s. What we hoped to find here were movements consistent with each country's position on the development spectrum. Divergence of regional income *per capita* levels should generally hold true for those countries below the middle income group, while convergence should be the case for those above the middle income range. That is, India at low levels of *per capita* income and regional disparity should exhibit increasing regional dualism and a rising V_w as she

19. In this case,

$$M_w = \frac{\sum_i |y_i - \bar{y}| \frac{f_i}{n}}{\bar{y}} \times 100$$

where f_i = population of the ith region,
n = national population,
y_i = 'income *per capita*' of the ith region,
y = national income *per capita*.

proceeds through her early stages of modern development; the mature U.S. economy at high *per capita* income levels should be undergoing a further diminution in what is already a low degree of regional inequality and imbalance.

And indeed this is most strikingly the case: the nations in groups I and II exhibit either stability or a weakening in their North–South problems. Seven of the ten nations in these two groups underwent a decline in V_w. Those in the middle income group show a variety of change consistent with the pivotal nature of that level of development: Brazil underwent a decline from a 'secular peak' in regional inequality, Italy exhibited stability in V_w at a high level, and Spain experienced regional convergence.[20]

Table 2
Secular Changes in V_w During the Postwar Period

Income class	V_w rising	V_w stable	V_w falling
I		Australia United Kingdom	Canada United States Sweden
II		France	Finland West Germany Netherlands Norway
III			
IV		Italy	Spain Brazil
V	Japan Yugoslavia		
VI			
VII	India		

Source: See Appendix and Table 5.

The remaining nations of the low income groups all reveal tendencies towards divergence in regional income levels.

We should note, at this stage of our discussion, that there is a significant amount of information for the currently underdeveloped nations which this study has not employed (either due

20. Lasuen implies that Spanish experience has been just the opposite. He suggests that regional divergence has been the case for the past decade. See Lasuen (1962), pp. 169—88.

to its unreliability or due to its non-quantitative nature). For example, there does exist some information which indicates the increasing problem of regional divergence in Pakistan's postwar development. The figures below are meant only to be suggestive, not conclusive, but they do stress regional divergence in growth rates between East and West Pakistan.[21]

Table 3
Pakistan (*per capita* quantum indices)

	West Pakistan	East Pakistan	Pakistan
1951–52	100	100	100
1952–53	101	103	102
1953–54	107	115	111
1954–55	115	105	110
1955–56	114	91	103
1956–57	118	116	117
1957–58	124	109	117
1958–59	125	96	111
1959–60	128	112	120

At any rate, these short-term time series movements appear to be consistent with our international cross-section results.

United States Cross-Section Analysis: 1950 and 1960

If we treat the states within American borders as nations themselves, and define *counties* as the regional unit, we ought to be able to perform an independent cross-section test. Using the median family income and population estimates which are enumerated in the United States census by county, we can then determine the degree of regional inequality that exists in each state at varying levels of *per capita* income and development. This test has a number of advantages over the international cross-section analysis summarized above. First, the sample size is twice as large, since it includes forty-six states (see footnote to Table 4). Second, the sample has the advantage of utilizing both more reliable income and population data as well as more comparable income data,

21. See Khan (1961) Tables I and II. Furthermore, population redistribution has been in favor of West Pakistan during this decade.

making a cardinal ranking of state income *per capita* and the use of regression analysis less objectionable. Third, the states themselves differ significantly from nations in terms of their control over economic activity. For this reason, any relationship between levels of state development and intercounty income differentials is more likely to be attributable to 'natural' forces rather than governmental policy with regards to spatial inequality.[22]

At the same time, however, the data present us with significant disadvantages. First, we have already mentioned that county income data is expressed, approximately, in terms of personal income (rather than 'national' income) and per family (rather than *per capita*). The use of median income *per family* may introduce a significant bias if there are substantial state differences in rural–urban family size differentials. Thus, there *may* be a systematic bias which tends to minimize the observed size of intercounty income differences in the poor states. The second disadvantage is that the income range from poorest to richest state is much more narrow than that for our international cross-section. In particular, the U.S.'s poorest state, Mississippi, is significantly above the Kuznets middle income range, and for that reason alone we cannot expect to find evidence which would shed light on that part of the hypothesis which predicts rising inequality during early stages of economic growth. What we should find is that the more developed states in the Northeast and Midwest have very small intercounty differences in income levels relative to the lower income states.

The results of these tests for both 1950 and 1960 seem to throw

22. This does not mean that governmental policy cannot appear as an important explanatory variable of intercounty income differentials. Each state *does* have some autonomy of control over economic activity, and, furthermore, the national government may itself influence intercounty income differentials via central government policies. As an example of the impact which state government may have over regional inequality, many of the currently industrializing Southern states are attempting to diversify their new industry spatially. The Mississippi Agricultural and Industrial Board has overtly given regional balance as one of its primary goals by 'bringing industry to the people'. That is, they have expressed an interest in spreading industrial projects evenly throughout the state, rather than further stimulating the flow of intrastate migration into the major urbanized counties.

added support behind our contentions concerning regional inequality. Table 4a summarizes the results by listing the computed regional inequality measures by state (where V_w is determined in precisely the same fashion as under 'International cross-section analysis', page 111. For 1950, the range lies between a low degree of regional inequality for Connecticut, 0.0627, and a high V_w for Georgia, 0.3965. Table 4b aggregates this evidence into a summary table where the inverse relationship between levels of state development and regional inequality seems fairly clear. On the average, the eight lowest income states have a coefficient of intercounty inequality approximately two and one-half times that of the richest seven. The same pattern holds true for the 1960 data, where again severe interregional differentials are associated with relatively low levels of development.

Using simple univariate regression analysis, the inverse correlation between state income *per capita* and our index of interregional inequality is significant for both years:

$$(1950) \quad V_w = 0.52792 - 0.000131 \ Y_{pc}^{50}, \quad R = 0.760$$
$$(0.000017)$$

$$(1960) \quad V_w = 0.46791 - 0.000139 \ Y_{pc}^{60}, \quad R = 0.687$$
$$(0.00022)$$

This presents us with a second question: What role does state size play in determining the degree of regional inequality? At first blush, the results were definitely negative, and geographic size did not appear to be a significant determinant of intercounty income differentials. Geographic size is either a poor proxy variable for measuring, say, diversity of state resources, or the importance of that independent variable in the international cross-section simply does not appear in a comparative analysis among American states. It is the former which seems to explain our poor results, since when we exclude the Mountain and Pacific states plus Texas, geographic size becomes a significant determinant of V_w.[23] The justification for this exclusion is approximately the same as our treatment of Australia in the international cross-section. For most, but certainly not all (e.g. California), of these states, large geographic

23. The states excluded here are Arizona, California, Colorado, Idaho, Montana, Nevada, New Mexico, Oregon, Texas, Utah, Washington, and Wyoming.

size is not identical with varied resources or significant localism but with empty regions of semi-desert.

At any rate, for the states east of the Mississippi and on the Great Plains, size is a significant determinant of regional inequality. The higher the level of development and the smaller the state, the lower is the index of regional inequality[24]

$$(1950) \quad V_w = 0.4384 - 0.000113 \ Y_{pc}^{50} + 0.001205 \ S,$$
$$(0.000019) \quad\quad (0.000461)$$
$$R = 0.791$$

One more question remains to be answered. Has the pattern of change in intrastate inequality been consistent with each state's position on the development spectrum? Furthermore, is it consistent with the postwar experience of the United States with *interstate* inequality trends? Both of these questions may be answered in the affirmative. Column 4 of Table 4a exhibits the change in V_w for each state between the terminal years of the decade 1950–60. In only nine of the forty-six states did the size of regional inequality increase, and there appears to be no common factor among them: Iowa, Minnesota, Nebraska, North Dakota, Texas, and West Virginia are the major exceptions, while Massachusetts, North Carolina, and Pennsylvania exhibit minor increments in V_w over the decade. During a decade when regional inequality *among* the states was declining sharply (see under 'The Historical Patterns: One', page 130), regional inequality *within* the majority of the states was declining as well. And to repeat, these postwar movements are consistent with the fact that all of the U.S. states are above the middle income range and in relatively mature states of economic growth.

The cutoff points defining income groups in Table 4b are taken from Kuznets (1963).

24. It has been suggested that the number of regional units, counties, within each state may significantly affect our statistic of regional inequality. That is, the greater the number of counties within the state, everything else being equal, the larger the V_w. Given that state income *per capita* and the number of counties within the state are independent, then is it possible that our 'size' variable does nothing more than reflect the impact of the number of counties upon state V_w? Interestingly enough, however, state size and number of counties are also independent of each other (Spearman rank correlation coefficient is 0.077).

The state income *per capita* figures (Y_{pc}) are official government estimates and can be found in the *Survey of Current Business*.

Table 4a

United States Cross-Section, 1950 and 1960

State	V_w (1950)	V_w (1960)	ΔV_w	Y_{pc} (1950)	Geographic size (land area: 1,000 sq. miles)
(1)	(2)	(3)	(4)	(5)	(6)
Alabama	0.3529	0.280	− 0.0729	1,956	51.1
Arizona	0.1639	0.112	− 0.0519	2,375	113.6
Arkansas	0.3356	0.292	− 0.0436	1,315	52.7
California	0.1045	0.099	− 0.0055	3,021	156.7
Colorado	0.1659	0.163	− 0.0029	2,514	103.9
Connecticut	0.0627	0.053	− 0.0097	3,155	4.9
Florida	0.2171	0.147	− 0.0701	1,950	54.3
Georgia	0.3965	0.300	− 0.0965	1,649	58.5
Idaho	0.1378	0.121	− 0.0168	2,685	82.8
Illinois	0.1686	0.167	− 0.0016	3,163	55.9
Indiana	0.2005	0.136	− 0.0645	2,827	36.2
Iowa	0.1663	0.201	+ 0.0347	2,612	56.0
Kansas	0.2389	0.211	− 0.0279	2,377	82.1
Kentucky	0.3908	0.352	− 0.0388	1,774	39.9
Louisiana	0.2916	0.267	− 0.0246	1,810	45.2
Maine	0.1269	0.110	− 0.0169	2,213	31.0
Maryland	0.2483	0.223	− 0.0253	2,811	9.9
Massachusetts	0.0854	0.092	+ 0.0066	2,909	7.9
Michigan	0.1791	0.124	− 0.0551	3,195	57.0
Minnesota	0.1980	0.236	+ 0.0380	2,683	80.0
Mississippi	0.3862	0.366	− 0.0202	1,028	47.2
Missouri	0.3622	0.301	− 0.0612	2,200	69.2
Montana	0.1686	0.146	− 0.0226	2,718	145.9
Nebraska	0.1617	0.238	+ 0.0763	2,389	76.7
Nevada	0.1243	0.094	− 0.0303	2,982	109.8
New Hampshire	0.1067	0.056	− 0.0507	2,405	9.0
New Jersey	0.1440	0.110	− 0.0340	3,285	7.5
New Mexico	0.3293	0.227	− 0.1023	2,301	121.5
New York	0.1739	0.152	− 0.0219	3,055	47.9
North Carolina	0.2696	0.274	+ 0.0056	1,846	49.1
North Dakota	0.1461	0.204	+ 0.0579	2,446	70.1
Ohio	0.1599	0.120	− 0.0399	3,024	41.0
Oklahoma	0.3129	0.252	− 0.0609	2,050	69.0
Oregon	0.0921	0.077	− 0.0151	2,943	96.3
Pennsylvania	0.1339	0.138	+ 0.0041	2,834	45.0
Rhode island	0.1066	0.050	− 0.0566	2,650	1.1
South Carolina	0.3102	0.229	− 0.0812	1,647	30.3
South Dakota	0.3037	0.252	− 0.0517	2,337	76.5
Tennessee	0.3160	0.288	− 0.0280	1,749	41.8
Texas	0.1755	0.242	+ 0.0665	2,273	263.5
Utah	0.1443	0.109	− 0.0353	3,001	82.3
Vermont	0.1135	0.094	− 0.0195	2,101	9.3
Washington	0.1351	0.112	− 0.0231	2,955	66.8
West Virginia	0.2181	0.230	+ 0.0119	2,344	24.1
Wisconsin	0.2102	0.183	− 0.0272	2,860	54.7
Wyoming	0.1384	0.115	− 0.0234	2,964	97.5

Table 4b

Income groups	Average V_w (1950)	Average V_w (1960)	No. of states in group
I	0.1367	0.114	7
II	0.1510	0.123	8
III	0.2000	0.179	8
IV	0.1585	0.159	7
V	0.2616	0.217	8
VI	0.3134	0.286	8

Source: Of the continental states, this group does not include Delaware, due to the small number of counties in that state (three), or Virginia, due to a unique method of regional classification (into urban units). The 1950 and 1960 median income per family and population data for counties are from Tables 36 and 35 in the 1950 and 1960 *United States census of population*, United States Department of Commerce, Bureau of the Census, 'Detailed characteristics by state'. In some of these states a few counties are eliminated from the computations, since the census does not estimate median family income if the population size is below a low minimum.

The Historical Patterns: One

The question now arises as to whether the long-run historical experience of nations is consistent with our cross-section results. As the currently more mature national economies underwent the early process of economic development, did they experience first increasingly severe North–South dualism which eventually reached a peak and declined thereafter during their advanced stages of growth? Did the 'empty' countries with ever-expanding frontiers trace out changing patterns of regional inequality quite different from those of the settled parent nations in Europe?[25]

25. Commenting on the hypothesized inverted 'U' traced out by historical experience with secular income structure, Kuznets has said, 'This long secular swing would be most pronounced for older countries where the dislocation effects of the earlier phases of modern economic growth were most conspicuous; but it might be found in the "younger" countries like the United States. . . .' With regard to spatial income distribution, this is apparently not the case for the 'younger' Latin American nations. They have had historically more severe cases of regional dualism than that of the older European states such as Germany, France, and even Italy. However, it is

Does the experience of these nations with regional inequality appear to be one of a smooth trend, or is the degree of spatial inequality widely disturbed by such random factors as war, discovery, and political change?

The problems surrounding this methodological approach are immense, the most significant of which is the predictable lack of data necessary to extend a time series study for any nation back into its formative or adolescent years of economic development. Even where such regional population and income data are available, their reliability is usually very questionable. Although there may well be sources which we left untapped, we were able to find historical data for only ten nations which extended their experience with regional income differentials back for more than two decades. Our quantitative measures of regional inequality for these nations are presented in Table 5, and they cover the following periods: United States (1840–1961), United Kingdom (1937–59/60), France, (1864–1958), Canada (1926–60), Netherlands (1938–58), Sweden (1920–61), Norway (1939–60), Italy (1928–60), Brazil (1939–59), and Germany (1900–60). Only six of these cover periods which extend back significantly before World War II, and of these six it would appear that only the United States, France, and Germany cover sufficiently long periods to encompass the three hypothesized stages of regional dualism (increasing, stable, and declining regional inequality), with Sweden and Italy dubious possibilities.

The first observation of interest might be the apparently consistent pattern of change in regional inequality between the 1930's and the immediate postwar period. With the predictable exceptions of Italy and Brazil,[26] each of these nations exhibit tremendous changes towards reduced regional disparity during that decade; all of them experienced significant convergence in regional income

clear that both Canada and the United States have not had as severe problems with regional income inequality as the Scandinavian and Continental European nations (excluding Germany); see immediately below under 'International cross-section analysis' and 'The historical patterns: two', pages 112 and 141. See Kuznets (1955) also.

26. Italy and Brazil, of course, do not belong to the same high income groups as the other eight nations. The German series suffers from too much discontinuity between 1936 and 1950 to enable us to include it in the analysis which follows below.

levels. Surely a large part of the apparent lessening in regional inequality during this period can be explained by the unusually high levels of regional disparity reached by most nations during the 1930s. The 'short-run' effects of the Great Depression were felt much more severely in the agricultural regions of each country, especially the United States and Canada, and a large part of the regional convergence in *per capita* incomes from the 1930s to the 1940s was due simply to a movement back to national full employment.[27] A good part of this convergence may also be explained by the war itself, which tended to strengthen secular forces towards convergence. How much of this apparent convergence is due to overt government policy and concern with regional inequality is debatable: no answer regarding causation is attempted at this stage.

Let us move on to the major question. What has been the long-term relationship between regional inequality and economic development?

In spite of the fact that the United States has undergone a growth experience somewhat unique among nations, being an 'empty' country exhibiting unusual regional aspects in its development process, it traces out a 'classic' pattern of regional inequality (Easterlin, 1960). Column 1 in Table 5 presents regional inequality measures over time, but where the regional units are defined according to the Bureau of the Census (these include nine geographic units; see footnote to Table 5). The inequality in column 1 exhibits a definite secular pattern over the whole development spectrum; during the early stages of growth, 1840–80, regional inequality increased or regional divergence was the rule; from 1880 to 1920, the degree of inequality stabilized and even revealed a significant decline; the 1920–60 experience has been varied, to be sure, but generally the evidence suggests a secular decline in the North–South problem, the rate of which has accelerated from the mid–1930s to the present.

It should be noted first that the tendency towards regional divergence, prevalent in our early and mid-nineteenth century

27. It has long been recognized among politicians and economists alike that national depressions or periods of stagnation have inequitable effects upon the distribution of income, and this is true, too, of the regional impact of such periods.

history, cannot be explained entirely by the Civil War and the bitter period of reconstruction which followed. Regional divergence was the case *prior* to the Civil War; the tendency towards increasing North–South dualism is evident, although not striking, between 1840 and 1860.[28] The sharpest increase in regional inequality does occur, however, between 1860 and 1880, a period covering both Civil War and Reconstruction.[29]

What can we say about the varied time pattern of American regional inequality between 1900 and 1940? The Great Depression temporarily halted the secular tendency towards a reduction in geographic income differentials because of the relatively severe effects of that period upon the agricultural regions in the United States; by 1940, we had recovered a relatively low degree of regional inequality which had been achieved by 1920. Indeed, Easterlin has shown us that when our data is adjusted by use of National Bureau reference cycle averages, the 1930's do not seriously interrupt the great secular decline in regional dualism which has persisted for almost eighty years. (Easterlin, 1960). Yet the 1920s still remain a significant exception. This unusual decade in American history experienced regional divergence, contrary to the long-run trend towards convergence, and this was hardly a period of stagnation like the decade which followed.

The second column presents our measure of regional inequality where the regional units are the states themselves. This series, based upon smaller regional units, exhibits a higher measure of regional inequality throughout our nineteenth- and twentieth-century history. The divergence, or increasing North–South dualism, from 1840 to 1880 is clear in both series, however, and the tendency towards increased regional inequality during the 1920s and 1930s is also pronounced in each. In both cases, the decline in regional inequality and tendency towards convergence has been most impressive during the twenty-five years, 1935–60, a period of active federal concern with regional dualism where public transfers to 'depressed areas' has been most significant.

28. Nevertheless, it should be pointed out that if the American South is excluded from our regional measurement, regional inequality becomes very slight and, furthermore, the 'classic' pattern all but disappears.

29. The estimates of regional income inequality for 1860 are not given here. See Easterlin (1961), p. 528.

This so-called 'classic' pattern also seems to hold for Swedish experience. The degree of regional inequality increased sharply during the decade of the 1920s, from 0.440 to 0.539 in 1930.[30] One could argue that this decade is the terminal one for the early and adolescent stage of Swedish growth. Although the period is admittedly short, we might then argue that the increasing regional inequality from 1920 to 1930 is entirely consistent with our hypothesis. This conclusion is strengthened by the high degree of inequality that *was* prevalent during this period of Swedish history (only the current middle-income nations have North–South problems as severe as that which Sweden experienced in the 1920s). It should be emphasized here that the trend towards increasing regional divergence is not the result of the dominating performance of a small sample of regions, but reflects consistent divergence throughout Sweden. With only two major exceptions, all of the counties below the national 1920 averages suffered further decline during the decade. Although the Stockholm region was clearly the most dynamic *'pôle de croissance'*, all the highly developed Swedish areas show relative improvement, with the exception of Malmöhus län, which underwent a decline in relative income *per capita* (120.4 to 118.4 per cent of the national average).

During the three decades following 1930, and during a period of mature development, Sweden has undergone a tremendous decline in regional dualism: V_w fell from 0.539 in 1930 to 0.192 in 1961. This aggregate pattern is again strikingly supported by individual performance; over these three decades each of the high income regions underwent a decline relative to the national average, while every Swedish region with a 1930 *per capita* income less than that of the national average exhibited a trend approaching that average.

Both Italy and Brazil also seem to have undergone experience with regional inequality consistent with our results thus far. Italian income data on a regional basis is available only from 1928. Our Index of Italian regional inequality rises from a fairly high level in 1928, 0.313, to an average figure of 0.360 for 1950–60.

30. The year 1930 is not one of severe depression, and therefore our estimate of regional inequality should not be excessively biased by the effects of the Great Depression.

Table 5
Time Series: Ten Nations

United States

	V_w (by region)	V_w (by state)		V_w (by region)	V_w (by state)
1840	0.231	0.279	1942		0.269
1880	0.321	0.355	1943		0.258
1900	0.299	0.322	1944		0.236
1919		0.276	1945	0.211	0.227
1920	0.291	0.331	1946		0.236
1921		0.373	1947		0.226
1929		0.369	1948		0.214
1930	0.338	0.389	1949		0.212
1931		0.395	1950	0.193	0.218
1932		0.410	1951	0.194	0.213
1933		0.394	1952	0.189	0.209
1934		0.369	1953	0.191	0.212
1935	0.310	0.337	1954	0.182	0.208
1936		0.344	1955	0.182	0.207
1937		0.326	1956	0.184	0.211
1938		0.329	1957	0.184	0.208
1939		0.331	1958	0.171	0.201
1940	0.263	0.331	1959	0.172	0.196
1941		0.306	1960	0.176	0.195
			1961	0.167	0.192

Canada

	V_w
1926	0.176
1930	0.221
1935	0.237
1940	0.220
1945	0.189
1950	0.199
1955	0.192
1960	0.175

Italy

	V_w
1928	0.313
1938	0.345
1951	0.363
1952	0.384
1953	0.323
1954	0.331
1955	0.346
1956	0.348
1957	0.344
1958	0.348
1959	0.356
1960	0.372

Norway

	V_w
1939	0.424
1947	0.253
1952	0.238
1957	0.233
1958	0.221
1959	0.209
1960	0.186

United Kingdom

	V_w
1937	0.116
1949/50	0.074
1954/55	0.064
1959/60	0.071

Netherlands

	V_w
1938	0.302
1946	0.151
1950	0.123
1955	0.142
1958	0.128

Sweden

	V_w
1920	0.440
1930	0.530
1944	0.311
1950	0.229
1955	0.180
1961	0.192

France

	V_w (Taxable income per family)	V_w (Personal income per capital)
1864		0.260
1938	0.658	
1946	0.436	
1951		0.289
1954		0.245
1955/56		0.305
1958		0.299

Brazil

	V_w
1939	0.502
1947	0.693
1948	0.689
1949	0.713
1950	0.732
1951	0.725
1952	0.781

	V_w
1953	0.703
1954	0.711
1955	0.692
1956	0.690
1957	0.665
1958	0.635
1959	0.663

Germany

	V_w, Old Empire	V_w, 'New' W. Germany	V_w, 'Old' W. Germany
1900	0.220		0.160
1907	0.242		0.177
1913	0.226		0.165
1926	0.181		0.132
1928	0.186		0.136
1932	0.176		0.128
1934	0.164		0.116
1936	0.196		0.148
1950		0.221	
1951		0.218	
1952		0.213	
1953		0.202	
1954		0.197	
1955		0.196	
1960		0.191	

Sources:

(1) *United States.* The first column, 'by region', is computed by using nine regions as defined by Bureau of Census (see footnote to Table 1). V_w was computed from data in Easterlin (1960), T–D–1 and T–D–2, 136–7 for the years 1840, 1900, 1920, 1940, and 1950. The years 1935 and 1945 are derived from Swartz and Graham (1960). See footnote to Table 2 for sources of 1951–61 data. The second column, 'by states', is from three sources: 1840, 1880, and 1900 are derived from Easterlin (1960), T–A–1, pp. 97–104; 1919–54 are from Hanna (1959), T–3, p. 36; see footnote to Table 1 for sources of the 1955–61 data.

(2) *Netherlands.* See footnote to Table 1.

(3) *Norway.* See footnote to Table 1.

(4) *Sweden.* See footnote to Table 1 for the source of the data used to compute the figures for 1950, 1955, and 1961. For 1920, the income data is from the Statistiska Centralbyrån, *Folkrakningen den 31 December 1920*, IV (Stockholm, 1926), T–F, pp. 38–9, and the population data is from the same source, T–A, pp. 22–3. For 1930, the income data is from the Statistiska Centralbyrån, *Folkrakningen den 31 December 1930*, VII (Stockholm (1938), T–Ae, pp. 86–7, and the population data is derived from the same source, T–G, p. 16, and p. xv. See footnote to Table 1 for regional definitions.

(5) *France.* See footnote to Table 1 for regional classification and for sources of 1954, 1955/56, and 1958 data. The 1864 data is also from Delefortrie and Morice (1959), cols. 30 and 51, pp. 18–19 and 85–6, and is based on personal income *per capita*. The 1938 and 1946 taxable

income per family data is taken from *Etudes et Conjuncture* (September 1949), T–8, pp. 83–4.

(6) *United Kingdom*. All these estimates are based on earned income per taxpayer. The 1937 figure is derived by a different regional breakdown than the later years: it includes thirty county groupings and excludes North Ireland. Clark (1965), T–5, 104–105. The 1949/50, 1954/55, and 1959/60 estimates are based on earned income per taxpayer figures: for these years the 'standard regional classification' is used (including North Ireland) and is from the *95th, 100th*, and *105th Reports of the Commissioners of Her Majesty's Inland Revenue* (see footnote to Table 1).

(7) *Canada*. See footnote to Table 1.

(8) *Brazil*. See footnote to Table 1.

(9) *Italy*. See footnote to Table 1 for 1951–60 data. The regional units for 1928 and 1938 are the same as those for the postwar years: Associazione per lo Svilluppo dell 'Industria nel Mezzogiornia (Svimez) *Un Secolo di Statistiche Italiane Nord e Sud, 1861–1961*, Capitolo XI (Roma, 1961), T–295, p. 770.

(10) *Germany*. See footnote to Table 1 for 1950–60 data and for description of regional units encompassed by West German border. Because of periodic changes in the national boundary, as well as in the nature of the regional units themselves, it would be impractical and not very meaningful to attempt to construct a continuous time series from 1900–60. The 'Old' West Germany series includes Schleswig-Holstein, Hannover, Westfalen, Hessen-Nassau, Rheinprovinz, Bayern, Würtemberg, Baden, Hessen, Hamburg, Oldenberg, Braunschweig Bremen, Lippe, and Schaumburg-Lippe (approximately 56 per cent of total pre-war Germany in terms of income). The 'Old Empire' series includes East Prussia, West Prussia and Posen, Berlin-Brandenburg, Pommern, Schlesien, Provinz Sachsen, Schleswig-Holstein, Hannover, Westfalen, Hessen-Nassau, Rheinprovinz, Sachsen, Würtemberg, Baden, and Hamburg. These income and population data (1900–36) are from the following sources: Statistichen Reichsamt, 'Das deutsche Volkseinkommen vor und nach dem Kriege', *Einzelschriften zur Statistik des Deutsches Reichs*, No. 24 (Berlin, 1932), Table 12, 15, and 16, pp. 72 and 76; Statistischen Reichsamt, *Wirtschaft und Statistik, Neunzehnter Jahrgang* (Berlin, 1936), p. 565; Statistischen Reichsamt, *Statistisches Jahrbuch für das Deutsche Reich* (Berlin, 1932), Table F–16, p. 525. There are also some scattered observations for the years 1854, 1875, and 1896, but the number of German regions was so limited no attempt was made to use them: see Procopovitch (1926), 69–82.

Throughout the period 1928–60 it was Piemonte, Liguria, and Lombardia which were the leaders in the North, while in the postwar era both Lazio and Emilia-Romagna have joined them.

The decade pattern *within* the 1950s is confused, to be sure, but the relative stability of V_w between 1951 and 1960 suggests that Italy has reached a plateau with respect to her North–South problem. This would be consistent with her position on the development spectrum. For that matter, it is difficult to determine whether the sharp increase in V_w from 1938 to the early 1950s is part of a secular trend, peaking in the 1950s, or whether it is due in part to the disproportionate regional effects of World War II. While Piemonte, Liguria, Lombardia, Lazio, and Emilia-Romagna enjoy increasing *per capita* income relatives during the period, they do so partly at the expense of Toscana, Friuli-Venezia Giulia, and Trentino-Alto Adige, which undergo relative declines. Furthermore, although all of the underdeveloped southern Italian regions find their relative positions slightly worsening, the most serious declines appear in Umbria, Basilicata, Calabria, and Sicily, which apparently suffered most severely from the war.

Hopefully for such institutions as the *Casa per il Mezzogiorno* and the spirit of the Vanoni Plan, the Italian North–South differential has at least seemingly stabilized during the postwar era, although the relative importance of public policy as the causative factor is almost impossible to isolate. This evidence on Italian regional dualism suggests optimistic projections regarding the future size of the North–South problem as Italy passes into mature stages of growth and rapidly ascends into high-income classes.

Brazilian experience is less encouraging. Divergence was the case from 1939 to the early-mid 1950s (or perhaps even from the drought of 1877–9), but surprisingly, slight convergence has been the rule during the short period since. Brazilian regional income data may not be reliable enough to make strong conclusions from such short-term periods, but in any case it seems clear that the conditions which produced these two opposite trends are themselves quite different. From 1939 to 1952 the increase in our aggregate measure V_w is accompanied by consistent movements in the disaggregate; with very few exceptions, the advanced southern states increased their *per capita* income relatives, while the underdeveloped states to the North suffered relative declines. This consistency of pattern is less true of the recent period of declining V_w, 1952–60. Four of the five advanced regions did exhibit relative declines in income *per capita*, but in large part this was due to the extremely rapid development of Rio Grande do Sul. Among the poorer regions there was a considerable lack of conformity of movement. Most of the underdeveloped states showed only slight increases in their relative positions, while Espirito Santo, Mato Grosso, Amazonas, and Para underwent very severe declines. It appears, then, that North Central suffered a considerable decline, while the North East gained only slightly. Thus the mild decline in V_w over this brief period is all the less encouraging, since it hardly represents a general trend towards convergence in state income *per capita* levels.

One might suggest that the inverted 'U' traced out by Brazil's passage through the later years of her early development stage may be due entirely to governmental policy, on the one hand, and movements of the external terms of trade, on the other. We might also comment here that Brazilian concern with its North–South problem (explicitly revealed by the inauguration in 1959 of SUDENE by Kubitschek) is highly unusual relative to the historical experience of other nations. At similar levels of national income *per capita* and development, few countries have tended to devote increased attention to regional dualism at the expense of other national goals; yet the five year plan of SUDENE involves a heavy net transfer of funds from the Center-South to the North-east as well as external aid from the United States (Hirschman, 1963; Baer, 1964).

Quantitative information on French historical experience with regional income inequality is very thin, and we shall discuss it only briefly here. We have one observation for 1864 (based on very suspect data), where V_w is computed as 0.260, while the next comparable observation is not available until *ninety* years later; in 1951, the coefficient of variation is 0.289. We would have predicted that French regional inequality increased significantly during its modern period of development after the mid-19th century.[31] We would also expect a period of convergence to have set in during her mature stage of growth long before the 1950s. The

31. The lone observation for 1864 does suggest a contradiction of the popular view among European economic historians that France was typified by 'polarization' and regional inequity long before her industrial revolution, since the computed V_w of 0.260 for 1864 does not indicate severe dualism. Regional concentration may still, of course, have been the case.

estimates of V_w for 1864 and 1951 are at least consistent with the notion.

If we utilize evidence which is less direct and which does not involve regional income data, we find strong support for the hypothesis that France has experienced the 'classic' pattern of regional income distribution over the past one hundred years. In an excellent study of internal migration patterns. L. M. Goreux presents data which is extremely pertinent to our problem. Goreux computed coefficients of variation based upon the regional wages of agricultural laborers and also upon regional indices of agricultural production per male laborer. Although his measures of regional inequality are less universal than ours, since they are based only on the agricultural sector, they may still prove to be helpful.[32]

If this data can be interpreted without qualification then it suggests that regional inequality became increasingly severe from the 1860s to World War I. Thereafter, secular convergence appears to have been the rule, excluding the temporary interruption of World War II and reconstruction. This pattern is not only consistent with the experience of other presently developed nations, but it is extremely similar with the time path of German regional distribution (see below).

Canada does not reveal any significant trends towards either divergence or convergence during the thirty-five year period, 1926–60, for which regional income data are available. Given Canada's size and relative immaturity compared with the United States, V_w was surprisingly low in the 1920s, and the index of regional inequality for 1960 was almost precisely that of 1926. Recognizing that the increasing level of V_w to the 1930s simply reflects the effects on the depression on the Prairie provinces and that the decline in V_w thereafter reflects a reversal of those conditions, the Canadian case remains a curious one still. If we artificially separate the period into 1926–35 and 1935–60, the

32. These figures are from Goreux (1956), pp. 331 and 343, respectively. The observations are weighted by the distribution of the agricultural labor force by department. Given the information which follows under 'Regional Labor Participation and Sectoral Distribution', page 152, a true estimate of V_w based upon regional *income* inequality would be somewhat lower in level but similar in movement to those estimated by Goreux based only upon conditions in the agricultural sector.

disparate patterns become striking. In the earlier period, the 'backward' eastern provinces show a mixed performance, with New Brunswick and Prince Edward Island just barely maintaining their relative income *per capita* positions, while Nova Scotia and Quebec reveal an impressive improvement. The severe effects of the depression upon the Prairie provinces, however, dominates our aggregate measure (e.g. Saskatchewan declines from 102.4 to 63.1 per cent of the national average), and increasing inequality is the general rule. The same lack of consistency among the under-

Table 6

France

(V_w based on agricultural wages, including room and board, by department

1862	0.285	1948	0.109
1882	0.303	1949	0.100
1892	0.368	1950	0.158
1929	0.225	1951	0.140
1938	0.201	1952	0.160
1947	0.095	1953	0.160

(V_w based on agricultural product per male agricultural laborer by department

1882	0.427
1910	0.406
1929	0.391
1948	0.342

developed regions appears in the latter period as well. The Prairie provinces undergo impressive improvement, while the Maritime provinces just barely hold their own and Quebec suffers a significant decline. In summary, apart from the interlude of the 1930s, stability in V_w has been the rule, with Quebec and the Maritime provinces barely maintaining growth rates equivalent to those of Ontario and British Columbia, while the Prairie provinces reveal extreme instability producing fluctuations around the national average. We will say more about Canadian experience and its dissimilarity with U.S. history in the next section.

The German data does not cover the largest portion of her earlier stages of modern development, but begins only with 1900.

Generally, V_w did experience a minor increase during the decade and a half prior to World War I. Our hypothesis would suggest that this period would be a terminal one following four decades of development and concomitant regional divergence. This seems extremely unlikely, given the low level of regional inequality which existed in 1900 (less than or equal to the V_w's of those nations currently in Kuznets' income class II). Furthermore, the mild increase in V_w prior to World War I does not describe a period in which all the developed states are growing at rates exceeding the national average. Only Berlin-Brandenberg shows a significant improvement in relative income *per capita*, while Hamburg, Hessen-Nassau, Rhein province, and Saxony all reveal stability. Nevertheless, regional inequality declined fairly consistently from 1907 to the mid-1930s. The puzzling phenomena is not so much the *time pattern* of German regional inequality, but its low *level* throughout the period 1900–60. None of the other European countries appears to have had similar experience with geographic income differentials. It is interesting to note that German experience with *size* distribution of income is strikingly similar to what we have already described as her experience with regional inequality. Kuznets' estimates of German size distribution reveal fairly low indices of concentration during the late nineteenth and early twentieth centuries compared with other nations at similar stages of development. Furthermore, it appears that Germany underwent increasing inequality of size distribution up to the period 1896–1912 (Kuznets, 1963, table 16, pp. 60–62).

With the exception of Germany and perhaps Canada, what slim historical evidence we do have seems to be at least consistent with the results of our cross-section analysis.[33]

33. Quantitative evidence describing this aspect of British economic history is not available. However, Arthur Redford in his classic study on British nineteenth-century interregional migration suggests that the development of Great Britain's industrial centers in the first part of that century tended to increase regional dispersion in wage rates. See Redford (1926) and Goreux (1956), p. 343. Commenting on Spanish experience with regional development, Lasuen implies that regional divergence was initiated with the early development of the heavy metal industries in the Bilbao area and the textile industries in the Barcelona area, both of which began their regional development almost fifty years ago. Furthermore, secular divergence may still be the case, for 'although a little spreading has taken place (mainly

It would be of major interest to us to know more about the experience of planned economies with regional inequality, although any comparative study involving the East European or Soviet economies would involve questionable indirect evidence and conjecture. It seems highly unlikely that the Communist nations have sacrificed rapid national growth for the 'secondary' Marxian goals of (1) introducing industrialization throughout the country in order to achieve the necessary conditions for socialism on a nationwide scale and (2) achieving idealistic equalitarianism implied by the socialist society (Dziewonski, 1962, p. 45). In the case of Poland, what little evidence we have concerning regional resource-allocation suggests that goals of reducing regional dualism have been subordinated to national development goals, and that increasing regional divergence has been the case in the postwar period of early industrialization. It appears that Poland has been concentrating her incremental resources in the Upper Silesian Industrial District (Dziewonski, 1962, pp. 43–57). Furthermore, now that Soviet Russia has reached a relatively mature stage of growth (equivalent to the middle-income nations or higher), has that nation undergone any tendency towards convergence in regional development levels and reduction in regional dualism? It may turn out that Russia, given its size and income level prior to World War II, actually did not undergo as sharp a movement in regional divergence as, say Brazil. This seems a likely supposition, given Russian difficulties with inland transportation during the 1930s and increasing stress upon regional self-sufficiency, as well as the military insistence upon regional decentralization. Whatever the case, we do know that the Seven Year Plan in 1959 included in it significant regional goals, and also the 1956 movement toward decentralization itself may imply a serious attempt to reduce regional inequities generated by the fabulous growth of three decades. Finally, we have already seen that in spite of official pronouncements and alleged effort, Yugoslavia underwent increasing regional divergence between 1956 and 1960 (see Appendix and Table 2).

around Barcelona, less so around Bilbao) the backwash effects are probably stronger than ever'. With regard to the last phrase, we have already expressed some disagreement (see under 'International cross-section analysis', p. 119, and Lasuen, 1962, p. 177.)

The Historical Patterns: Two

We did attempt to extend our historical evidence by the substitution of a variable which would approximate regional income *per capita* or level of development. By using this very imperfect substitute, the share of agricultural laborers in the total labor force by regions, we were able to lengthen considerably our time series for Canada, Italy, and Brazil. We derived a rough index of regional inequality by using the square of the differences between regional shares of agricultural employment in the labor force (hereafter termed A/L) and that of the nation as a whole.[34]

A glance at Table 7a gives an idea of just how imperfect, as an approximation of income *per capita*, A/L is in computing inequality indices. In this limited cross-section sample, the rank correlation (Spearman's coefficient) between our V_w based on income *per capita*, and Δ_w based on A/L, is hardly impressive: $r = 0.576$, and when the major offender, Brazil, is eliminated, $r = 0.758$. Although A/L may be a poor substitute as a measure of regional income inequality, this should not imply at the same time that the correlation between A/L and income *per capita* is poor between regions and *within* nations. On the contrary, for all nations which have such data available income *per capita* and the A/L share revealed highly significant inverse correlations similar to the results of the Chenery–Kuznets–Clark *international* cross-sectional studies.[35] Nevertheless, the slope of the function estimating the relationship between regional A/L and income *per capita* varies

34. More precisely, this index of regional inequality, Δ_w, is the following:

$$\Delta_w = \sqrt{\sum_i [(A/L)_i - (A/L)]^2 \cdot \frac{f_i}{n}} \times 100$$

where $(A/L)_i$ = share of agricultural labor in total labor force of ith region,
(A/L) = share for the nation as a whole,
f_i = population of the ith region,
n = national population.

35. Assuming a simple linear relationship of the form

$$\frac{A}{L} = \beta_0 + \beta_1 Y$$

where $\frac{A}{L}$ is the proportion of the labor force employed in agriculture in each considerably between countries. In the cases of Finland and Austria, the regional variations in A/L are much more wide than those of income *per capita* compared with such nations as Brazil, Italy, and Sweden. To put it in another way, for some nations (most notably Brazil) regional disparities in agricultural productivity are almost as important as the regional role of manufacturing employment in explaining geographic differences in income *per capita* levels.[36]

Table 7a

Index of Regional Inequality Using Agricultural Labor Force As a Share in Total Labor Force: Cross-Section

Country	Year	V_w (using Y_{pc})	Δ_w (using A/L)
Italy	1951	0.363	14.22
Brazil	1950	0.732	13.10
Canada	1951	0.192	10.19
Finland	1950	0.331	23.20
Great Britain	1951	0.141	5.31
Austria	1957	0.225	15.55
Spain	1957	0.387	22.69
United States	1950	0.218	9.46
Japan	1959	0.259	16.59
Sweden	1940		14.12
	1944	0.311	

region, and Y is the income *per capita* of each region, we get the following results:

Country	No. regions	$\hat{\beta_1}$
Great Britain	10	—0.1587 (0.0495)
Austria	9	—0.7071 (0.0546)
Sweden	25	—0.0266 (0.0029)
Brazil	20	—0.2126 (0.0675)
Italy	16	—0.4024 (0.0514)
Canada	9	—0.3272 (0.0571)
Finland	23	—0.8514 (0.0569)

36. The $\hat{\beta_1}$ coefficients above do not precisely show this. It would appear that Sweden and Great Britain exhibit even less variation in A/L relative to income *per capita* variation than Brazil. Clearly, the absolute importance of the agricultural sector is small for all regions in Sweden and Great Britain, while this is not the case for Brazil. This interesting topic is pursued further under 'Regional labour participation and sectoral distribution', p. 152.

Table 7b
Time Series for Canada, Italy, and Brazil: Δw

Canada		Italy		Brazil	
1901	7.14	1861	6.55	1920	7.76
1911	9.88	1871	7.88	1940	8.20
1921	12.35	1881	6.76	1950	13.10
1931	12.68	1901	7.84		
1941	12.60	1911	9.41		
1951	10.19	1921	10.94		
		1931	12.14		
		1936	12.72		
		1951	14.22		

Source of labor force data:

(1) *Brazil. The development of Brazil*, Joint Brazil–United States Economic Development Committee (Washington, D.C., 1953), Tables VIII and XI, pp. 291–2.

(2) *Italy.* Svimez, *Cento anni di statische sulle regioni d'Italia* (Rome, 1961), Table 10, pp. 18–22.

(3) *Canada.* Dominion Bureau of Statistics, *Census of Canada, 1951* (Ottawa, 1953), vol. IV, Table 2, and vol. 1, Table 1.

(4) *Spain.* Banco de Bilbao, *Renta nacional de España y su distribucion provincial, 1957* (Bilbao, 1958), pp. 46–7.

(5) *United States. U.S. census of population, 1950*, vol. II, part I, Table 83.

(6) *Japan.* See footnote to Table 1.

(7) *Austria.* 'Die Verteilung des Volkseinkommens nach Bundesländern', *Monatsberichte des Oesterreichischen Institutes für Wirtschaftsforschung*, Supplement no. 60 (December 1959), Table 15, p. 17.

(8) *Finland.* Wahlbeck (1955).

(9) *Sweden.* Statistiska Centralbyrån, *Statistisk Arsbok för Sverige, 1945* (Stockholm, 1945), Table 27, pp. 36–7.

(10) *Great Britain. Census of England and Wales, 1941*, Occupational Tables (London: Her Majesty's Stationery Office, 1956), Table 20, pp. 152–67.

In spite of these qualifications, we did make use of the A/L index, Δw, to extend our quantifiable historical series backwards for the three nations exhibited in Table 7b. It is interesting to note that Brazil *had* been undergoing divergence in regional income levels for two decades prior to 1940, while the most violent increase in regional dualism occurred during her modern era of industrialization, 1940–50 (the data for the decade 1950–60 was not available to us). This again appears to support our hypothesis. The use of A/L data also helps solve some of the mystery surrounding Canadian historical experience: Δw increased rapidly during a very impressive period of Canadian growth, from 1901 to World War I (or more accurately, to 1921).[37] Stability in regional inequality was indeed the case from 1921 to 1941, and the decline since World War II does appear to be part of a secular trend, rather than a short-term movement. Finally, the movement of Δw in Italy from unification to the modern postwar era seems consistent with the 'classic' relationship between regional inequality and national development. There is only a mild increase in regional dualism from unification to the turn of the century: Δw increases from a low level in 1861, 6.55, to 7.84 by 1901. The rapid increase in regional inequality occurs during the first really impressive period of modern Italian growth from the late nineteenth century to World War I. Incidentally, if we heroically assume that North–South differentials in labor productivity were the same in Italy in 1861 as in the United States in 1950, it would appear that the North–South problem was less serious in Italy at the turn of the century. Keeping in mind the restrictiveness of our assumptions concerning productivity, it would seem that there is a great deal of truth to the contention that serious Italian regionalism was not inherited at the time of unification, nor was it significantly increased by governmental policy during the last four decades of the nineteenth century (Eckaus, 1961). Whatever the case, Δw increased continually after 1921, but at a slower rate. All of this appears to be consistent with our qualitative evidence concerning Italian regional development during the national growth process.

Measurement: Economic Significance or Political Reality?

There are a number of alternative statistical measures one can use for determining the extent of regional inequality and its change over time. The preference for an unweighted index over a weighted

37. It might prove fruitful to examine the nature of the tremendous inflow of foreign capital and labor into Canada during the period to learn more about the impact of those factor imports upon regional inequality. *Source:* See Tables 1 and 2.

one, we think, is indefensible. The choice of an index which squares regional deviations about the national means is less clear. In an earlier section we defended our use of the former, since it was helpful in analysis of variance which we pursued elsewhere in the research; in any case, the behavior of M_w and V_w is so similar in both cross-section and time series that the discussion becomes academic. More serious is the choice of our measure of regional levels of development in computing aggregate indices of regional inequality. Although an index which is based upon regional income *per capita* relatives may have more meaning in understanding the process of regional inequality over the development spectrum, it may not be *politically* meaningful. It is quite possible and hardly uncommon that a period of convergence in regional income *per capita relative to a national average* may at the same time be one of increasing absolute differentials. An index based on the former will be determined by regional growth differentials; one based on the latter will be influenced by a mixture of regional growth-rate differentials and initial absolute differentials.

If political decision-makers are indeed motivated by absolute differentials in regional income, then a comparison of our index computed from income relatives with that computed from absolute differentials might be helpful. The empirical evidence below compares the movement in M_w, a weighted mean deviation based upon income relatives, and in M_w^a, a weighted mean deviation based upon absolute income differentials.[38] To illustrate the divergent movements we have used the recent experience of the United States, Canada, Sweden, and Italy as examples.

As the reader can verify by looking at Table 8, although the

38. To be more precise,

$$M_w^a = \frac{\sum_i |y_i - \bar{y}| \dfrac{f_i}{n}}{P}$$

where y_i = income *per capita* of the ith region,
$\bar{y}$ = national income *per capita*,
n = national population,
f_i = population of the ith region,
P = index of the general price level.

It should be emphasized that M_w^a cannot be used for between-country comparisons, since money incomes are deflated only by a general national price index – they have not been converted into common currency units.

United States and Canada have both recently undergone considerable convergence in regional income *per capita* relatives, neither have had any success in reducing absolute differentials between regions. The poorer regions have managed to grow at rates so much higher than the richer ones, however, that absolute differentials have stabilized. Given that in 1951, for instance, the Northeastern region of the United States had a *per capita* income level half again as large as that of the South, the stability in the absolute differential represents quite a considerable effort. The same description appears to hold for Sweden as well. Given much

Table 8

Comparative Behavior of M_w and M_w^a

United States			Canada		
	M_w	M_w^a		M_w	M_w^a
1951	17.6	263.7	1950	17.8	169.3
1955	17.0	281.2	1955	17.2	175.8
1961	14.8	264.4	1960	15.5	169.2

Italy			Sweden		
	M_w	M_w^a		M_w	M_w^a
1951	30.3	519.4	1950	17.7	617.3
1955	30.1	610.2	1955	14.0	576.8
1960	32.4	846.7	1961	14.9	671.3

higher initial regional differentials for Italy, the divergence between M_w and M_w^a is much sharper. Although Italian regional inequality based on income relatives declined slightly between 1951 and 1955, absolute income *per capita* differentials increased sharply.

To summarize this brief section, we have tried to show that, to have any economic meaning and to be useful in explaining the behavior of this aspect of the growth process, an analysis of regional inequality and geographic dualism must be based upon income relatives and thus upon growth rate differentials. We recognize that absolute income differentials may have more political meaning, but to expect that the regional convergence typical of national maturity will also produce reductions in these absolute differentials is to expect a great deal indeed. Thus it would be folly to assume that the strain of economic development upon regional dualism will lessen as the young nation moves into self-sustained growth or into income class IV, for even the highly integrated American economy, with its trend towards regional convergence, has not been able to reduce the *absolute* gap between North and South.

Population Redistribution *versus* Income Growth

Recall that our index of regional inequality has two components. First, the index is an aggregate measure of the dispersion of regional levels of *per capita* income (or A/L) about the national mean. Second, each regional observation is weighted by its importance, that is, by its share in the national population. The question therefore arises of the relative contribution of changes in regional *per capita* income over time versus the contribution of population redistribution in producing these historical variations in V_w. Is it differentials in regional *per capita* income growth which generally dominate our measure of regional inequality, or does population redistribution and changing regional population weights play a significant role?

It should be made clear immediately what we do *not* intend to investigate here. It should be obvious that internal migration may have significant effects on the regional distribution of the national population over time. But internal migration also should effect wages and income *per capita* in both the sending and receiving region. In this section, we are implicitly assuming that population redistribution has *no* causative effect upon income *per capita* in the regions themselves. Our goal is therefore a much more limited one. We are asking whether changes in regional population weights over time (due either to differential natural rates of growth, internal migration, or external migration) significantly effect the historical pattern of V_w in the course of national development.

To measure the relative importance of population redistribution versus income growth we have used analysis of variance. Changes in the weighted variance of regional income *per capita* about the national mean can be artificially decomposed into three separate components: changes in variance due to shifting population weights, changes in variance due to divergent regional income *per capita* growth, and, an indefinable component necessary to preserve additivity, changes in variance due to the interaction of both income and population change.[39] The results of these computations are given in Table 6. Ten countries were examined for different time periods in their growth experience, and in three cases the A/L data was used in addition to the income data.

In Table 9 each of these three components is given as a percentage of the change in total variance. Using Italy as an example, and using the available income data, during the period 1951–60, 29.0 per cent of the change in total regional variation appears to be due to population redistribution or changes in regional population weights. This turns out to be an unusual case, since the historical experience of most nations has been that population redistribution has a relatively insignificant effect upon changes in regional inequality of income distribution. Indeed, in the twenty-one cases exhibited in Table 9, nine show that changes in variance due to population redistribution acted in a fashion opposite to that of changes in total variance.[40] For that matter, only seven

39. Between two time periods $t = 0$ and $t = 1$, the increase or decrease in total regional variance can be decomposed in the following fashion:

$$\sum_i (y_i^1 - \bar{y}^1)^2 f_i^1 - \sum_i (y_i^0 - \bar{y}^0)^2 f_i^0 = \sum_i (y_i^0 - y^0)^2 (f_i^1 - f^0) +$$

$$\sum_i f_i^0 \left[(y_i^1 - \bar{y}^1)^2 - (y_i^0 - \bar{y}^0)^2 \right] + \sum_i (f_i^1 - f_i^0)[(y_i^1 - \bar{y}^1)^2 - (y_i^0 - y^0)^2]$$

where y_i^1 is the income *per capita* of the ith region in $t = 1$,

   $\bar{y}^0$ is the income *per capita* of the nation in $t = 0$,

   f_i^1 is the share of the ith region's population in the population for $t = 1$.

Obviously what we have done was to fix regional income differentials at levels existing in the initial period and then allowed the population weights to vary; similarly, we fixed population weights at those of the initial period and then allowed variations in regional income growth to occur; finally, both were then allowed to vary over the time period. These three components should then sum up to total change in regional variation between $t = 0$ and $t = 1$ computed independently.

40. For example, Italian experience between 1901 and 1936 was such that population redistribution tended to *diminish* regional inequality while the measure of total regional inequality *increased*. The eight other cases are Canada (1926–33), Brazil (1952–9 and 1920–50), France (1864–1954), Germany (1907–36), Sweden (1944–61), Norway (1939–60), and the United

of the twenty-one cases exhibit population redistribution playing a significant role; but in only one case, India, does population redistribution dominate changes in total variation. In all other cases disparity in regional *per capita* income growth is the major explanation of variations in V_w, regional income inequality.

To repeat, no inference should be drawn concerning the effect of internal labor migration upon regional inequality, since we would expect labor migration to effect income *per capita* levels as well as to change regional population weights.

Table 9

Decomposition of Variance: Population Versus Income Growth for Ten National Time Series

Country	Absolute variance (1)	% variance[e] (2)	Absolute variance (3)	% variance (4)	Absolute variance (5)	% variance (6)
Italy (Income)	*1951–60* 18.7992[a] 44.7204[b] 1.4048[c] 64.9244[d]	29.0 68.9 2.2				
Italy (A/L)	*1861–1901* 1.9874 58.7439 −6.8552 53.8761	3.7 109.0 −12.7	*1901–36* −2.5432 517.3368 1.2250 516.0186	−0.5 100.3 0.2		
Canada (Income)	*1926–33* −7.567 427.991 5.180 425.604	−1.8 100.6 1.2	*1933–48* −48.650 −462.201 54.895 −455.956	10.7 101.4 −12.0	*1951–61* −10.396 −82.146 2.463 −90.079	11.5 91.2 −2.7
Canada (A/L)	*1911–31* 87.34 695.69 99.92 882.95	9.9 78.8 11.3				
Brazil (Income)	*1939–52* 98.440 3,311.903 166.642 3,576.985	2.8 92.6 4.7	*1952–59* 140.111 −1,790.994 −51.792 −1,702.675	−8.2 105.1 3.0		
Brazil (A/L)	*1920–50* −1.6390 −77.9969 2.0165 78.3744	−2.1 −99.5 2.6				

States (1880–1920). There is no consistency, furthermore, with regard to where these time periods fall on the inverted 'U': for Brazil it is during a period of rising regional inequality, for Sweden a period of declining inequality, and for the United States a period of relative stability.

148

Country	Absolute variance (1)	% variance^e (2)	Absolute variance (3)	% variance (4)	Absolute variance (5)	% variance (6)
France (Income)	*1864–1954*					
	477.9323	−613.7				
	−273.7338	351.5				
	−282.0777	362.2				
	−77.8792					
Australia (Income)	*1949/50–59/60*					
	0.1064	0.7				
	14.4680	99.9				
	−0.0889	−0.6				
	14.4855					
Germany (Income)	*1907–36*		*1950–60*			
	6.8119	−3.3	−1.4930	1.2		
	−196.3604	96.4	−122.3828	100.9		
	−14.0842	6.9	2.6185	−2.2		
	−203.6327		−121.2573			
Sweden (Income)	*1944–61*					
	52.4709	−8.7				
	−614.6234	103.0				
	−34.6402	5.8				
	−596.7927					
Norway (Income)	*1939–60*					
	68.3723	−8.1				
	−931.9665	109.8				
	14.8386	−1.7				
	−848.7556					
United States (Income by state)	*1930–61*					
	−47.0053	4.2				
	−1,107.2758	98.8				
	34.1195	−3.0				
	−1,120.1616					
United States (Income by region)	*1840–60*		*1880–1920*		*1920–30*	
	12.972	12.1	315.58	−44.0	22.81	7.8
	175.930	164.7	−668.24	93.2	277.41	94.9
	−82.067	−76.8	−364.45	50.8	−8.05	−2.8
	106.835		−717.11		292.17	
India (Income)	*1950/51–60/61*					
	465.41	50.8				
	204.92	22.4				
	245.81	26.8				
	916.14					

a. Variance attributable to population redistribution.
b. Variance attributable to income *per capita* (or A/L) changes.
c. Variance attributable to both population and income changes. See text.
d. Total variance.
e. This column gives a, b, and c as a percentage of d.

Note: The data used in deriving the variance estimates above are taken from the same sources as indicated in earlier tables. The reader will note further that in three cases A/L has been used as the 'income' variable. Finally, the regional units underlying the estimates in this table are those used in Table 1.

Regional Labor Participation and Sectoral Distribution

This section involves two additional steps which attempt to increase further our understanding of the relationship between regional inequality and economic development. The first attempts to isolate the role of regional variations in labor participation rates and their contribution to spatial differences in income *per capita* levels. Given significant geographic income *per capita* differentials, one would anticipate high rates of participation in the rich North and low rates in the South for much the same reasons that labor participation rates tend to be relatively low in low-incomes countries.[41] The question then arises, how much of these observed regional inequalities are explained by productivity differentials and how much by participation rates?

Column 7 in Table 10 throws some light on this question. Here we have a small sample of thirteen countries. Column 3 exhibits the computed index of inequality using regional income *per capita* and weighting by regional population shares. Column 4 presents a different index of inequality based on labor productivity: this index measures regional variation in income (or product) per worker, and each regional variation is weighted by regional labor force shares in the national labor force.[42] Column 7 is simply a ratio of the inequality index based on income *per capita* to that which is based on labor productivity. At a variety of national development levels and in all cases but two, Japan and the United States (1900), the inequality index is lower when computed from regional productivity data. Labor participation rates appear to play a significant role in explaining regional dualism at all levels of national development.

We might interject the remark that the positive correlation between income levels and labor participation rates tends to be stronger between regions within national boundaries than between nations themselves (two exceptions are discussed below). Furthermore, the range of variation in regional labor partici-

41. The correlation between national levels of development and labor participation rates is, however, far from perfect.

42. As under 'International cross-section analysis', page 111,

$$V_w = \frac{\sqrt{\sum_i (y_i - \bar{y})^2 \frac{f_i}{n}}}{y}$$

but where f_i = labor force of ith region,
$\quad\quad\quad n$ = national labor force,
$\quad\quad\quad y_i$ = income per worker in the ith region,
$\quad\quad\quad \bar{y}$ = national income per worker.
The indices in columns 3 and 4 use the same regional income or product data.

pation rates is apparently greater than between nations. Using Kuznets' post-war data (Kuznets, 1957), the range in labor participation rates (including unpaid family labor and expressed in percentages) is something like the following: France – 51.5; United Kingdom – 46.2; Germany – 46.3; and the United States – 39.8; compared with Mexico – 32.4; Chile – 36.9; Brazil – 33.0; and Egypt – 37.6. Contrast this with the range of regional labor participation rates in, for example, Italy and Sweden: in Italy (1951) the range lies between 48.0 (Piedmont) and 50.0 (Venice), on the one hand, and 33.0 (Sicily) and 34.0 (Sardinia), on the other; in Sweden (1944) the range lies between 55.1 (the Stockholm region) and 48.6 (Mälmohus), on the one hand, and 39.9 (Norrbottens) and 42.2 (Västerbottens), on the other. The suggestion here, of course, is that in the light of the much smaller range in regional development levels, the range in regional participation rates appears to be significantly larger. Does this suggest that higher rate of internal, relative to external, migration plays a consistent role in tending to generate regional labor participation rate differentials due to its selective nature?[43]

Note, too, the effect that changes in regional participation rates can have upon historical experience of national economies with spatial income *per capita* differentials. Although Italian interregional disparities in income *per capita* increased slightly between two isolated postwar years, 1951 and 1960, productivity disparities declined! If participation rates had remained unchanged during the 1950s, Italian attempts to reduce the North–South schism would have shown more notable success. Notice also that the perverse change in regional participation rates in Canada has dampened what might otherwise have been a very sharp decline in Canadian regional income disparities during the two decades 1931–51. The opposite appears to have been the case for Sweden from 1944 to 1960.

In summary, not all of the North–South problem in these countries is due to productivity differentials: systematic regional differentials in age structure patterns and the like tend to further widen the regional gap already produced by productivity differentials. As we have already noted, Japan is one exception to the

43. See under 'Expectations', p. 100, for a brief theoretical discussion of the selective nature of migration.

Table 10

Labor Participation and Sectoral Distribution: By Regions

Country (1)	Year (2)	Income/capita (V_w) (3)	Income or prod./worker (V_w) (4)	Agric. prod./agric. lab. (V_w) (5)	Indus. prod./indus. lab. (V_w) (6)	(3)÷(4) (7)	(5)÷(6) (V_w) (8)	(5)÷(6) (V_{uw}) (9)
Australia	1954/55	0.055	0.024			2.292		
Spain	1957	0.387	0.304	0.373	0.148	1.273	2.520	3.949
Brazil	1950	0.732	0.571	0.578	0.297	1.282	1.946	2.424
Italy	1951	0.363	0.321			1.131		
	1960	0.372	0.303	0.357	0.227	1.228	1.573	1.334
Japan	1959	0.259	0.372	0.177	0.283	0.696	0.625	0.573
Finland	1958	0.313	0.228	0.147	0.141	1.373	1.043	0.994
Sweden	1944	0.311	0.213			1.460		
	1960	0.192	0.133			1.444		
Yugoslavia	1959	0.332	0.103	0.470	0.160	3.233*	2.938	2.573
United States	1900	0.322	0.384	0.461	0.160	0.839	2.881	1.941
France	1951	0.327	0.285	0.331	0.254	1.147	1.303	1.398
Canada	1931	0.272	0.272			1.000		
	1951	0.206	0.179			1.151		
Colombia	1951	0.604	0.568			1.063		
Austria	1957	0.225	0.194			1.160		

rule (as she is to almost any economic generality). With regard to the United States observation for 1900, Easterlin's data should help in explaining the second apparent contradiction to the above

Sources (refers only to data not used in previous tables):
(1) *Spain.* The data used to derive columns 4, 5, and 6 are taken from Banco de Bilbao, *Renta nacional de España y su distribucion provincial, 1957* (Bilbao, 1958), pp. 20–21 and 46–7. The regional units are the same as in Table 1.
(2) *Brazil. Revista Brasileira de economia*, Ano 14, No. 1 (March 1960), p. 119; and *Annuario estatistico de Brasil, 1960.* See Table 1 for regional units.
(3) *Italy* (1951). Tagliacarne (1961), pp. 81–4; and Svimez, *Cento anni di statische sulle regioni d'Italia* (Roma, 1961), p. 22. (1960) Tagliacarne's 1960 estimates, pp. 48–50 and 44–6. See Table 1 for regional units.
(4) *Japan.* See Table 1.
(5) *Finland.* Finland's officiella statistik, *Inkomst-och förmögenhets-statistik, 1958* (Helsinki, 1961), Table 2, pp. 52–3; based on sixteen 'economic regions'.
(6) *Sweden.* (1944) Uses 1940 participation rates derived from Statistiska Centralbyrån, *Statistisk arsbok för sverige, 1945* (Stockholm, 1945), T–27, pp. 36–7. (1960) Statistiska Centralbyrån, *Skattetaxeringarna samt fördelningen av inkomst och förmögenhet, 1961* (Stockholm, 1962), T–18, p. 48. See Table 1 for regional units.
(7) *Yugoslavia.* The figure in Column 4 is very suspicious. The data was taken from *Statisticki godisnjak FNJR*, 1961 (Beograd, 1961), pp. 316 and 350; based on eight provinces. The reader should note that it is possible for both columns 5 and 6 to exceed column 4, since we have not examined the service industry.
(8) *United States.* Derived from Easterlin (1960).
(9) *France.* Derived from *Etudes et conjuncture*, Supplement (1955), pp. 18–19 and 85–7; see Table 1 for regional units.
(10) *Canada.* (1931, 1951) Dominion Bureau of Statistics, *National accounts: income and expenditure, 1926–1956* (Ottawa, 1958), T–28, pp. 64–5, and Appendix T–1, pp. 100–101; Howland (1957). See Table 1 for regional units.
(11) *Colombia.* Uses 1951 population weights and labor force estimates, but 1953 income estimates. *Estudio sobre las condiciones del desarrollo de Colombia*, Mision Economia y Humanismo (Bogatá, 1958), pp. 19 and 326.
(12) *Austria.* Uses 1951 population and labor force estimates. Österreich-ischen Statistischen Zentralamt, *Statistiches Handbuch für die Republik Österreich*, 1958 (Wien, 1958), p. 10. See Table 1 for regional units.

generalization. It seems likely that the 1900 observation lies within a pivotal era in United States history. Before the turn of the century, labor force participation rates tend to be higher in the south. After 1900 and up to 1960 this pattern reverses itself and becomes consistent with the results outlined in Table 10; the poorer Southern states are then typified by low participation rates relative to the North and West.

Columns 5 and 6 represent the results of decomposing regional income into a number of economic sectors and an examination of two of these sectors, agriculture and manufacturing. In these columns our V_w measures the degree of regional inequality where agricultural (or industrial) productivity differentials are weighted by the regional share of the agricultural (or industrial) labor force in the national agricultural (or industrial) labor force. Is regional dualism more prevalent in a traditional sector, agriculture, and one in which technology is more localized by regional resource endowment?

The answer to this question is most definitely in the affirmative, although we base it on a very limited sample, because of the rare appearance of regional income data with sector breakdown. The computed ratio of agricultural V_w to industrial V_w is given in column 8. In six out of the eight cases, regional dualism is much more severe in agriculture. The most extreme examples are Yugoslavia, Spain, Brazil, and the United States (1900), where regional income inequality in the agricultural sector is approximately two to two and a half times that of industry.[44] In postwar Finland, regional inequality in agriculture is only slightly greater than that of industry, while, again, Japan is the exception – regional dualism in industrial production is more severe.

Our conclusions are not significantly altered if we compare unweighted indices of sectoral inequality. The ratio of regional productivity variation in agriculture to that of industry, without weighting, is given in column 9. Here again, regional dualism more striking in the traditional sector, where regional natural resource endowment plays a significant role. At the risk of oversimplification, it appears that the persistence of high degrees of regional income disparities in such countries as Spain, Brazil, Italy, Yugoslavia, and the United States (at the turn of the century) can be

44. Based on somewhat different information, this generalization seems to hold historically for France. Goreux derived regional dispersion indices for both agricultural and industrial wages, Goreux (1956). The ratio of V_w in agriculture to that of industry ranges between 1.5 and 2.0 over the period 1862–1926.

further decomposed into two parts: (1) tremendous differentials in agricultural productivity, and (2) significant regional differences in economic structure (the relative importance of manufacturing employment). It would appear that regional 'dualism' in the industrial sector plays a minor role, and that its significance has been grossly exaggerated in much of the current development literature.

Summary

This concludes our investigation into the nature of regional dualism. What we have done thus far is to simply describe the nature of the so-called 'North–South problem', giving particular attention to the relationship between regional dualism and national economic development. There is a consistent relationship between the two: rising regional income disparities and increasing North–South dualism is typical of early development stages, while regional convergence and a disappearance of severe North–South problems is typical of the more mature stages of national growth and development.

More specifically, both our cross-section approaches and our time series analysis suggest that there is a systematic relation between national development levels and regional inequality or geographic dispersion. In the international cross-section, the degree of regional inequality is very high in Kuznets' middle income class, but consistently lower as we move to higher levels of development. Although our evidence is much less extensive, it also appears from this sample that those nations below the middle income class have not yet generated the high levels of regional inequality associated with Spain, Italy, Colombia, and Brazil. The U.S. cross-section lends support to the international cross-section, in that the states with lowest income *per capita* are also typically those with the greatest inter-county inequality. The historical evidence on regional productivity or income *per capita* differentials is much more difficult to collect, but what little information we have on nineteenth- and twentieth-century Italian, Brazilian, U.S., Canadian, German, Swedish, and French experience suggests that increasing regional inequality is generated during the early development stages, while mature growth has produced regional convergence or a reduction in differentials. Finally, we have seen

155

that regional dualism or inequality is much more extensive within the agricultural than within the industrial sector, and that labor participation rates in part contribute to regional income *per capita* differentials.

This leaves us with a number of interesting related questions which are left unanswered in this study. The most pressing question is, of course, why does this pattern of regional inequality persist? What is the mechanism by which regional income differentials increase in early development stages, then stabilize, and then diminish in mature periods of growth? Have economic institutions in the past been of such a nature to cause capital to first flow in an interregional fashion, so as to increase the income gap between North and South, and then to cause this flow to reverse? Are presently developing nations sufficiently aware of the conflicts between national growth optimization and regional equality? If they are, are they aware of the costs necessary to reduce such inequities in early development stages? What historical role have central governments played in contributing to these patterns of regional inequality, and can contemporary developing nations derive benefit from that knowledge? What role do changing patterns in regional income distribution play in contributing to changes in national size distribution?[45]

But the most important question, one which is related to those enumerated above, has not yet been posed. If, indeed, contemporary underdeveloped nations are attempting to achieve industrialization on a weaker and more unstable socio-political scaffolding, 'can . . . the underdeveloped societies withstand the strain which further widening of income inequality is likely to generate?' (Kuznets, 1955, p. 26).

These questions seem extremely important. Hopefully, economists will continue to find them interesting enough so that some answers will appear in future research.

45. See Smolensky (1961). Some historians have even suggested the use of regional income inequality indices to approximate the historical patterns of national size distribution!

Kuznets, of course, has emphasized the importance of intersectoral distribution as a contributor to size distribution trends. Given the information here contained on regional inequality, is it possible that *changes* in national size distribution are dominated by a combination of changing regional differences within sectors and changes between sectors?

References

BAER, W. (April 1964) 'Regional inequality and economic growth in Brazil', *Economic development and cultural change*, 12, no. 3, pp. 268–85.

CHENERY, H. B. (September 1960) 'Patterns of industrial growth', *American Economic Review*, 50, Table 1, p. 632.

CLARK, C. (April 1945) 'The economic function of a city', *Econometrica*, 23.

DELEFORTIE, N., and MORICE, J. (1959) 'Les revenus départementaux en 1864 et en 1954', *Recherches sur L'Economie Français*, no. 1.

DZIEWONSKI, K. (1962) 'Theoretical problems in the development of economic regions', *Regional Science Association Papers*, 8.

EASTERLIN, R. A. (1960) 'Interregional differences in *per capita* income, population, and total income, 1840–1950', *Trends in the American economy in the nineteenth century*, Princeton University Press, pp. 73–140.

EASTERLIN, R. A. (1961) 'Regional income trends, 1840–1950', in S. Harris (ed.), *American economic history*, McGraw-Hill.

ECKAUS, R. S. (September 1961) 'The north–south differential in Italian economic development', *Journal of Economic History*.

FRIEDMAN, J. (1959) 'Regional planning: a problem of spatial integration', *Regional Science Association Papers*, 5, pp. 167–79.

GOREUX, L. M. (April 1956) 'Les migrations agricoles en France depuis un siècle et leur relation avec certains facteurs économiques', *Etudes et conjuncture*.

GRAVIER, J. F. (1947) *Paris et le desert Français*, Le Portulan.

HANNA, F. A. (1959) *State income differentials*, 1919–1954, Duke University Press.

HIRSCHMAN, A. O. (1958) *The strategy of economic development*, Yale University Press, ch. 10.

HIRSCHMAN, A. O. (1963) *Journeys towards progress: studies of economic policy-making in Latin America*, The Twentieth Century Fund.

HOWLAND, R. D. (1957) *Some regional aspects of Canada's economic development*, p. 78.

HUGHES, R. B. (July 1961) 'Interregional income differences: self-perpetuation', *Southern Economic Journal*, 22, p. 41.

KHAN, S. U. (Autumn 1961) 'A measure of economic growth in East and West Pakistan', *The Pakistan Development Review*, 1, no. 2, pp. 50–51.

KINDLEBERGER, C. P. (1964) *Economic growth in France and Britain 1851–1950*, Harvard University Press, pp. 259–60.

KUZNETS, S. (March 1955) 'Economic growth and income inequality', *American Economic Review*, 45, pp. 1–28.

KUZNETS, S. (July 1957) 'Quantitative aspects of the economic growth of nations. II. Industrial distribution of national product and labor force', *Economic development and cultural change*, 5, no. 4, Appendix Table 8, pp. 106–7.

Regional Development in Particular Countries

KUZNETS, S. (1960) *Population redistribution and economic growth: United States, 1870–1950,* pp. 270–71.

KUZNETS, S. (January 1963) 'Quantitative aspects of the economic growth of nations. VIII. Distribution of income by size', *Economic development and cultural change,* 11, no. 2, part 2.

LASUEN, J. R. (1962) 'Regional income inequalities and the problems of growth in Spain', *Regional Science Association Papers,* 8, pp. 69–88

LEBERGOTT, S. (1964) *Manpower in economic growth: the United States record since 1800,* McGraw-Hill, esp. ch. 3, pp. 74–130.

MYRDAL, G. (1957) *Economic theory and underdeveloped regions,* chs. 3–5.

PERROUX, F. (1955) 'Note sur la nation de "pole de croissance"', *Cahiers de L'Institut de Science Economique Appliquée,* series D, no. 8.

PROCOPOVITCH, S. N. (March 1926) 'The distribution of national income', *Economic Journal,* no. 36.

REDFORD, A. (1926) *Labour migration in England, 1800–50,* Manchester University Press.

SMOLENSKY, E. (1961) 'Industrialization and income inequality: recent United States experience', *Regional Science Association Papers,* no. 7, pp. 67–88.

SWARTZ, C. F., and GRAHAM, R. E. (September 1960) 'Personal incomes by states, 1929–54', *Survey of current business.*

TACHI, M. (January 1964) 'Regional income disparity and internal migration of population in Japan', *Economic development and cultural change,* 12, no. 2, pp. 186–204.

TAGLIACARNE (December 1961) *Moneta e credito.*

WAHLBECK, L. (1955) 'Om inkomstniväns geografi i Finland är 1950', *Ekonomi och samhalle, skrifter utgivna av svenska handel skogskolan,* no. 2, Soderstrom & Co., Table 2, pp. 576–7.

5 G. H. Borts and J. L. Stein

Regional Growth and Maturity in the United States:
A Study of Regional Structural Change

G. H. Borts, and J. L. Stein, 'Regional growth and maturity in the United States: a study of regional structural change', *Schweizerische Zeitschrift für Volkswirtschaft und Statistik*, vol. 98 (1962), pp. 290–321.

Introduction

This article summarizes and interprets a study of regional growth and maturity in the United States which the authors have recently completed. We shall present the analytical techniques employed, the explanations we have found to be fruitful, and our view of the process by which regions grow and decline. It is our belief that the techniques and conclusions will prove to be useful in the analysis of growth differentials among any set of regions, subnational or national units, which are connected together by liberal trading arrangements. It would be presumptuous of us to attempt to develop here the full implications of this analysis for recent developments in Western Europe. Nevertheless, we hope to suggest possible applications in the hope that the techniques may be improved and used more widely.

We shall define the term economic growth to mean an increase in the total real value of income in a region. We are also assuming the existence of full employment. The value of output will increase as a result of three changes; increase in the supplies of capital and labor, technological change, and increases in economic efficiency. The latter consists of gains in output secured when resources move from lower to higher paying employments. Conceptually it is difficult to isolate efficiency gains from the first two causes of growth, for these operate on the economic system by generating price differentials. Nevertheless, the identification of efficiency gains is crucial to an understanding of the way in which regional growth occurs. At any moment in time, except in the stationary state, gains in output are potentially available through resource shifts of this type.

Regional Growth Patterns in the United States

It is possible to observe stable patterns of economic growth among regions of the United States over the last fifty years. For the sake of historical analysis, we have used the forty-eight continental states as statistical observations. We shall speak of the states as constituting individual regions, although it is true that for many purposes larger groupings may be relevant. Nonetheless, the basic unit of analysis will be the individual state, considered itself as a region of the United States.

Certain states have consistently grown more rapidly than others over the entire period. On occasion, the slowly growing states have actually declined, and this decline has begun to attract public attention. Many of the nation's surplus labor areas are located in the declining regions. The declining areas do not fit any neat classification pattern. Some, such as West Virginia and Pennsylvania, have suffered through the loss of employment in the coal industry. The states in New England have experienced a geographical shift of textile mills and shoe factories to areas where labor costs are relatively lower. Others, such as North and South Dakota, have declined due to the exhaustion of agricultural fertility and the migration of farm population.

The declining regions share certain common economic attributes, namely lower than average rates of growth of employment, of population, and of income.

The growing regions of the country also fail to fit any neat classification pattern. Some grow through the industrialization of a burgeoning population which is shifting from farm to non-farm occupations. These areas are found in the South east. Some grow by attracting both human and non-human resources out of other regions. Among the latter, some grow as a result of the discovery or development of resource-based industries, e.g. petroleum refining and petro-chemical processes. The Gulf Coastal areas of Texas, Louisiana, and Alabama are developing in such fashion. Still others develop as a result of the attractiveness of climate, e.g. Southern California and Florida, or the lure of employment in government installations, e.g. Cape Canaveral and Los Alamos.

The growing regions also share certain common characteristics, namely higher than average rates of growth of employment, of population, and of income.

The movement of human resources between regions

Population movements in the United States are fed from two types of regions. As one might expect, population tends to leave the older, declining regions such as New England and Pennsylvania, which have in the past experienced continually lower growth rates. The inducement to migrate is, however, complex. One cannot simply point to wage differentials in favor of the growing regions and unfavorable to the older declining regions. There are sound reasons for this. Wage levels do not drop suddenly in areas where unemployment has appeared. Instead, wage levels fail to grow as rapidly in the declining regions. While one might expect wage differentials to appear in favor of growing regions, this is limited by the growth of labor supply in these regions, and by the initial wage level and labor market characteristics of the declining regions. As expected, all that can be observed at the moment is the differential in rates of growth of wages, but we cannot yet observe the appearance of positive differentials in favor of growing regions. The inducement to migrate must therefore be understood in terms of the growth of employment opportunities and in terms of the returns to capital invested in small business. The small businessman (lawyer, accountant, construction contractor, etc.) will migrate in anticipation of absolutely higher returns to his enterprise and in anticipation of future growth in such returns. For these reasons, we may expect areas with high rates of unemployment to be unattractive to migrants, no matter how high their wage level at the present time.

The second type of region which feeds the supply of migrants is predominantly rural. Migration is induced by opportunities for higher incomes in urban occupations. The destination of these migrants is either the urban areas of their native regions, or the urban areas of the Pacific Coast, the Southwest, the North Central States, and the Atlantic Coast. Areas which supply out-migrants are found in the South East, particularly states in the Appalachian Mountain region, and in the West North Central states. In the latter areas, there has been a movement of population off the farm, out of such states as the Dakotas, Nebraska, and

Montana, in the direction of the Pacific Coast and the metropolitan areas of the North Central States: Chicago, Milwaukee, Minneapolis, and Detroit.

The movement of human resources within regions

Because of the complex migration patterns mentioned above, there is no relationship between the growth of a region and its wage structure. It is not possible to say, for example, that the low-wage areas are growing faster than the high-wage areas. The reason is that the low-wage areas are experiencing a simultaneous shift of resources within and between regions, tending to raise *per capita* levels of income. On the one hand, rural population moves toward the urban centers of the same region, but on the other, population migrates out of the region entirely. The effect of the first type of movement is to stimulate investment in manufacturing and other urban economic activities within the low-wage area. Moreover, state *per capita* real income is increased as a result of the transfer of labor from low-wage industries. This migration has been a potent source of economic growth. It is observed that the greater the misallocation of resources, at the initial period, the greater has been the rate of growth of *per capita* income. As our measure of misallocation, we used (*a*)—the wage differential between sectors, and (*b*)—the fraction of the labor force initially employed in the low-wage sector. The effect of the second type of movement is to stimulate investment in the destination areas of the population movement. The first effect, if it operated alone, would yield a more rapid growth of low-wage than high-wage regions, for the low-wage regions would be investing more rapidly. However, this is offset by the second type of movement, which yields rapid growth in the high-wage areas which receive population migration. Thus, evidence exists for the belief that the interregional growth differentials operate through a self-perpetuating process. These possibilities will be explored later through a formal model.

A second phenomenon which has been observed in different regions concerns the wage structure of the region. In those regions where manufacturing occupies a small share of the labor force relative to other non-farm activities, the wage in manufacturing markedly exceeds the wage paid in these other occupations. On the other hand, where manufacturing occupies a substantial share of the labor force, the differential is narrow. Such a relation is also observed over time. In those regions which have experienced rapid growth of employment in manufacturing, the sectoral wage differential has narrowed. It is true that nationwide there has been a narrowing of the wage differential between manufacturing and other non-farm occupations. Nevertheless, the nationwide pattern does not suggest the selective narrowing process occurring among regions. The nationwide pattern could also have occurred with simultaneous narrowing of the differential among all regions. In fact, the narrowing of the differential appears to be related to the pace of economic development in different regions. This suggests the strong linkage which must exist between farm wages and unskilled wages generally. It is true in the United States, as in other industrialized countries, that farm occupations pay less than urban occupations, although the differential has narrowed over time. It is also true that rural birth rates have been higher than urban birth rates, and that employment on the farm has grown less rapidly than employment in urban areas. We suggest that the following set of relationships influence the wage differential within the region: As labor leaves the farm it moves first into non-manufacturing occupations. These are the unskilled service trades requiring relatively low levels of training. The wage rate in these occupations will be lower than in manufacturing. There are two reasons for this: first, the costs to the worker of acquiring skills impose a barrier to movement between non-manufacturing and manufacturing sectors. Second, the conditions of market competition and expansion limit the desire of employers of skilled labor to undertake the training of the unskilled.

The differential between the sectors will be influenced by the shift of workers between them. In a perfect labor market, which is in a state of equilibrium the differential would reflect only costs of training. Our analysis suggests that the market is not in static equilibrium. Supply is growing in the non-manufacturing sector through movements off the farm. Supply is growing in the manufacturing sector through shifts from the non-manufacturing sector. Demand for labor in the two sectors is growing as a result of the growth in demand for the region's exports and non-export products. When the differential widens, it means that labor is moving off the farm into the non-manufacturing sector faster than it is being absorbed into manufacturing. The differential has also been observed to widen in declining industrialized areas as a result of the downgrading of labor previously employed in manufacturing, now forced to seek employment in the service industries. A possible additional factor is that due to the decline of manufacturing, migrants from farms are forced to seek work in the non-manufacturing sector. Wages are more flexible in the non-manufacturing than manufacturing occupations. Hence the differential widens.

When the differential narrows, it means that labor is shifting into manufacturing out of non-manufacturing faster than farm emigration refills the supply in non-manufacturing. Alternative explanations for this phenomena might be sought in terms of differential changes in the demand for manufacturing and non-manufacturing labor. However, the above analysis appears consistent with the evidence cited previously. The differential in wages between manufacturing and unskilled occupations is smallest in those regions where the labor force is the most industrialized. In these regions the growth of the labor supply due to interregional shifts out of agriculture is the smallest. These regions have already at some time in the past industrialized their labor supply. Consistent with this is the behavior over time: the differential in wages between manufacturing and unskilled occupations narrows most rapidly in those regions with the most rapid growth of manufacturing, and with the most rapid industrializtion of the farm labor supply.

Movements of capital

In addition to the labor market patterns observed above, it is also possible to observe certain stable patterns of behavior in the capital market. In the first place, many of the newer regions appear to be net debtors to the older regions. That is to say the social product of the newer region exceeds the income payments to residents of the newer region.[1] The differential represents net payments on

1. Write Z = regional product M = imports
                C = consumption S = savings
                I = investment D = net income payments to
                E = exports   foreign owners of domestic
                                                    capital

income account to absentee owners of capital. This is hardly surprising, for a new region cannot very likely generate out of domestic income the savings necessary for capital information. The notable exceptions to this observation occur in such states as California and Florida, which, due to the attractiveness of climate, have experienced an immigration of many older people. The second stable pattern is the movement of capital from declining to growing regions. That is, the supply of goods and services for domestic uses tends to exceed the social product in growing regions, and to fall short of the social product in declining regions.[2] The reasons are: first, the conscious decision by savers in all parts of the country to seek the highest return on their new investment; and, second, the decision by firms to create capital in those employments where rates of return are highest. By any reasonable standard, the capital market in the United States is almost a perfect one, so that the above-mentioned regional flows are quite consistent with equalization of marginal rates of return on investment. Nevertheless, differentials in interest rates do appear among regions. While small, they suggest the directions in which capital is moving. Yield differentials on marketable residential mortgages indicate higher yields in the West and South. The same differentials appear in interest charges for commercial bank loans.

Regional growth differentials and governmental policies

Governmental policy on the federal level has faced in two directions in the past. On the one hand, the expenditures by the federal government have been enormously influential in the regional distribution of economic activity. This has been particularly the case in wartime, when governments stimulated the development of new industries and directed the movements of individuals in the military establishment. While government sponsored activities, such as shipyards and airframe plants, decayed when no longer needed, the individuals and firms concerned frequently remained in their new locations. The Pacific Coast and Southwest areas

Then by definition $Z = C + I + E - M$
$$Z = C + S + D$$
where $C + S$ = Received income payments.

2. Define $C + I$ = goods and services for domestic use. Then $Z = C + I + E - M$. If $E - M$ is positive then $Z > C + I$.

received strong stimuli from this development. Second, the federal government has supported the incomes of many agricultural groups, thus contributing to the incomes of their regions. Because of technological developments in agriculture, the government programs have not led to increased agricultural employment.

On the other hand, the federal government has also, slowly at first, taken a hand in the problems of depressed areas. An attempt is now being made, under the Area Development Act, to reverse the decline of employment opportunities in the most sorely afflicted areas. Retraining programs have been started in coal-mining regions, and federal loans are made available to construct new production facilities in depressed areas. At the moment, the federal program is small in scope relative to the number of areas which could use this aid. This is partly due to the broad coverage of the legislation, and partly a result of the funds available. It is fair to say, however, that depressed urban areas are also aided by urban renewal programs which apply to all urban regions. Under these programs federal funds are available for the reconstruction of blighted urban areas.

Despite the potential power of the federal government, most of the active governmental policy affecting depressed areas is carried out at the state and municipal level. Two devices have been employed. One is the use of tax rebates or allowances as a means of attracting new industries. The second is the formation of semi-governmental lending authorities, and industrial development corporations. These agencies make loans at low rates of interest, insure loans, provide second mortgages, and, in some cases, construct facilities for lease to industrial users. The hope of these programs is that they will attract new firms which will promote permanent employment opportunities.

A possible difficulty with the state and local programs is a tendency for the efforts to cancel out in a competitive bidding for new firms. As in the case of many types of advertising, those who fail to advertise suffer a loss of markets, and those who do advertise are not appreciably better off. Nevertheless, the proponents of such industrial development stimuli can point to new firms as evidence that their programs are worthwhile. There is no clear cut evidence that these programs have had positive marginal returns. Whatever the answer, it is clear that state and local development programs have not halted the patterns of decline in the depressed areas. They may, however, have mitigated the worst aspects of decline – namely, high local levels of unemployment.

Explanations of Regional Growth Patterns

The goal of our study is to explain the economic phenomena associated with regional growth differentials in terms of an economic model. A model is a theoretical simplification of the economic relationships in operation. The purpose of constructing a model is to isolate the forces at work which generate the observable behavior of the various regions. The usefulness of a model is twofold. If relationships are stable over time, we are able to make predictions about future behavior, and to make intelligent prescriptions for government policy. Secondly, a model contains the structure of relations which generate the behavior studied. Once the model is accepted, it may be compared with models which have been used to explain other aspects of growth. The goal of comparison is the possibility of finding more general types of explanations which bring together a wide variety of phenomena. One goal in the investigation of models of regional growth is to discover whether growth differentials among nations are explainable in terms of the same set of relationships.

In this section, we shall explore a number of different models which have been brought to bear on the regional growth problem. In the following section, we shall synthesize the results of our inquiry into a more general model of regional growth.

The models to be presented are derived from the assumptions that the economy may be described in terms of a set of competitive markets subject to certain empirical constraints. The techniques to be used are therefore derived from the theory of resource allocation under assumptions of profit maximization and atomistic competition. It is our belief that these provide a powerful tool for the understanding of regional development in advanced market economies.

One-product economies

A simple and venerable explanation of regional growth patterns is based on the assumption that each region produces the same product for a national market. Let us assume that:

(a) the production function for the product is homogeneous of the first degree in the inputs of capital and labor;

(b) units of labor are identical in terms of quality within and between regions;

(c) capital consists of the accumulation of outputs produced in the past;

(d) there are no regional differentials in the price of output. Effectively this means that there are no transport costs;

(e) perfect competition exists.

Under these conditions, regional differences in the real wage and in the return to capital result from differences in relative resource endowments. A region with a relatively high ratio of capital to labor will experience a relatively high real wage and a relatively low marginal physical product of capital. The converse will be true in a region with a relatively low ratio of capital to labor. The equalization among regions of returns to labor and returns to capital will follow from the migration of resources between regions. When the capital–labor ratio is identical among regions, these differentials in resource prices will be eliminated. On the basis of the above assumptions, we may expect capital to move from high-wage to low-wage regions, and labor to move from low-wage to high-wage regions. The growth differentials among regions will therefore depend upon the relative mobility of the two types of resources. If labor is immobile among regions, while capital is mobile, then the low-wage regions will grow more rapidly than the high-wage regions in terms of *per capita* real income, for capital will move to the low-wage regions. Conversely, if capital is immobile among regions, while labor is mobile, we may expect the high-wage regions to grow more rapidly in terms of employment. In a later section we shall examine the predictions of this model in terms of the evidence on regional behavior.

Multi-product economies

A wider variety of growth patterns may be generated if we relax the unrealistic assumption that each region produces one identical commodity. Suppose instead that we think of a variety of production activities in each region. The regional composition of output will be determined by resource endowments, transport cost differentials, regional differences in production functions and internal demand conditions. Under these less restrictive conditions, alternative growth patterns are possible.

(a) The differentials in regional growth rates may stem from differential growth rates in the demand for various regional exports. If, for example, the demand for automobiles grows more rapidly than the demand for coal, then regions producing automobiles will grow more rapidly than those producing coal. Note that this model is capable of contradicting the pattern of behavior generated under the assumption of one-product economies. For, in this example, if the area producing automobiles were a high-wage area, wage levels would diverge. That is, capital would be attracted into the automobile industry, even though it is a relatively high-wage industry, and the high-wage region would grow more rapidly than the low wage. This pattern of divergence would be accelerated by the migration of labor from low-wage to highwage areas. Increases in a region's labor supply enhance the inducement to invest in many local industries which serve domestic markets. This pattern will be investigated in a later section.

(b) Differentials in regional growth also stem from autonomous differences in the rates of growth of the labor supply. In region A the labor supply may be growing at 1 per cent per annum, and in region B at 3 per cent per annum. Let us assume that the two regions (among many) produce the same export commodity for sale to the rest of the country. Let us also make the same assumptions about the production and sale of this export commodity as were made previously about the one-product economies. However, assume that capital goods are separately identifiable commodities available at the same price in the two regions. Under these circumstances, capital and employment in the export sector will grow more rapidly in the region undergoing the more rapid growth of the labor supply. If this happens to be a high-wage region, then the high-wage region will grow more rapidly in terms of employment and capital than will the low-wage region. Note that under conditions prevailing in the American economy, the labor supply of this high-wage region would have grown more rapidly as a result of interregional migration of labor. Conversely, if the region undergoing the more rapid increase of labor supply had been the low-wage region, then the low-wage region would grow more rapidly in terms of capital and employment.

This analysis implies that when the export industry in the two regions reaches an equilibrium, the industry will pay the same wage in each region.[3] However, until the industry arrives at a position of long-run static equilibrium, it will continue to expand capacity in the region with the more rapidly growing labor supply. It is possible that in this region the wage will be lower than its long-run equilibrium level while the expansion is taking place. This will most likely be the case if the expansion of the labor force available to the export sector is generated through the fertility of the domestic population, or the shift of resources from inferior employments.

This conclusion raises a further question. If, in the long-run competitive equilibrium, wages must be equalized among the export sectors of the regions, must they not also be equalized within the two regions as well? For otherwise the labor markets would be imperfect within each region. If the labor markets were perfect, could regional wage differentials occur? The answer to this has partly been provided. Wage equalization may in fact occur between regions A, B, C, and D, because they share export industry 1. Wage equalization may also occur between regions E, F, G, and H, because they share export industry 2. But no mechanism other than the migration of labor between regions will equalize wages between the two groups of regions.

This conclusion, while valid, still hides the process of reallocation going on within regions, The process of economic growth consists of the movements of resources to superior employments. The process generates differentials in resource prices through changes in demand, technology, and resource endowments. Resources change employments in response to the resulting price differentials. Within region A, for example, the growth of the labor supply to the export industry may result from the fertility of its population, from interregional migration, or from the transfer of resources out of inferior employments. We have already

3. This follows from the assumptions of perfect competition, identical prices of output and capital goods, and a production function which is homogeneous of the first degree in the inputs of capital and labor.

seen that the latter source of labor supply growth is an important source of regional expansion.

The American economy has, in the last fifty years, experienced a transfer of population from farm to non-farm employment, and from rural to urban locations. Causes of the movement off the farm have been explored thoroughly by other writers and need only to be reviewed briefly: the higher rural population reproduction rates, the introduction of labor-saving technology on the farm, and the low-income elasticity of demand for farm products. As mentioned in the first section of this paper, these developments have generated a long lasting differential in wages between farm and non-farm employments. Thus the farm has provided a ready source of new labor for non-farm employment. When the development of non-farm economic activity does occur in such regions, it can call upon a highly expansible supply of labor, which is available at a wage slightly above the wage on farms. These considerations lead us to believe that wage equalization among export sectors, as discussed above, is consistent for long periods of time with intraregional wage differentials between sectors. It also leads us to conclude, or rather, predict, that those regions with large rural populations will experience the most rapid growth of non-agricultural employment. For, as indicated earlier, manufacturing wages have been higher historically than other non-farm wages, and relatively highest in those regions where manufacturing was least developed. While it is true that not all manufactures are exported, it is also true that the manufacturing wage indicates the wage paid by a majority of the non-farm export industries. Thus we feel secure in using the historical data on manufacturing wage relations to derive inferences about the behavior of certain export industries.

Consistency of Explanations with Evidence on Regional Growth Patterns

In this section we shall examine more closely data which we have prepared on growth patterns. Our concern is the ability of the above three models to predict the behavior of regions. The test of such a prediction must be made with reference to historical events. In a sense, the strongest of the models presented above is the first, since it leads to clear-cut and refutable predictions of behavior. The multi-product model is a looser framework which leads to predictions only when quite narrow specifications are made concerning certain relationships. For example, the multi-product is, under conditions described above, capable of imitating the outcome of the one-product model. The purpose of using this model is the wider range of behavior which it draws together in one explanation.

In the following table, we present the actual regional growth patterns for four intervals within the period from 1919 to 1957. We shall concentrate on the non-agricultural sector of each state. The period 1919–57 is broken into shorter intervals marked by business cycle peaks as the initial and terminal dates. We measure growth as the percentage change of a variable between two periods. Such changes are independent of cyclical movements during the interval, in the sense that intervening cyclical troughs do not influence the statistical measurement of growth from one peak date to the next. The intervals chosen are 1919–29, 1929–48, 1948–53, and 1948–57. While the last two periods overlap, they are included because of certain differences in behavior they demonstrate. Several statistics were calculated for each state:

1. the growth of non-agricultural capital (C^*)[4];

2. the growth of non-agricultural employment (L^*);

3. the growth of non-agricultural wages and salaries per non-agricultural employee (w^*);

4. the growth of the ratio of capital to labor in the non-agricultural sector (C^*-L^*);

4. The growth of non-agricultural capital is approximated through the growth of income payments to owners of non-agricultural capital. We shall present a model in a later section which indicates the conditions under which the income payments to capital grow as rapidly as the stock of capital. Note that the measure of income used is a received concept, identifying the location of the capital with the residence of the owner. A better measure would be a produced concept, identifying the location of the capital with the area of its employment. Unfortunately, data on produced income by region are not available for a large number of years. No government statistical source provides this information. Estimates of produced income for the years 1929 and 1953 are to be found in Borts (1961). While produced and received income do diverge at any moment, they also appear to grow at similar rates. Consequently, the use of received income to capital in the text is satisfactory.

5. the volume of migration of native born population in the preceding period *per capita* of the initial year population (M^*);

6. the growth of population in the preceding period as a per cent of the initial year population (P^*).

The periods covered by M^* and P^* are shown in the table.

For each period, the forty-eight states were divided into two groups, those with above and those with below average wages and salaries per employee.

The following data are shown in this form.

Table 1

		High-wage areas	Low-wage areas
		1919–29	
	C^*	60%	53%
	L^*	22%	23%
	$C^*–L^*$	38%	30%
	w^*	43%	36%
(1920–20)	M^*	5.49%	— 3.99%
(1910–20)	P^*	21.19%	10.66%
		1929–48	
	C^*	86%	139%
	L^*	31%	29%
	$C^*–L^*$	55%	110%
	w^*	168%	220%
(1930–50)	M^*	12.05%	— 10.16%
(1930–50)	P^*	33.52%	18.98%
		1948–53	
	C^*	37%	32%
	L^*	13%	13%
	$C^*–L^*$	24%	18%
	w^*	29%	28%
		1948–57	
	C^*	69%	67%
	L^*	20%	23%
	$C^*–L^*$	49%	44%
	w^*	55%	58%

Let us examine each of these periods. We see that in only one period does behavior conform to the model of a one-product economy. From 1929 to 1948, the low-wage areas grew more rapidly than the high wage; the non-agricultural wage per em-ployee, the stock of capital, and the capital–labor ratio all grew faster in the low-wage regions. The data on $M*$ and $P*$ confirm this pattern. From 1930 to 1950, the low-wage regions exported population and in fact grew less rapidly in terms of population than the high-wages regions. The other three periods examined do not display the same patterns. In the period 1919–29, a pattern of wage divergence occurred. Wages per employee grew more rapidly in high-wage states than low-wage states. The capital–labor ratio also grew more rapidly in high-wage states. The period 1948–53, and 1948–57, show virtually no pattern in wage growth, but there is a greater growth of the capital–labor ratio in high-wage states.

Examination of the evidence on wage growth, employment growth, and capital growth indicates that none of the preceding models provides a completely satisfactory explanation. The first model of a one-product economy appears consistent with the data between 1929 and 1948. However, it is clearly inconsistent with the behavior observed between 1919 and 1929, between 1948 and 1953, and between 1948 and 1957. Our investigations have shown that the second model – a demand-growth model – explains be-havior between 1948 and 1953.[5] However, neither the one-product model nor the demand-growth model suitably explains what hap-pened between 1948 and 1957, or between 1919 and 1929. While wages were diverging between 1919 and 1929, the simplest models presented above do not explain why. Further, in all periods but 1929–48, the capital–labor ratio grew more rapidly in high-wage states – a phenomenon not yet explained, but explainable in a

5. In the period 1948–53, high-wage regions grew more rapidly than low-wage regions. An analysis of national industrial behavior leads to the con-clusion that this was a demand induced phenomenon, undoubtedly associated with the Korean War and high levels of employment. The analysis pro-ceeded from the findings of other investigators that high-wage regions tend to be heavily dependent upon employment in high-wage industries, and similarly for low-wage regions. Our investigation showed that in this period the high-wage industries enjoyed a more rapid growth of prices and wages than low-wage industries. This occurred in a period of rising national demands, and led us to conclude that demand for high-wage products grew more rapidly than demand for low-wage products. Thus we concluded that demand changes were responsible for the regional behavior.

later model. If any stable pattern appears, it is the domination of the labor reallocation phenomena discussed in the third model. Looking solely at manufacturing for the moment, it appears that the most rapidly growing regions in terms of manufacturing employment were of two types: those which experienced migration of labor from other regions, and those which enjoyed the internal reallocation of labor from farm to non-farm activities.

Why did not all regions share this type of growth? There are two answers: Certain regions have already exhausted the possibility of internal transfer of labor. These are the highly industrialized areas of the North East. In this situation, regions must continue their growth through the attraction of labor from the outside. For this group, the role of demand for exports is crucial. They may suffer a loss of demand for two reasons: either a declining national market for the product or the growth of rival sources of supply elsewhere. The first factor would explain the fate of the coal industry since the Second World War. Another important factor in coal is the high rate of development of labor-saving technology. The second factor, rival sources of supply, has played a role in driving textiles and shoes out of New England; hosiery, gloves, and carpets out of New York and Pennsylvania. It is also beginning to affect the production of steel, glass, and cement in Western Pennsylvania and West Virginia. The failure of the export sectors to grow in these states led to a failure of wage levels to grow as fast as wage levels elsewhere. It has also led to high levels of unemployment. While these are still 'high wage' areas, they remain so due to the industrial composition of their labor force. They are not at the moment attractive areas for new migrants seeking industrial jobs. Thus the North East has witnessed a shrinking of employment opportunities in industry. This has not yet affected the major coastal cities – Boston, Newark, New York, Philadelphia, and Baltimore. These areas have gained population at the expense of the shrinking industrial towns, and have gained through the migration of population from the South. They also contain a large number of sustaining and growing activities which are keyed to growing national markets. Witness the growth of electronics and plastics in Boston, electronics and aviation products around New York, and petroleum refining and steel producing in the Philadelphia–Baltimore complex.

A second factor in the failure of all regions to share in growth is the absence of urban development in certain heavily rural areas. These states have simply lost population almost as rapidly as it increased due to natural fertility, so that they have had roughly the same population over a forty year period. The population of the United States has increased by approximately 70 per cent between 1920 and 1960. Yet it has declined or grown by less than 20 per cent in such heavily rural areas as Vermont, North and South Dakota, Iowa, Nebraska, Arkansas, and Oklahoma. The population of these states has migrated to other regions or to the urban areas of nearby regions. Thus they have fed the economic growth of adjacent regions.

Returning now to our three models it seems clear that, as the allocative process continues, the events explained by the multi-product models will take on increasing importance. In the American economy we are moving toward an urbanized society. The possibilities of regional growth through the internal shift from farm to urban occupations is a self-limiting process. Eventually the inducement to migrate will diminish. Growing demands for food from a growing urban population and a diminishing farm population will eventually eliminate the wage inducements to leave the farm. In addition, the rural birth rate will decline as farmers take on more of the living patterns of urban dwellers. Whether the monetary differential will ever disappear is not an issue; it is not clear what differential is stable in terms of the non-pecuniary compensations of rural life.

As a factor influencing regional growth, this type of intraregional labor force shift will become less important. This means the elimination of one of the strongest factors tending to cause a difference in wages among regions. Suppose, for example, all regions were to become completely industrialized with no internal wage differentials, and no regional birth rate differentials. Wage differentials would reflect mainly differences in occupational structure. Future growth differentials would depend upon interregional migration from one urban area to another. This would in turn depend upon changes in the demands for regional exports and upon differences in tastes with regard to place of residence. Regional growth differentials will certainly continue in the future. But in the American economy, they will change their form as the major reallocations of the past have been completed.

A Synthetic Model of Regional Growth

In this section we shall present a model of economic growth which synthesizes the previous material. We shall use the concepts and findings of the earlier analysis to provide the structure and assumptions of the model.

In our view, a model of economic growth should accomplish the following objectives. First, it should show the equilibrium time paths of accumulation and resource allocation of individual regions. Second, it should demonstrate the interactions between resource allocation, the payments to resources, and the other determinants of growth. Third, it should show the reactions of the economic system to changes in the data. Fourth, it should indicate the instrumental variables in the system which are amenable to influence by government policy.

In constructing a growth model for a multi-regional economy, an additional and narrower group of specifications must be satisfied. First, the model must generate a pattern of interregional resource shifts consistent with observations. Second, the model must show the reallocative processes which occur within growing and declining regions: movements between farm and non-farm sectors, and within the non-farm sectors; between manufacturing and other non-farm occupations; the corresponding changes in wage differentials; the influence of the rate of return on investment; and the influence of changes in the supply of labor. Third, the model must show the influence of changes in export demands and changes in technology on the equilibrium growth paths of the region.

In the following model we shall examine the growth of a group of regions under highly artificial conditions. These restrictive assumptions can be relaxed at a later stage of the analysis. We shall first assume that they are growing along stable time paths. Next we shall introduce disturbances into these time paths and indicate the reactions of the regions in subsequent periods. Our goal is to demonstrate how the observed time paths are generated by the disturbances.

We shall assume that each region produces two kinds of goods, an export good which is sold to other regions, and a domestic good which is only sold at home. It is assumed that the export good is an industrial product, and we shall abstract from the export of agricultural products between regions. That is, all agriculture is assumed to be domestic. There is no reason for all regions to produce the same export good. Consequently a region will sell its export good to other regions, and buy their exports in return. We also assume that the particular region to be examined in detail imports its capital goods from other regions. Obviously, this assumption cannot be maintained for all regions, and we shall at a later point examine the role of regions which export capital goods.

We shall assume that the regions share a common money unit of account, and that balance of payments surpluses or deficits are settled by transfer of private debt. There are no gold flows or flows of interregional short-term balances. In fact, the assumptions to be made provide only a minor equilibrating role for interregional money flows of any type. We shall assume that all interregional prices are determined in competitive national markets, and that no region is large enough to influence these prices. That is, the regions do not have any monopoly or monopsony power to influence what they buy or sell. The only prices which are determined primarily by conditions of demand or supply within the region are the prices of domestic products.

We shall assume that capital goods are employed in the production of the export good, but not in the production of the domestic good. This is a rather extreme assumption to make for a number of reasons. First, a number of non-exported products do indeed make heavy use of capital. The examples which come to mind are railways, telephone systems, and electric and gas utilities. We shall not analyze these, and exclude them from our abstract model. Secondly, agriculture uses capital in the form of land, buildings, improvements, and livestock. For the sake of simplification, we shall abstract from this, assuming that agriculture uses only labor. At a later stage, we can relax these rather severe assumptions.

We shall assume that the production function for the export

commodity is homogeneous of the first degree in the inputs of labor and capital, and that for the domestic commodity is homogeneous of the first degree in the input labor. We shall assume that the national capital market is perfect and that the same rate of return on investment is earned in each region. If the same return were not earned, capital resources would of course be reassigned until returns were equalized.

Note that the above assumptions eliminate the role of money, because they have already provided us with a concept of a regional price level. Assume the full employment of resources within the region and the equalization of wages between the two sectors. The export price is fixed, the price of capital goods is fixed, and the rate of return on investment is fixed. In the long run this determines the money wage in the export industry.[6] Assuming a perfect labor market within the region, the money wage in the domestic sector equals that in the export sector. This determines the price of output in the domestic sector.[7] Thus at full employment the domestic price level is determined without influence from the money supply of the region. The supplies of capital and labor in the region, and the characteristics of the production function, determine a transformation function between domestic and export

---

6. Let $x = f(K, L)$ be the production function for exports x, homogeneous of the first degree in L, labor, and K, capital; with f_L and f_K representing first partial derivatives. Let P_x and P_K represent the prices of exports and of capital goods respectively. Let r represent the rate of return on investment and w_x the wage per worker in exports. The conditions of *long-run* equilibrium in the export industry require that

a. $rP_K = P_x f_K$. This determines a value of f_K, since r, P_K and P_x are determined outside the region. The value of f_K determines L/K, which in turn determines f_L. This follows from the concept of homogeneity of degree 1. Thus we have the money wage in exports, since we know P_x.

b. $w_x = P_x f_L$.

7. Let w_x indicate the money wage per worker in the domestic sector. Then assuming a perfect labor market.

c. $w_x = w_y$

In addition $P_y = w_y \left[\dfrac{L_y}{y} \right]$, where P_y is the price of domestic products, and

$\dfrac{L_y}{y}$ the inverse of the average product of the domestic sector labor force which we shall assume is a given constant. Thus we know the price of domestic sector outputs.

goods. With the assumptions embodied in the footnotes, this is a continuous function concave to the origin. In addition, the determination of P_x, the price of exports, implies a value for P_y, the price of domestic goods. These imply a point on the transformation function, and consequently imply the quantities of the outputs of the two commodities. In order to satisfy the conditions of equilibrium in the two output markets, this allocation of labor between the domestic and export sectors must be consistent in the long run with the expenditure by domestic consumers on domestic products. In turn this will determine the value of borrowing or lending between this and other regions.

We shall begin our analysis of growth by assuming that all regions neither borrow nor lend; that is, domestic capital formation is completely financed out of domestic savings, and exports equal imports.[8] We shall also assume that the labor supply grows at a constant and equal rate in all regions, and that the stock of capital grows at a constant and equal rate in all regions. Further, we shall assume, at least initially, that the export sector maintains a constant share of each region's labor force. In conjunction with the requirement of an equal rate of return on investment in all regions, this implies that the capital stock grows at the same rate as the labor supply.[9] Note we are excluding the possibility that the rate of return alters simultaneously in all regions through unequal growth of labor and capital. Finally, note that

8. Write Z = regional product = value of export output plus value of domestic output. Note we assume that all Domestic Output is consumed as, a final product.

Then $Z = C + I + E - M$, where C = consumption, I = investment, E = exports, M = imports.

We also know that $Z = C + S + D$

where C = consumption, S = savings, D = net overseas income payments on capital account. Assume $D = 0$, initially.

Then $S = I + E - M$, so that if investment equals savings, then exports equal imports.

9. Recall that $rP_K = P_x f \cdot_K$ Using starred superscripts to denote percentage rates of change over time, this implies that $f_k^* = 0$. Now f_K is a function of $\frac{L_x}{K_x}$ where L_x, K_x refer to the stocks of labor and capital in the export sector. Because we assume this sector to maintain a constant share of the labor supply, L_x must grow at the same rate as the labor supply. To keep f_K unchanged, K_x must grow at an equal rate.

these assumptions imply a time path of growth of regional product and investment at a rate equal to the growth of the labor supply. If we assume savings to be a constant fraction of income, then savings too grow at the same rate as investment. This means that exports continue to equal imports over time with no net borrowing or lending.

Let us now disturb this stable and uniform growth pattern. The disturbance assumed is a rise in the demand for a region's exports. This increased demand comes from other regions. Under stable monetary conditions, it implies a reduction in the demand for other export products, which we regard as produced by regions other than the particular one we shall examine.

The ordinary analysis of the balance of payments adjustment would lead to the examination of money flows, income multipliers and sectoral price levels. It would lead to the conclusion that the region with higher export demands undergoes a domestic price-level inflation, an increase in its money stock, and a rise in its imports. It would arrive at a new equilibrium level of income where exports exceeded or at best equalled imports. In the present model, an entirely different approach is required. For the present non-Keynesian model is a long-run analysis of the effects of higher export demands under conditions of full employment. In this model, the rise of export prices in fact will destabilize the balance of payments such that imports grow more rapidly than exports. The result is that the growth of export prices leads to an increase in the growth of the region's capital stock, and consequently to an increase in the region's rate of growth.[10] Why does this occur? It will be recalled that we assumed the export sector to be in long-run equilibrium, and that the price of exports, the price of capital goods, and the rate of return are determined nationally. The rise in export prices makes it profitable to increase the stock of capital relative to the number of workers in the export sector.[11] The total increase in capital will be determined by the magnitude of the rise in export prices, the growth of the region's labor supply,

10. These statements will be demonstrated in the mathematical appendix to this section, page 191.

11. Recall the static equilibrium condition $rP_K = P_x f_K$. Assuming r, and P_K unchanged, we have $0 = P_K^* + f_K^*$. Since the change of export prices, P_x^* is positive, the marginal physical product of capital must decline. This occurs through a fall in the ratio L_x/K_x.

and the shift of the labor force of the region from the domestic to the export sector.[12] The amount of labor which shifts between sectors will depend upon the income elasticity of demand for domestic sector products. In the extreme case where this elasticity is zero, all future growth of the labor supply will move into the export sector, and ε^* will be positive. We shall see in the appendix that when the income elasticity is unity, ε^* may be zero, and will be positive only if the elasticity of substitution in the export sector production function falls short of unity. In addition, the smaller the growth in demand for domestic goods, the greater the movement of labor into the export sector. Note that each worker who moves into the export sector increases the amount of capital to be used in that sector, and consequently under our assumptions increases the amount of capital to be accumulated in the region. Recall our basic assumption that the domestic goods use no capital. We shall return to this point below when we discuss public utilities and agriculture.

We have seen that an increase in export prices leads to an increase in the amount of capital employed in the export sector; consequently there is an increase in the region's stock of capital. How is this financed? If savings rise in equal proportion to the rise in investment, then no borrowing from other regions is necessary. In fact, if we assume that savings rise proportionately to income, then it will be insufficient to finance the increased investment. Therefore, an import capital will have to occur.[13] Thus our model satisfactorily incorporates the following phenomena: the movement of capital from declining to growing regions, and the shift of resources within growing regions toward capital-using sectors. In addition, the capital–labor ratio will rise in growing

---

12. Write $0 = P_x^* + f_K^*$; now let $u = f_K^*/Q^*$, where $Q = L_x/K_x$, and u is the elasticity of the marginal productivity of capital. Therefore, $0 = P_x^* + uQ^*$,
or $0 = P^* + uL^* - uK^*$
$K^* = P_x^*/u + L_x^*$
Now recall we assumed $L_x/L = \epsilon$, where L is the region's labor force, and ϵ is the share in the export sector. Assume this share changes. We have $L_x^* = \epsilon^* + L^*$, where L^* is the growth of the region's labor force
Therefore $K^* = P_x^*/u + L^* + \epsilon^*$ or
$\varDelta K = I = K_x[P_x^*/u + L^* + \epsilon^*]$.
13. See mathematical appendix, page 191.

regions, leading to a rise of money wages above the level in other regions.

Up to now we have assumed a uniform growth rate of population among regions. We now see that the rise in money wage levels resulting from the process described above, implies an inducement for workers to migrate to this area. This provides an additional stimulus to capital formation over and above those described earlier. For as we saw in the previous footnote, any factor tending to increase the growth of the region's labor supply will tend to increase the amount of capital accumulated in the export sector. It will also increase the amount of capital accumulated in the export sector. It will also increase the amount of capital imported.

How does the above process end? Does it lead to a new stable and uniform growth pattern with all regions again growing at the same rate, capital and labor growing at this rate as well? The answer is no. The reason is that investments exceed savings permanently. How does this occur? It will be recalled that the growth process set into motion by the rise of export prices results in a faster increase of investment relative to the increase in savings. In response to the new higher level of export prices, there is a new expanded quantity of capital in the export sector. After this new level of capital stock is reached, investment and the stock of capital again grow at the same rate as the supply of labor. There will be two reasons why these future investment levels will permanently exceed the future levels of domestic savings. First, investment originally equalled savings and grew at the same rate as savings under our stable time path of growth. As a result of the disturbance examined above, investment and the stock of capital have grown more rapidly than the growth of savings. When the adjustments to the disturbance are completed, investment will again grow at the same rate as savings. However, investment will be absolutely larger by the factor of the amount of capital financed through net borrowing from other regions. The second reason is that a discrepancy now appears between the region's produced income and its received income. The difference represents the net external income payments on borrowed capital. As this discrepancy grows, the region's received income grows at a slower rate than its produced income. Following the adjustment to higher export prices, produced income again grows at the same rate as the labor force. Consequently, received income must grow at a slower rate. Recall that we earlier regarded domestic savings to be a constant fraction of income without the need to distinguish between produced and received. It is now necessary to do so, and it seems most reasonable to regard savings as a constant fraction of received income. Consequently savings grow less rapidly than produced income, and therefore less rapidly than investment.

What this means is that the forces we have outlined produce a permanent divergence of regional growth rates. The only way in which growth rates might converge is through the role played by other autonomous forces operating within the framework of such a set of economic relations.

Three alternative disturbances might be considered within the framework of the present model: autonomous migrations of labor between regions; autonomous shifts of labor between sectors of a given region; and technological changes. These will be considered in turn.

(a) An autonomous migration is one which is not in response to the economic variables of our system. For example, population might migrate from A to B because of pleasant climate. Starting from the stable, uniform time patterns which we initially assume, the effect of an autonomous migration is to produce a permanent divergence in growth rates. For now, we may no longer assume that the labor force grows at the same rate in each region.

Where labor grows more rapidly, so must capital grow more rapidly in order to maintain uniformity in the rate of return on investment. Furthermore, shifts of this type induce a movement of capital between regions. We recognized earlier that these shifts increased the magnitude of any capital movement which is going on for other reasons. In addition, by themselves, population migrations set into motion, within the framework of our model, the forces which lead investment to exceed savings. The reason is that the migration induces the growth rate in income, savings, and the stock of capital, all to rise to the new higher rate of growth of the labor supply. In adjusting to this new growth rate of the stock of capital, investment must grow more rapidly than the stock of capital.[14] Note that this conclusion is independent of the possi-

14. Let starred superscripts denote percentage rates of change. Initially we assumed that along the stable time path $S^* = I^* = K^* = Z^* = L^*$;

bility that migrants bring capital with them. For this would imply that the capital movement is as autonomous as the migration itself.

(b) Autonomous shifts of labor between sectors of a region are capable of setting a growth process into motion. This will occur when labor shifts from low to high capital using industries. We saw earlier that such shifts take place within the framework of the model, under appropriate values of the income elasticity of demand for domestic sector goods. However, we now wish to consider cases where the shifts are autonomous in the sense that they take place without the rise of export prices and its consequent train of adjustments. We have discussed at length in an earlier part of the paper how labor might shift from non-manufacturing to manufacturing occupations in regions where the non-manufacturing sector is itself fed from emigration off the farm. Within the context of the present model this implies a wage differential in favor of the export sector, with a shift of labor from the domestic sector. This movement is capable of generating a growth process. It is also capable of initiating the import of capital, for it will induce investment to rise more rapidly than savings. Finally, it is capable of leading to changes in interregional growth patterns which produce an equalization of returns to labor. For as labor shifts to the export sector, wages will rise in the domestic sector. Thus the average wage in the region will come to equal the export sector wage, and this will come to equal the wage in other regions sharing the same type of export sector. Further equalization of wages among regions then requires interregional migration.

(c) The third type of disturbance which can lead to a growth process is technological change within the export sector. As an example, if we had neutral technological change and a perfectly elastic demand for the region's products, then we would have

---

where S = Savings, I = Investment, K = Capital, Z = Regional Product, and L = Labor Force. Now let L^* rise to $L^* + \alpha$; consequently K^*, S^*, and Z^*, must rise to $L^* + \alpha$. However I must rise more rapidly. $I = \Delta K$; initially $I = KL^*$ and $\Delta I = L^* \Delta K$. So that $I^* = L^*$. In order that capital grow at the higher rate, investment must grow more rapidly. For now $\Delta I = L^* \Delta K + K \Delta L^* = L^* I + K\alpha$; so that $I^* = L^* + \frac{\alpha}{L^*}$, and this exceeds S^*.

exactly the same type of process as outlined originally when export prices rose.[15] In fact, almost any technological change will lead to a growth process if it leads to an increased demand for capital in the export sector. This can occur even with capital-saving innovations, for the lower costs will induce an expansion of the scale of the export sector.

Before ending this section, let us return to two simplifying assumptions which were made originally, and examine the effect on our model of eliminating them. We assumed out of existence such capital-using domestic goods as railways, telephones, and electric utilities. Further, we assumed agriculture to be a domestic good which used no capital.

Turning first to capital-using domestic goods: we could introduce these into the model provided that the income elasticity of demand for these goods were very high. Alternatively, if the income elasticity of demand is very low, we must assume that the capital embodied in these industries is fixed, or at least cannot be withdrawn rapidly. Under these assumptions, if labor is induced to enter these industries, there will be an increase in the demand for capital similar to the increased demand for capital in the export sector. On the other hand, if labor leaves these industries, there will be no appreciable withdrawal of free capital for investment in the export sector. These assumptions will therefore not alter the picture of the growth process already presented. For the one event which would negate the process is the transfer of capital to the export sector from other sectors within the region.

These conclusions also explain the unusual treatment accorded to agriculture. If agriculture is now regarded as an export sector, there is no change in our conclusions provided that it is more capital intensive than other sectors from which labor is drawn. On the other hand, if labor is moving out of agriculture, for familiar reasons, there is to be no transfer of capital out of agriculture. Under these conditions, our original analysis is unchanged.

15. The initial growth process was set into motion by $P_x^* > 0$, with the adjustment to the new equilibrium described by the equation $0 = P_x^* + f_K^*$.

Let us write the production function for exports as $X = Af(K, L_x)$, where A is a multiplicative factor which embodies technological improvements. Then $X_L = A \cdot f_L$ and $X_K = A \cdot f_K$.

Consequently the adjustments to the disturbance induced by technological change may be written $0 = X_K^* = A^* + f_K^*$.

Let us now re-examine an assumption we introduced at the beginning of the discussion. We assumed that the region imports capital goods from other regions at unchanged prices, and that it does not produce capital goods domestically. The purpose of this assumption is to provide a direct link between the rise in export prices and the rise in the inducement to invest in the export sector. If the price of capital rose in equal proportion to the price of exports, there would be no growth process of the type specified. The only inducement to grow faster would then come from a shift of labor to the capital intensive sector. Such would have been the case, had we specified capital goods to be a domestic product. It would then require an expanding wage differential between exports and domestic goods to prevent a rise in the price of capital goods. We could make some concession to reality and allow some capital goods to be produced domestically. Nevertheless, to have the growth process specified above, enough capital goods must be imported at unchanged or slowly rising prices to allow a rise in the ratio of export to capital goods prices. Of course these restrictions do not apply so narrowly when growth is induced by the other autonomous factors. In the case of growth induced by technological change, the restriction is that capital goods must rise in price at a rate slower than the rate of technological change in the export sector. In the case of growth induced by a sectoral shift or interregional migration, the restriction is that capital goods must rise in price at a rate slower than the increase in the marginal productivity of capital.

How do these considerations affect the regions which export capital goods? How will they grow without a rise in the prices of their exports? This question must be handled in two parts. If there is only one type of capital good in the whole economy, then a rise in its price will not induce a rise in the capital–labor ratio used in its manufacture.[16] However, a rise in its price will induce the expansion of the industry's scale at the expense of the domestic sector. If the industry is competitive, the price rise will increase export sector wages, attract labor from the domestic sector and

16. Recall the long-run equilibrium condition: $rP_K = P_x f_K$. For the industry producing such a capital good, this expression becomes $r = f_K$.

Consequently, f_K and L_x/K will change only in response to a change in the rate of return on investment.

consequently increase domestic sector wages. In addition, the rise of export sector wages will attract population from other regions. Consequently a growth process can occur even if the region produces its own capital.

However, let us turn to the second and more reasonable possibility: that many types of capital goods are produced, some in this region, some in others. Under these circumstances, the growth of regions producing capital goods is no different conceptually from the growth of regions producing any type of export good. All that is necessary is that the region's exports rise in price relative to capital goods which are imported.

Note that this interregional model always assumes stable monetary conditions, so that if the demand for one type of exports expands, the demand for another type contracts. Thus no special expansion of the nation's capital goods is implied by the regional growth patterns we have generated. This ignores second order effects arising from possible differences in the capital intensity of different types of export goods.

Possible Applications of the Model to Conditions in Western Europe

The model we have presented is derived from a study of growth patterns among United States regions, over the past fifty years. Nevertheless we feel that it contains a structure which may be useful in the analysis of growth in Western Europe. The purpose of this last section is to provide a bridge for the reader who wishes to analyze European experience in terms of the model.

In the first place, Western Europe, like the United States, contains regions with disparate rates of growth of population, employment, and stocks of capital. These differences extend to the industrial and wage structures of the regions as well. To the outside observer, Europe appears to be undergoing the same type of simultaneous growth and reallocation process as is the United States. Labor is moving from the farm to non-farm occupations. Within non-farm occupations, labor is shifting to manufacturing. Low-wage regions are exporting labor to high-wage regions, and simultaneously undergoing an industrialization. The best example of this process appears to be Northern Italy. While the present authors have not examined statistical data on wage structure, these patterns would suggest a narrowing of sectoral differentials in the regions undergoing this type of change. These patterns would lead us to expect the highest wages to be paid in highly industrialized growing regions which have exhausted domestic sources of expanding labor supply. An example of this might be in Switzerland itself.

What about the balance of payments among European countries, and between Europe and the rest of the world? Does not the existence of separate currencies, separate money markets, and separate central banks prevent us from applying the preceding analysis?

This would certainly bc the case if there were serious violations of the conditions we established previously. However, with fixed exchange rates and free currencies, how far does the situation in Western Europe depart from the conditions of the model? It may still be possible for different rates of return on investment to prevail in different countries. Nevertheless, if these rates and their differences remain unchanged, our analysis should apply. We should expect a rise in demand for a country's exports to set into motion the same growth process, eventually leading to an import of capital. What appears today in Western Europe as an embarrassment of plenty in foreign exchange funds may therefore be viewed as the first step in the process which proceeds from increased exports to such a large rise of investment that capital imports occur. Casual evidence in support of this proposition comes from the behavior of American and British private investors and business firms in the last three years. Certainly their quest for Western European securities and branch plants would support the notion that the profitability of investment has risen markedly in Western Europe. Nevertheless one may wonder at the large rise in foreign exchange reserves and ask why the process of capital import has not begun. In terms of our framework, two answers are possible. Either savings has risen by a greater proportion than assumed; that is, savings has risen by a greater proportion than income. The other possibility is that investment has failed to rise by as great a proportion as contemplated in the model. There are two possible reasons for the first occurrence; either the savings function shows savings as a rising fraction of income; or the role of taxation and tax policy has made savings plus taxes rise more rapidly than income. Our original model ignored the role of government spending and taxation. Once they are brought into the picture, the appearance of capital imports will require that private investment and government spending grow more rapidly than private savings and taxes. If taxes are an increasing fraction of income, this may not occur.[17]

The second occurrence may be due to a number of factors which violate the model or which are external to the model. First, if the region undergoing the export boom produces its own capital goods, then the price of capital goods may rise sufficiently to wipe out the increased volume of investment. The capital stock will continue to grow at its old rate, which in our model is the growth of the labor force. This possibility is, however, contradicted by the behavior of non-continental firms in attempting to construct or acquire productive facilities on the continent. A second and more likely possibility is the unwillingness of monetary authorities to allow the process to work to completion, out of fear of domestic inflation. The process which our model describes is an inflationary process. The price level in the region undergoing growth rises relative to the price level in other regions. In the view of anyone seeking to halt inflation, it is appropriate for the government to use fiscal and monetary measures to prevent the rise of investment beyond what appears

17. Write Z = national product = $C + I + G + E - M$; where C, I, E, and M are as before, and G = government spending.

Further, $Z = C + S + T + D$, where C, S, and D are as before, and T represents taxes. Further, assume $D = 0$. Then we have $S + T = I + G + E - M$.

Assume that initially, savings equal investment, taxes equal government expenditures, and exports equal imports. What changes are necessary for Imports to exceed Exports? The above expression may be written $M - E = I + G - S - T$ or $\Delta M - \Delta E = \Delta I + \Delta G - (\Delta S + \Delta T)$.

We wish to show that although savings rise as rapidly as income, savings plus taxes will rise more rapidly than income, if the tax collection is an increasing fraction of income. Assume savings are a fraction of income after tax.

Let $S = a[Z - T]$, $T = BZ - \gamma$, where a, B and y are positive constants, and a, B are less than unity.

Then $S = aZ - aBZ + a\gamma$ and

$S + T = aZ - aBZ + a\gamma + BZ - \gamma = Z(a - aB + B) - \gamma(1 - a)$. *Quod erat demonstrandum.*

to be a level consistent with price-level stability. Within the framework of our model, it means that money income is held down to that level at which domestic prices must be stable. For we assume that exports are not consumed at home, so that the price of exports does not enter a price index of the consumer budget. Such a policy can only succeed either by rationing investment or by raising interest rates high enough to choke off the demand for capital.[18] This is not the place to evaluate policies, which in fact we have invented to explain the possible discrepancies between the model and actual behavior. It is an interesting test of our model to confirm that such policies exist. Our purpose has been to show how the model might be extended to explain growth among individual countries which have control over their monetary units.

Mathematical Appendix

I. We wish to show first that the rise of export prices will lead to an increase in investment which exceeds the increase in savings. The labor force, L, grows at a rate L^*. Further we assume S to be a constant fraction of regional product, Z. Therefore, it will suffice to show that I rises more rapidly than Z [$I^* > Z^*$], as a result of the increase in export prices.

We shall define Z, the regional product, in terms of the payment to factors of production.

a. $Z = W + R$, where W is the wage bill, and R the total payment to capital.

The percentage change Z^* may be written:

a'. $Z^* = AW^* + (1 - A) R^*$, where $A \equiv W/Z$.

18. Recall that P_y, the price of domestic sector goods $= w_y \left[\dfrac{L_y}{y} \right]$, where w_y is the domestic wage, and $\left[\dfrac{L_y}{y} \right]$ the inverse of the average product of domestic sector labor. We wish to keep P_y constant. This means we must keep w_y constant. Assume a perfect labor market, with wage equality in the two sectors. Then w_x must be kept constant. However, $w_x = P_x f_L$. Since P_x has risen, the marginal product of labor, f_L, must fall. This means that enough labor must move into the export sector to raise L_x/K. But this will raise f_K, the marginal product of capital. Initially in equilibrium, we had $rP_K = P_x f_K$. But now, P_x and f_K both rise. Either investment must be rationed, or r must be raised to offset these increases.

In addition, the wage bill is defined as:

b. $W = wL$, where w is the wage rate and L the labor force.

Therefore the growth of the wage bill is:

b′. $W^* = w^* + L^*$.

Therefore:

c. $Z^* - L^* = Aw^* + (1 - A)(R^* - L^*)$.

Let us now examine the growth of investment. Recall from an earlier footnote that capital increases in the export sector according to the following relation:

d. $\Delta K = K[L^* + P_x^*/u + \epsilon^*]$.

The first term in the bracket shows us the secular growth of capital induced by the growth of the labor force. The second term shows the increment in the demand for capital due to the increase of export prices; the third term shows the effects of shifts of the labor force from the domestic to the export sector. The second and third terms together provide a discontinuity (a jump) in the growth of the capital stock. That is, there is a once and for all change in the rate of growth of capital, after which it again grows at its secular rate. This change is shown as occurring in the period Δt, in the chart below.

It can be seen that the growth of the capital stock consists of two parts: S, the secular part proceeds at L^*; while D, the disturbed part, has a value of $P_x^*/u + \epsilon^*$. Ordinarily, if we ignored the disturbance, capital would grow at L^*, and investment would also grow at L^*. However, in order to bring capital stock up to its new higher level, investment must during this period, increase by more than KL^*. Consequently, the disturbed increment to the stock of capital, D, is also a disturbed increment to investment. A simple numerical example will make this clear. Suppose the stock of capital were constant over time at 100 units. Then it rises during a period from 100 to 110. Thereafter it remains constant at 110. Then investment rises from zero to ten, and then falls back to zero. In the period when investments rises from zero to ten, the growth of investment is also plus 10. This implies that the increment to investment is negative when the new permanent level of capital 110 is reached. In terms of our model it means that I^* is at first equal to L^*, then exceeds L^* by the disturbed term. When the adjustments are completed, I^* becomes negative. However, as

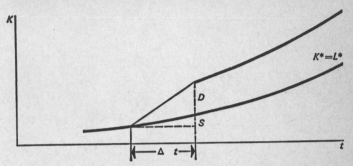

Figure 1

indicated earlier, this does not reverse the capital flow for even at its lower long-term level, investment still exceeds savings.

We may derive the expression for I^* which includes both secular and disturbed terms. Note that we are using expressions for continuous changes to describe what is essentially a discontinuity. The increment to investment I is comprised of a secular plus a disturbed term.

e. $\Delta I = \Delta I_S + \Delta I_D$,

The secular term is derived as follows: under stable conditions of long-term growth, $K^* = L^*$, where $K^* = I/K$. Consequently, $I = KL^*$ and $\Delta I = L^*$. $\Delta K = L^* L^* K$. In addition the disturbed term is the disturbed increment to the stock of capital.

$$\Delta I_D = K[P_x^*/u + \epsilon^*].$$

Therefore we have:

e′. $\Delta I = L^* L^* K + K[P_x^*/u + \epsilon^*].$

We therefore have the following expression for I^*

e″. $I^* \equiv \dfrac{\Delta I}{I} = \dfrac{\Delta I}{KL^*} = L^* + \dfrac{P_x^*/u + \epsilon^*}{L^*}.$

This may also be written $I^* - L^* = \dfrac{P_x^*/u + \epsilon^*}{L^*}.$

Return now to the definition of R, the return to capital.

f. $R = r P_K K$.

Therefore, with no change in r, or P_K,

f'. $R^* = K^*$.

Making use of expression d,

g. $R^* - L^* = K^* - L^* = P_{\bar{x}}^*/u + \epsilon^*$.

Therefore, we have

h. $I^* - L^* = \dfrac{R^* - L^*}{L^*}$.

Let us combine this with expression a' to determine whether investment rises more rapidly than income.

i. $I^* - Z^* = \dfrac{1}{L^*} \left\{ (R^* - L^*) \left[1 - (1 - A) L^* \right] - w^* A L^* \right\}$.

This term may be simplified as follows:

g. $R^* - L^* = P_{\bar{x}}^*/u + {}^*\epsilon$. We can prove that $P_{\bar{x}}^*/u = \sigma w^*$, where σ is the elasticity of substitution between labor and capital.

Proof: Start with the condition:

1. $r P_K = P_x f_K$. Therefore, holding r and P_K constant:

2. $0 = P_{\bar{x}}^* + f_K^* = P_{\bar{x}}^* + u Q^*$, where $u = f_K^*/Q^*$, as defined in an earlier footnote in the text.

Therefore 3. $P_{\bar{x}}^*/u = - Q^*$.

From the definition of the wage:

4. $w = P_x f_L$, we have:

5. $w^* = P_{\bar{x}}^* + f_L^* = P_{\bar{x}}^* + v Q^*$; where $v = f_L^*/Q^*$. v is the elasticity of f_L with respect to the labor–capital ratio. Substituting from 3 above,

6. $w^* = -u Q^* + v Q^* = -Q^* (u - v)$
    or $- Q = w^*/u - v$.

However, $\dfrac{1}{u - v} = \sigma$, the elasticity of substitution. Therefore

7. $-Q^* = w^* \sigma$. *Quod erat demonstrandum.*

It is easily seen that, in fact, $\sigma = \dfrac{1}{u - v}$. Proof: The elasticity of substitution is defined as minus one times the ratio of the per cent change in the factor ratio to the per cent change in the relative prices of the factors. Or:

8. $\sigma = \dfrac{-[L/K]^*}{[f_L/f_K]^*} = \dfrac{-Q^*}{f_L^* - f^*} = \dfrac{-Q^*}{vQ^* - uQ^*} = \dfrac{1}{u - v}.$

Quod erat demonstrandum.

Return now to expression g.

g′. $R^* - L^* = \sigma w^* + \epsilon^*.$

Therefore expression i may be written:

i. $L^*[I^* - Z^*] = (\epsilon^* + \sigma w^*)[1 - (1 - A)L^*] - AL^*w^*.$

This decomposes into two expressions; in ϵ^* and in w^*.

1. $\epsilon^*[1 - (1 - A)L^*]$. We assume that ϵ^* be either positive or zero. That is, the growth process raises or leaves unchanged the share of the labor force in the export sector. In addition, the bracket is positive, since $1 - A$ is less than unity, and L^* is less than unity. Therefore this expression is positive.

2. $w^*[\sigma(1 - L^*) + AL^*(\sigma - 1)]$. We know that w^* is positive. In addition, the bracket will be positive, if $\dfrac{\sigma}{1 - \sigma} > A\dfrac{L^*}{1 - L^*}$. We know A to be less than unity, and L^* to be less than unity. Consequently the inequality is satisfied if the left side exceeds unity. Such will be the case when $\sigma > \frac{1}{2}$. A less stringent requirement for σ is imposed by using empirical values of A and L^*. Let A, the share of income paid to labor, be $\frac{2}{3}$, and L^* be one per cent per annum. Then the expression on the right side of the inequality will be exceeded when $\sigma > .0067$. Thus we may conclude that I^* exceeds Z^*. Under our assumption, $I^* > S^*$, and capital imports will occur.

II. We now wish to investigate the conditions under which ϵ^* will be positive. Let us specify the demand conditions for the domestic sector. We shall assume an income elasticity of demand equal to h.

a. $[YP_y]^* = hZ^*$.   Now:

b. $Y = L_y \left[\dfrac{Y}{L_y} \right]$, where the bracketed term is the assumed constant average productivity of labor, and L_y is the domestic sector labor force. We assume Y/L_y to be constant, because we assume Y to be produced with no capital. Consequently:

b'. $Y^* = L_y^*$. In addition, write:

c. $L_y = (1 - \epsilon) L$, where $\epsilon = L_x/L$.

We therefore have:

d. $L_y^* = L^* - \epsilon^* L_x/L_y$.

We also know, from constant average productivity that:

e. $P_y^* = w_y^*$; and from a perfect labor market.

e'. $P_y^* = w_x^*$.

Finally, employing the definition of Z^*.

f. $Z^* = AW^* + 1 - A(R^*)$,

$Z^* = A[w^* + L^*] + (1 - A)(L^* + P_x^*/u + \epsilon^*)$.

So that expression a may be rewritten:

a. $\dfrac{Y^* + P_y^*}{h} = Z^*$.

a'. $\dfrac{1}{h} \left[L^* - \epsilon^* \dfrac{L_x}{L_y} + w^* \right] =$
$$A[w^* + L^*] + (1 - A)[L^* + P^*_x/u + \epsilon^*].$$

Let us assume h, the income elasticity of demand, to be unity, and examine the conditions under which ϵ^* is positive.

a'. $L^* - \epsilon^* \dfrac{L_x}{L_y} + w^* = L^* + Aw^* + (1 - A)[P^*/u + \epsilon^*]$.

We may first cancel the term in L^*. Next substitute $\sigma w^* = P_x^*/u$, as proved earlier. Then collect terms and solve for ϵ^*. We have:

$$\epsilon^* = w^* \left[\frac{(1 - A)(1 - \sigma)}{(1 - A) + L_x/L_y} \right].$$

It is clear that all terms on the right are known positive except $(1 - \sigma)$. If $\sigma < 1$, then ϵ^* will be positive. If $\sigma = 1$, then ϵ^* is zero. It can also be shown that for a given σ, the value of ϵ^* grows as h becomes smaller.

References

BORTS, G. H. (1960), 'Returns equalization and regional growth, *American Economic Review*, 50.

BORTS, G. H. (1961), *The estimation of produced income by state and region*, presented to the Conference on Research in Income and Wealth, April.

BORTS, G. H., and STEIN, J. L. (1961) 'Investment return as a measure of comparative regional economic advantage', in W. Hochwald (ed.), *Design of regional accounts*, Johns Hopkins, for Resources for the Future, pp. 69–103.

STEIN, J. L. (1958) 'Interregional comparisons of the marginal product of capital', *Southern Economic Journal*, 25.

STEIN, J. L. (1960) 'A theory of interstate differences in the rates of growth of manufacturing employment in a free market area', *International Economic Review*, 1.

STEIN, J. L., and SCHUPACK, M. B. (1959) *Forecast of New England's machinery industry in 1970*, Federal Reserve Bank, Boston.

6 H. B. Chenery

Development Policies for Southern Italy

H. B. Chenery, 'Development policies for Southern Italy', *Quarterly Journal of Economics*, vol. 76 (1962), pp. 515–47.

Despite the current popularity of policies for promoting development, there has been little systematic study of the effects of such policies on the actual course of economic growth. This situation is due in large part to the relatively short period over which most development programs have been in operation. Only a handful of countries has followed a fairly consistent policy for a period of as long as ten years, which is perhaps the minimum required for even a preliminary judgment of the effectiveness of a particular approach.

Within this small group, Southern Italy is of considerable interest because there the Italian government has attempted to carry out the theoretically attractive procedure of developing external economies by a massive dose of public works while leaving the direct investment in commodity production to private individuals. In this policy it has received substantial support from the U.S. government, the World Bank, and other international agencies. Since the program got under way in 1951, Southern Italy has had an import surplus equal to 25 per cent of its regional income, indicating one of the highest levels of external assistance in the world.

With a population of eighteen million and a separate historical tradition, Southern Italy is a distinct economic entity having a *per capita* income somewhat below that of the average for Latin America. In cultural heritage, social structure, and resistance to institutional change, it has many other parallels to Latin American countries.[1] In particular, the conflict between left- and right-wing elements of the Italian government over the lines of Southern development policy has led to a compromise that might be called

1. It will be recalled that Southern Italy was also under Spanish rule until 1861.

'intervention without planning', which finds its counterpart in many Latin American countries.[2] Certain objectives of southern development were set out in the Vanoni 'Plan' of 1954,[3] but the measures necessary to achieve them were not specified and the scheme has had little practical effect. Despite the fact that it has authority to spend three billion dollars over a fifteen-year period, the Southern Development Agency (the *Cassa per il Mezzogiorno*) makes no overall economic analysis against which to judge its past accomplishments and current program. In general, the government has preferred to follow a policy of unplanned growth and of influencing resource allocation in industry and agriculture by fiscal instruments rather than by more direct measures.

A considerable debate is now in progress over the success of southern development policies to date and the direction that they should take in the future.[4] Although the rate of growth of regional income has been substantial (4 per cent per year), it has been somewhat less than that of the rest of Italy and no higher than the average for other Mediterranean countries that receive much less outside assistance. The stated objective of southern policy – to develop as fast as or faster than the north – has not yet been met, and in fact *per capita* income in the south has fallen from 63 per cent to 56 per cent of the national average in the past decade. It is not clear whether it is the direction of policy that has been wrong, or whether the time period of ten years is just too short for a proper test.

The present paper will be concerned with three aspects of development policy in Southern Italy: (i) the significance of the differences between Southern Italy and the typical economy of its income level; (ii) the explanation of the lower rate of growth in output in the South, and the extent to which it results from the policies followed in the past decade; (iii) the nature of the

2. Current American efforts to use economic aid to achieve specific social objectives in Latin America encounter many of the same political and institutional obstacles that similar efforts met with in Southern Italy ten years ago. The analysis of current aid policy may therefore benefit from a study of the effects of U.S. policies in Italy in a period when it was receiving very large amounts of American aid.

3. Comitato dei Ministri per il Mezzogiorno (1961).

4. For a range of views see: Buffa (1961), Di Simone (1960a), Lutz (1960). Pescatore (1961), Saraceno (1961a), and Wellisz (1960).

structural changes needed for more successful development in the future. A simple interregional growth model will be used as a basis for the analysis of development policy.

Southern Italy as an Underdeveloped Economy

An underdeveloped region of a more advanced national economy has important differences from as well as similarities to a country of the same income level. Before trying to explain the pattern of southern growth, I shall therefore make a statistical comparison of Southern Italy with low-income countries and try to show how its economic structure is influenced by being part of a more advanced national economy. Further differences will be brought out by comparing Italian development policies with those of other countries.

The structure of the Southern economy

Although there has been much discussion of the economic structure of Southern Italy, it is only in the past year that the Central Institute of Statistics (ISTAT) has published a detailed study of regional income and its components for 1951–9 (Instituto Centrale di Statistica, 1960). Since 1951 is also the year in which the southern development program got under way, I shall take it as the starting point for the present analysis.[5]

In 1951, the region traditionally defined as the South ('Mezzogiorno') had a *per capita* income of 125,000 lire, or about $200 (Instituto Centrale di Statistica, 1960, p. 138). This income level was in contrast with $500 *per capita* in the industrial Northwest and $320 *per capita* for the country as a whole.[6] The difference in

5. The Cassa per il Mezzogiorno was established in 1950, but expenditures on a significant scale began only in 1951.

6. One important innovation in the ISTAT study is the division of the nation into three regions – Northwest, Center-Northeast, and South – instead of the North–South division that has been used up to now. The North (Piemonte, Lombardia, Liguria, Valle d'Aosta) contains the highly industrialized 'industrial triangle' of Milan, Turin, Genoa. The South (Abruzzi, Campagnia, Puglie, Lucania, Calabria, Sicilia, Sardegna) is the area traditionally called the 'Mezzogiorno', for which there is a separate development agency and policy. The Center comprises the remaining provinces (Tre Venezie, Emilia, Romagna, Marche, Toscana, Umbria, Lazio).

the available resources is substantially less, however, because there has been a continuing transfer of income from north to south by means of taxes and public expenditure. In 1951 this transfer reduced the regional resources *per capita* (i.e. the total of regional consumption and investment) to $415 in the north and raised regional resources to $235 *per capita* in the south. In subsequent years (as shown in Table 3, p. 204), the interregional income transfer has become considerably larger as the programs for developing the south have gotten under way.

Since one of the main problems of the south is lack of industry, it is interesting to compare the industrial output of the region with that of countries having similar income levels. This can be done most accurately by utilizing the results of a statistical comparison of production by sector in fifty countries (Chenery, 1960), which gives regression equations relating value added by sector to the income level and population of the country. The actual levels of total demand (regional income plus import surplus) and population in Southern Italy can be substituted in these equations to estimate the 'normal' productive structure of a country having these characteristics. The results of these calculations for 1951 and 1959, along with the actual values for Southern Italy, are given in Table 1.[7] The ratios of actual to normal in the main branches of production – 1.12 for primary production and .84 for industry in 1951 – show somewhat less industrial development than would be found in the typical country, but the deviations are no greater than those in many other countries in the original sample (Chenery, 1960, Table 6).

The effect on Southern Italy of being part of a more advanced national economy is more noticeable in the composition of industrial output. In 1951 regional specialization within the Southern Italian economy is shown by the relatively high values of agriculture and food processing, reflecting exports from the south to the north, and low values of textiles, metals, paper, and nonmetallic mineral products, reflecting relatively high imports of these

7. Since the level of total demand (consumption plus investment) is the main factor influencing sector output, I have used this variable instead of the regional product (income) in the regression equations. The international comparison is based on *per capita* income, but on the average there is little difference between the two. If income is used, however, the south had a ratio of 1.06 to the normal for all industry in 1951 and 1.29 in 1959.

Table 1

Actual and Normal Value Added by Sector in Southern Italy, 1951 and 1959

(In dollars *per capita*)

Sector	1951			1959		
	Actual value added[1]	Normal value added[2]	Actual ÷ Normal	Actual value added[1]	Normal value added[2]	Actual ÷ Normal
	(1)	(2)	(3)	(4)	(5)	(6)
Primary Sectors						
1. Agriculture	80.70	70.90	1.14	94.19	83.22	1.13
2. Mining	2.93	3.99	0.73	6.10	5.41	1.13
Total primary	83.67	74.89	1.12	100.29	88.63	1.13
Industry						
3. Food and tobacco	17.07	11.21	1.52	22.90	16.11	1.42
4. Textiles	0.93	4.33	0.21	0.93	7.10	0.13
5. Clothing and leather	2.10	2.55	0.82	3.15	4.44	0.71
6. Wood products	2.58	1.66	1.55	3.78	2.97	1.27
7. Metals	1.11	2.69	0.41	2.42	5.59	0.43
8. Metal products	4.48	2.72	1.65	9.12	6.37	1.44
9. Nonmetallic mineral products	1.21	1.72	0.70	2.85	2.94	0.97
10. Chemicals, rubber and petroleum refining	3.16	3.18	0.99	6.15	5.63	1.09
11. Paper	0.29	0.54	0.54	0.56	1.33	0.42
12. Other manufacturing	0.60	1.82		1.19	3.17	
Unclassified small industry		6.13			6.36	
Total (3–12)	33.93	38.55	0.88	53.06	61.96	0.86
13. Construction	7.69	10.75	0.72	17.65	15.64	1.12
14. Electricity, gas and water	4.48	(5.00)		7.65	(8.00)	
Total industry (3–14)	45.73	54.30	0.84	78.36	85.60	0.92
15. Transportation	13.70	14.00	0.98	19.30	21.34	0.90
16–20. Services	65.01	81.50	0.80	80.29	115.10	0.70
Total[3]	209.24	224.69		278.21	310.67	

1. Columns (1) and (4) are based on data from Instituto Centrale di Statistica (1960). Total value added in each sector was converted to 1953 dollars at the exchange rate of 625 lire per dollar and divided by the population of 17.65 million in 1951 and 18.99 in 1959.

2. Columns (2) and (5) are computed by substituting values of $235 *per capita* income and 17.65 population for 1951, and $326 and 18.99 for 1959, in the regression equations given in Tables 2 and 3 of Chenery (1960).

3. The differences in the totals are due to the fact that the total of the regression estimates is some 10 per cent less than the corresponding level of total value added, plus the fact that there is an import surplus of $35 in 1951 and $70 in 1959.

products into the south from the rest of the country. By 1959 the deviation in non-metallic mineral products was eliminated, but the pattern of specialization in the remaining sectors showed little change.[8]

8. Construction increased very markedly in this period, but this reflects an increase in local demand rather than a change in specialization.

It will be shown in the subsequent analysis that this pattern of specialization is a distinct handicap to southern growth, and in this respect belonging to a national economy will be a liability if it inhibits future changes in the economic structure. However, two other features of economic integration are definite assets, which should in the future outweigh any handicap resulting from the existing structure of production. The first, of which mention has already been made, is the income transfer to the south from the north,[9] which has contributed 20 per cent of the total resources

Table 2
Demographic Movements, 1951–9
(In thousands)

	North		Center	South	Italy
Population Physically Present[1]					
Total 1951		29,766		17,459	47,225
Natural increase		1,136		2,092	3,228
External migration		−470		−743	−1,213
Internal migration	(+790)	610	(−180)	−610	
Total 1959		31,042		18,198	49,240
Index $\frac{1959}{1951}$:		104.3		104.2	104.3
Annual rate of:					
Natural increase		0.49		1.42	0.83
External migration		−0.19		−0.51	−0.33
Internal migration		+0.25		−0.48	
Net increase		0.54		0.52	0.54
Resident Population[2]					
1951	11,720		18,040	17,651	47,411
1959	12,650		18,839	18,991	50,480
Index	107.9		104.4	107.6	106.5
Rate of increase	0.96		0.54	0.92	0.79

1. Source: SVIMEZ.
2. See Instituto Centrale di Statistica (1960), Table 17.

available in the south for the period 1951–60. As shown in Table 3 on page 205, a substantial part of this income transfer goes to finance consumption, which is somewhat larger than the total income produced in the region. Even so, since 1954 gross investment has averaged 20 per cent of total resources or 25 per cent of regional income, which is much higher than the level achieved in the typical country of this income level.

The second difference from other underdeveloped countries is

9. There is no detailed analysis of the financing of this import surplus, but the principal elements are social insurance payments and public works expenditures.

the higher emigration rate that is made possible for the south by being part of a larger political unit. The rate of natural increase in the south of about 1.4 per cent in recent years is close to the median population growth for Mediterranean countries of its income level,[10] although much lower than the rates of over 2.5 per cent that now prevail in the Near East and Latin America. However, the rate of population increase in the south over the past decade was lowered to 0.5 per cent by emigration (to the north and abroad), as shown in Table 2 above. This rate is much lower than the normal for an underdeveloped country. Internal migration has thus had the effect of equalizing population growth in the different regions of the country, and in the short run at least it makes the problem of raising *per capita* income in the south easier.

Southern and national growth, 1951–60

When we turn from the productive structure to the rate of growth in the past decade, the effect on the south of belonging to a national economy is even more noticeable. The growth of the Mezzorgiorno has been stimulated by the fact that gross national product in Italy as a whole has been increasing at 5.6 per cent per year, as shown in Table 3. The factors producing this high rate

Table 3

Sources and Uses of Regional Resources, 1951–60
(In billions of lire)

Northern and Central Italy

	1951[1]	1960	Per Capita[2] 1960	Increase 1951–60	% of increase in net resources	Annual rate of growth
Gross Product[3]	8,020	13,630	426	5,611		6.07%
Net Exports	283	1,174		890		17.3%
Net Resources	7,737	12,456	389	4,719	100	5.44%
Consumption	6,086	9,099	284	3,013	63.8	4.58%
Gross Investment	1,651	3,357	105	1,706	36.2	8.21%

10. For the period 1953–7, percentage rates of population increase in the Mediterranean were: Spain, 0.8; Portugal, 0.8; Greece, 0.9; Jugoslavia, 1.4; Algeria, 2.0; Egypt, 2.4; Turkey, 2.8; and Lebanon, 3.0.

Southern Italy

	1951[1]	1960	Per Capita[2] 1960	Increase 1951–60	% of increase in net resources	Annual rate of growth
Gross Product[3]	2,366	3,351	175	985		3.95%
Net Imports	382	1,203	63	821		13.6%
Net Resources	2,748	4,555	238	1,807	100	5.77%
Consumption	2,297	3,476	182	1,179	65.3	4.70%
Gross Investment	451	1,079	56	628	34.7	10.19%

Italy

	1951[1]	1960	Per Capita[2] 1960	Increase 1951–60	% of increase in net resources	Annual rate of growth
Gross Product[3]	10,386	16,982	332	6,596		5.62%
Net Imports	99	29		−70		
Net Resources	10,485	17,011	333	6,526	100	5.51%
Consumption	8,383	12,575	246	4,192	64.2	4.60%
Gross Investment	2,102	4,436	87	2,334	35.8	8.65%

1. See Instituto Centrale di Statistica (1960).
2. Resident population in 1960 was 32,013 thousand in the North and Center, 19,138 in the South, and 51,151 in all Italy. See Comitato dei Ministri per il Mezzogiorno (1961).
3. Total consumption has been recalculated by correcting the income from housing where statistical criteria have changed on the basis of the ratio of 1959 noncorrected figures to corrected figures; this brought about a corresponding change in gross product.

affect the south differently from the north, however, and on balance cause it to lag behind.

The rapid growth of the Italian economy since 1950 has been due to a number of factors: a relatively high rate of savings and investment, the initial existence of unused capacity in a number of sectors, unemployed labor, trade, liberalization, and an unexpectedly rapid growth of exports of goods and services (Presidenza del consiglio dei ministri, 1957; Saraceno, 1916b). From 1950 to 1956, one of the main factors that set a limit to growth was the balance of payments, which prevented a more rapid absorption of the excess labor supply because of the danger that import requirements would outrun exports.[11] The rapid growth of exports removed this limitation after 1957 and also provided the stimulus for continued growth of output (Presidenza del Consiglio dei Ministri, 1960).

The factors determining the growth of the Mezzogiorno are quite different. It has a relatively small share of national production in the sectors that have contributed the bulk of the increase in exports – metals and metal products, chemicals, tourism. Although it benefits indirectly from the income growth in the north and center, its exports to the rest of the country and abroad have not grown so fast as its imports since it produces commodities having lower income elasticities of demand. In this respect the south resembles the typical underdeveloped country. Local demand in the south has however been stimulated by the investment program of the Cassa per il Mezzogiorno and by increases in other types of government expenditure.[12] The nature of this relationship between the south and the rest of the country will be analyzed more fully under 'A model of regional development' page 211.

The differences between the south and the rest of the country are shown very clearly in the pattern of investment over the period 1951–9 and its effects on output, which are summarized in Table 4. In the distribution of investment by sector, the south has a higher than average proportion in overhead facilities (34 per cent versus 25 per cent). In large measure, this difference stems from the lack of transportation, communications, and other public facilities in the south and the need to improve them before commodity production can be increased. Within the sectors of commodity production, a much higher proportion goes to agriculture and a lower proportion to industry in the south than in the rest of the country. The increase in value added per unit of investment is significantly lower in the south, both in agriculture and in industry. The average profitability of this investment

11. This was one of the main conclusions of the analysis of development prospects by the U.S. government in 1952 (see Chenery, Clark, and Cao Pinna (1953)); and of the Vanoni Plan in 1954 (see Presidenza del consiglio dei Ministri (1957).

12. The mechanism by which expenditure in the south is translated into production and income in both north and south is analyzed in detail in Pilloton (1960).

Table 4
Gross Fixed Investments and Increases in Output (1951–9)[1]

	Commodity production		Overhead facilities			Other	Total
	Agriculture	Industry	Transportation and trade	Public works	Housing		
	1	2	3	4	5	6	7
a) Gross fixed investment (In billions of lire)							
North	534	3,653	1,425	446	2,319	553	8,929
Center	1,248	2,745	1,362	830	2,709	572	9,467
South	1,284	1,242	1,026	988	1,041	310	5,891
Italy	3,065	7,640	3,813	2,264	6,069	1,435	24,286
b) Percentage of total investment by regions							
North	5.97	40.91	15.96	4.99	25.97	6.20	100.00
Center	13.18	29.00	14.38	8.77	28.62	6.05	100.00
South	21.80	21.08	17.42	16.77	17.67	5.26	100.00
Italy	12.62	31.46	15.70	9.32	24.99	5.91	100.00
c) Ratio of increase in value added to gross fixed investment							
North	0.233	0.340			0.141		0.228
Center	0.319	0.314			0.150		0.220
South	0.176	0.241			0.139		0.169
Italy	0.244	0.315			0.144		0.211
Ratio of south to Italy	0.722	0.765			0.964		0.801

1. See Instituto Centrale di Statistica (1960).

was probably lower as well, since differences in wage rates can hardly have made up for the substantial difference in value added.[13]

All three of these factors – the large share of overhead facilities, the lower proportion of industry, and the lower return on investment in both agriculture and industry – combine to give a lower increase in output per unit of investment in the south than in the rest of Italy. The marginal capital–output ratio for this period (measured as gross investment/increase in gross product) is about 6 for the Southern economy as a whole and 4.8 for commodity production, both of which are high in comparison with most other underdeveloped countries.

Regional development policy

It is in the field of policy rather than in its economic structure that Southern Italy differs most significantly from the typical under-developed country. In principle, the objective of raising regional income as rapidly as possible is common to both. In Southern Italy, however, this objective must be reconciled with the interests of the rest of the country, and the instruments by which it is pursued are therefore limited by the type of policy chosen for the nation as a whole. The result is quite a different approach to development from that which is currently popular in Asia and Latin America.

The principal postwar objective of government policy in the south, stated most clearly in the Vanoni Plan (Presidenza del Consiglio dei Ministri 1957), has been to reduce the difference in consumption and income levels between the south and the rest of the country. The Cassa per il Mezzogiorno was set up for this purpose in 1950.[14] At that time, it was assumed that substantial progress could be made toward this objective within a period of ten years, and this assumption was incorporated in the projections of

13. The social profitability of the investment in the south was not necessarily lower, particularly in the field of industry, because there was probably a substantial difference between the opportunity cost of labour and its wage rate in the south and little or none in the north.

14. The Cassa was strongly supported by the U.S. government at its inception, and half of its financing in its first two years came from the counterpart funds generated by U.S. aid (see Chenery, Clark, and Cao Pinna, 1953, p. 97).

regional income that were made for the Vanoni Plan in 1954. These showed income in the south increasing by 8 per cent over the period 1954–64 as compared with 4 per cent in the center and north and 5 per cent for the country as a whole.

As the years have passed without any gain in the growth rate of the south over the rest of the country, official statements on development policy have tended to shift this goal to an indefinite time in the future and to stress the establishment of a self-sustaining process of growth as the main objective (Pescatore, 1961; Saraceno, 1961a). The integration of the south into the national economy remains the ultimate goal, however, and this implies that income levels cannot be allowed to get too far out of line between the two regions.

The means by which the goal of southern development is pursued are limited by the general principles guiding national economic policy. Italy's notable economic success over the past fifteen years has been based on orthodox economic policies of fiscal restraint, price stability, and the freeing of trade in accord with other members of the O.E.E.C. and the Common Market. These national policies imply the lessening of protection and reliance on subsidies and tax incentives in sectors where it is desired to promote production and investment. The most common instrument of development policy, the protection of local industry, has therefore not been used in the south. The alternative (and theoretically more desirable) means of stimulating industry have not been applied very vigorously, however.

One reason for not actively promoting industry in the south has been the difficulty for private entrepreneurs in setting up new plants to compete with the established firms in the north. The initial program of the Cassa per il Mezzogiorno made no provision for industrial investment, and measures to promote industry are still limited to tax incentives and loans at low interest rates.[15] The principal exception to this general policy has been the provision that the state-owned industrial holding companies (I.R.I. and

15. In 1953 special regional institutions (IRFIS, CIS, and ISVEIMER) were set up to provide industrial credit at favorable terms to industry in Sicily, Sardinia, and the rest of the south respectively. These and other measures to favor industrial development are summarized in Associazione per lo Svilluppo dell'Industria nel Mezzogiornia (1954) and Wellisz (1960).

E.N.I.) should make 40 per cent of their total industrial investments in the south.[16]

These factors have combined to produce a regional development policy that is devoted primarily to improving the economic environment. Over the past ten years the principal expenditures under the Cassa per il Mezzogiorno have been as follows (in billions of lire)[17]

Land reclamation	305 (31.6%)
Land reform	280 (29.0%)
Water supply and sewage disposal	127 (13.1%)
Roads	118 (12.2%)
Railways and shipping	72 (7.5%)
Mountain basins	42 (4.3%)
Tourism	22 (2.3%)
Total	966 billion
	($1,516 million)

It is estimated that only about 25 per cent of these expenditures has a direct effect on commodity production (Di Simone, 1960b). The remainder will have an indirect impact over an extended period.

As shown in Table 4, this program has been successful in reducing somewhat the gap in public facilities between the south and the rest of the country. The distribution of these facilities within the south has, however, been guided to a large extent by the political necessity of providing some immediate improvement in public services in all areas. The further contribution which overhead facilities make to increasing output must be judged by the increase in commodity production that has taken place in the south and will take place in the next decade.

Although the Cassa per il Mezzogiorno administers the bulk of the government's programs for southern development, its policy-making functions are limited to the sectors of the economy covered by its appropriations. The general scope of southern development policy is established by an interministerial committee

16. According to Law No. 634, July 1959.

17. Summarized in Pescatore (1961), p. 23 through December 1960 and given in detail in Cassa per Opere Straordinarie di Publico Interesse nell'Italia Meridionale (1961).

(the Comitato dei Ministri per il Mezzogiorno). Since there is no overall program for southern development, the committee tends to formulate policy on an *ad hoc* basis without being able to judge the total impact of various measures on the regional economy.[18] This procedure may partially explain the very high proportion of government expenditures that is devoted to public works and welfare expenditures in comparison with the development programs of other underdeveloped countries. Few countries having active development policies place such heavy reliance on the market mechanism to bring about the changes in the economic structure that are needed to promote growth.

In summary, the past decade has been characterized by a substantial transfer of resources to Southern Italy, devoted very largely to making up the deficit in public facilities of all sorts and to increasing private consumption. It had been hoped that the increase in local demand resulting from these expenditures would lead to the development of local industry without the need for more direct intervention. At the end of the decade, this policy had not yet produced much change in the structure of the southern economy, and there has recently been a tendency to use more direct measures to promote industrialization.

A Model of Regional Development

One of the lessons of the past decade is that the development policies followed have so far proved to be inconsistent with the objective of reducing the regional gap in income. The principal reason for this result has been the failure to take account of the development of the rest of the economy in planning for Southern Italy. The relation between the two can best be established by means of a simple model of regional growth.

The first requirement of a regional model is to show the way in which an increase in national income is translated into increases in production in each region. Once this structural pattern has been established, actual and potential government policies can be analyzed in terms of the changes that they bring about in the existing structure of supply and demand.

18. The need for a more comprehensive program to guide the Cassa has recently been stressed by its director. See Pescatore (1961).

Design of a regional model policy

The discussion of the previous section shows that it is more realistic to regard regional development policy in Italy as a modification of national policy than as an effort to maximize the growth of Southern Italy. In this respect, the model to be suggested is basically different from that which I used in 1954 to investigate the optimum allocation of resources in Southern Italy (Chenery, 1955). The earlier study determined the pattern of investment and production that would lead to a given growth in southern income with a minimum of investment from the north, but it did not take account of the difficulty of changing existing supply patterns. The present model focuses on the stability of established supply patterns rather than on the availability of investment resources as being the main limit to growth. The results of the previous analysis will, however, be used to give an indication of the different investment patterns that might result from different policies.

Existing and potential regional development policies are reflected in the model in the following ways:

(i) in the total growth of national income in Italy and its effects on commodity demand in each region;

(ii) in the transfer of resources from the rest of Italy to the south to increase consumption or investment;

(iii) in increases in the production of specific commodities in the south resulting from investment incentives or direct government investment;

(iv) in the rate of migration from Southern Italy to the rest of the country and abroad.

These elements will be described by 'policy variables'. The latter are chosen to reflect the main alternatives available to the government, such as migration versus increased local production, even though a phenomenon such as migration is susceptible to only limited and indirect government influence. Although the concept of a policy variable is less specific than the 'instrument variable' used by Tinbergen (Tinbergen, 1956), which the government is supposed to control directly, the policy variable performs a similar function in the model, that of specifying a given government action. The value given to the policy variable may be the predicted outcome of a *laissez-faire* policy (e.g. the emigration rate), or the result of specific intervention by the government (e.g. state investment in steel production in the south).

The form of the structural relations to be assumed is limited by the data available in the ISTAT breakdown of production and income by region (Instituto Centrale di Statistica, 1960). Commodity supply can be divided among the three regions, but demand can be calculated only for the country as a whole. The extent to which demand is localized must be estimated mainly from the nature of the commodity, and sectors will be assumed to have either a regional or a national market. The more realistic assumption of varying proportions of the two is ruled out by lack of data. Since differences in the rate of growth of total demand in the three regions have not been large, however, this simplification is not very important to the analysis of regional growth over the past decade.

In analyzing past developments, the values of the policy variables are given. The equations comprising the model show how they have determined the growth of income in each region. In analyzing future possibilities, alternative values for the policy variables, representing different directions of policy, will be assumed.

Formal statement of the model

The regional model determines levels of output in twenty sectors and three regions of Italy, but its form is quite general. Sectors 1–12 have national markets; the others are regional. The following variables will be used in the analysis (the subscripts i and R denote commodity an 1 region;[19] the superscript t denotes time):

X_i Total national production in sector i ($i = 1 \ldots 20$).

X_{iR} Production of commodity i in region R ($R = N, C, S$).

M_i Imports of commodity i from abroad.

Z_i Total supply of commodity i in the nation (sectors 1–12).

Z_{iR} Total supply of commodity i in region R (sectors 13–20).

D_i Domestic final demand for commodity i in the nation.

E_i Exports of commodity i.

W_i Intermediate demand for commodity i in the nation.

19. The regions are designated North (N), Center (C), South (S), and are defined in footnote 6, p. 200.

V_{iR} Value added in sector i in region R.

V_R Total value added in region R (gross regional product).

Y_R Total regional resources (gross regional product plus transfers).

T_R Net transfer of resources to region R (excess of regional imports over regional exports).

V Total value added in the nation (approximately gross national product).

For the regional analysis, gross national product (V), (national) exports (E_i) and regional transfers (T_R) are taken as given. For convenience, I assume a constant growth rate in GNP and exports, so that their values in any year can be expressed as a function of their initial values and their rates of growth:

Gross national product

(1) $\qquad V^t = (1 + g)^t\, V^o$

where g is the annual growth in GNP

Exports of commodity i

(2) $\qquad E_i^t = (1 + e_i)^t\, E_i^o$

where e_i is the annual growth in exports of i.

The structural relations and equilibrium conditions comprising the model are as follows:

Total demand and supply for commodity i (national sectors)

(3) $\qquad Z_i = D_i + W_i + E_i = X_{iN} + X_{iC} + X_{iS} + M_i$
$\qquad\qquad\qquad\qquad\qquad\qquad\qquad (i = 1 \ldots 12)$.

Total demand and supply for commodity i (regional sectors)

(4) $\qquad Z_{iR} = D_{iR} + W_{iR} = X_{iR}$

Regional production of commodity i (national sectors)

(5) $\qquad X^t_{iR} = s^o_{iR} Z^t_i + \varDelta s^t_{iR} Z^t_i,$

or

(5a) $\qquad \varDelta X^t_{iR} = X^t_{iR} - X^o_{iR} = s^o_{iR} \varDelta Z^t_i + \varDelta s^t_{iR} Z^t_i$
$\qquad\qquad\qquad\qquad\qquad\qquad\qquad (i = 1 \ldots 12)$,

where s^t_{iR} is the supply coefficient[20] (fraction of total supply of

20. An alternative definition that would be equally plausible in some sectors would take the supply coefficient as the share of *national* supply,

commodity i that is furnished by region R in period t) and Δs^t_{iR} is the change in this fraction from time o to time t. The change in the supply coefficient will be treated as a policy variable. This procedure implies that growth in regional output proportional to total demand ($s^o_{iR} \Delta Z_i^t$) is the normal pattern and that policy is concerned with changes in this pattern. (There is no implication that changes in the supply pattern result only from deliberate policy, however).

Domestic demand (national sectors)

$$
(6a) \qquad D^t_i = D^o_i \left(\frac{V^t}{V^o}\right)^{\eta_i} \qquad\qquad (i = 1 \dots 12).
$$

$$
(6b) \qquad W^t_i = \sum_j a_{ij} X^t_j \qquad\qquad (i = 1 \dots 12).
$$

The first of these equations assumes for each commodity i a constant average income elasticity (γ_i) of total final demand (private consumption, government consumption, and investment).[21] The second, for intermediate demand, is the standard form of input–output equation in which the input coefficient, a_{ij}, measures the amount of commodity i required per unit of output of j. In the absence of inter-industry estimates in Italy for the whole period, it will be necessary to use a cruder estimate of intermediate demand. I shall therefore assume a constant income elasticity for total demand as a first approximation and shall replace equations (6a) and 6b) by:

$$
(6) \qquad (D^t_i + W^t_i) = (D^o_i + W^o_i) \left(\frac{V^t}{V^o}\right)^{\eta_i},
$$

where η_i is the average income elasticity of total demand in sector i. So long as the weights of the different demand components do not change greatly, the average income elasticity (which is a weighted average of the income elasticities γ_i of all sectors using the commodity) will be reasonably constant.

---

which would not be affected by a change in import proportions. The concept chosen has some significance in the analysis of agriculture, in which the share of imports has increased in Italy, but it makes little difference in other sectors.

21. No allowance is made for changes in the rate of population growth, so that total income can be used in place of *per capita* income.

Domestic demand (local sectors)

$$(7) \qquad (D^t{}_{iR} + W^t{}_{iR}) = (D^o{}_{ir} + W^o{}_{iR}) \left(\frac{Y^t{}_R}{Y^o{}_R}\right)^{\eta^{iR}},$$

where the total regional resources Y_R replaces the gross national product as the explanatory variable.

Sector value added

$$(8) \qquad V_{iR} = v_{iR} X_{iR},$$

where v_{iR} will be assumed constant among regions in all sectors except agriculture in the Italian application of the model.

Regional value added

$$(9) \qquad V_R = \Sigma V_{iR}.$$

Total regional resources

$$(10) \qquad Y_R = V_R + T_R,$$

where T_R, the net resource transfer to region R, is a policy variable.

These ten equations comprise a policy-oriented version of the type of regional input–output model used by Leontief and others to explain regional production levels in different sectors (Chenery, Clark and Cao Pinna, 1953). The model serves to allocate a given growth in gross national product among sectors and regions according to the value of the parameters e_i, η_i, η_{iR}, $s^o{}_{iR}$, and $s^t{}_{iR}$ and the regional transfers, T_R. Alternatively, targets can be set for the relative growth of GNP by region and solutions made for feasible values of the policy variables. This approach is followed in 'Implications for development policy', page 223.

The simplicity of this regional model derives from the fact that it omits the analysis of factor use and of changes in prices. The increase in regional income is measured in constant prices, which precludes any effect of changes in the terms of trade between regions.

The Pattern of Regional Growth

This model will now be applied to the Italian economy for the period 1951–9 to determine its usefulness in explaining past regional growth and hence in judging future policy. The basic assumption of the model is that regional supply patterns change very slowly in the absence of deliberate measures to alter them. To test the validity of this assumption, it will be useful to maintain the division of Italy into the three regions that are given in the ISTAT study even though my primary concern is with Southern Italy.

The analysis is based on data for the three regions and twenty sectors of the Italian economy in the years 1951 and 1959. After a study of the values of the variables and the supply patterns in the intervening years, I decided that estimates based on the terminal years only would be sufficiently accurate.[22] The results of the analysis are aggregated into nine sectors in the present paper. The values of the parameters pertaining to the south and the national economy are shown in Table 5.[23]

Equation (5a) breaks down the growth in sector output into two parts. The first term, $s^0_{iR}\Delta Z^t_i$, may be called the *demand effect*, since it assumes no change in the regional supply coefficients; output in each sector is therefore assumed to increase at the same rate in all regions. The second term, $\Delta s^t_{iR}Z^t_i$, measures the change in regional output at a constant level of total demand due to the change in the regional supply coefficient. It will therefore be called the *supply effect*.[24]

22. This assumption was tested further by breaking the period into two parts, 1951–6 and 1956–9, but the breakdown added little to the one-period analysis and was subsequently dropped.

23. An appendix to this paper, giving the data and calculations for twenty sectors and all three regions, is available on request to the Secretary, Research Center in Economic Growth, Stanford University, Stanford, California. The more complete analysis is published in Italian (Chenery, 1962).

24. In Chenery (1955), I defined 'import substitution' for a national economy in a similar way. 'Import substitution' refers to the change in the fraction of the local market that is supplied from regional sources; the 'supply effect' measures the change in the share of the national market. It thus includes increased exports as well as reduced imports. A similar distinction is made by Perloff, Dunn, Lampard, and Muth (1960), p. 71, in analyzing shifts in regional employment. Their 'net differential shift in employment' corresponds to my supply effect, while their 'proportionality shift' is the difference between my total demand effect and proportional regional growth. They do not utilize these concepts in the framework of a specific regional model, however.

Table 5

Selected Parameters for the South and Italy[1]

Sector	Export growth E_i %	Demand elasticities η_i	η_{is}	Southern supply coefficients		
				1951 s_{is}^{51}	1959 s_{is}^{50}	Change Δs_{is}
National Sectors						
1. Agriculture	7.1	0.67		0.309	0.284	−0.025
2. Mining	1.5	2.00		0.155	0.152	−0.003
3. Food and tobacco	4.1	1.05		0.319	0.294	−0.025
4. Textiles	3.2	0.37		0.026	0.023	−0.003
5. Clothing and leather	17.7	0.99		0.198	0.193	−0.005
6. Wood products	3.4			0.194	0.191	−0.003
7. Metals	16.8	1.89		0.049	0.055	+0.006
8. Metal products	12.8	1.68		0.062	0.074	+0.012
9. Nonmetallic mineral products	7.2	1.90		0.115	0.132	+0.017
10. Chemicals, rubber, petroleum refining	12.4	1.98		0.079	0.070	−0.009
11. Paper		1.70		0.068	0.074	+0.006
12. Other manufactures	9.6	2.16		0.052	0.043	−0.009
Regional Sectors						
13. Construction			2.09	0.241	0.223	
14. Electricity, gas, water			1.41	0.183	0.214	
15. Transportation			0.96	0.252	0.251	
16. Trade			0.84	0.207	0.203	
17–19. Other services			0.26	0.221	0.214	
20. Public administration			0.71	0.313	0.321	

1. Estimated from Instituto Centrale di Statistica (1960). See 'References', p. 233.

The effects of demand on regional growth

Since the usefulness of this regional model depends on supply coefficients being relatively stable, I shall first compare the rates of regional growth that would be predicted from the observed growth of sector demand alone, with no change in the supply pattern, with the actual rates. This is done in Table 6.

Table 6

Predicted and Actual Regional Growth Rates, 1951–9

(In percentages)

	North	Centre	South	Italy
Predicted growth Rates with no supply effects				
1. Nation sectors[1]	6.6	5.9	5.1 (4.95)[3]	
2. Total output[2]	6.1	5.5	5.0 (4.9)[3]	
Actual growth rates				
3. National sectors	6.3	6.6	4.3	5.9
4. Total output	5.8	5.8	4.6	5.5
Differences from national growth of total output				
5. Predicted[4]	+0.6	0	−0.5 (−0.6)[3]	
6. Actual[5]	+0.3	+0.3	−0.9	

1. Predicted output in national sectors derived from demand effects in Table 5.
2. Predicted total output is based on average relations of local to national sectors except in the south, where allowance is made for the increase in the income transfer.
3. Predicted values if agriculture is treated as a local sector.
4. Differences between values in line 2 and 5.5 per cent.
5. Differences between values in line 4 and 5.5 per cent.

The 'demand prediction' is that total output in the south will grow at 89 per cent of the national average (4.9 per cent) whereas the actual rate was 83 per cent of the national average (4.6 per cent). (Since constant income elasticities are assumed, the actual rate of growth is irrelevant to this prediction, which would be the same proportion of any national rate.) For the north the demand prediction is also too optimistic, whereas for the center it is overly pessimistic. Over half of the total variation in the regional rates from the national average is explained by the change in demand and the existing supply pattern, however, and for the south in particular the demand prediction provides a useful point of departure.

The reason why the south lags behind the north and center on the basis of demand factors alone is readily seen from Tables 7 and 8. The south provides only 9 per cent of the national supply of manufactured goods (apart from food) and 16 per cent of the supply of minerals. These are the only sectors in which the elasticity of total demand is substantially greater than 1. Conversely, the weight of agriculture, for which the elasticity of total demand has been 0.70 in the past decade, is much higher in the south than in the rest of the country. For the national sectors, the ratio of 'normal' southern growth to national growth of 0.87 can be interpreted as a weighted average of the demand elasticities in the south in sectors 1–12 compared with the national average for the same sectors. Since the same elasticities are used, the difference is entirely due to the difference in weights. The income transfer to the south, which affects only the local sectors in this model, raises the 'normal' (i.e. the relative growth rate without change in the supply pattern) somewhat, but not enough to offset the existing supply structure.

Effects of supply changes on regional growth

The way in which supply effects modify this basic pattern is shown in Table 7. For Italy as a whole, the supply effects can be interpreted as the change in the proportion of imports in the total supply of each commodity. This proportion has increased for agriculture and consumer goods and diminished for minerals and basic industrial goods, with a net rise of less than 0.8 per cent for all the national sectors. The rising ratio of imports to GNP (from 0.125 to 0.148) therefore represents primarily a demand effect rather than a change in import proportions of individual commodities. The most significant increase is in agriculture, in which imports have risen from 11.5 to 12.9 per cent of total supply.

The principal result of changes in the regional supply pattern has been to increase the share of the center in both primary production and manufacturing. In primary production, the gain of the center has been at the expense of the south, while in manufacturing it has been at the expense of the north. In the latter case, it is only the producer goods industries that are becoming more evenly distributed, with the share of the north dropping from 62 to 59.5 per cent and the other two regions making gains in proportion to their initial shares. In the consumer goods industries (including food) there has been on balance almost no change in the supply pattern, with a slight fall in the share of the south and a rise in imports.

As a result of these supply changes, it is the center rather than the south that has achieved the objective of closing the gap in the growth rate between itself and the traditional industrial area of the north. Some of the main elements in this process have been the discovery of natural gas in the Po valley, the development of a petrochemical industry in the center, and the decentralization of the metal-working industries. Since population has increased somewhat less rapidly in the center than in the other two regions, the gain in *per capita* income is even higher here than in the north.

In the south, the supply effects shown in Tables 5 and 7 were exactly the opposite of the pattern of development that the Cassa was expected to induce. Ten years after the start of the regional development program, the production of agricultural products and consumer goods has not kept up with the growth of either regional or national demand.[25] Without exception, the supply effects in these sectors are negative, and together they account for the difference between the demand prediction and the actual rate of growth of total income. It is only in the field of producer goods, for which the market is a national one, that the growth rate in the south has more than kept up with the national average. Since this group of industries starts from a small base, their contribution to the growth of regional income in this period is relatively small, but it promises to increase in the future. Even though in consumer goods production, local demand is more important, plants are typically smaller, and entry is generally easier, these sectors have not responded adequately to the rise in local demand and the fiscal concessions made by the government. Therefore the policy of induced

25. In analyzing the period 1951–9 in the south, it makes little difference whether sectors are assumed to be regional or national because the regional growth in total demand is about the same as the national growth, due to the increase in transfers.

Table 7 Causes of Increase in Regional Output, 1951–91 (In billions of lire)

Sectors	North Demand effect	North Supply effect	North Total	Center Demand effect	Center Supply effect	Center Total	South Demand effect	South Supply effect	South Total	Italy Demand effect	Italy Supply effect	Italy Total
I. Primary Production												
1. Agriculture	155	−31	124	323	74	397	327	−101	226	805	−58	747
2. Mining	19	22	41	44	47	91	41	− 1	40	104	68	172
Subtotal	174	− 9	165	367	121	488	368	−102	266	909	10	919
II. Manufacturing²												
3. Food	114	22	136	97	−4	93	106	− 23	83	317	− 5	312
4, 5, 6, 12. Other consumer goods	230	−32	198	150	7	157	45	− 6	39	425	−31	394
7-11. Producer goods	930	−61	869	478	47	525	121	16	137	1,529	2	1,531
Subtotal	1,274	−71	1,203	725	50	775	272	− 13	259	2,271	−34	2,237
III. Local Sectors												
13. Construction	230	0	230	231	0	231	125	0	125	586	0	586
10-15. Utilities	135	0	135	216	0	216	119	0	119	470	0	470
16-19. Service	234	0	234	224	0	224	106	0	106	564	0	564
20. Government	71	0	71	152	0	152	119	0	119	342	0	342
Subtotal	670	0	670	823	0	823	469	0	469	1,962	0	1,962
Total	2,118	−80	2,038	1,915	171	2,086	1,109	−115	994	5,142	−24	5,118

1. Derived from equation (5a) applied to data for 20 sectors.
2. Other consumer goods include textiles, clothing, wood products, 'other', producer goods include metals, metal products, nonmetallic mineral products, chemicals and petroleum refining, and paper.

development by means of demand increases cannot yet be counted a success.

Effects of other factors

Several factors that are omitted from the regional model must be added in order to round out the picture of regional income growth. As shown in Table 2 the rate of population increase has been nearly equal in all regions, and therefore there is little difference between relative rates of growth by region and relative rates of *per capita* growth. A second omitted factor, changes in the 'terms of trade' among regions, has also been relatively small in this period (Saraceno, 1961b; Segrè, 1959). Productivity rises have been more rapid in industry than in agriculture, but this difference has been offset to some extent by the greater price rise in agriculture.

In one respect, the evaluation of the development of the south in terms of current output has a substantial downward bias. Since many of the overhead investments require a long period before they become fully productive, the presently unused capacity in these facilities should be given a value. A start has been made toward providing the housing and public services needed to move the population away from the overcrowded hilltop towns to which they were once driven by the prevalence of malaria in the lowlands. A much better base for future agricultural and industrial development therefore existed in the south by 1960 than in 1950.

Implications for Development Policy

The experience of Southern Italy in the past decade shows the seriousness of the obstacles that must be overcome to change the economic structure of a country or region. Despite the large transfer of resources to the region, the investment in overhead facilities, the rapid growth of consumption and investment, the considerable incentives given to private investors, and substantial use of northern technicians, the composition of output has changed relatively little since 1950. If the large income transfer were to be cut off next year, it is probable that the south would revert to a considerably lower growth rate than its present 4 per cent because of the limited demand for the commodities which it produces. Whatever judgment may be passed on the program of the Cassa per il Mezzogiorno when more complete information becomes available, it is clear that in its first decade it has not really come to grips with one of the most basic southern economic problems: the concentration of production in sectors that do not offer the possibility of rapid growth.

As Saraceno has recently pointed out (Saraceno, 1961a), the main objective of development policy in the south should be to achieve an economic structure capable of sustained growth rather than a particular ratio between the growth rate in the south and in the north. The first requirement of a viable economic structure in Southern Italy is that the normal increase in export demand plus internal demand should generate a satisfactory rate of growth in production and income without excessive reliance on income transfers. The growth rate that is considered 'satisfactory' cannot be much lower than that in the rest of the country, however, if it can be shown that parity can be achieved with a different allocation of given resources. The present economic structure is deficient in this respect because if an income growth of say 5 per cent per year is initiated (by whatever means), the growth of regional exports will be inadequate to cover the growth of demand for commodities that are now imported, and the growth in total expenditure can only be sustained by continued external financing of a large import surplus.

To judge from official statements on the subject, the magnitude of the structural changes required to produce self-sustaining growth in the south has not been appreciated by the government. The extent of those changes and the direction that future policy should take can be ascertained only from a comprehensive analysis of the economic structure. Aggregate projections of the type used in the Vanoni Plan tend to conceal some of the difficulties involved and do not provide an adequate guide to the execution of policy.

A second requirement of a viable economy is that local savings plus 'normal' income transfers should cover investment needs. Although it is impossible to estimate the level of local savings that would be forthcoming with a smaller import surplus in relation to regional income, this requirement seems to be easier to meet in

Southern Italy than the structural problem. The following analysis therefore concentrates on the need for structural change.

The principal lines of policy

There are three principal policies of structural change to be considered, which may for simplicity be identified as:

(1) agricultural development,
(2) industrial development,
(3) increased emigration.

Although the best development policy probably consists of a combination of all three, it is useful to consider them first in isolation.

Under 'A model of regional development', page 211, these policies of structural change may be defined as follows:

(1) Growth of agricultural production in an amount and composition that will permit the south to supply a larger share of total Italian internal and external demand.

(2) Growth of industrial production sufficient to permit the south to supply a larger fraction of the total Italian market (which in most sectors implies supplying a larger proportion of the regional market also).

(3) Increasing emigration in an amount sufficient to make up for any short fall in the growth of production.

Although other possible development policies might be advanced, such as price support for southern agriculture, they are of a palliative nature and conflict with the national policy of freer trade and economic integration with the rest of Europe.

The policy of the past decade was primarily one of agricultural development, with increasing attention to industrial development by the end of the decade. The analysis under 'The pattern of regional growth', page 216, showed that the results fell short of maintaining the 1951 share of the south in the national output of both agriculture and industry. One way to indicate the magnitude of the problem is to calculate how much additional output (or reduced population) would have been required under each policy to achieve a growth rate of *per capita* output in the south equal to the national average:

Under policies (1) and (2), this objective would have required an additional value added of 260 billion lire in the south in 1959. In each case it may be assumed that 45 per cent will be produced in local sectors, as indicated by the elasticity of demand for their products (Table 5). Under policy (1), the remaining 140 billion lire of value added is assumed to be produced in agriculture and food processing, while under policy (2) it would be produced in the remaining sectors of manufacturing industry. The results of successfully carrying out these policies in the period 1951–9 would have been as follows, compared with the actual results:

	Actual		*Required*	
	Growth rate	*Δs*	*Growth rate*	*Δs*
Policy (1) Growth of agriculture	2.9%	−0.025	4.0%	0
Growth of food processing	4.7%	−0.025	6.5%	+0.017
Policy (2) Growth of other manufacturing	8.8%	+0.005	13.5%	+0.039

Adequate agricultural development would have required a growth rate of 4 per cent and maintenance of the southern share in total agricultural supply. Adequate industrial growth would have involved an overall growth rate of 13.5 per cent outside of food processing, and an increase of nearly 4 per cent in the share of southern manufacturing in the national supply. Achieving equal growth in *per capita* output by means of emigration alone would have necessitated an increase in the rate of *per capita* growth of 3.6 per cent to the national average of 4.7 per cent. To achieve this result, population would have had to remain constant in the south, with a total emigration of 2,100,000 instead of the 750,000 recorded.[26]

Although it is unlikely that any one of these three results could have been achieved by itself within the existing institutional framework, a combination of the three would probably have been feasible within the resources available. It is more useful, however,

26. This calculation is based on the 'resident' population in Table 2, which underestimates the emigration that has taken place. On the basis of population physically present the total emigration would have to have been 2,500,000 instead of the observed 1,400,000.

to turn our attention to future development policies than to speculate on what might have been.

The role of industrialization in future policy

Since only demand limitations are taken into account in the
present regional model, additional information on supply is
needed to narrow down the range of policies to be considered. A
recent study by Saraceno (Saraceno, 1961b) gives some idea of the
possibilities for future agricultural development in the south,
taking into account the investments already made by the Cassa.
A comprehensive study of energy demand and supply (Paretti,
Cao Pinna, Cugia and Righi, 1960) also indicates some of the
possibilities for mineral expansion.

If an economic limit is set to the growth of primary production,
based on demand factors, natural resources, and costs of production in the south, the main policy alternatives for achieving a given
per capita income in the south are industrial development and
emigration. Since the output of the local sectors is limited by the
growth of local income, they cannot be considered as a separate
alternative, but must be assumed to vary with the level of value
added in sectors 1–12.

To indicate the rates of growth required of the industrial sectors
under various assumptions, I shall repeat the analysis of Table 7
for the period 1959–70, aggregating the regional model into five
sectors. Greater detail would, of course, be needed in making an
actual development program, but the more aggregated model is
adequate to indicate the quantitative significance of different lines
of policy.

The basic assumptions common to all the projections are:

(i)   a national growth rate of GNP of 5 per cent per year (or
of 4.2 per cent in *per capita* income) for 1959–70;

(ii) roughly the same patterns of demand increase in the next
decade as in the past (as shown in the demand elasticities in
Table 8);

(iii) a target for regional growth in *per capita* income of 5 per
cent per year;

(iv) increase in transfers to the south in proportion to the
growth in income.

227

Table 8 Alternative Regional Projections for 1970 (In billions of lire)

Sector	Italy — Value added					Southern Italy — Program A[1]				Program B				Program C			
	Income elasticity	1959	Index	1970	Growth rate %	1959	s_s	V_s	Growth rate %	Δs_s	ΔV_s	V_s	Growth rate %	Δs_s	ΔV_s	V_s	Growth rate %
Primary production																	
1. Agriculture		3,250	1.31	4,280	2.5	1,120	0.3	1,470	2.5	0.013	60	1,530	2.9	0.013	60	1,530	2.9
2. Mining		250	2.28	580	7.8	70	0.29	160	7.8	0		160	7.8	0		160	7.8
Total primary		3,500	1.33	4,860	3.0	1,190	0.34	1,630	2.6	0.012	60	1,690	3.2	0.012	60	1,690	3.2
Manufacturing																	
3. Food processing	1.03	880	1.74	1,530	5.2	270	0.31	470	5.2	0.013	20	490	5.6	0.013	20	490	5.6
4–12. Other manufacturing	1.33	4,160	2.04	8,510	6.7	360	0.09	740	6.7	0.030	260	1,000	9.8	0.074	630	1,370	13.0
Total manufacturing	1.29	5,040	2.00	10,040	6.5	630	0.12	1,210	6.1	0.028	280	1,490	8.1	0.065	650	1,860	10.4
Local sectors																	
13–20.	0.95	6,090	1.665	10,120	4.7	1,480		2,230	3.8		230	2,460	4.7		490	2,720	5.7
Total	1.71	14,630	1.71	25,020	5.0	3,300		5,070	4.0		570	5,640	5.0		1,200	6,270	6.0
Migration rate[2]									−2.4%				−1.4%				−0.5%

1. Under Program A, the ratio of southern production to national production in 1970 is the same as that in 1959 in all sectors ($\Delta s_s = 0$).
2. Based on resident population and the past rate of natural increase of 1.4 per cent.

The national growth rate assumed in GNP is lower than the 5.5 per cent of the past decade, but is still rather optimistic. The regional target for *per capita* income is 20 per cent above the national rate, but it falls short of the rate of 6 per cent that would be needed to stop the widening of the regional gap in *per capita* income by 1970.

The three southern development programs illustrated in Table 8 are based on the following hypotheses as to technical possibilities and policy direction:

Program A represents a continuation of past policies and may be labeled a 'demand projection'. It assumes that output will be determined by the growth of demand and the existing productive structure, maintaining fixed supply coefficients.[27] (The forecast growth rate of 2.5 per cent in agriculture in both regions is somewhat more optimistic than Saraceno's estimate of 2.3 per cent.)

Program B is intended to establish the minimum structural change that will suffice to produce a growth of 5 per cent in GNP over the period. It therefore makes an optimistic assumption as to the growth of southern agriculture, which is assumed to be higher than that in the rest of the country. The growth of manufacturing and of local production are determined from the model, taking total growth as given.

Program C determines the minimum structural change (Δs_s) required to achieve the income objective with no increase in the emigration rate. The same assumptions about primary production are made as in Program B.

The growth of the south under Program A[28] lags more behind the national growth rate than has the actual development of the past decade because there is less projected increase in income transfers. The emigration rate required to achieve the target of *per capita* income growth is more than three times the present rate and would probably result in a very unfavorable population structure in the south, since people of working age constitute the bulk

27. For simplicity, the supply coefficient is redefined as the ratio of output in the south to total output, thereby ignoring further changes in the proportion of imports.

28. This type of program is implied by Mrs Lutz's recommendations to develop the north instead of the south. See Lutz, V. (1960).

of the migrants. It would also reduce investment incentives in the south because of the lower growth rate.

Program B requires an increase of 2.8 per cent in the share of total industry located in the south, which would raise the growth rate in sectors 4–12 to 9.8 per cent, slightly above its recent level. In Program C, on the other hand, the share of industry in the south must be increased by 6.5 per cent of the national total, which is equivalent to producing 25 per cent of the increase in industrial output in this region. Under the last assumption, the growth rate in sectors 4–12 would rise to 13 per cent and the supply effect would nearly equal the demand effect in causing the growth of industry.

To select the 'best' development program requires an analysis of the social costs in both north and south and of the institutional implications of the alternatives being considered. In my previous analysis of development possibilities in Southern Italy (Chenery, 1955), I calculated the pattern of production that would lead to a 5 per cent growth in output with a minimum investment cost. On the assumptions of that study, the increase in output under the optimum program was divided between agriculture and industry in the ratio of 30:70. This is very close to the proportion that results from Program C, and in contrast with the 50:50 ratio that has characterized the past decade. Both analyses therefore support the idea that a much higher share of industry in the southern development program would be consistent both with the demands of the country and the supply conditions in the south. This shift in emphasis seems to be essential if the south is going to become a viable economy without really massive emigration.

Conclusions

Southern Italy provides one of the first cases in which we can see the results of a deliberate policy of giving heavy emphasis to overhead facilities and relying on them to stimulate commodity production. Although the government's expectations as to the outcome of this program were never formulated in precise terms, it is clear that this approach to development has serious weaknesses when it is carried to such extremes as it has been in Southern Italy. In the first place, the capital required per unit of increase in regional output has proven to be very high, yielding a gross capital–

output ratio of between 5 and 6 in comparison with the ratio of between 3 and 4 obtaining in the rest of Italy and the even lower values in most underdeveloped countries. Secondly, the high proportion invested in sectors in which there is a long interval before the investment reaches full utilization (agriculture and overhead facilities) means that domestic production and saving increase more slowly under this approach, and a greater reliance on outside assistance is necessary to maintain a given growth in income. Finally, the 'overhead approach' either ignores the other structural changes that are needed in the rest of economy or assumes that they will take place automatically. In Southern Italy the failure of the increase in local demand to stimulate import substitution is very clear in the first decade, although one may hope that it will begin to take place in the second. Since investment has been limited mainly to commodities that the south already produces, for which demand is growing slowly, there is considerable evidence that actual investment has fallen short of utilizing fully the available resources, which have therefore been invested elsewhere.

The drawbacks to the approach that has been followed in Southern Italy stem largely from the fact that the area is not a administrative unit and that there is no overall plan for its development. An overall plan would enable judgments to be made as to the comparative advantage of different types of production, based on the opportunity costs of labor, capital, and the available natural resources. To the extent that this analysis indicated the desirability of developing types of production that are not profitable at current market-prices – as it almost certainly would in Southern Italy – an independent government would have a much wider choice of instruments (subsidies, tariffs, wage policy, devaluation, etc.) than does the region at present. Although there has been ample political support for increasing the total resource transfer to the south, there has been considerable resistance to developing the industries that would be rational for the south, which might increase competition with the established plants in the north. Because of this reluctance to plan realistically for the south, much of the overhead investment has gone for facilities that would not be of high priority in an integrated approach.

The central government is now challenged to provide some of these advantages within the framework of an integrated national economy. So far it has not devised a substitute for the protection of infant industries that is an effective stimulus to development, and the working of comparative advantage is further hindered by the national wage policy.[29] The channeling of investment resources into less productive uses has therefore offset to a considerable degree the large capital inflow from the rest of the country.

In more general terms, the experience of Southern Italy over the past decade shows that a change in the productive structure must be put on a par with an increase in total investment as an immediate objective of development policy. The development of overhead facilities is only one aspect of the total change that is needed.

References

ASSOCIAZIONE PER LO SVILUPPO DELL' INDUSTRIA NEL MEZZOGIORNIA (SVIMEZ) (1954) *Measures to promote industrialization in Southern Italy*

BUFFA, A. (1961) *Tre Italie.*

CASSA PER OPERE STRAORDINARIE DI PUBLICO INTERESSE NELL' ITALIA MERIDIONALE (1961) *Bilancio, 1959–60.*

CHENERY, H. B. (May 1955) 'The role of industrialization in development programs', *American Economic Review, Papers and Proceedings*, **45.**

CHENERY, H. B. (September 1960) 'Patterns of industrial growth', *American Economic Review*, **50.**

CHENERY, H. B. (1962) *Politiche di sviluppo per l'Italia meridionale*, Giuffrè.

CHENERY, H. B., CLARK, P. G., and CAO PINNA, V. (1953) *The structure and growth of the Italian economy*, U.S. Mutual Security Agency, Special Mission to Italy for Economic Co-operation.

COMITATO DEI MINISTRI PER IL MEZZOGIORNO (1961) *Relazione al parlamento presentata dal presidente del comitato dei ministri per il mezzogiorno.*

DI SIMONE, G. M. (April 1960a) 'Integrazione economica e sviluppi comparativi: nord-sud', *Mondo Economico*, no. 16.

DI SIMONE, G. M. (1960b) 'Sviluppo economico del mezzogiorno e sviluppo economico Italiano', *L'Industria*, no. 3.

FUCHS, V. R. (May 1962) 'The determinants of the redistribution of manufacturing in the United States since 1929', *Review of Economics and Statistics*, **44.**

29. The great importance of wage differentials and induced changes in supply patterns of low-wage industries in the recent development of the Southeastern United States is shown in Fuchs (1962).

INSTITUTO CENTRALE DI STATISTICA (1960) *Primi studi sui conti economici territoriali.*

LUTZ, V. (October 1960) 'Italy as a study in development', *Lloyds Bank Review*, no. 58.

PARETTI, V., CAO PINNA, V., CUGIA, L., and RIGHI, C. (1960) *Struttura e prospettive dell' economica energetica italiana.*

PERLOFF, H., DUNN, E., LAMPARD, F., and MUTH, R. (1960) *Regions, resources and economic growth*, Johns Hopkins.

PESCATORE, G. (1961) *Dieci anni di esperienze della cassa per il mezzogiorna.*

PILLOTON, F. (1960) *Effetti moltiplicativi degli investimenti della cassa per il mezzogiorno*, Giuffrè.

PRESIDENZA DEL CONSIGLIO DEI MINISTRI (1957) *Documenti sulla programma di sviluppo economico*, 2nd edn.

PRESIDENZA DEL CONSIGLIO DEI MINISTRI (1960) *Riconsiderazione dello schema vanoni nel quinto anno dalla sua presentazione*, Rapporto del Presidente del Comitato per lo Sviluppo dell' Occupazione e del Reddito.

SARACENO, P. (March 1961a) 'Dopo un decennio di intervento nel Mezzogiorno', *Nord e Sud*, no. 15.

SARACENO, P. (May 1961b) 'Linee di sviluppo del' economia italiana e ruolo dell' agricoltura e della bonifica', *Proceedings of the Naples Conference on La Bonifica nello Sviluppo del Mezzogiorno.*

SEGRÈ, C. (1959) *Produttivá e prezzi nel processo di sviluppo – l'esperienza italiana* 1950–1957, SVIMEZ, Giuffrè.

TINBERGEN, J. (1956), *Economic policy: principles and design*, North Holland Publishing Co.

WELLISZ, S. (June 1960) 'Economic planning in the Netherlands, France and Italy', *Journal of Political Economy*, 68.

Part Three Inter-regional and International Trade

Regions are less self-sufficient than nations, so that trade is even more important for regions than for nations. But though the importance of inter-regional trade was recognized early and indeed was emphasized in the title of a seminal work on trade theory, Bertil Ohlin's, *Interregional and international trade*, 1933, most of the theoretical work and almost all of the empirical studies on trade have explicitly concentrated on trade between nations rather than between regions. Part of the explanation is that the policy problems associated with inter-regional trade were much less obvious (see p. 240 below) and apparently less urgent than those arising from international trade. In addition, there is comparatively little statistical information on inter-regional trade flows, in turn a consequence of the absence of customs and excise duties on trade between regions.

Of the two papers in this section, the first, by Ingram, examines some monetary aspects of trade; the second, by Moroney and Walker, is concerned with non-monetary aspects. Using regional data, the authors attempt in this article to test a well-known hypothesis that seeks to explain the commodity composition of trade. The paper is of interest, not so much because of the results of the tests performed – the results are rather inconclusive – but because of the full explanation given of the trade hypothesis, the review of trade literature and the illustration of the problems involved in attempting to test economic hypotheses.

7 J. C. Ingram

State and Regional Payments Mechanisms

J. C. Ingram, 'State and regional payments mechanisms', *Quarterly Journal of Economics*, vol. 73 (1959), pp. 619–32.

The close similarity between interregional and international trade has long been recognized, and the theory of balance-of-payments adjustment has been thought applicable to regions within a nation as well as to separate nations. So it is, in a general sense, but general statements of the theory tend to become taxonomic.[1] Such a variety of circumstances may exist that the number of policy alternatives becomes unmanageably large.

The purposes of this paper are, first, to examine the payments mechanism for a single state within the United States in order to see how policy alternatives are limited by the position in which the state finds itself; and, second, to examine the implications of the analysis developed in the case of a state for the nation-member of a customs union.

I

When we take a single state of the United States as our geographic entity, many of the policy variables in ordinary balance-of-payments analysis are fixed by the legal and political structure in which the state exists. This fact considerably reduces the number of possibilities and enables us to talk more concretely about what the probable mechanism of adjustment will be.

Specifically, the following assumptions become 'reasonable' ones to make for the purpose of analyzing the balance of payments of a state. (In what follows we use North Carolina as our example.)

---

1. See J. E. Meade, *The balance of payments* (London: Oxford University Press, 1951), and the review by H. G. Johnson, 'The taxonomic approach to economic policy', *Economic Journal*, vol. 61 (December 1951).

(a) The exchange rate is fixed at a par of unity. No exchange controls exist. Convertibility is complete and unhampered.

(b) The money supply is outside the control of state authorities. It will tend to respond 'automatically' to conditions of trade and payments. While the total supply will be determined by a supra-state agency (the Federal Reserve System or Treasury), it is unlikely to be varied because of the balance-of-payments conditions existing in North Carolina.

(c) Commercial policy is not available as a tool for balance-of-payments adjustment. Certain barriers exist, largely in forms of agricultural and administrative protection, but there is little or no scope for manipulation of these restrictions in order to exert a deliberate influence on trade.

(d) Prices are in large part fixed in the 'world' market. North Carolina is assumed to comprise so small a part of the total market for U.S. and world goods that variations in her demand will not affect their prices. Similarly, North Carolina output is so small relative to the world market that the prices of North Carolina exports will not change in balance-of-payments adjustment. In short, foreign demand for North Carolina goods and foreign supply of North Carolina imports are both assumed to be perfectly elastic.[2]

(e) Labor is largely immobile in the short run because of cultural factors. Although wage rate differentials between North Carolina and the United States will induce movements of labor in the longer run, we will omit the effect of such movements in the following discussion. Wages are sticky in both directions.

(f) Some goods, and a number of services, do not or cannot enter into trade between North Carolina and the United States. The prices of such goods and services may change in the process of balance-of-payments adjustment.

These assumptions, along with a little casual empiricism, imply that North Carolina's marginal propensity to import is large, and that the rate of interest will differ only marginally in North Carolina from its level in the United States, especially for securi-

2. This may not be true of some states – e.g. Texas in oil, Michigan in automobiles, or even North Carolina in tobacco – but it is a convenient place to begin.

ties sold in national financial markets. Interest rate differences on such securities will be quickly erased by movements of funds, which are highly fluid and virtually costless.[3]

Within the framework of these assumptions, we shall analyze in a conventional way the mechanism of adjustment to a disturbance in the balance of payments. As the first example, let us take the classic case of a long-term capital movement. Starting from an initial equilibrium in which both internal and external balance exist, suppose U.S. capitalists decide to invest $1.0 billion in new plants to be constructed in North Carolina. (This is an addition to whatever capital flows existed in the initial equilibrium.)

As the new plants are constructed, expenditures are made for domestic North Carolina resources and for imported machinery and supplies. The former will cause incomes to rise in North Carolina and, to the extent that these expenditures are for non-traded materials and services, North Carolina prices will tend to rise. The reserves of North Carolina banks will rise by approximately the same amount as North Carolina demand deposits, thus increasing excess reserves of North Carolina banks. Since this increase in reserves is likely to be regarded as temporary, and since North Carolina banks may not be able or willing quickly to expand local loans, the banks are likely to acquire short-term assets through U.S. money markets. Consequently, the North Carolina money supply will not have a tendency to expand by a multiple of the increased reserves resulting from the capital movement, nor will the U.S. money supply tend to contract by such a multiple.

As domestic sellers of materials and services dispose of their increments of income, imports will rise. A large fraction of the increased consumption outlays is likely to be spent on imports since North Carolina is highly specialized and dependent upon U.S. suppliers for much of her consumer goods. A portion will also be spent on goods previously exported. Thus the banks will soon find it necessary to sell their newly acquired short-term assets to cover the drain of reserves to the United States. However, it may take some time for the induced rise in imports to equal the increase in reserves resulting from the initial outlays for

3. Interest rate differentials on 'local' loans may persist, just as do wage differentials. These do not much affect the following analysis, however, unless the size of the differential varies significantly.

domestic material and services; and, to the extent that North Carolina residents save their income increments, North Carolina banks will be left with increased reserves (or foreign assets).[4]

The remainder of the planned construction outlay will be spent for imports of machinery and supplies for installation in North Carolina. To this extent the real capital inflow occurs immediately. (Labor and other services required from North Carolina factors have been included in the first category, above.) No direct change in North Carolina income or money supply in associated with this part of the capital inflow.

So far this descriptive account of the capital movement suggests that the bulk of the 'real transfer' is effected through the shift in purchasing power and the rise in North Carolina incomes. Only a small role is played by the price effect of classical price–specie-flow analysis. Our two regions are so closely linked that the disparate price movements of classical theory cannot occur, except in a small way as prices of nontraded goods and services rise in North Carolina. Similarly, the monetary systems are so closely linked that North Carolina banks, having acquired excess reserves, are content (or even prefer) to acquire U.S. short-term assets, thus preventing disparate movements in the money supply such as would be expected under the gold standard. To the extent that it involves an increase in expenditure in North Carolina, the capital movement brings about a rise in North Carolina money income, but a cumulative rise is quickly stopped by a high marginal propensity to import. Meanwhile, a large part of the capital inflow is initially spent for imported capital goods, thus producing no (immediate) income effect in North Carolina.[5] The institutional structure makes possible a smooth and rapid real transfer

4. North Carolina banks will be willing to hold large quantities of U.S. assets, even for long periods of time. The failure of equilibration to be 'complete' in this sense therefore need cause no difficulties, either in theory or practice. Cf. F. Machlup, *International trade and the national income multiplier* (Philadelphia: Blakiston, 1943), pp. 41–2.

5. Income in the United States will rise as a result of these capital goods purchases, unless U.S. domestic investment outlays fall when the new investment in North Carolina is made. We ignore the 'foreign repercussions' since they are likely to be very small in any case. (E.g. if U.S. income rises, the marginal propensity to import North Carolina goods is likely to be so small that little further change in North Carolina income will be induced.)

of capital with almost no price effect, not much of an income effect, and with no monetary phenomenon that is exactly equivalent to a gold flow. Equilibrating capital movements perform a much larger role in the adjustment process than was true in the classical gold standard case.[6]

As our second example, let us suppose that an increase in North Carolina domestic investment of \$1.0 billion occurs, but without a prior decision by U.S. capitalists to finance the investment. The key question then becomes: how is the new investment financed? Several possible answers may be given:

(a) North Carolina owners of U.S. assets may decide to sell them, using the proceeds to finance domestic plant construction.

(b) The North Carolina state government may float a bond issue in U.S. money markets, and use the proceeds to finance domestic plant construction (either directly or by lending to private firms).

(c) North Carolina banks may decide to make loans to North Carolina business to finance the new construction. Without initial excess reserves, they will have to liquidate other assets such as U.S. securities. This then becomes a special case of (a) above.

(d) Funds for new investment expenditure may be released by reductions in consumption or current government expenditures. This might occur through: a spontaneous and voluntary increase in private savings out of given incomes, increased taxes which force such reduction in consumption, reduction in current government expenditures, or through a combination of these possibilities.

The first three of these alternatives, (a), (b), and (c), essentially involve a long-term capital inflow into North Carolina, and the analysis developed above will apply. The only difference – an important one – is that the initiative is taken by a different group or agency. In our original example foreign (U.S.) capitalists held the initiative. In (a), (b), and (c), respectively, the initiative is taken by North Carolina capitalists, the North Carolina government, and North Carolina banks. Only in the case of government initiative

6. While it is true that the classical mechanism allowed for equilibrating short-term capital movements, their motivations (movement of the exchange rate toward the gold points, interest rate differentials in the two money markets) were not the same as in the present case. It is essentially the institutional structure that makes the difference.

is any deliberate planning for a large-scale expansion of North Carolina domestic investment likely to be feasible. North Carolina capitalists and banks are likely to respond to about the same incentives as U.S. capitalists, and if one is willing to finance new investment the other will also be willing.

The fourth possibility is, of course, the traditional prescription for capital accumulation. In the case of a state, however, it is unlikely that the fiscal weapons will be effective. Both increased taxes and reduced current expenditures are likely to frighten away as much foreign and domestic capital as they encourage or facilitate by releasing resources from other uses. Furthermore, if a spontaneous reduction of consumer expenditures occurred, North Carolina residents would be as likely to purchase U.S. assets as to finance North Carolina capital formation, if not more so. Where the saver and investor (purchaser of real capital) are one and the same person, a spontaneous reduction in consumption will probably mean an increase in North Carolina capital formation. This condition will hold where capital formation takes place in small business units, but it will rarely hold where large-scale plants are involved. Financing of the latter is likely to be dispersed (where it involves security sales to a wide public) or concentrated in business organizations whose decisions to invest are little affected by the geographic location of the physical plant (so long as it is within the United States).

We may conclude that, where a single state is concerned, the supply of capital is much less critical than the expected rate of return in determining the rate of investment. Paraphrasing Keynes, one may say that if Opportunity and Incentive are present, Thrift and Investible Funds will take care of themselves. Or, in other words, a state has access to a large pool of investible funds whose owners, both in the United States and in North Carolina, will respond to clear economic opportunities. When such funds are attracted to a state, existing institutions allow a smooth and rapid real transfer to occur. No 'transfer problem' exists.

It also seems to follow that a state can do little to promote capital formation within its borders. The main thing it can do is to make itself as attractive as possible to the owners of investible funds. That states have recognized this rudimentary fact is apparent when one examines the activities of state and local development-planning agencies. The only difficulty seems to lie in determining what will please the prospective investor. Some put their faith in low taxes, cheap labor, and free land or buildings, while others rely on good schools, abundant public services, and skilled labor. Unfortunately, our analysis furnishes no clues to this problem.

But what if North Carolina rejects this passive and waiting role? What if state authorities are determined to take positive steps to expand capital formation? We have noted that the North Carolina government could issue bonds and use the proceeds for domestic investment. This constitutes a long-term capital inflow (if bonds are sold through the national capital markets) and presupposes sound state credit and willingness on the part of U.S. residents to buy the bonds. We have also noted that North Carolina could raise taxes or lower current state expenditure in order to raise funds for investment. Both of these seem limited in scope, especially since they may cause a drop in the existing rate of capital inflow from the United States.

A third approach is more similar to plans and proposals now being advanced by underdeveloped nations anxious to promote economic growth. The state government might *create* additional loanable funds within North Carolina by reducing reserve requirements for state banks (not members of the Federal Reserve System), or by permitting such banks to count new issues of North Carolina bonds as part of their reserves.[7] Both actions enable nonmember banks in North Carolina to expand their loans and deposits.

Let us suppose that reserve requirements are lowered sufficiently to create $10 million of excess reserves in North Carolina

7. This is, of course, not offered as a 'practical' proposal, but merely for illustrative purposes. The scope for such action is small, in any case, and it would be violently opposed as an extremely radical move. In earlier times, before the federal government achieved clear supremacy in the monetary field, states sometimes used such means to expand the supply of money. These experiments often ended disastrously, as was the case in 1858 when Minnesota, anxious to promote railway construction, made a special issue of state bonds eligible to be used as collateral for the notes of state banks. These bonds dropped far below par and were finally defaulted. Cf. Charles S. Popple, *Development of two bank groups in the central northwest* (Cambridge, Mass.: Harvard University Press, 1944), pp. 11–12.

banks, and that loans of this magnitude are made to finance domestic investment. As before, we assume that the new expenditure is used partly for direct purchases of imports and partly for domestic goods and service. Both direct and induced imports will cause North Carolina banks to run adverse clearing balances with U.S. banks. It is now necessary to discuss several cases:

(a) Imports are paid for with checks drawn on non-member North Carolina banks.

(1) Non-member North Carolina banks keep their reserves in U.S. banks. In this case adverse clearings will reduce reserves of North Carolina banks. In the limiting case, adverse clearing balances will reach the amount of initial excess reserves (and thus equal the amount of new loans made), and the North Carolina money supply will return to its former level. The increased imports will have been paid for with a reduction in short-term assets abroad – i.e., with a short-term capital inflow.

It is possible that this limit will not be reached – i.e., that the North Carolina money supply will remain higher than before, in which case part of the initial excess reserve will become required. Imports will have risen by less than the amount of new loans made.

(2) Nonmember North Carolina banks keep their reserves in North Carolina member banks. In this case adverse clearing balances of nonmember North Carolina banks will reduce their reserves. But North Carolina member banks, which must settle the checks drawn in favor of U.S. residents, will suffer a drop in their reserve deposits with Federal Reserve Banks. To cover the deficiency in reserves they will probably sell short-term (U.S.) assets in the necessary amount. Thus the net effect is that increased imports are financed by the short-term capital inflow as before.

(b) Imports are paid for with checks drawn on North Carolina member banks. This case is the same as (a. 2) above, except that the preliminary clearings between nonmember and member banks are omitted. The net effect is to reduce U.S. assets held by member banks in an amount sufficient to cover increased imports.

None of these cases is likely to appear in pure form. Instead, a mixture of them, along with other variations and complications, is to be expected. It seems clear, however, that North Carolina holdings of short-term assets in the United States will decline.[8] If no such assets are available for this purpose, a balance-of-payments 'problem' will arise.

The description of the last alternative – deliberate expansion of credit within a single state – probably suffices to show its impracticality. The reserves of nonmember state banks are small;[9] the expanded deposits (and excess reserves) would quickly be lost through adverse clearings resulting from a high marginal propensity to import; the action could not be repeated; and such a move would frighten away foreign capital and probably cause a net decline in North Carolina capital formation.

The interregional payments mechanism is thus marvelously effective in facilitating the transfer of capital. Given the motivation for capital to move into a state, its transfer can take place smoothly and efficiently; but the existence of this mechanism for transfer does nothing to set in motion a flow of long-term capital. The determinants of such a flow are not to be found in a study of the short-run mechanism of adjustment in the balance of payments.

II

The above analysis suggests that one of the chief reasons why 'transfer problems' and other balance-of-payments pressures are not currently a source of much concern in the United States is the existence of a large stock of financial claims, readily transferable from place to place. The growth of such a stock of 'generalized' claims may indeed be of more importance than the Federal Reserve System in promoting smooth regional balance-of-payments adjustments. While the rediscount facilities of the Federal Reserve enable banks to convert 'local' claims into transferable funds, a strong banking tradition has limited the use of this method. The other contribution of the Federal Reserve that is

8. Of course, the definition of 'short-term' is arbitrary, and any claim linking North Carolina and the United States could serve the purpose.

9. As of 31 December 1958, North Carolina had 156 nonmember state banks with cash and demand balances totaling $240 million, and deposit liabilities (demand and time) totaling $1,216 million. (Figures supplied by Mr Ben R. Roberts, North Carolina Commissioner of Banks.)

often mentioned in this connection – namely, the provision of rapid clearing facilities – is to be attributed more to developments in communication than in banking. It is, indeed, an interesting coincidence that the Federal Reserve System came into existence at about the same time that commercial banks began to hold significant stocks of 'generalized' financial claims. Thus the Federal Reserve may have been credited with improvements in inter-regional payments which actually belong to other institutional developments. The relative importance of 'generalized' claims is shown in Table 1 for selected dates. The liquidity of 'other securities' has probably increased considerably since 1914, as the capital market has developed and matured.

Table 1

All Commercial Banks
Ratio of 'Generalized' Claims to Total Loans and Investments

Date	U.S. securities	All securities
June 30, 1914	4.9 per cent	21.9 per cent
June 30, 1919	16.2 per cent	29.6 per cent
June 30, 1925	11.2 per cent	28.3 per cent
June 30, 1930	10.2 per cent	29.4 per cent
June 30, 1935	36.8 per cent	56.9 per cent
June 30, 1940	40.2 per cent	57.7 per cent
June 30, 1950	54.0 per cent	63.2 per cent
June 30, 1958	35.6 per cent	46.7 per cent

Sources: Banking and Monetary Statistics, 1943, Board of Governors, Federal Reserve System, p. 19; Federal Reserve Bulletin, various issues.

That interregional payments problems existed prior to 1913 is well known. The nature and causes of these disturbances may be interpreted in terms of the analysis so far developed. Along the moving frontier the demand for capital was intense. Some capital movements did take place from the older regions to the developing regions, but institutional arrangements had not yet been developed to allow absentee capitalists to participate in many types of investment. The capitalist and entrepreneur were still one and the same person, to a large extent, and most eastern capitalists were not inclined to expose themselves to frontier life.

The intense demand for investible funds, not being satisfied through autonomous capital movements, exerted great pressure upon banks and state governments. When these agencies yielded to the temptation to create loanable funds, money incomes and imports swiftly rose in the expanding regions. The rise in imports was augmented by price and accelerator effects. The necessity to remit funds to U.S. banks to pay for the rising volume of imports caused reserves to fall in frontier banks. Since their assets were almost wholly in 'local' claims, these banks had no way to settle the drafts to U.S. banks except by drawing down their reserve balances in those banks. A regional 'dollar shortage' therefore appeared. Sporadic efforts were made to develop institutions to bridge this gap. For example, in the nineteenth century mortgage dealers bought mortgages from frontier banks in the central northwest and sold them to eastern banks and investors. Such mortgages '. . . were, in fact, readily salable and in many cases were considered a secondary reserve. Whenever the demand for so-called commercial loans in the territory increased, the banker sold real-estate mortgages to raise funds for local loans.'[10]

Had a Federal Reserve System existed at this time, the frontier banks could have converted local claims into funds for settling adverse clearings through the rediscount operation. But this would have simply underwritten the creation of credit by frontier banks. If the tradition of quick repayment of bank debt to Federal Reserve Banks had been in force, no real solution would have been provided by the Federal Reserve, *per se*. On the other hand, if the assets of frontier banks had included 'generalized claims', or if eastern banks had been willing to hold claims on frontier firms and persons, the payments problem would have been readily handled. While this is a short-run argument, with clear limits to its usefulness, it seems legitimate to argue that the present easy transfer relations among U.S. regions is due less to the Federal Reserve System than to the development of a huge stock of 'generalized' financial claims.[11]

Even in fairly recent times, equilibrating short-term capital

10. Popple, op. cit., pp. 58–9. Such arrangements were likely to break down just when they were most needed.

11. After showing that reserve and correspondent balances do not perform this function, Douglas Hellweg asks: '. . . What other assets . . . can banks liquidate to accommodate a deposit outflow? What assets are held by the First National Bank of Podunk which are readily marketable in other

movements have sometimes not performed their vital role. For example, just after World War I, commercial banks in the Ninth Federal Reserve District were faced with large and persistent adverse clearing balances because of the sharp decline in prices of the agricultural exports from this district. 'If the banks had owned some exportable assets, such as Government securities, the persistent deposit outflow might have been accommodated without the large number of bank failures which were actually suffered. As it was, the earning assets of most district banks consisted almost entirely of paper with a very limited market, paper which could not be exported or sold in other districts to help minimize the clearing house deficits which were encountered.'[12]

It thus appears that the disappearance of the kind of regional payments pressures formerly experienced within the United States is the result of the development of large holdings of 'generalized' claims and the attendant development of an integrated capital market. These developments have caused the payments position of individual states and regions to be less like that of separate nations (as usually analyzed in international trade textbooks), and more like that of parts of a fully integrated economy. Thus the multiple expansions and contractions of money so often stressed in balance-of-payments theory are not experienced by U.S. states and regions.[13]

III

The regional adjustment mechanism within the United States appears to lie midway between the mechanism of adjustment for

districts and thus can be used to produce credits at the inter-district settlement fund? Government securities, of course, have the necessary characteristics.' See Douglas Hellweg, 'Comments on task force report', in *Record of the Federal Reserve System Conference on the Interregional Flow of Funds* (Washington, D.C., 1955).

12. Ibid.

13. 'Under the fractional reserve system, primary losses or gains of deposits and reserves would lead to multiple swings in bank deposits within the region if the process of banks' liquidating secondary reserves (or borrowing) outside the region to meet the primary losses . . . did not result in an equilibrating flow.' – Norman N. Bowsher, J. Dewey Daane, and Robert Einzig, 'The flows of funds between regions of the United States', *Regional Science Proceedings*, vol. 3 (1957), 140.

separate nations and the mechanism in a completely integrated economy. The chief difference involved in this comparison concerns the nature of the banking system. In an integrated economy, where a small number of banks have nationwide branch-banking facilities, payments from one region to another create no difficulties because total reserves and deposits are unaffected. In the U.S. system, payments from North Carolina to the United States reduce North Carolina reserves and deposits and increase U.S. reserves and deposits, but North Carolina banks can forestall any pressure toward multiple contraction by selling U.S. securities or other secondary reserves in the United States. Because of this equilibrating capital movement, the net effect is the same as in an integrated economy. But when payments are made from one nation (*A*) to another (*B*), the fall of *A*'s reserves and deposits is more likely to set in motion a multiple contraction because the assets of *A*-banks may not be readily saleable in *B*, or because of restrictions on such sales by *A*-authorities, or because *B*-banks and other financial institutions are not allowed to hold 'foreign' securities. In short, financial claims tend to be 'localized' rather than 'generalized', and this operates to separate the two economic systems in such a way as to produce payments pressures.

Our analysis serves to throw into sharp relief the crucial role of the capital market in balance-of-payment adjustment.[14] It carries with it policy implications for any group of nations, such as the European Common Market, anxious to minimize payments pressures among its members. First, this analysis implies a need for an integrated capital market with facilities for quick sales of securities, for establishing standard measures of investment quality for widely different types of securities, and for establishing ethical codes to govern dealers and issuing firms and agencies. Second, eligibility rules for asset-holdings of banks, insurance companies, pension funds, and other financial institutions need to be modified to enlarge the market for the securities of any single nation and thus to convert localized (national) claims into generalized (internationally acceptable) claims. Third, restrictions on capital movements need to be removed, since they directly conflict with

14. This has been stressed in a similar context by T. Scitovsky, 'The theory of the balance of payments and the problem of a common European currency', *Kyklos*, vol. 10 (1957), no. 1.

the mechanism by which payments pressures may be lessened. Existing provisions of the International Monetary Fund are, of course, in conflict with this requirement.

Equilibrating capital movements are likely to be most effective under a regime of fixed exchange rates. This is likely, not for theoretical but for institutional reasons. If exchange rates are free to fluctuate, it is less likely that the regulatory authorities of a nation will allow financial institutions to hold securities denominated in foreign currencies. Since the free movement of such securities is a vital part of the adjustment process, fixed rates are also vital.

In a recent article, Meade discusses prospective balance-of-payments problems in a European free-trade area, and mentions several possible solutions.[15] Four of these are the traditional alternatives: (a) an increase in international reserves, (b) the gold standard approach, (c) direct controls on payments, and (d) exchange-rate adjustments. Meade approves of (a) and (d), at least in some degree, and he prefers (c) to (b), which is his bête-noir. His antagonism to the gold standard approach is based on the belief that it requires a multiple contraction of money in the deficit country, with this monetary stringency leading to lower incomes and prices, in order to correct a deficit. 'This solution is dangerous', he writes, and 'the probable outcome . . . would in fact be the breakdown of the free-trade arrangement'.[16]

Meade's fifth alternative is to integrate European financial arrangements 'so as to make it easy for a Frenchman to pay a German . . . as it is for a Welshman to pay an Englishman. . . .'[17] To achieve this goal, Meade thinks it would be necessary to have a single currency and banking system and a single authority to fix uniform monetary and fiscal policies, control the overall balance-of-payments, and remedy any 'depressed-area problems' that may arise. Because these requirements imply a single European government, Meade doubts that this alternative is now feasible.

Our analysis implies that considerably less stringent requirements may be sufficient to make it as easy for a Frenchman to pay

15. J. E. Meade, 'The balance-of-payments problems of a European free-trade area', *Economic Journal*, vol. 67 (September 1957).

16. Ibid., p. 385.   17. Ibid.

a German as it is for a Tarheel to pay a Texan. Integration of capital markets in the several partner countries, plus removal of restrictions on the movement of claims, will enable equilibrating capital movements to perform their vital role. This involves a vast increase in 'liquidity', but not in the usual sense. The entire stock of securities held by a nation's banking system (or other financial institutions) becomes a potential source of foreign exchange to settle a deficit. It also involves a part of the gold standard mechanism, but neither the multiple contraction feature nor the cumulative deflation of income and prices is necessary. While close co-ordination of fiscal and monetary policies would be highly desirable in any case, this proposal does not require a single authority. A nation could engage in deficit financing, although it would have to pay the going rate of interest to attract buyers for its bonds. For example, individual states pursue widely different fiscal policies within the United States. Total debt of state and local governments rose from $14.4 billion to $46.7 billion between 1947 and 1957. This is considerably larger than the net increase in federal debt over the same period.[18]

It would be a mistake to minimize the difficulties in the way of such a proposal, however, Much study and negotiation would be necessary to determine the exact scope for independent monetary and fiscal policies in each country, and to specify the kinds of institutional adjustments necessary to make this payments system function smoothly. Our present argument is that it can work, that it is consistent with recent moves toward economic integration, and that it would be a pity to see no proper hearing given merely because of fears associated with past experience with the gold standard.

18. *Economic Report of the President*, January 1958, p. 170.

8 J. R. Moroney and J. M. Walker

A Regional Test of the Heckscher–Ohlin Hypothesis

J. R. Moroney, and J. M. Walker, 'A regional test of the Heckscher–Ohlin hypothesis', *Journal of Political Economy*, vol. 74 (1966), pp. 573–86.

1. Introduction

There are currently two important theories of comparative advantage as a basis for international or interregional trade. The first to be developed is the classical doctrine of comparative costs, which stems from Ricardo (1951, chap. vii) and Mill (1929, pp. 574–606).[1] More recently, the so-called Heckscher–Ohlin Theorem has received extensive study as an alternative theoretical basis for trade (Heckscher, 1919, 1949; Ohlin, 1933).[2] Regarded as empirical propositions potentially useful for predicting the course of a nation's (region's) development, the two theories diverge because they offer different explanations of the basis for comparative advantage.[3] Specifically, the comparative-cost doctrine holds that a country (region) possesses a comparative advantage in producing those commodities in whose production its 'real' labor costs (in the sense of the inverse of average productivity of labor) are relatively lower than those of other countries.[4] On the other

1. An excellent review of the literature on comparative costs appears in Caves (1960, pp. 6–22). More detailed discussion is found in Mason (1926), Taussig (1927, esp. pp. 43–68), and Viner (1932, 1937).

2. The Heckscher–Ohlin theory is succinctly treated in Caves (1960, pp. 23–30). Geometrical and algebraic versions of the two theories of trade appear in pp. 30–57 of this work. Further discussion of the classical and Heckscher–Ohlin theories is found in Bhagwati (1964).

3. The two theories are discussed in a developmental context by Chenery (1961).

4. Capital costs were largely ignored or were accorded secondary importance in most treatments of comparative costs. Similarly, international wage differentials that might serve to offset international labor-productivity differentials were generally regarded as unimportant in explaining patterns of commodity trade. Caves points out that the schism between 'real' labor costs and money costs, especially predominant in the work of Mill and Marshall, bothered Cairnes and certain continental economists (see Caves

hand, the Heckscher–Ohlin theory of comparative advantage depends upon (a) different productive factor endowments among countries and (b) different factor intensities of production processes for different goods.[5]

This paper is concerned with the empirical content of the Heckscher–Ohlin hypothesis applied to regional manufacturing in the United States. The empirical framework of our test is new, yet it relies on most of the traditional Heckscher–Ohlin postulates. We feel that our framework is preferable on four grounds to most tests conducted with international data: (1) It avoids the assumption that production coefficients are fixed and identical in the two trading areas. (2) It avoids the assumption that demand functions for all commodities are identical in the two trading areas. (3) It utilizes regional data in the United States. These data are more likely than international data to reflect common industry production functions, an essential condition for meaningful interpretation of results. (4) It avoids the problem that actual international trade is obstructed by tariffs.

Section II briefly reviews tests of the Heckscher–Ohlin hypothesis using international data, section III presents the basis of our tests using regional data, section IV suggests some advantages in testing the hypothesis with regional instead of international data, and section V presents the test results.

1960, p. 13). Nevertheless, the classical emphasis on 'real' costs, construed as the inverse of labor productivity, continued through the writings of Taussig and Viner. Yet Viner seems to feel that several classical predecessors abandoned the simple labor-cost theory of value in favour of money costs of production in order to explain the actual course of trade (see, for example, Viner, 1936, p. 6). In empirical tests of the classical labor-cost theory, the studies by MacDougall (1951, 1952), Kravis (1956a and b), and Balassa (1963) tend to confirm the primary importance of labor-productivity differentials and the secondary role of wage differentials in explaining international trade. On the contrary, the study by Forchheimer (1947) finds relative wage differentials to be a somewhat more important determinant of comparative advantage in selected industries. See particularly his discussion on p. 24 (Forchheimer, 1947).

5. It should be noted that Heckscher did not regard his contribution as a radical departure from the classical theory but rather as a modification and addendum to the classical labor-cost theory. Ohlin (1933, pp. 33–4) disagrees, contending, 'As a matter of fact, I do not think it [Heckscher's paper] can be fitted into the labour-cost theory at all.'

II. International Tests of the Heckscher–Ohlin Hypothesis

The purpose of reviewing international tests is twofold: first, to indicate the controversial status of the hypothesis tested with international data and, second, to provide the background for criticisms of i ·ernational tests and to show why our regional tests seem preferable.

MacDougall (1951, 1952) was the first economist to test empirically the Heckscher–Ohlin hypothesis. Using horsepower as an index of capital, MacDougall postulated that the United States had more capital per worker than the United Kingdom. According to the hypothesis, then, the United States should have a larger relative share of exports in the world market for capital-intensive goods. MacDougall, however, found no such systematic relationship; consequently he rejected the hypothesis as an explanation of comparative advantage.

Kravis (1956b) also tested (indirectly) the Heckscher–Ohlin hypothesis. He showed that wages are high in U.S. export industries relative to import-competing industries. If these high wages stemmed from relatively much capital per unit of output (and presumably per worker) in these industries, this finding would be consistent with the hypothesis. Kravis, however, was unable to find any relationship between capital per unit of output and exports.

A third study bearing on the hypothesis was conducted by Tarshis (1959). Instead of studying exports in the light of factor endowments, Tarshis focused on relative internal commodity prices within nations. He found that price ratios of capital-intensive goods relative to labor-intensive goods were lower in the (presumably capital abundant) United States and were higher in less capital-abundant countries. Consequently his results, although not a direct test of the hypothesis, are consistent with its implications.

The most extensive tests of the Heckscher–Ohlin hypothesis are those of Leontief (1953, 1956). Given that the United States has more capital per unit of labor than any country with which it trades, the hypothesis asserts that the United States has a comparative export advantage in capital-intensive goods and should import labor-intensive goods. To test the hypothesis, Leontief assumed that both U.S. exports and imports are reduced by one million dollars. He reasoned that the export reduction should release relatively more capital and relatively less labor than would be absorbed (assuming fixed capital–labor input coefficients) by import-replacement industries.

Surprisingly, Leontief found that 'an average million dollars' worth of our exports embodies considerably less capital and somewhat more labor than would be required to replace from domestic production an equivalent amount of our competitive imports. America's participation in the international division of labor is based on its specialization on labor intensive, rather than capital intensive, lines of production. In other words, this country resorts to foreign trade in order to economize its capital and dispose of its surplus labor, rather than vice-versa' (1953, p. 343).

Instead of interpreting his results as inconsistent with the relative-factor-proportions hypothesis, Leontief contended that in fact the United States is *relatively labor abundant* in the sense that U.S. labor is roughly three times as efficient as foreign labor. Thus, the U.S. labor force can be multiplied by three to yield internationally comparable labor efficiency units; labor becomes the relatively abundant productive factor in the United States; and the Heckscher–Ohlin hypothesis is saved because the United States exports labor-intensive goods, which is consistent with the prediction of the hypothesis.[6]

6. Leontief presents no evidence that three is the correct index of U.S. labor efficiency compared to foreign labor. Moreover, he contends that the relatively greater efficiency of U.S. labor cannot be attributable simply to greater capital per man in the United States. Instead, he asserts that the probable explanation lies in the area of 'entrepreneurship and superior organization' but recognizes that this explanation is not wholly convincing since these forces also tend to increase the efficiency of U.S. capital (Leontief, 1953, pp. 334–45). The recent empirical study by Kreinin (1965) indicates that U.S. labor may be 1.2 or 1.25 times as efficient as foreign labor but that Leontief's multiple of three is much too high. Two other studies are pertinent. The international study of Diab (1956) tends to confirm Leontief's assertion that the United States is relatively labor abundant. Diab estimated capital–labor ratios in several countries using a Cobb–Douglas production function and assuming capital productivity is equivalent in all nations. On the other hand, Bhagwati (1963) used Diab's procedure but assumed that *labor* productivity is comparable across nations and found that the United States is relatively *capital* abundant.

An alternative resolution of the so-called Leontief Paradox is suggested by a few economists, including Ellsworth (1954), Becker (1962), Colberg (1963), and especially Kenen (1965). Each of these write s feels that U.S. exports have been improperly identified by Leontief as 'labor intensive'. Instead, they contend that these commodities are 'material capital plus human capital' intensive; therefore, the U.S. export mix is consistent with the factor-proportions hypothesis. Although the papers of Ellsworth, Becker, and Colberg are only suggestive on this point, Kenen skilfully analyzes the material– and human–capital content of U.S. exports in drawing this conclusion.

Four further studies in the spirit of Leontief's work should be mentioned. Using a 1951 input–output table for Japan, Tatemoto and Ichimura found that 'an average million yen's worth of Japanese exports embodies more capital and less labor than would be required for the domestic replacements of competitive imports of an equivalent amount' (1959, p. 445). If one postulates that Japan is relatively labor abundant, this conclusion is consistent with the Leontief Paradox and inconsistent with the Heckscher–Ohlin hypothesis. However, the authors were able to dispel the paradox by a more careful examination of Japanese exports and imports. First, they observed that Japan's capital–labor endowment is intermediate between advanced and underdeveloped nations. Consequently, she should have a comparative advantage in labor-intensive goods when trading with the former and in capital-intensive goods when trading with the latter. Then they observed that 75 per cent of Japan's exports were to underdeveloped countries, the remaining 25 per cent going to advanced countries. Since they found that Japan's exports to the United States were indeed relatively *labor* abundant and her exports to countries other than the United States were relatively *capital* abundant, their results are consistent with the Heckscher–Ohlin hypothesis. Their paper is the first of four more 'specific' than Leontief's in the sense that each one studies more carefully the destination of exports.

Stolper and Roskamp (1961) conducted an input–output study of East German trade. They found that exports are capital intensive and imports labor intensive. They concluded that this finding is consistent with the hypothesis since three-quarters of East Germany's trade is with the Communist bloc, among whose countries she is probably the most capital intensive.

Wahl (1961) conducted a similar study for Canadian industrial products. He found that Canadian exports in 1949 'embodied more capital and less labour than would have been required to replace an average million dollars' worth of total Canadian competitive imports with domestic production' (p. 353). Since this finding pertains to trade specifically with the United States as well, it is presumably inconsistent with the hypothesis.

Finally, the study by Bharadwaj (1962) of Indo-U.S. trade yielded results inconsistent with the hypothesis, since it found Indian exports to the United States to be capital intensive and imports from the United States to be labor intensive.

It is clear that international tests of the Heckscher–Ohlin hypothesis have displayed mixed success. The tests by MacDougall, Kravis, Leontief, Wahl, and Bharadwaj have, on balance, been negative, while those by Tarshis, Tatemoto, and Ichimura, and Stolper and Roskamp generally have been consistent with the hypothesis.

It should be recalled that the tests by MacDougall, Kravis, and Tarshis were not 'direct' tests of the hypothesis. On the other hand, those by Leontief and several others were. Leontief's test procedure, incorporated in several of the above studies, has evoked a barrage of criticisms. Since a number of these criticisms are questionable and irrelevant to our test, we shall not repeat them. However, a number of comments on Leontief-type studies merit consideration, since they bolster the case for regional tests of the hypothesis. These comments are discussed in detail in section IV.

III. Basis for Regional Tests

International trade theory is generally based on the assumption that productive factors are imperfectly mobile. Indeed, the lack of factor mobility gives rise to comparative advantage in the Heckscher–Ohlin framework. If factors were fully mobile among nations, they would migrate so that in general competitive equilibrium the ratios of marginal physical products to factor–price ratios would be equal in all nations. If all nations used similar production techniques, they would have the same comparative costs for all goods and there would be no basis for trade.

The theory of trade resting on imperfect factor mobility among nations is equally applicable to regions in the United States because productive factors have never been fully mobile among regions. If full factor mobility among regions occurred, factor–price equalization would result. Some evidence on the absence of factor–price equalization is presented in the remaining part of this section.

The hypothesis we propose to test might be regarded as the simple factor-proportions view of comparative advantage. In particular, we shall first test the null hypothesis that there is no correlation between relative regional factor endowments and regional location of manufacturing in the southern and non-southern regions of the United States. Our second test concerns regional factor endowments and relative regional *growth* of manufacturing. The basis for our tests is that the South (that is, the East South Central, South Atlantic, and West South Central census regions) is relatively labor abundant, while the non-South is relatively capital abundant.

Evidence of the relative labor abundance in the south may be found in the wage differentials between the south and non-south. We computed an index of this differential using data from the *Census of Manufacturers, 1958* (U.S. Bureau of the Census, 1961). The average hourly wage of production workers in the south was 78 per cent of the non-south average. Similarly, average annual non-production worker salaries in southern manufacturing were 87 per cent of the corresponding non-south average. These differentials are consistent with the results of the studies by Fuchs and Perlman (1960) and by Gallaway (1963).

The wage differential is explained, according to the Heckscher–Ohlin hypothesis, by different relative regional supplies of labor (factor endowments). It is possible, however, that the lower southern wage rates are attributable to lower demand schedules for labor relative to the non-south. Presumptive evidence indicates that differences in regional supplies of labor may be the more important explanation. In particular, Hanna (1957) found that unexplained interstate differences in hourly earnings in manufacturing industries 'stem chiefly from differences in pay rates for similiar skills' (p. 152). Moreover, Gallaway (1963, pp. 269–70) tentatively rejected the hypothesis that observed regional wage differentials were attributable to dissimilar regional demand schedules for labor. Indeed, he concluded that 'by implication it has been established that the capital–labor ratio of the south is less than that of the North' (p. 270). The only circumstance under which the south might be relatively capital abundant is if the relative cost of capital in the south were even lower than the relative cost of labor. This seems to be most unlikely since casual inspection of regional interest rates indicates that, if anything, the absolute (and therefore relative) cost of capital tends to be higher in the south than in the non-south.

IV. Advantages of Regional Tests

In theory, the Heckscher–Ohlin Theorem depends fundamentally on the assumption that any commodity is produced according to a single, linearly homogeneous (constant-returns-to-scale) production function common to all countries.[7] Leontief's (and others') input–output analyses presume this is so. Obviously, it would be impossible to identify a nation's relatively abundant factor of production in terms of *observed* capital and labor data if its factor efficiencies were different from those in another nation. Valavanis-Vail (1954, p. 528) commented on this point: 'When technologies are very different, no simple relationships hold between [relative factor endowments]. . . . In this case, relative endowments have little meaning, for the transformation curves themselves tell us all there is to know about both the endowments and the technologies'.[8] It is significant, therefore, that two recent studies of capital–labor substitution using international data found that different countries producing the same International

7. We think it is fair to conclude that both Heckscher and Ohlin regarded this as a reasonable approximation to reality, although both recognized the possibility of intercountry differences in efficiency (see Heckscher [1949, esp. pp. 277–9] and Ohlin [1933, pp. 14–15, 29–30]). Ohlin also recognized the possibility of production indivisibilities and economies of scale, particularly in his discussion on pp. 52–8.

8. Although the implications for the hypothesis of dissimilar production functions have not been fully explored, some are discussed by Laursen (1952, pp. 556–7), Robinson (1956a, pp. 173–4), and Laing (1961).

Standard Industrial Classification three-digit product operate with different levels of (neutral) technology, that is, on different production functions (Arrow, Chenery, Minhas, and Solow, 1961, esp. pp. 242–3; Fuchs, 1963). The interpretation of the results of tests of the factor-proportions hypothesis that use international data consequently seems hazardous. On the other hand, our application to regional data may be more appropriate since it seems plausible that regional production functions in the United States are similar.[9]

A second objection to international studies of the factor-pro-proportions hypothesis involves 'factor-intensity reversal'. If two trading areas each produce two commodities with either Leontief fixed proportions or Cobb–Douglas production functions, it can be demonstrated that, if one commodity is produced with a higher capital–labor ratio than the other at any set of factor prices, it is so produced at all sets of factor prices. This is Samuelson's (1948, 1949) so-called strong factor-intensity assumption. If, however, the relevant production functions are of the constant-elasticity-of-substitution form (with different elasticities of substitution in the two industries), relative capital–labor intensities (that is, equilibrium capital–labor ratios) for two commodities may reverse as relative factor prices change. If such reversals in factor intensities are empirically important, one is unable to classify (and consequently to rank) commodities as uniquely capital or labor intensive since relative factor intensities may switch with changes in relative factor prices. Indeed Minhas (1962; 1963, ch. iv) raised this specific objection to the traditional Heckscher–Ohlin hypothesis.[10] He argued that if factor-intensity reversal is *unimportant*

9. Although there have been no extended studies covering this proposition, Gallaway (1963) rejected the hypothesis of dissimilar regional production functions in U.S. census regions as an explanation of regional wage differences.

10. Although Lerner (1952) did not utilize the constant-elasticity-of-substitution (CES) production function, he was perhaps the first to recognize the possibility of factor-intensity reversal in a paper written in 1933 but not published until 1952. Further discussion of factor-intensity reversal appears in Pearce and James (1951–2) and the subsequent paper by Samuelson (1951–2). Although he did not use the CES production function explicitly, but specifically recognized differences in 'facility in substituting capital for labour' among industries, Johnson (1957) also demonstrated theoretical factor-intensity reversal.

empirically there should be a strong positive rank ordering of capital–labor ratios by industry in different countries. He performed a rank correlation test for twenty industries common to both Japan and the United States. He obtained a Spearman ρ of $+0.328$ using direct plus indirect capital in his capital–labor ratios. On the other hand, he found ρ to be $+0.730$ using only direct capital in computing capital–labor ratios. The first value is not significantly different from zero at $P \leqslant .10$, and the second is judged to be sufficiently different from unity 'to provide room for reversals in relative capital-intensity to take place' (Minhas, 1962, p. 148). Consequently, Minhas rejected the strong factor-intensity hypothesis; by doing so, he rejected one of the bases of the Heckscher–Ohlin hypothesis. Minhas' conclusion, however, is open to serious criticism. In the first place, his test data are taken from input–output tables that, *in pure theory*, do not permit factor-intensity reversal. Our judgment is that his data are not suitable for the test he performs and that they actually indicate only that Japanese and U.S. industries operate on different production functions. In the second place, Leontief (1964) feels that some of Minhas' other data may be used to support the strong factor-intensity hypothesis. Ball (1966), on the other hand, feels that Minhas' tests neither support nor refute the strong factor-intensity hypothesis.[11]

Nevertheless, since factor-intensity reversal might vitiate the meaning of our regional test of the hypothesis, we ranked the 1958 two-digit-industry capital–labor ratios given by Ferguson (1964, pp. 429–33) for the south and non-south.[12] Kendall's τ is $+0.78$, significantly different from zero at $P \leqslant 0.00001$. Apart from its statistical significance, we feel that this value is very high

11. Ball (1966) shows that, by removing the agricultural and foodstuffs industries from Minhas' tests, the rank correlation between factor intensities of Japanese and U.S. industries increases appreciably. He further argues that these industries *should* be deleted from the tests and that the strong factor-intensity hypothesis remains neither rejected nor accepted on the basis of these tests.

12. It should be noted that the regional capital estimates in this study were estimated by use of the CES production function which *specifically allows* for reversal of factor intensities. 'Southern' capital–labor ratios were weighted averages of South Atlantic, East South Central, and West South Central ratios given by Ferguson. 'Non-southern' capital–labor ratios were weighted averages of those in the remaining regions.

considering the gross nature of the capital–labor ratios from which it is computed. Therefore, we cannot reject the strong factor-intensity hypothesis and we feel that factor-intensity reversal should not obscure our test results.[13]

A third objection to international tests of the Heckscher–Ohlin hypothesis concerns the assumption that the countries under observation have similar demand functions for the commodities traded. If demand functions are different between the two trading areas so that one country demands relatively more commodities whose production requires much of its relatively abundant factor, then trade may fail to occur as predicted by the hypothesis. Valavanis-Vail (1954) aptly describes this possibility as a country's *physically* abundant factor being *economically* scarce.[14] Since our study concerns comparative advantage in terms of production *location* and does not specifically identify regional *trade* (that is, commodity flows) of manufactured goods, it avoids this fundamental criticism of international tests.

V. Statistical Tests of the Hypothesis

As framed in section II, the Heckscher–Ohlin hypothesis predicts that the south will specialize in the production of goods requiring relatively much labor because such goods can be produced at lower money cost in the south than in the non-south.

As an empirically testable proposition, the hypothesis implies that commodities requiring in production a relatively low capital–labor ratio are concentrated more heavily in the south than industries requiring in production a relatively high capital–labor ratio.

13. Although the strong factor-intensity hypothesis is accepted in this regional test, factor reversals remain an empirical possibility at the international level. Mordechai Kreinin suggested to one of us that factor reversals are less likely to occur in regional than in international tests because of relatively smaller variation in relative factor prices in the former.

14. Robinson (1956a, pp. 184–7) demonstrated that 'biased' demand functions are not a necessary condition that a country export its scarce factor-intensive commodity. It is only necessary that countries have different income levels and non-linearly homogeneous utility functions. As a historical point, frequently overlooked, it should be noted that Ohlin (1933, pp. 16 ff.) recognized that different regional demand conditions could cause differences in 'relative scarcity' of similar physical endowments of 'industrial agents'.

To test this hypothesis, one must develop a measure of relative concentration of southern manufacturing industries and obtain estimates of the capital–labor ratio in each industry.

Capital–labor ratios for 1957 were computed from the capital and employment estimates given in the *Census of manufactures, 1958* (U.S. Bureau of the Census, 1961). The Census capital-stock data were obtained from a sample survey of manufacturing establishments to determine accumulated depreciation and the gross book value of depreciable and depletable assets as of 31 December 1957. The gross book value of such assets is available by two-digit industry and was used as the numerator in the capital–labor ratios.[15] The labor input used as the denominator is full-time equivalent man years of employment. Employment data for 1957 are given in U.S. Bureau of the Census (1961). Although the capital–labor ratios are national, not regional, estimates, their rankings are maintained in the south and non-south because of the strong factor-intensity hypothesis.

For the same two-digit industries, a measure of regional output concentration was computed for 1949 and 1957 by dividing *per capita* value added in the south for each industry by *per capita* value added in the nation for each corresponding industry.[16] If the resulting quotient is greater than 1, *per capita* production concentration is greater in the south than in the non-south. If the quotient is less than 1, the converse holds.

The industry capital–labor ratios and location quotients used for the statistical tests appear in Table 1. Before we proceed to tests of the hypothesis, a few comments on the test data are in order. First, one notices that in 1949 the south had location quotients exceeding 1 in only four industries. In 1957 this was also true in four industries. The south obviously had less than its *per capita* 'share' of total U.S. manufacturing. As one might expect however, the south increased its *per capita* 'share' of manufacturing in every industry under review with the single exception

15. Net-capital-stock figures could have been used. The gross figures seem preferable, however, because net capital stocks partially reflect legal (as opposed to economic) depreciation rates. Accordingly, gross capital stocks may be the better choice as proxies for services of capital.

16. Regional value added was taken from U.S. Bureau of the Census (1952, 1959). Regional population figures were obtained from U.S. Bureau of the Census (1954, 1964).

of industry 24, as shown by the pervasive increases in industry location quotients during 1949–57.

Because of the so-called lag in southern economic development, particularly in manufacturing, one should not really expect the

Table 1

Census Capital–labor Ratios: 1957; Industry Location Quotients: 1949, 1957; Percentage Changes in Location Quotients: 1949–57

Industry*	1957 Capital–Labor ratios (Dollars /man year)	Location quotients		Percentage change in location quotients (1949–57)
		1949	1957	
20. Food and related products	6,952	0.6173	0.7236	+ 17.22
21. Tobacco products	4,535	2.4543	2.8359	+ 15.55
22. Textile products	5,039	1.4312	1.8176	+ 27.00
23. Apparel	796	0.3919	0.6144	+ 56.77
24. Lumber	4,518	1.0997	0.9780	− 11.07
25. Furniture	2,777	0.6026	0.9101	+ 51.03
26. Paper and pulp	12,718	0.6958	0.8628	+ 24.00
27. Printing and publishing	4,267	0.3806	0.4434	+ 16.50
28. Chemicals	17,308	0.9592	1.1447	+ 19.34
29. Petroleum and coal	42,770	1.1047	1.4482	+ 31.09
30. Rubber products	6,858	†	†	....
31. Leather and leather products	1,290	0.2794	0.3533	+ 26.45
32. Stone, clay, and glass products	9,804	0.6327	0.6738	+ 6.50
33. Primary metal products	13,624	0.4442	0.4564	+ 2.75
34. Fabricated metal products	5,131	0.3006	0.3806	+ 26.81
35. Machinery (except electrical)	5,521	0.1930	0.2800	+ 45.08
36. Electrical machinery	3,771	0.1312	0.2480	+ 89.02
37. Transportation equipment	4,893	0.2583	0.3697	+ 43.13
38. Instruments	4,111	0.0240	0.0600	+150.00
39. Miscellaneous	4,012	0.0908	0.1640	+ 80.62

Source: U.S. Bureau of the Census (1952, 1954, 1959, 1961, 1964).

* Two-digit industries listed in the U.S. Bureau of the Census (1961).

† Information insufficient to develop a location quotient.

south to have a location quotient greater than 1 in all industries in which it possesses a comparative advantage. A more reasonable expectation, in light of the different development stages between the south and non-south, is that the south possesses *comparatively* larger location quotients (although these quotients may be less than unity) in those industries in which it enjoys a comparative advantage.[17] An empirical test of the Heckscher–Ohlin hypothesis may be deduced from the following theorem developed by Jones (1956–7, p. 6): 'Ordering the commodities with respect to the capital/labor ratios employed in production is to rank them in order of comparative advantage' (1956–7, p. 6). Because of the theorem's rank-ordering nature, rank-correlation tests seem more suitable than parametric ones. Accordingly, with reference to the data in Table 1 we test the following hypothesis: *Hypothesis 1: There is an inverse rank ordering between capital–labor ratios and location quotients*.

Kendall's τ was computed between industry capital–labor ratios and corresponding location quotients for 1949 and 1957. In the first case τ is $+0.3216$; in the second, $+0.2865$. In neither case is τ significantly different from zero at $P \le 0.05$. Nevertheless, τ is significantly positive in the first test at $P \le 0.06$ and in the second at $P \le 0.10$. However, τ is of the 'wrong' sign. That is, the data display a *positive* rank ordering between capital–labor ratios and location quotients. The main reason is that three of the most capital-intensive industries (petroleum and coal, chemicals, and paper products, ranking 1, 2, and 4 in capital–labor ratios) are relatively highly concentrated in the south (ranking among the seven most concentrated in terms of location quotients).

17. This formulation also permits the south to have commodity demand functions different from the rest of the nation. This represents a distinct advantage over international tests performed from input–output tables. For example, the test in this paper does not attempt to identify southern *exports* or *imports*; instead, it identifies only the relative concentration of industry location. As mentioned before, Valavanis-Vail (1954) suggested that dissimilar commodity demand functions between two trading regions might cause a region to *import* a good requiring in production much of its relatively abundant factor provided its demand were biased in favor of the good in question. Consequently he suggested that the Heckscher–Ohlin hypothesis be reworded to read: 'A country tends to *produce* relatively more of the product that uses relatively more of its abundant factor' (p. 525). Our test conforms to this suggestion.

One might argue that these industries, along with tobacco, are based on 'natural resources' more than other industries are (see, for example, Fuchs, 1962, pp. 250–54). Consequently, their location might be more influenced by availability of natural resources than by relative abundance of capital and labor as defined in this study. We removed these four industries from the sample and recomputed τ. Using 1949 location quotients τ is $+0.2000$, and using 1957 location quotients τ is $+0.1429$. Thus, even after arbitrarily removing these industries from the sample, τ is still of the 'wrong' sign. But in neither test is τ significantly different from zero at an acceptable level of probability.[18]

As an auxiliary test of hypothesis 1, we performed rank correlations between location quotients in Table 1 and capital–labor ratios computed from the 1953 capital and employment estimates of Creamer, Dobrovolsky, and Borenstein (1960, pp. 270–73).[19] These capital-stock data include the book value of owned land, buildings, and equipment based primarily on original cost less depreciation. They differ in detail from the U.S. Bureau of the Census (1961) data mainly on two grounds. First, the Creamer *et al.* estimates are net capital stocks while the Census estimates are gross. Second, the Creamer *et al.* estimates are derived from corporate *firm* reports collected by the Internal Revenue Service and reported in U.S. Treasury Department (1955), while the Census data are collected from a sample of *establishments* (plants) which may be only subsidiary components of multiplant firms. The Creamer *et al.* employment figures do, however, correspond to the Census employment estimates in that they cover all employees measured in man-years.[20]

18. Certain 'market-oriented' industries (for example, food and related products, primary metals, and fabricated metals) were also removed from the sample, but positive rank correlations (not statistically significant) were still obtained.

19. These capital–labor ratios are not given in detail in this paper but are available from us on request.

20. The Creamer *at al.* (1960) employment data group together industries 24 and 25 (lumber and furniture) and industries 33 and 34 (primary and fabricated metals). Furthermore, Creamer *et al.* have no employment estimates for industry 38 (instruments). Thus, Creamer *et al.* group four two-digit industries into two classifications (24 and 25 and 33 and 34) and exclude industry 38. To test for consistency between the two sets of capital–labor ratios, we grouped industries 24 and 25 and 33 and 34 and excluded

The rank correlation between the Creamer *et al.* (1960) capital–labor ratios and industry location quotients is +0.1667 using 1949 location quotients, and +0.2000 using 1957 location quotients. Neither of these values is statistically significant. Moreover, both have the 'wrong' sign, as did the values of τ computed from Table 1. The Heckscher–Ohlin hypothesis, tested by hypothesis 1, clearly must be rejected on the basis of either the Census or the Creamer *et al.* (1960) capital–labor ratios.

The foregoing tests of hypothesis 1 are conducted in a static framework. That is, the tests are performed with static capital–labor ratios and location quotients at two different dates. In the comparative static sense, the widespread increase in southern location quotients was mentioned. Thus, within a *developmental context* the Heckscher–Ohlin Theorem implies that those industries in which the south has the greatest comparative advantage should be developing relatively more rapidly in that region. Using data in Table 1 we test this corollary: *Hypothesis 2*: *There is an inverse rank ordering between capital–labor ratios and* percentage changes *in location quotients*.

We calculated the rank correlation between capital–labor ratios and percentage changes in location quotients listed in the last column of Table 1. Industry 24, the only one showing a *decrease* in the magnitude of its location quotient, was ranked last in terms of percentage change. The calculated value of τ is -0.3216, significantly different from zero at $P \leqslant 0.06$. Thus τ is not only significant at an acceptable level of probability but is also negative as the hypothesis predicts. There is some evidence, therefore, that the south tended to attract more strongly the relatively labor-intensive industries during the period under review.[21] This result is

---

industry 38 from the Census data. We then computed the rank correlation between the Creamer *et al.* capital–labor ratios and comparably classified Census capital–labor ratios. Kendall's τ was $+0.5000$, significant at $P \leqslant 0.01$. Therefore, the *rankings* are reasonably consistent, although the *magnitudes* of the capital–labor ratios differ because of reasons mentioned in the text.

21. This conclusion, of course, rests on statistical tests using percentage changes in location quotients. Regional scientists often criticize the use of location quotients because, for example, location quotients usually change if the comparative 'base' changes. Although this criticism is justified in certain cases, it seems less applicable in the present one. Either relative *per*

consistent with Fuchs' study (1962, pp. 124–5), which found that during 1929–54 the south attracted comparatively low-wage four-digit industries in which the wage bill was a significant part of value added (that is, industries that were labor intensive).

Hypothesis 2 was also tested using the Creamer *et al.* (1960) capital–labor data. The rank correlation between capital–labor ratios and percentage changes in location quotients is − 0.0667, negative as the hypothesis predicts but not statistically significant. We regard the test using the Census data as preferable to that using the Creamer *et al.* data because of more complete and accurate industrial coverage in the former.

VI. Conclusion

It is emphasized that the hypothesis tested in this paper is of course not fully comparable to the factor-proportions theorem attributable to Heckscher and Ohlin. Specifically, the model tested includes as productive factors only labor and material capital. Heckscher, on the other hand, included as 'factors of production' not only broad categories of land, labor, and capital but different *qualities* of each. Similarly, Ohlin envisioned mineral deposits, land suitable for growing particular products, and climate as contributing to different factor endowments. Thus, the full-dress Heckscher–Ohlin Theorem is far more comprehensive in its inclusion of 'productive factors' than our hypothesis. It is consequently more elegant and at the same time more tautological. For if all of the 'productive factors' contemplated by Heckscher and Ohlin are accounted for, the theorem becomes an exhaustive description of trade conditions; it is no longer a potentially fruitful hypothesis capable of empirical refutation.

Framed as an empirically testable proposition, hypothesis 1

capita value added or regional share of value added (value added in south/ value added in nation) seems to be the most appropriate base for testing the Heckscher–Ohlin hypothesis. Although the location quotients do indeed change if the regional share base is used, the *rankings* and *rankings of percentage changes* are identical for both bases. Since our conclusions rest *only* on rankings and on rankings of percentage changes, they are not affected by the change in base. Nevertheless, the percentage changes in location quotients refer to the period 1949–57 and might be altered somewhat if different dates were used.

fails to predict the areas of manufacturing where the south's comparative advantage lies, at least in terms of homogeneously defined capital and labor alone. Indeed, there is some indication that the south experiences a comparative advantage in relatively *capital-intensive* industries.

The truth seems to be that natural resources as well as capital and labor 'endowments' represent an important determinant of comparative advantage.[22] Petroleum, chemicals, tobacco, and paper products cannot be produced in areas lacking the natural resources (including climate) necessary for their production. Therefore, the complete Heckscher–Ohlin Theorem properly 'predicts' that the south possesses a comparative advantage in producing those commodities requiring in production an abundance of 'southern conditions'. These conditions apparently include much more than a relative abundance of labor.

Once the basic structure of comparative advantage is determined in view of climate and availability of natural resources, as well as in view of capital and labor 'endowments', a corollary of the Heckscher–Ohlin Theorem seems to be supported. Specifically, hypothesis 2, tested with Census data, indicates that the south tends to attract more strongly the relatively more labor-intensive industries, as the theorem implies.

The combined results of testing hypotheses 1 and 2 indicate that perhaps the initial endowment of natural resources may be more important than relative abundance of material capital or labor in determining the *initial structure* of comparative advantage. After this initial structure is established, however, relative endowments of material capital and labor are important in influencing the pattern of industrial growth. Finally, as certain natural resources are depleted and new ones are discovered, and as capital and labor migrate in response to regional factor–price differentials, the concept of 'initial endowment' loses meaning. Consequently, modifications in the overall structure of regional comparative advantage might be expected in the long run. Nevertheless, the

22. This is one of the principal points made by Kravis (1956b, esp. pp. 148–50) and by Vanek (1963). Viner (1937), of course, feels that natural resources may be even more important than relative abundance of capital and labor in determining comparative advantage (see, for example, pp. 503 ff.).

Heckscher–Ohlin hypothesis seems to have some value in predicting regional patterns of industrial development.

References

ARROW, K. J., CHENERY, H. B., MINHAS, B. S., and SOLOW, R. M. (August 1961) 'Capital–labor substitution and economic efficiency', *Rev. Econ. and Statis.*, XLIII, 225–50.

BALASSA, B. (August 1963) 'An empirical demonstration of classical comparative cost theory', *Rev. Econ. and Statis.*, XLV, 231–8.

BALL, D. S. (February 1966) 'Factor-intensity reversal in international comparison of factor costs and factor use', *Journ. Polit. Econ.*, LXXIV, 77–80.

BECKER, G. S. (October 1962) 'Investment in human capital: a theoretical analysis', *Journ. Polit. Econ.*, Supplement, 9–49.

BHAGWATI, J. N. (1963) 'Some recent trends in the pure theory of international trade', in R. Harrod and D. Hague (eds.) *International trade theory in a developing world*, New York: St Martin's Press.

BHAGWATI, J. N. (March 1964) 'The pure theory of international trade: a survey', *Econ. J.*, LXXIV, 1–84.

BHARADWAJ, R. (October 1962) 'Factor proportions and the structure of Indo-U.S. trade', *Indian Econ. J.*, X, 105–16.

CAVES, R. (1960) *Trade and economic structure*, Cambridge, Mass.: Harvard Univ. Press.

CHENERY, H. B. (March 1961) 'Comparative advantage and development policy', *Amer. Econ. Rev.*, LI, 18–51.

COLBERG, M. R. (January 1963) 'Human capital as a southern resource', *Southern Econ. J.*, XXIX 157–66.

CREAMER, D., DOBROVOLSKY, S. and BORENSTEIN, I. (1960) *Capital in manufacturing and mining*, Princeton, N.J.: Princeton Univ. Press.

DIAB, M. A. (1956) *The United States capital position and the structure of its foreign trade*, Amsterdam: North Holland Publishing Co.

ELLSWORTH, P. T. (August 1954) 'The structure of American foreign trade: a new view examined', *Rev. Econ. and Statis.*, XXXVI, 279–85.

FERGUSON, C. E. (1964) 'The elasticity of substitution and regional estimates of capital and capital ratios in American manufacturing industry, 1954–1958', in M. L. Greenhut and W. T. Whitman (eds.). *Essays in southern economic development*; Chapel Hill: Univ. of North Carolina Press.

FORCHHEIMER, K. (November 1947) 'The role of relative wage differences in international trade', *Quart. Journ. Econ.*, LXII, 1–30.

FUCHS, V. R. (1962) *Changes in the location of manufacturing in the United States since 1929*, New Haven, Conn.: Yale Univ. Press.

FUCHS, V. R. (November 1963) 'Capital–labor substitution: a note', *Rev. Econ. and Statis.*, XLV, 436–8.

FUCHS, V. R., and PERLMAN, R. (August 1960) 'Recent trends in southern wage differentials', *Rev. Econ. and Statis.*, XLII, 292–300.

GALLAWAY, L. (August 1963) 'The north–south wage differential', *Rev. Econ. and Statis.*, XLV, 264–72.

HANNA, F. A. (1957) 'Analysis of interstate income differentials: theory and practice', in Conference on Research in Income and Wealth, *Regional income*, Studies in Income and Wealth, vol. XXI, Princeton, N.J.: Princeton Univ. Press (for the National Bureau of Economic Research.

HECKSCHER, E. (1919) 'Utrikeshandelns verkan på inkomstfordelningen', *Ekon. Tidskrift*, XXI, 1–33.

HECKSCHER, E. (1949) 'The effect of foreign trade on the distribution of income', in H. S. Ellis and L. A. Metzler (eds.). *Readings in the theory of international trade*, Homewood, Ill.: Richard D. Irwin, Inc.

JOHNSON, H. G. (September 1957) 'Factor endowments, international trade, and factor prices', *Manchester school econ. and social studies*, XXIV, 270–83.

JONES, R. W. (1956–7) 'Factor proportions and the Heckscher–Ohlin theorems', *Rev. Econ. Studies*, XXIV, 1–10.

KENEN, P. B. (October 1965) 'Nature, capital, and trade', *Journ. Polit. Econ.*, LXXIII, 437–60.

KRAVIS, I. B. (February 1956) 'Wages and foreign trade', *Rev. Econ. and Statis.*, XXXVIII, 14–30 (a).

KRAVIS, I. B. (April 1956) '"Availability" and other influences on the commodity composition of trade', *Journ. Polit. Econ.*, LXIV, 143–55 (b).

KREININ, M. (March 1965) 'The Leontief scarce-factor paradox', *Amer. Econ. Rev.*, LV, 131–39.

LAING, N. F. (September 1961) 'Factor price equalization in international trade and returns to scale', *Econ. Record*, XXXVII, 339–51.

LAURSEN, S. (September 1951) 'Production functions and the theory of international trade', *Amer. Econ. Rev.*, XLII, 540–57.

LEONTIEF, W. W. (September 1953) 'Domestic production and foreign trade: the American capital position re-examined', *Proc. American Philosophical Soc.*, XCVII, 332–49.

LEONTIEF, W. W. (November 1956) 'Factor proportions and the structure of American trade: further theoretical and empirical analysis', *Rev. Econ. and Statis.*, XXXVIII, 386–407.

LEONTIEF, W. W. (June 1964) 'An international comparison of factor cost and factor use', *Amer. Econ. Rev.*, LIV, 335–45.

LERNER, A. P. (February 1952) 'Factor prices and international trade', *Economica*, XIX, 1–15.

MACDOUGALL, G. D. A. (December 1951) 'British and American exports: a study suggested by the theory of comparative costs' (Part I), *Econ. J.*, LXI, 687–724.

MACDOUGALL, G. D. A. (September 1952) 'British and American exports: a study suggested by the theory of comparative costs' (Part II), *Econ. J.*, LXII, 487–521.

MASON, J. S. (November 1926) 'The doctrine of comparative costs', *Quart Journ. Econ.*, XLI, 63–93.

MILL, J. S. (1929) *Principles of political economy* (edited by W. J. Ashley New York: Longmans, Green & Co).

MINHAS, B. S. (April 1962) 'The homophypallagic production function, factor-intensity reversals, and the Heckscher–Ohlin theorem', *Journ. Polit. Econ.*, LXX, 138–56.

MINHAS, B. S. (1963) *An international comparison of factor costs and factor use*, Amsterdam: North Holland Publishing Co.

OHLIN, B. (1933) *Interregional and international trade*, Cambridge, Mass.: Harvard Univ. Press.

PEARCE, I. F., and JAMES, S. F. (1951–2) 'The factor-price equalization myth', *Rev. Econ. Studies*, XIX, 111–20.

RICARDO, D. (1951) *The principles of political economy and taxation*, in *The works and correspondence of David Ricardo*. P. Sraffa (ed.) Cambridge: Cambridge Univ. Press.

ROBINSON, R. (May 1956) 'Factor proportions and comparative advantage', (Part I), *Quart. Journ. Econ.*, LXX, 169–92 (*a*).

ROBINSON, R. (August 1956) 'Factor proportions and comparative advantage' (Part II), *Quart. Journ. Econ.*, 346–63 (*b*).

SAMUELSON, P. A. (June 1948) 'International trade and equalisation of factor prices', *Econ. J.*, LVIII, 163–84.

SAMUELSON, P. A. (June 1949) 'International factor-price equalisation once again', *Econ. J.*, LIX, 181–97.

SAMUELSON, P. A. (1951–2) 'A comment on factor–price equalisation', *Rev. Econ. Studies*, XIX, 121–22.

STOLPER, W., and ROSKAMP, K. (November 1961), 'An input–output table for East Germany with applications to foreign trade', *Bull. Oxford University Institute Statis.*, XXIII, 379–92.

TARSHIS, L. (1959) 'Factor inputs and international price comparisons', in *The allocation of economic resources*, M. Abramovitz *et al.*, (eds.), Stanford, Calif.: Stanford Univ. Press.

TATEMOTO, M., and ICHIMURA, S. (November 1959) 'Factor proportions and foreign trade: the case of Japan', *Rev. Econ. and Statis.*, XLI, 442–6.

TAUSSIG, F. W. (1927) *International trade*, New York: Macmillan Co.

U.S. BUREAU OF THE CENSUS (1952) *Annual survey of manufactures, 1949 and 1950*, Washington: Government Printing Office.

U.S. BUREAU OF THE CENSUS (1954) *The statistical abstract of the United States, 1954*, Washington: Government Printing Office.

U.S. BUREAU OF THE CENSUS (1959) *Annual survey of manufactures, 1957*, Washington: Government Printing Office.

U.S. BUREAU OF THE CENSUS (1961) *Census of manufactures*, 1958, Washington: Government Printing Office.

U.S. BUREAU OF THE CENSUS (1964) *The statistical abstract of the United States, 1964*, Washington: Government Printing Office.

U.S. TREASURY DEPARTMENT (1955) *Statistics of income*, Washington: Government Printing Office.

VALAVANIS-VAIL, S. (December 1954) 'Leontief's scarce factor paradox', *Journ. Polit. Econ.*, LXII, 523–8.

VANEK, J. (1963) *The natural resource content of United States foreign trade, 1870–1955*, Cambridge, Mass.: M.I.T. Press.

VINER, J. (1932) 'The doctrine of comparative cost', *Weltwirtschaftliches Archiv*, XXXVI, 356–414.

VINER, J. (1936) 'Introduction: Professor Taussig's contribution to the theory of international trade', in *Explorations in economics*, New York: McGraw-Hill Book Co.

VINER, J. (1937) *Studies in the theory of international trade*, New York: Harper & Bros.

WAHL, D. F. (August 1961) 'Capital and labour requirements for Canada's foreign trade', *Canadian J. Econ. and Polit. Sci.*, XXVII, 349–58.

Part Four **Regional Stabilization Policy**

Regions vary greatly in the fluctuations in unemployment that they experience over the business cycle and many writers, from Rutledge Vining in the mid-1940s onwards, have sought to explain the causes of the variation and to suggest remedial measures. Engerman, in the following paper, reviews the explanations that have been advanced and argues that differences in regional unemployment over the cycle cannot be explained wholly in terms of differences in industrial composition between the regions, and this view is consistent with the findings of a similar study on British regions (see p. 385 below). But the effectiveness of policies to reduce unemployment in particular regions will be affected by the degree to which expenditure in any one region 'spills over' into other regions through an increased demand for imports from those other regions. Using a simple model of interregional trade, Engerman examines how the effectiveness of particular fiscal measures in attaining given policy ends is affected by different assumptions about regional marginal propensities to import and to consume.

9 S. Engerman

Regional Aspects of Stabilization Policy

S. Engerman, 'Regional aspects of stabilization policy', in R. A. Musgrave, ed., *Essays in fiscal federalism*, The Brookings Institution, 1965, pp. 7–62.

Most writers on cyclical stabilization are concerned with the movements of national aggregates and the responses of these national aggregates to the policies of national fiscal and monetary authorities. They explicitly or implicitly assume either that these responses affect the national economy in ways which are uniform (however defined), or that specific industrial or regional responses do not concern the policymaker. Deliberately selective policies intended to affect specific industries or areas are said by such writers to be 'structural' policies, as distinguished from cyclical stabilization policies.

This paper is an examination of the implications, for cyclical stabilization policy, of regarding the nation as a network of related regions rather than as one market. The first section indicates the extent and causes of regional variation in cyclical patterns, and the manner in which these causes affect the efficiency of regional stabilization policies. The second is an analysis of the formulation of stabilization targets and policies when the regional distribution of cyclical unemployment is uneven and when the regional distribution of changes in employment resulting from fiscal and monetary policies concerns the policymaker. This concern would be greatest either when regional differentials in unemployment rates are large, so that some regions are at a 'distress' level, or when the national unemployment rate is close to, but above, a maximum socially acceptable level, so that the pattern of unemployment differentials is a crucial factor in determining the compatibility of 'full' employment with price level stability. This section also makes use of a simple model of interregional trade to compare the levels of efficiency of various fiscal policies in achieving specified goals. In a final section, some estimates of efficiency are derived on the basis of input–output data.

Since this study is focused on the unemployment aspect of stabilization, it employs a sectoring of the economy by geographic regions. A similar sectoring is not as relevant to a discussion of other aspects of stabilization policy. In the discussion of inflation, for example, sectoring by industries has been found most practical (Schultze, 1959), but the argument that a similar breakdown should be used in analyzing policies to reduce unemployment ignores differences between the two problems. Inflation tends to be more evenly diffused than unemployment, and, among regions, there are larger intra-industry differences in unemployment than in prices because goods are more mobile than labor, especially in the short run. Thus, a regional approach seems more appropriate to a discussion of unemployment than to a discussion of inflation.

Regional Differences in Unemployment

An analysis of the postwar period indicates considerable variations in regional behavior. Although the findings are more suggestive than conclusive, they are useful in placing the subsequent discussion in the context of the recent United States experience. Much of the following section is covered in greater detail in Chapters II through V of my dissertion (Engerman, 1962).

What is a region?

Three criteria are customarily used in the delineation of regions: factor mobility, commodity mobility, and political boundaries. Each is useful for certain purposes, and, to some extent, the regional concept in this paper will involve all three criteria. Despite imprecision in defining the nature of the ideal regional concept to be used, the problem of geographic differences in unemployment rates obviously exists under each criterion.

The first and most obvious approach to an analysis of unemployment would focus upon regions defined in terms of labor mobility. If the national rate of unemployment is a function of the locational pattern of the labor force, an increase in labor mobility would reduce the national rate, or at least narrow regional differentials in unemployment rates. Similarly, the location of any increases in demand for output leading to increased demand for labor would not be as crucial a concern in the presence of labor mobility as when such mobility is absent. Insofar as the national goal of policy is 'full' employment of the labor force, the existence of different labor market areas becomes a key consideration.

A second approach to regional classification is based on the concept of the sales market area. This should prove useful to the extent that the output of firms is directed largely towards purchasing units located within a specific area. It is relevant in analyzing the spread (or spillover) of the effects of policy changes among regions. The larger the market area for products produced in regions of high unemployment, the less necessary and desirable may be pinpointed policies, and the more these regions benefit from expenditure changes occurring in other regions. A major difficulty of this approach is that the relevant market areas will differ among products so that no one set of boundaries would suffice for all purposes. However, if certain key industries were meant to be aided by policy measures, then a knowledge of the specific market area for products of the producing units in these industries would be important in determining the expected geographic incidence of policy measures.

Imprecise as this criterion may be when applied to a complicated network of transactions (particularly since the market area itself may vary with cyclical phases), it again suggests that the geographic distribution of policy effects will depend upon the location at which the measure is introduced; and that, insofar as production in any one industry may occur at several locations, the customary assumption of national uniformity of response to all policy changes is unrealistic. It should be noted, again, that this inequality of response would not be so important if labor were mobile, meaning that for policy purposes these two criteria – labor mobility and commodity mobility – are interrelated.

A third approach is based upon administrative units for policy-making. Since the important consideration here is the institutional framework within which policies are designed and implemented, this approach requires recognition of political boundaries particularly within the context of a federal system. While such political boundaries frequently encompass areas which otherwise are not meaningful economic units, they may nevertheless be important for purposes of policy action, as in the case of state or local fiscal measures, or with respect to federal policies implemented at lower levels of government. While most fiscal policies involve direct relationships between the federal government and individual economic units, either individuals or firms, there are grant programs in which payments are made to the states *qua* states. Thus, aside from their independent roles in formulating their own tax and expenditure policies, states also serve as administrators and conduits for federal government policies.

While some recent legislation, notably that involving aid to the so-called depressed areas, recognizes labor market areas – essentially cities and their immediate suburbs – as the locale of federal policies, direct federal–regional relationships are not as common in our political system as are federal–state relationships. Although political and economic relationships between the federal and state governments are more important than those between the federal government and other political units, this fact need not be an inherent aspect of federalism as a political process.

Whatever may appear theoretically to be the most useful criteria for regional delineation in any specific case, most empirical studies use states or census regions, which are aggregated from states, as the primary units of observation. An important exception is the use of Federal Reserve districts when monetary factors are being considered. Generally, however, the greater availability of data on the state level for most economically significant variables limits most studies to states as the basis for regional classification. Much of our information about regional cyclical behavior, for example, comes from studies using states as the basic units, improper as this may seem when judged by rigorous theoretical standards (Borts, 1960; Hanna, 1959; Vining, January and July 1946, and July 1945). As noted above, the use of states as the fundamental units of observation is justifiable in a discussion of policy measures. For this reason, the empirical study summarized below will employ state data.

Postwar regional cyclical behavior

The data in the following tables were taken from state reports, prepared for the Bureau of Labor Statistics, of employment in non-agricultural establishments. They were used to calculate changes in levels of employment, and the decline from peak to trough in employment was used to indicate the rate of cyclical unemployment. Owing to difficulties in adjusting the data for seasonal variations, annual averages of employment in each state were used. Each state's employment was not adjusted for trend, but instead, observations over each cycle were averaged according to the National Bureau of Economic Research method. The following information is presented: comparisons of the timing of turning points in the annual data; the relative share of recession unemployment of three contiguous census regions; rates of expansion and decline and average annual amplitudes of state employment for the two cycles between 1949 and 1958.

The timing of turning points. The use of annual data for a survey of behavior within the period of a business cycle is admittedly crude, particularly for a discussion of the timing of turning points. Nevertheless, inspection of Federal Reserve bank reports and of the various state employment agency publications, which present monthly data, substantiates the conclusion that differences in timing were usually minor.

The data show a moderately high degree of uniformity among turning points of cyclical movements in various states. This conclusion follows from Table 1, which lists those states where changes in employment for each year were in a direction opposite to that shown by total national employment. The large number of deviant states which had over 20 per cent of their experienced labor force in agriculture in 1950 are noted accordingly in the table.[1] Similarly, those states whose growth rankings were 1 to 4 (from 1949 to 1958) are also noted.[2] The behavior of the agricultural states in recession years is not directly explained, however, by a difference in behavior between agricultural and industrial sectors. While agricultural income increased in 1958, it declined both in 1949 and 1954, not only at the national level but also, excepting Nebraska in 1954, in every deviant state in both years.[3] The deviance of these states may possibly have resulted from

1. The state ratios of labor force in agriculture to total experienced labor force are from Lee and others (1957).
2. See Table 8 for the rankings of the states by growth rates.
3. See U.S. Department of Commerce (1956) for the 1949 and 1954 income changes. For the changes in the next recession, see Graham (1959).

small employment samples and consequently unreliable data; thus apparent declines may simply be inaccurate measurements. In each of the highly ranked growth states, a deceleration in the rate of growth occurred in the recession years. For this reason, these apparent deviations are attributable to the failure to adjust for trend.

Special conditions affected the patterns in 1952 and 1957. The timing of the downturns for all manufacturing and for total non-agricultural employment differs in the recession phase of the cycle of 1954–8, thus rendering interpretation of that period difficult. It should be noted that the behavior of the states from the peak – whether in 1956 or 1957 – to the trough in 1958 is consistent with the behavioral patterns in the other two postwar recession periods.[4] The other period of divergence, 1952, resulted from sharp declines of about 6 per cent in employment in each of three key manufacturing industries – lumber and wood products, primary metals, and textile mill products – which were important in certain of the states (U.S. Bureau of Labor Statistics, 1961). The deviance of states in 1952 can be explained by the declines in employment in a 'key' industry in each state – textiles in Vermont and Massachusetts, primary metals in Pennsylvania, and mining in West Virginia – which exceeded the increases in all other employment. While, for reasons given above, too much importance should not be attached to the 1957 pattern, it should be noted that eight of the states are included in the fourteen-state area discussed in the next section, which includes those states in which manufacturing claims a large share of the labor force.

The conclusion suggested by this summary is that the postwar cycles, though comparatively minor by prewar standards, are still pervasive and affect nearly all of the states during a given period of time. The differential behavior of specific industries explains

4. Manufacturing employment reached a peak in October 1956, and total nonagricultural employment in September 1957. Thus manufacturing employment in 1957 fell below that in 1956, while the opposite is the case with total nonagricultural employment. See U.S. Bureau of Labor Statistics (1961). Because of this the 1957 movement in each state was not of the divergent movements in manufacturing and nonmanufacturing employment. The possibility exists that a greater severity in decline in employment within 1957, rather than a difference in timing of the turning points, accounts for most of the divergent movement.

Table 1

States Whose Total Employment Changed in a Direction Opposite to the Direction of Change of Total National Employment, 1949–58[1]

1949	1950	1951	1952	1953	1954	1955	1956	1957	1958
District of Columbia	—	—	Idaho²	Arkansas²	Arizona³	North Dakota²	Michigan	Connecticut	Arizona³
Kansas²			Massachusetts	District of Columbia	Florida³			Delaware	Arkansas²
Idaho²			Pennsylvania	Idaho²	Montana²			Georgia³	Florida³
Louisiana			Vermont	Maine	Nebraska²			Illinois	Mississippi²
Montana²			West Virginia	Rhode Island	Nevada³			Indiana	New Mexico³
New Mexico³				West Virginia	North Dakota²			Iowa³	South Dakota²
North Dakota²					South Dakota²			Kansas	
Oklahoma								Maine	
South Dakota²								Massachusetts	
								Michigan	
								Mississippi²	
								Missouri	
								Nebraska²	
								Oklahoma	
								Oregon	
								Rhode Island	
								South Dakota²	
								Tennessee²	
								Vermont	

Source: Bureau of Labor Statistics.

1. The total of national employment for all industries declined in 1949, 1954, and 1958. Employment increased in all other years.
2. Over 20 per cent of the state's experienced labor force in agriculture.
3. Growth ranking 1 to 4.

283

almost all of the apparent deviations, and since industry movements occur at about the same time, this makes tenable the previous assumption of national uniformity in the timing of cyclical behaviour.

The share of the 'manufacturing belt' in recession unemployment. To indicate the unevenness of the regional distribution of unemployment in the postwar recessions and its concentration in the northeastern manufacturing region, comparisons between shares

Table 2

Proportions of Employment and Employment Declines in the Fourteen 'Manufacturing Belt' States in Three Recessions, 1949, 1954, and 1958

(In per cent)

	Proportion of	
	National employment (peak year)	Decline in national employment
1949:		
Total	55.5	73.2
Manufacturing	66.8	74.6
Durable goods	72.5	75.9
1954:		
Total	53.9	75.9
Manufacturing	65.0	81.5
Durable goods	70.4	82.6
1958:		
Total	52.2	81.8
Manufacturing[1]	62.7	84.3
Durable goods[1]	67.8	88.2

Source: Bureau of Labor Statistics.
1. Peak year 1956.

of employment and shares of recession declines in employment were made for the three recession years, 1949, 1954, and 1958. The 'manufacturing belt' is a term frequently used by economic geographers to refer to the fourteen states in the New England, Middle Atlantic, and East North Central census regions.

Table 3   Rates of Expansion and Decline and Average Annual Amplitudes by States, 1949–54

(In per cent)

State		Rate of expansion[1]		Rate of decline[2]		Average annual amplitude[3]
Alabama	(26)	13.43	(24)	2.22	(27)	5.58
Arizona	(2)	28.00	(46)	+1.16	(12)	7.16
Arkansas	(30)	11.37[4]	(11)	3.86	(25)	5.72
California	(5)	22.14	(40)	0.48	(21)	6.02
Colorado	(6)	20.27	(31.5)	1.37	(17)	6.44
Connecticut	(14)	18.14	(16)	2.84	(11)	7.38
Delaware	(8)	20.02	(13)	3.13	(10)	8.14
District of Columbia	(39)	9.19[4]	(2)	7.38	(14)	6.75
Florida	(3)	24.79	(48)	+4.33	(4)	10.53
Georgia	(13)	18.44	(27)	1.76	(19)	6.37
Idaho	(36)	9.50[5]	(10)	4.04	(20)	6.10
Illinois	(33)	10.68	(12)	3.71	(18)	6.38
Indiana	(12)	18.46	(3)	7.35	(2)	11.97
Iowa	(46)	7.45	(31.5)	1.37	(45)	3.23
Kansas	(9)	19.71	(37.5)	0.80	(24)	5.73
Kentucky	(21)	15.50	(7)	5.41	(6)	9.29
Louisiana	(27)	13.18	(42)	0.35	(43)	3.65
Maine	(40)	9.10[4]	(22)	2.28	(39)	4.17
Maryland	(17)	16.45	(28)	1.72	(23)	5.83
Massachusetts	(42)	8.17[6]	(15)	3.00	(34)	5.04
Michigan	(10)	19.29	(5)	5.96	(3)	10.78
Minnesota	(29)	11.82	(30)	1.47	(38)	4.43
Mississippi	(23)	14.58	(37.5)	0.80	(37)	4.45
Missouri	(25)	13.87	(14)	3.04	(16)	6.51
Montana	(48)	6.10	(44)	+0.53	(49)	2.05
Nebraska	(28)	12.07	(43)	+0.03	(46)	3.05
Nevada	(1)	32.48	(49)	+6.56	(1)	14.68
New Hampshire	(44)	7.87	(39)	0.70	(47)	2.67
New Jersey	(24)	14.42	(29)	1.67	(32)	5.28
New Mexico	(4)	23.40	(20)	2.45	(8)	8.30
New York	(43)	8.04	(26)	1.97	(41)	3.98
North Carolina	(16)	16.48	(34)	1.14	(33)	5.26
North Dakota	(45)	7.59	(47)	+1.65	(44)	3.55
Ohio	(15)	16.94	(9)	4.23	(7)	8.47
Oklahoma	(22)	15.09	(41)	0.39	(40)	4.16
Oregon	(31)	10.88	(19)	2.72	(28.5)	5.44
Pennsylvania	(37)	9.43[6]	(6)	5.82	(9)	8.18
Rhode Island	(41)	9.07[5]	(4)	6.09	(15)	6.57
South Carolina	(7)	20.04	(8)	4.57	(5)	9.58
South Dakota	(47)	6.79	(45)	+ .76	(48)	2.46
Tennessee	(18)	16.33	(33)	1.29	(30)	5.37
Texas	(11)	18.72	(36)	1.02	(26)	5.70
Utah	(19)	16.08	(17)	2.83	(13)	6.85
Vermont	(38)	9.26[6]	(21)	2.32	(36)	4.64
Virginia	(20)	15.70	(25)	2.05	(22)	5.98
Washington	(32)	10.70	(35)	1.05	(42)	3.73
West Virginia	(49)	2.79[5]	(1)	12.12	(28.5)	5.44
Wisconsin	(34)	10.22	(18)	2.76	(31)	5.32
Wyoming	(35)	10.02	(23)	2.27	(35)	4.78
National total[7]		13.49		2.65		6.02
National total[8]		13.89		2.70		6.17

Source: Bureau of Labor Statistics.
Note: Numbers in parentheses indicate rankings in order of magnitude of movement.
1. Expansion = Peak minus Initial Trough ÷ Cycle Base.
2. Decline = Peak minus Terminal Trough ÷ Cycle Base.
3. Average Annual Amplitude = Average Annual Expansion (Expansion ÷ Number of Years in Upswing) + Average Annual Decline.
4. Peak in 1952   5. Peak in 1951.   6. Decline in 1952, peak in 1953.
7. National total given by the Bureau of Labor Statistics.
8. Total of state figures.

Table 4

Rates of Expansion and Decline and Average Annual Amplitudes by States, 1954–8

(In per cent)

State		Rate of expansion[1]		Rate of decline[2]		Average annual amplitude[3]
Alabama	(12)	10.48	(27)	2.36	(15)	5.85
Arizona	(1)	25.63	(49)	+5.12	(1)	13.66
Arkansas	(25)	6.91	(45)	+.43	(46)	2.73
California	(4)	14.56	(40)	0.72	(21)	5.57
Colorado	(7)	13.01	(36)	1.34	(19)	5.68
Connecticut	(32)	6.08[4]	(12)	4.39	(23.5)	5.24
Delaware	(6)	13.80[4]	(6)	5.40	(7)	9.60
District of Columbia	(46)	3.00	(37.5)	1.06	(47)	2.06
Florida	(2)	25.49	(47)	+1.72	(3)	10.22
Georgia	(17.5)	8.16[4]	(30)	2.26	(25)	5.21
Idaho	(14)	9.75	(37.5)	1.06	(31)	4.31
Illinois	(31)	6.09[4]	(7)	5.34	(18)	5.72
Indiana	(27)	6.54[4]	(5)	7.00	(11)	6.77
Iowa	(40)	3.98[4]	(25.5)	2.53	(42)	3.26
Kansas	(47)	2.83[4]	(17)	3.21	(43)	3.03
Kentucky	(15)	8.80	(15)	3.47	(13)	6.40
Louisiana	(8)	12.77	(18)	3.20	(9)	7.46
Maine	(42)	3.54[4]	(9)	5.21	(29)	4.38
Maryland	(13)	9.86	(29)	2.29	(20)	5.58
Massachusetts	(41)	3.91[4]	(14)	3.72	(36)	3.82
Michigan	(26)	6.67[5]	(1)	15.12	(2)	11.71
Minnesota	(28)	6.52	(33.5)	1.67	(35)	3.84
Mississippi	(20)	7.77[6]	(44)	+0.33	(44)	2.92
Missouri	(45)	3.22[4]	(25.5)	2.53	(45)	2.88
Montana	(22)	7.54	(22.5)	2.76	(22)	5.27
Nebraska	(48)	2.24[4]	(33.5)	1.67	(48)	1.96
Nevada	(5)	14.23	(16)	3.32	(8)	8.06
New Hampshire	(30)	6.16	(19)	3.19	(23.5)	5.24
New Jersey	(24)	7.29	(10)	4.94	(10)	7.37
New Mexico	(3)	17.79	(48)	+4.09	(4)	10.02
New York	(35)	5.54	(21)	2.89	(27)	4.74
North Carolina	(17.5)	8.16	(39)	0.96	(37.5)	3.68
North Dakota	(39)	4.03[7]	(43)	0.01	(49)	1.35
Ohio	(29)	6.36	(3)	7.73	(5)	9.85
Oklahoma	(33)	6.07[4]	(28)	2.33	(32)	4.21
Oregon	(23)	7.48[4]	(11)	4.91	(14)	6.20
Pennsylvania	(38)	4.22	(8)	5.27	(12)	6.68
Rhode Island	(49)	2.15[4]	(2)	7.84	(26)	5.00
South Carolina	(36)	5.09	(32)	1.76	(41)	3.46
South Dakota	(34)	5.75[6]	(46)	+1.18	(40)	3.47
Tennessee	(37)	4.67[4]	(24)	2.67	(37.5)	3.68
Texas	(11)	11.16	(41)	0.63	(30)	4.35
Utah	(9)	12.73	(35)	1.52	(16)	5.76
Vermont	(43)	3.40[4]	(13)	3.89	(39)	3.65
Virginia	(10)	11.75	(42)	0.21	(33)	4.12
Washington	(16)	8.41	(31)	1.81	(28)	4.61
West Virginia	(21)	7.55	(4)	7.25	(6)	9.77
Wisconsin	(19)	7.96	(20)	3.08	(17)	5.73
Wyoming	(44)	3.33	(22.5)	2.76	(34)	3.87
National total[8]		7.33		3.18		5.62
National total[9]		7.48		3.37		5.86

Source: Bureau of Labor Statistics.
1. Expansion = Peak minus Initial Trough ÷ Cycle Base.
2. Decline = Peak minus Terminal Trough ÷ Cycle Base.
3. Average Annual Amplitude = Average Annual Expansion (Expansion ÷ Number of Years of Upswing) + Average Annual Decline.

Table 2 shows the share of total nonagricultural employment, manufacturing employment, and durable goods manufacturing employment in this area in each of the peak years (1948, 1953, and 1956 or 1957) and the respective declines in the recession years. The disproportionately larger share of unemployment in these states, even after adjustment has been made for differences in industrial composition, should be noted, as should the fact that their relative share increased in each recession at the same time that their share of employment was declining.

Rates of cyclical change, by states. Tables 3 and 4 show the rates of expansion and decline and average annual amplitudes for each state in the cycles of 1949–54 and 1954–8. They were computed using the National Bureau method of averaging the observations over each cycle, with the terminal years given half-weight. The numbers in parentheses indicate the ranking of the state in order of magnitude of movement. Owing to variations in the timing of turning points, rates of expansion and decline were computed for entire phases, but amplitudes were computed from annual averages of the behavior in each cyclical phase. If the national turning point had been used, and annual rates of expansion and decline computed, the rankings shown in the tables would be little changed. These tables, along with those in Appendix A, page 327 form the basis of the rank correlations to be discussed below.

Influence of location

Two locational factors are important in analyzing the theories used later to explain regional differences in cyclical behavior. The first follows from the geographer's concept of the export base, with its distinction between local (or residentiary or service) industries and national (or export) industries (Isard and others, 1960). While this dichotomy may be exaggerated in some cases, it illuminates an important distinction between (1) those (national)

---

4. Peak in 1956.
5. Peak in 1955.
6. Decline in 1957, peak in 1958.
7. Trough in 1955, peak in 1957.
8. National total given by the Bureau of Labor Statistics.
9. Total of state figures.

industries which can be directly affected by demand conditions in other regions and (2) those (local) industries which respond directly to local demand conditions, including both the final demand of local consumers and the intermediate demand of locally situated national or other local industries. Local dependence may arise either because buyers and sellers must be closely proximate, owing to high transport costs (in the case of purely local industries), or because transport costs make it efficient for local purchasers to purchase from local producers.

Trade, construction, services, and utilities are usually considered local industries, and would be classified under (2) above. Most manufacturing and mining industries are considered national, or at least multi-regional, industries, with market areas extending beyond the immediate localities in which production occurs. These would be classified under (1).[5] The important point, for our purposes, is that increases in demand for certain firms arise mainly within immediate regions, while for others, increases in demand anywhere in the nation can affect regional production. Similarly, increases in expenditures within regions may purchase goods produced either by national industries located within the region or elsewhere, or those produced by local industries. The magnitude of interregional spillover of demand will depend upon the extent of expenditures for goods produced by national industries not located within the region under consideration.

Location is important, secondly, with respect to national industries. Within an industry there tends to be a negative correlation between the flow of expenditures between two regions and their distance from each other (Vining, 1953; Isard and other 1960). For an industry with producing units located in several regions, any initial increases in demand by any purchasing units should result in increased sales by that sales unit located closest to the source of the increase in demand. This expectation would rise with an increase in the ratio of transport costs to the delivered price of the goods. Such an effect may not occur if there is full employment in nearby regions, but during recessions, when all plants would be likely to have some under-utilized capacity, the corre-

5. For a detailed breakdown of the New York Metropolitan Area on this basis, see Lichtenberg (1960). The high non-local share of finance and service industries found in this study would not be expected for most other areas.

lation between distance and expenditures should exist. The relationship between expenditures, distance, and cyclical conditions is usually described as the problem of the marginal supplier – that unit of production which is last in and first out as a seller within certain markets, and which benefits from demand increases in some regions only after plants nearer the source of demand have approached capacity levels of output. It is for this reason that some distinction must be made between selective industrial and selective regional policies.

Theories used to explain regional differences

The theories discussed here are used most often to explain regional differences in cyclical behavior. Sometimes they have been viewed as complementary, sometimes as substitutes for each other, and it is often difficult to determine the specific relationship intended among them. For this reason each theory will be discussed separately, and implications of each will be first explored in isolation.

Industrial composition. Regional differences in cyclical behavior are most commonly explained in terms of differences in industrial composition. This explanation is stated most succinctly by Walter Isard, although he disputes it:

Differences in the intensity and timing of regional cycles are explained in terms of differences in the sensitivity and responsiveness of particular industries. Cycles of a regional economy are simple composites of the cyclical movement of the economy's industries, appropriately weighted (Isard, 1957).

As Isard points out, this implies that regional breakdowns are not functional, since only industrial behavior is significant. Any regional differences are to be explained by a weighted average of the national behavior of the industries located in the regions, with the weights reflecting the importance of each industry in the region's industrial base.[6] Thus the existence of differences in unemployment among regions simply reflects differences in industries'

6. For a study of regional cycles in manufacturing employment which uses this method for computing hypothetical regional cyclical behavior, see Borts (1960), pp. 151–211. Borts concludes that 'differences are in part

unemployment. The necessary assumption is that for any one downturn (upturn) there are equal percentage declines (increases) within an industry in all regions in which it is located, so that the location of the employment declines (increases) in any one industry is independent of the location of the forces leading to the declines (increases) in demand for the output of that industry.

Wide acceptance of this hypothesis has led to a lack of concern with the regional distribution of unemployment. Since the hypothesis assumes that responses of particular industries to stabilization measures would be evenly diffused among the various locations of these industries, the location of the initial increase in demand need not be considered independently in the design of stabilization policy. All regions will benefit similarly, independent of the location of the initial injection of expenditure changes, or of the changes in demand arising from tax changes or changes in monetary policy, insofar as these changes in demand occur in certain industries. It does not follow that aggregate policies suffice for the appropriate disaggregation in this case is in terms of industrial sectors rather than regions. Policies which discriminate appropriately by industries will be sufficient to aid all regions. The policymaker need not discriminate regionally because the market will provide the proper regional distribution of employment changes.

Even if this hypothesis is accepted in its extreme form, the behavior of each region is a function of the industries which it contains, and regional responses would still differ for alternative stabilization measures. Since the policy alternatives may give rise to different mixes of output, the stabilization decision cannot be neutral in its effects upon regional employment. A concern with regional factors in formulating stabilization policy may still be necessary, but could, again, be implemented through industry measures. Since industries are centered regionally, these measures carry regional implications.[7]

---

the result of differences in the types of manufacturing industry found in each state', but that 'a change in the trend of growth alters the cyclical behavior of state industries relative to their national counterparts'. Ibid., p. 152.

7. Thus proposals for excise tax variations to aid states producing consumer durable goods have been suggested as a contracyclical device.

While important, the industrial composition argument in its crudest form cannot be easily accepted, since it overlooks the locational factors discussed above. It assumes away the possibility of differences in the rates of decline in various regional locations in a given industry, as well as the distinction between national and local industries. Even if the hypothesis that national industries behave similarly in each region in which they are located were tentatively accepted, there remains the fact that changes in employment in local industries are related to changes in the resident national industries. Therefore, changes in local industries over the nation as a whole are not relevant in estimating changes in local industries within any region. The behavior of these local industries in any one region is dependent upon the initial change in the resident national industries via the customary multiplier and input–output processes. Thus, the larger the change in demand in national industries, the more the actual regional change in local industries will exceed the amount predicted by using national averages.[8] Since national industries located within the same region will also be linked, the same understatement in using national averages will occur. The presence of unstable national industries in a region should modify the behavior of the usually more stable

Similarly intended are proposals to reintroduce and vary consumer credit controls. Their efficiency from the regional point of view would depend upon the locational pattern of producing units as well as the price elasticities (or elasticities in response to changes in consumer credit terms) of demand for the products concerned. While possibly desirable from the aggregate national point of view, their regional impacts could be less than desirable. To the extent that production in affected industries is regionally concentrated these measures could provide for a more desirable pattern of employment changes as compared with an equivalent set of measures which are nonselective. However, an estimate of the specific magnitude of the effects would require more information concerning consumer spending habits in response to these changes. Selective industry measures applied to ubiquitous industries would not have this desired regional impact. For an interesting suggestion to make excise tax variation more effective from a regional standpoint, see Kreinin (1959).

8. In the case of 'chronically depressed areas' the Bureau of Labor Statistics comments that 'it is noteworthy . . . that even in chronically depressed areas at least a third of insured unemployment comes from [finance, services, and government] – not usually thought of as being directly subject to structural unemployment'. U.S. Bureau of Labor Statistics (1960). With allowance for lags the same should be true in the cyclical case.

national industries.[9] Applying weighted averages in these cases causes an understatement of the employment change in those states with large initial changes in demand for the products of national industries, and an overstatement in those with smaller initial changes.

Even if we were to concentrate upon the behavior of the national industries, equiproportionate decline in all regions would be a doubtful hypothesis in its extreme form. Because of the marginal supplier relationship, the initial declines in demand would not be evenly spread among the regions. The initial incidence of a decline in demand would be more likely to fall more heavily upon some suppliers than upon others, rather than be evenly spread among all suppliers. When the possibility is considered that the initial declines in expenditures may themselves be nonuniformly distributed among regions, there is a greater probability of nonuniform declines in employment within an industry. Although the industry change may be felt in all (or most) regions in which it is located, the magnitude of these declines should differ. For this reason, as well as the one discussed in the previous paragraph, regional cycles reflect more than simply industry cycles.

In the case of nonuniform industry declines among regions, the location of the initial expenditure increase in response to stabilization policy measures becomes more important. Since nationwide diffusion is not to be expected, pinpointed policies could be more effective in reducing unemployment than comparable policies applied on a nationwide scale. While the location of the initial expenditure increase is no doubt a consideration in discussing policy responses even when one accepts the weighted average hypothesis, different emphasis is placed here on the factors which would lead to disproportionate regional changes as opposed to nationwide diffusion. Also, to the extent that initial expenditures are made for purchases from local industries, nationwide measures may not be diffused, and the benefits in the areas of high unemployment will be reduced.

The data suggest a significant relationship between industrial composition and employment declines in the postwar period. Rank correlations between cyclical behavior of states and two in-

9. It should be noted, however, that Borts (1960, pp. 178–80) found this to be true in only three of the six cycles which he studied.

dices of industrial composition – share of employment in national industries (manufacturing and mining), and in durable goods manufacturing industries – are shown in Table 5. Although the rank correlations between these measures of industrial structure and the rates of decline accord with expectations, the negative correlations between the same measures and rates of expansion do not.[10] While substantially confirming the importance of industrial structure in recessions, the states' behavior in expansions indicates that other considerations must be introduced.

Diversification and trade involvement. The theme of stability through diversification is one that permeates the popular literature on geographic aspects of unemployment. The presumption seems to be that by increasing the degree of diversification within a region its stability will be increased, since diversified regions will tend to have smaller cyclical swings. In the absence of reference to specific industries, it is difficult to state whether this argument is intended to be a substitute for or a complement to the previously stated industrial composition hypothesis. On the one hand, it may mean that the process of diversification alters the cyclical behavior of particular national industries in such a way that the behavior of normally unstable industries is modified when they are located within the same region. This interpretation implies that diversification brings about a different relationship among industries when located in the same region than when located separately, so that the expectations of regional differentials in employment changes would not be based upon the behavior of the component industries. It is this which must be intended when the diversification argument is stated without specific details about

10. Since growth and industrial structure were negatively correlated in this period (a correlation of −0.39 between proportion of manufacturing and mining to total employment and growth, and −0.37 between the proportion of durables to total employment and growth), calculations were made using Kendall's Tau, which permits the calculation of partial rank correlation coefficients. The positive correlations between industrial structure and declines were slightly reduced, the positive correlations between amplitude and industrial structure were slightly increased, while the correlations between rates of expansion and industrial structure became slightly positive. The correlations between industrial structure and rates of decline are considerably greater than those between industrial structure and rates of expansion.

Table 5

Rank Correlation Coefficients (Spearman's Rho) Between Two Indices of Industrial Composition and Cyclical Behavior in Two Cycles, 1949–54 and 1954–8[1]

	Manufacturing and mining	Durable goods manufacturing
Rate of expansion:		
1949–54	−0.03	−0.07
1954–58	−0.18	−0.12
Rate of decline:		
1949–54	+0.56[2]	+0.46[2]
1954–58	+0.66[2]	+0.63[2]
Average annual amplitude:		
1949–54	+0.21	+0.14
1954–58	+0.23	+0.29

Source: Computed from Tables 3, 4, 9, and 10.

1. The rates of expansion and decline and average annual amplitudes for total employment, manufacturing and mining employment, and durable goods manufacturing employment in the two cycles are:

	Rate of expansion	Rate of decline	Average annual amplitude
All industries:			
1949–54	13.5%	2.6%	3.2%
1954–58	7.3	3.2	2.6
Manufacturing and mining:			
1949–54	17.8	7.8	5.1
1954–58	4.7	8.1	3.2
Durable goods manufacturing:			
1949–54	29.3	10.9	8.0
1954–58	7.3	11.3	4.7

2. Significance and the 1 per cent level. For $N = 49$ the significance levels are: 5 per cent, 0.28 and 1 per cent, 0.37.

industrial composition.[11] On the other hand, there is the interpretation which draws an analogy between the diversifications argument and the reduction of risk by diversification of portfolios,

11. For evidence bearing on this interpretation of diversification compare the statement of Leon Moses that 'the East North Central region is probably as good an approximation to the balanced region which reality affords', with the rates of employment decline for the states in this region shown in Tables 3 and 4. See Moses (1960).

an analogy which has little merit since the necessary randomness of individual industry behavior cannot be assumed to exist.

What remains to be explained is just why diversification should change relationships among industries. An alternative approach would stress the desirability of introducing more stable national industries into regions which are characterized by large cyclical declines. The diversification argument then becomes the same as the industrial composition hypothesis, since addition of stable industries to the industrial base reduces the instability of a region, regardless of the degree of diversification. The advantage of this approach follows from the fact that the cyclical behavior of industries is not random, nor do the characteristics of the industries affected vary among cycles to any great extent. Thus, Edgar M. Hoover, a strong advocate of diversification for long-term development, states that 'the character of products rather than the degree of diversification determines the impact of depression' (Hoover, 1948; Brecher and Reisman, 1957). It would seem that the diversification hypothesis, as usually expressed, does not explain regional differentials, but merely rephrases the industrial composition hypothesis. In a discussion of cyclical stability an abstractly defined diversification is not a useful concept.

Nevertheless, diversification may enter into the explanation o regional cyclical differentials in the following fashion. A high degree of diversification is likely to mean a relatively low marginal propensity to import. A highly diversified region would therefore find it more difficult to pass on internal declines in income to the outside via reduced imports. On the export side, depending upon the relative industrial composition of the region as contrasted with the rest of the nation, exports may or may not represent a large proportion of regional output. The larger the export share, and the greater the instability of the export industries, the more sensitive will a given region be to declining national demand; a low export share and lesser instability of those industries would mean less sensitivity. Thus diversification may lead either to greater or lesser stability, but a strong institutional factor would suggest the former alternative is more likely. Taking diversification in its usual meaning as the comparison of regional relative to national industrial structures, a diversified region (in the United States and other industrial nations) is likely to contain more industries which produce durable goods than is a nondiversified region. Since demand in these industries is cyclically unstable, and since diversification makes it difficult to export the decline in income which results from the decline in national demand, diversified regions (such as the East North Central region), with variable exports and a low marginal propensity to import, will experience greater fluctuations in employment than will a non-diversified region. Thus, the differential created by 'industrial composition' factors is accentuated by the low import propensity of such a region. In this case diversification will increase the need for regionally-oriented policies.

Diversification also has an important bearing on the efficiency of a regionally-oriented stabilization policy. The more diversified a region (in that it produces a larger assortment of goods to meet its final and intermediate demands), the greater will be the effects of any increase in expenditures within the region upon internal income. Given the probable relationship between diversification and the marginal propensity to import noted in the preceding paragraph, the spillover from a diversified region will be less than the spillover from a region which specializes in a narrow range of goods. Put differently, since high diversification implies a low marginal propensity to import, the more diversified a region, the more effective expenditures made within the region will be in changing that region's level of employment. Diversification within a region not only renders regionally-oriented stabilization policy more necessary, but also tends to make it more effective.

Growth differences. An hypothesis usually intended to supplement the industrial composition hypothesis relates differences in cyclical stability to differences in growth rates. Under this theory larger declines (and smaller expansions) than expected will occur in retarding regions, while rapidly growing regions will experience smaller declines (and larger expansions) than predicted on the basis of industrial composition. Two alternative explanations are given for these expectations; one stresses supply and cost factors and the other demand aspects. The implications of these alternative explanations differ; they postulate different relationships about comparative regional cyclical behaviour depending upon the magnitude of the national cycle.

The former explanation is based upon the presumption that the industrial movements which occur when regions are growing rapidly leads to the location of more efficient, lower-cost firms in the expanding regions. These firms, having lower average costs, will be better able to stay in business when prices decline. Thus, in times of falling demand their declines in production would be less than for higher-cost firms located in the regions with slower rates of growth.[12] The same result would follow if the decline in demand did not depress prices, since the lower-cost firms would be better able to absorb transport costs in recession, and thus would increase their market shares. Within an industry, then, firms located in expanding regions would suffer less than would firms in retarding regions which are the marginal suppliers. But larger expansions in retarding regions during periods of expansion would not be certain, since the more rapidly growing regions would be adding new capacity, hence their rate of expansion would not be limited by the preceding rate of decline.

The second explanation emphasizes the importance of population movements into growing regions as a source of demand for investment in housing, utilities, and other forms of social overhead capital, and/or the importance of investor's expectations of further expansion in the future, thus placing a floor under possible declines in investment. In retarding regions, by contrast, neither of these exogenous demand factors is present and differences in the initial declines in demand among regions will cause intra-industry differences in employment changes among regions. The higher floor under investment demand in rapidly growing regions means that declines in demand for firms in those regions will be less than the declines of firms in regions growing more slowly.[13] It

12. For a statement of this hypothesis, with the implication that these firms will have greater expansions than firms in more rapidly growing regions, see Borts (1960), pp. 181–2.

13. Examination of annual changes in manufacturing plant and equipment investment, and construction contracts awarded for all types of construction, public and private, do not accord with these expectations. However, nonfarm dwelling starts had a higher rate of increase in states with smaller employment declines in both recessions studied, with a sharper rate of decline when starts turned down. Thus the data on the relationship between growth and the recession behavior of investment appear inconclusive.

should be noted, however, that in large national declines this floor may not exist, and the previously more rapid expansion may lead to larger declines in growing regions. Unlike the explanation based upon cost differences, which would imply interregional differentials in the same direction regardless of the national cyclical amplitude, the explanation based upon the differential behavior of investment would imply larger declines in growing areas in large downturns and smaller declines when the national downturn is not substantial. That is, when the cyclical downturns do not lead to reductions in longer-term investment, areas growing more slowly will suffer from larger downturns because they lack the stabilizing factors of residential and other population-oriented expenditures and the more favorable long-term expectations associated with areas of rapid growth.

Table 6 shows that these expectations were borne out in the postwar period, when national declines were not substantial.

In both cycles there was a positive correlation between growth and rates of expansion and a negative correlation between growth and rates of declines.

The existence of regional differences in unemployment based upon differential growth rates points to a possible conflict between growth and stabilization criteria in the application of public policy. When rapidly growing regions experience the larger cyclical declines, both the stabilization of employment and the growth criteria are applicable to the same regions. But when declines are sharper in retarding regions, regionally-oriented policies may be necessary, since these regions may be less responsive to general monetary and tax measures than growing regions.

Similar considerations apply to the longer-run aspects of growth policy. To the extent that industrial relocation continues, the relative decline in the export base of regions growing comparatively slowly continues as well. Industry-oriented measures, therefore, may not be efficient in aiding these regions, and regionally discriminatory policies (for example, in the form of grants to state and local governments for necessary public works) may become most necessary at the very time when they are most in conflict with longer-run goals of regional adjustment. While a properly designed expenditure or transfer program may aid in spurring growth in these lagging regions, regional discrimination

Table 6

Rank Correlation Coefficients (Spearman's Rho)
Between Growth and Cyclical Behavior in Two Cycles, 1949–54
and 1954–8[1]

	1949–54	1954–8
Growth and:		
Rate of expansion	+0.71[2]	+0.78[2]
Rate of decline	−0.63[2]	−0.51[2]
Average annual amplitudes	+0.16	+0.32

Source: Computed from Tables 3, 4, and 8.

1. The measure of growth used here – the relationship between cycle
bases – is actually a measure of acceleration and retardation. This does not
affect the conclusions since the rank correlation between growth measured
in this manner and the peak-to-peak growth rates is +0.95.

2. Significant at the 1 percent level. For $N = 49$ the significance levels are:
5 per cent, 0.28 and 1 per cent, 0.37.

would also be needed to avoid the inflationary pressures of an increase in national aggregate demand large enough to accomplish
the same result.

Conclusions

Cyclical fluctuations in the United States during the postwar
years have been nationwide, with small differences in turning
points between regions (here defined as states), but the magnitude
of the movements within these fluctuations has differed considerably among regions. The foregoing discussion suggests three
major conclusions about the causes of regional differentials in
cyclical behavior, and the appropriateness of regionally-oriented
stabilization policy.

1. The industrial composition hypothesis, in its pure form,
holds that regional variations merely reflect the different weights
of various industries in the industrial structure of the region. It is
assumed that variations for any one industry are the same in all
its locations, and specific regional forces are excluded. If correct,
this would imply that regional objectives of stabilization policy
can be disregarded or need be approached via industry-oriented
measures. But this is not an adequate explanation. It is necessary

also to consider the complications created by the difference between national and local industries, and the importance of transportation costs which affect the pattern of demand for goods produced by the national industries. These considerations introduce an explicit regional factor into the explanation of cyclical differentials, and call for concern with regional factors in the determination and evaluation of stabilization policy.

2. Diversification was found to be a relevant explanation of regional differentials only to the extent that it represents a modified form of the industrial composition hypothesis, and to the extent that a resulting low marginal propensity to import reduces the region's ability to offset cyclical fluctuations in the national demand for durable goods. This relation between diversification and propensity to import will also prove a crucial factor in determining the effectiveness of regionally-oriented policies.

3. Growth differentials were found to play an important role in accounting for differences in regional cyclical behavior, and it was suggested that specific fiscal policy measures tied to regions may be more efficient than general or industry-based policies in securing stabilization. Similarly, it was found that regionally-oriented policies may be necessary to accelerate long-term growth.

It appears that regional cyclical differentials are of considerable importance, and that they are caused to a significant degree by specifically regional (as distinct from purely industrial composition) factors. This suggests that regionally-oriented stabilization policies would be desirable if feasible. This feasibility in turn depends on the extent (absence) of interregional spillover of income creating effects. It will therefore be useful to examine a simple model of interregional trade to see what it reveals about the probable results of certain policies, and about the resultant distributions of income changes among regions.

Comparative Statics of Alternative Fiscal Programs

In this section a simple model of interregional trade will be used to compare the regional effectiveness of several fiscal programs based upon various policy targets. For purposes of expositional simplicity, the analysis assumes only two regions, but the nature of the conclusions drawn would not be changed by the introduction of more regions.

Alternative regionally-oriented targets

Alternative stabilization targets may differ in the relative importance which is attached to the regional pattern of employment increases. If a policy preference for differential employment increases in different regions is introduced, interregional spillover of expenditure changes becomes a crucial consideration in the selection of appropriate policies. Spillovers may be helpful or harmful in simultaneously achieving desired targets, but in no case can they be overlooked by the policymaker.[14]

In the simplest case of two regions with equal labor forces, these alternative targets can be written as:

$$\text{I. } \Delta E_a + \Delta E_b$$

$$\text{II. } \Delta E_a$$

$$\text{III. } \Delta E_a + \Delta E_b, \quad \text{where} \quad \frac{\Delta E_b}{\Delta E_a} = \alpha$$

and a. $\alpha = 1$
   b. $0 < \alpha < 1$
   c. $\alpha = 0$
   d. $\alpha < 0$.

ΔE is the absolute increase in employment and the subscripts a and b refer to the two regions. With labor forces of equal size, the ratio of the absolute increases in employment also indicates the ratio of the change in employment rates in the two regions.

Target I, a maximum increase in national employment, is implicit in most discussions of stabilization policy. The regional distribution of employment increases is a matter of indifference to the

14. The discussion that follows is in terms of targets for two regions, with the national change in employment not explicitly introduced as a policy goal. It has been suggested that a more realistic approach to this problem would be to have a preference function which includes the national unemployment rate as well as the unemployment rates in each of the regions. The policymaker would then be 'trading-off' between a specific national rate and its distribution between the regions. It is possible that a higher national rate of unemployment with a more desirable distribution would be preferred to a lower national rate with a less desirable regional distribution, as in the third case of Target IIId.

policymaker, since increased employment anywhere in the nation is equally desirable. This target would be most appropriate when neither region is at a 'distress' level but when the national unemployment rate is high. Under such conditions there would be no great social urgency to reduce unemployment in one particular region. Moreover, increases in demand would lead to increases in employment in either region, without posing a price-stability problem. The policymaker could then afford to be indifferent to the location of employment changes – at least in the context of economic efficiency.

Target II, increased employment in one region, would be more relevant to a discussion of targets for each region treated in isolation. It is, of course, the target of any one nation in the world economy or, for that matter, the target of stabilization attempts by state or local governments. The focus of the policymaker is upon increasing employment in only one region, without concern for the effects of spillover into other regions. A policymaker concerned with the employment effects in two regions could hardly adopt this target since he could not be indifferent to the effects upon employment and prices in the other region.

The sub-targets listed under Target III would be the alternative aims of regionally-oriented stabilization policy. In each case the regional distribution of employment changes would be a key factor in the designing of the policy measures to be used to achieve these goals. Whereas Target I was specified only in terms of the national rate of unemployment, the national average would not be as important a concern under Target III as the rates in the component regions of the nation. Target IIIa would call for an equal increase in employment in both regions, a policy which would be appropriate if the two regions were equally above their bottleneck rates of unemployment and both were below (or similar with regard to) their 'distress' rate. Target IIIa might also represent a politically necessary solution, given the feelings which could develop over a conscious policy of regional discrimination. Target IIIb would be the most probable object of a regionally-oriented stabilization policy in recession periods. Employment increases in both regions would be desirable, but a greater increase in one than in the other region would be intended. This target would become more appropriate the closer the economy approached 'full' employment, and the more uneven unemployment was distributed, assuming both regions were still above their bottleneck rates of unemployment.

Targets IIIc and IIId would represent possible aims of a government faced with the unemployment–inflation dilemma. Increasing employment in one region would be achieved either (IIIc) without changed employment in the other or (IIId) with decreases in employment in the other region. Target IIId has three possible aspects: if $| \alpha | < 1$, national unemployment would be reduced; if $| \alpha | = 1$, national unemployment would be unchanged, but redistributed between the regions; or if $| \alpha | > 1$, the national unemployment rate would be increased and its burden shifted between the regions.

Target IIIc would be appropriate, in the cyclical setting, when there are significant differences in the regional unemployment rates; these would occur if the timing of regional cyclical turning points differed. As shown in the state data in the first section, above, this does not often occur. Yet during the 1956 employment decline in Michigan, which was attributable mostly to the decline in the demand for automobiles and to shifts in the placement of defense contracts, this target was a policy consideration. At that time, because of the concentrated regional pattern of production for automobiles, there was some discussion of the possible usefulness of excise tax reduction. This policy was considered unfeasible, however, because of fear of increasing the inflationary pressures in the rest of the economy. In the secular context. Target IIIc is an approximation of the goal of special 'depressed areas' legislation in times of cyclical expansion. By use of pinpointed construction projects, policymakers hope to maximize the increase in employment in these areas per dollar of government expenditure, while minimizing the effects upon the rest of the economy.

The discussion in the preceding paragraphs has obvious implications for the problem of stabilization policy in a common market with common fiscal and monetary policies. A country which is free to undertake its own independent policies would probably pursue Target II, aiming for domestic full employment (subject to a balance-of-payments constraint), with little concern for resultant internal effects in other nations. A common policy, however, would have to allow for external effects arising from attempts to stabilize each member, so that each member country would have to be satisfied with a less ambitious employment target. Thus, although for the common market as a whole, policy might be more efficient, each member would not necessarily be better off in terms of unemployment than if left free to pursue its own policy. A similar problem is faced by each state in the United States when it proclaims its view in national policy formulation. It may then be that a more nearly equal distribution of unemployment within the nation cannot be achieved without policies designed to encourage migration to comparatively fully employed regions.

Application to model

In the following analysis, one particular region is posed against another which represents the rest of the nation. The relative size of each region is important since it would be a determinant of the regional marginal propensities to import. That is, the smaller the region the larger would be its marginal propensity to import from another region, and the smaller would be the second region's marginal propensity to import from the region in question.

The trade model for this analysis is a standard Keynesian one:

$$(1) \quad Y_a = C_a + I_a + G_a + X_a - M_a$$
$$(2) \quad Y_b = C_b + I_b + G_b + X_b - M_b$$
$$(3) \quad C_a = c_a Y_a$$
$$(4) \quad C_b = c_b Y_b$$
$$(5) \quad M_a = X_b = m_a(C_a + I_a + G_a + X_a)$$
$$(6) \quad M_b = X_a = m_b(C_b + I_b + G_b + X_b),$$

in which I and G are exogenous. Y is income, C consumption, I investment, G government expenditures on goods and services, X exports, and M imports. The marginal ($=$ average) propensity to consume is c, and the marginal ($=$ average) import content of expenditures (here assumed to be equal for all expenditure categories) is m. The subscripts a and b refer to the two regions. No balance of payments constraint exists, since surplus regions will be willing to hold the balances of deficit regions.[15]

15. For illustrative purposes estimates of the upper limit to the marginal propensity to import out of consumption and other expenditures have been

In applying the model to the above targets, three comparisons would be of interest to the policymaker. Letting dY be the change in income, and dG the change in the government budget, with the subscripts a and b again referring to the regions, these comparisons are:[16]

---

derived. These hypothetical computations refer to a region in which there are only individuals who provide labor services in retail stores or in the service industries. If we assume all consumer expenditures to be made within the region, the estimated income generated locally would be equal to the labor income plus the profits received by the providers of services and the owners of retail establishments. This minimum local share for services is 50.5 per cent of expenditures (27.8 per cent for labor and 22.7 per cent for profits), and for retail purchases it is 14.7 per cent (10.8 per cent for labor and 3.9 per cent for profits). These represent pre-tax income. The service estimates are from U.S. Bureau of the Census, *Census of business: 1958*, vol. VI, part I: *Selected services, area statistics, U.S. summary and Alabama–Mississippi* (1961), pp. 1–5; and U.S. Internal Revenue Service, *Statistics of income 1958–1959: U.S. business tax returns* (1961), pp. 21, 35, 44. The retail estimates are taken from U.S. Bureau of the Census, vol. II, part I: *Retail trade; area statistics, U.S. summary and Alabama–Mississippi*, pp. 1–5; and U.S. Internal Revenue Service, ibid., pp. 20, 34, 44. The ratio of expenditures on these two categories will depend upon the relative distribution of consumer expenditures between goods and services. The average pattern for 1958 was 61 per cent for goods and 39 per cent for services, a pattern in which services are slightly above their decade average. See *Economic report of the President: January 1960*, p. 164. For this pattern the estimated local share is 28.7 per cent of expenditures. For the marginal pattern estimated by Suits (1962) in which the distribution is 86 per cent on goods and 14 per cent on services, the minimum estimate for the local share is 19.7 per cent of expenditures. To the extent that any goods are produced within the region, and that retail and services units have intermediate demands from each other, this ratio would, of course, be higher. The estimates for investment and government expenditures will depend upon the specific expenditure pattern discussed. Estimated on-site wage income for various construction projects ranges from 27 per cent of expenditures for multi-family residential dwellings to 58 per cent of expenditures for highway maintenance. See Strout (1958), for estimates based on the Bureau of Labor Statistics data prepared for the 1947 Input–Output Table. While the actual regional marginal propensity to import will be a weighted average of all expenditures, for simplicity it will be assumed that it will be the same for all expenditures in these multiplier comparisons.

16. For simplicity it is assumed that the relationship between income changes and employment changes is the same in both regions, and that a fixed relationship exists between income changes and employment changes.

$$(1) \quad \frac{\dfrac{dY_a + dY_b}{dG_a}}{\dfrac{dY_a + dY_b}{dG_b}} \qquad (2) \quad \frac{\dfrac{dY_a}{dG_a}}{\dfrac{dY_a}{dG_b}} \quad \text{and} \quad (3) \quad \frac{\dfrac{dY_a}{G_a}}{\dfrac{dY_b}{dG_a}}$$

The first comparison is between the effect on national income of an initial increase in expenditures (due to increased expenditures by the government or those induced by tax changes) in region a with the effect of an increase in b. The assumption, consistent with Target I above, is that the policymaker is interested only in the total increase in national income and not in its regional distribution. Regional differences in parameters are relevant only to the extent that they cause differential increases in total national income. If ratio (1) exceeds 1, the larger increase in national income will occur if expenditures are concentrated in region a. The opposite will occur if ratio (1) is less than 1. If the ratio is equal to 1, policy can be indifferent (with regard to effects on national income) to the region in which expenditures are made.

The second comparison, consistent with Target II above, is directed at achieving an increase in income in region a, with no concern for effects upon the other region. The policymaker here must choose the region in which the expenditure change is to be made to achieve this target. If ratio (2) is greater than 1, income in a will be increased most by an expenditure made in region a. A ratio of less than 1 would mean that it would be more efficient to increase expenditures in b. If the ratio were equal to 1, the same increase in a's income would occur regardless of where the expenditure was made, and the choice could be based upon other criteria, such as the effects upon income in region b. In this comparison, unlike the first, the region is important both in specifying the target and in determining the means by which the target is to be pursued.

The third comparison, which is important in determining the feasibility of the targets listed above under III, gives a measure of the spillover from an expenditure made in region a. The higher ratio (3), the smaller would be the spillover of income increases into region b. A ratio greater than 1 means that over 50 per cent of the income increase has occurred in region a, and a ratio of 1 that the income increase is evenly divided between the two regions. Ratio (3) and the corresponding ratio for expenditures in b, is of particular interest, since it will determine the possibility of the achievement of a target specifying changes in both regions. If all stabilizing expenditures are to be incremental and the existing budget cannot be changed, the policy problem involves the solution of the following pair of simultaneous equations for dG_a and dG_b:

$$\frac{dY_a}{dG_a} dG_a + \frac{dY_a}{dG_b} dG_b = dY_a$$

$$\frac{dY_b}{dG_a} dG_a + \frac{dY_b}{dG_b} dG_b = dY_b,$$

subject to both dG_a and dG_b being greater than, or equal to, zero. In accord with the previous discussion of regional targets, the policymaker is looking for that combination of dG_a and dG_b which meets the goal $dY_b = adY_a$ where the desired income increases are in a fixed ratio. For any value of α this target can be achieved only if:

$$\frac{\dfrac{dY_b}{dG_a}}{\dfrac{dY_a}{dG_a}} \leqslant \alpha \leqslant \frac{\dfrac{dY_b}{dG_b}}{\dfrac{dY_a}{dG_b}}$$

If α is equal to either ratio all expenditures will occur in one region. If α falls within the range given by the two ratios, the target can be achieved by some combination of expenditures in both regions, while if α is outside the range, the target cannot be achieved. In that case either the target must be amended, or greater flexibility in the use of budgetary means must be introduced. These may involve either a shift in expenditures between regions – a shift which still allows higher incomes in both regions than existed in an initial unemployment situation, or, possibly, some combination of taxes and expenditures which could make consistent the achievement of the two targets.[17]

17. This last point would be an argument for the efficiency of equal changes in taxes and expenditures, since taxes would be collected in both regions, while the expenditures are made in only one. Thus a nationally

In solving our model for these ratios, a distinction is drawn between expenditure programs involving imports and programs where the initial outlay is on local products only.

Expenditure programs involving imports

The first ratio. The first ratio is:

$$\frac{\frac{dY}{dG_a}}{\frac{dY}{dG_b}} = \frac{(1 - m_a)\,[1 - c_b\,(1 - m_b)\,] + m_a\,(1 - m_b)}{(1 - m_b)\,[1 - c_a\,(1 - m_a)\,] + m_b\,(1 - m_a)}.$$

The ratio will differ from 1 only if there is a difference in the two regional marginal propensities to consume. If the marginal propensities to consume are the same in both regions, the increase in national income will be the same regardless of where the initial expenditure is made. If they differ, the increase in national income will be the highest if it is made in the region with the higher marginal propensity to consume. In these cases the value of the ratio will be affected by the size of the regional marginal propensities to import. Excluding the possibility of the import propensity in each region being equal to or greater than 1, the extreme values of the ratio will occur when neither region has imports from the other. The greater the regional marginal propensities to import, the smaller will be the effect of differences in regional consumption propensities (the closer the ratio to 1).

This, of course, is the basis of the argument that (in the absence of differences in marginal propensities to consume) government expenditures in areas of labor surplus do not have a different effect upon national income than do expenditures in areas of high employment, since (given this condition) there are no differential effects upon aggregate demand. If there is no presumption that marginal consumption propensities differ with levels of unem-

---

balanced budget increase may not only be expansionary, but could have the effect of shifting income among regions and permitting different income changes in the two regions. While this point is frequently discussed in the context of the redistributional effects of the federal budget, the stabilization potential when there are differences in regional conditions should also be noted.

ployment, and assuming a model with constant wages and prices, the regional pattern of expenditures is a matter of indifference to the policymaker concerned only with effects upon national income and total employment. Once price and wage flexibility in an upward direction is allowed for, however, these conclusions may need to be modified to allow for the effects of differences in the levels of unemployment upon changes in prices as opposed to changes in employment.

The second ratio. The second ratio is:

$$\frac{\dfrac{dY_a}{dG_a}}{\dfrac{dY_a}{dG_b}} = \frac{1 - c_b(1 - m_b)}{m_b}.$$

In order to increase income in a, an expenditure made in a is more efficient than an equal expenditure made in b if $(1 - c_b)(1 - m_b) > 0$. This condition is met unless either c_b or m_b, but not both, is greater than 1. The efficiency of an expenditure in a increases as c_b and m_b are smaller. If c_b is greater than 1, the two regional marginal propensities to consume cannot be equal, or the system will be unstable.[18] If c_b and m_b are less than 1, a given desired increase in Y_a can be most cheaply achieved if expenditures are made directly in a. It is to be noted that the relative efficiencies of the policies do not depend upon any of the parameters in a.

In order to obtain some idea of the sensitivity of this ratio to changes in the parameters, c_b and m_b, the ratio of

$$\frac{\dfrac{dY_a}{dG_a}}{\dfrac{dY_a}{dG_b}}$$

was computed for several hypothetical values:[19]

18. See Schelling (1951). This holds for both marginal propensities to import less than 1.
19. A marginal propensity to consume of 0.7 represents an approximation to the marginal propensity to consume found by Suits. See Suits (1962). The marginal propensity of 0.5 is introduced for purposes of comparison.

	$c_b = 0.7$	$c_b = 0.5$
$m_b =$		
0	∞	∞
0.2	2.20	3.00
0.4	1.45	1.75
0.6	1.20	1.33
0.8	1.08	1.13

In a region having a small amount of induced exports in response to expenditure changes in other regions, it would be necessary to increase expenditures. Even as the level of induced exports rises it remains more efficient to increase expenditures within that region unless the induced exports exceed the initial expenditure.

The third ratio. The 'spillover ratio' is given by:

$$\frac{\dfrac{dY_a}{dG_a}}{\dfrac{dY_b}{dG_a}} = \frac{(1 - m_a)\,[\,1 - c_b(1 - m_b)\,]}{(m_a)\,(1 - m_b)}.$$

This ratio will be higher (the spillover will be less) as m_a and c_b are smaller and as m_b is larger. The ratio is independent of the marginal propensity to consume in a.

In order to see how this ratio varies with the different values of m_a, m_b and c_b calculations were made using several combinations of values for these parameters:

| | $c_b = 0.7$ | | | | | | $c_b = 0.5$ | | | |
	$m_a =$						$m_a =$			
	0	0.2	0.4	0.6	0.8		0	0.2	0.4	0.6	0.8
$m_b =$						$m_b =$					
0	∞	1.20	0.45	0.20	0.08	0	∞	2.00	0.75	0.33	0.13
0.2	∞	2.20	0.83	0.37	0.14	0.2	∞	3.00	1.13	0.50	0.19
0.4	∞	3.87	1.45	0.65	0.24	0.4	∞	4.67	1.75	0.78	0.29
0.6	∞	7.20	2.70	1.20	0.45	0.6	∞	8.00	3.00	1.33	0.50
0.8	∞	17.20	6.45	2.87	1.08	0.8	∞	18.00	6.75	3.00	1.12

It is to be noted that as the openness of both economies increases, the interregional spillover becomes larger, and the restriction placed upon the pursuit of differential regional policies becomes greater. Even if both regions have equal marginal propensities to import, the higher these propensities, the less feasible differential regional policies become.

A related calculation which is of interest is the estimation of the value of region a's propensity to import, which – given the other parameters – is consistent with any distribution of the income increase among regions. If, for example, the target is distribution of income equally between the regions for an expenditure made in a, then m_a must equal

$$\frac{1 - c_b(1 - m_b)}{2 - c_b(1 - m_b) - m_b}.$$

Using the hypothetical values of c_b and m_b, for the various combinations, m_a must equal the following:

	$c_b = 0.7$	$c_b = 0.5$
$m_b =$		
0	0.23	0.33
0.2	0.36	0.43
0.4	0.49	0.54
0.6	0.64	0.67
0.8	0.81	0.82

For values of m_a less than those shown, over 50 per cent of the income increase will be in a. As is obvious, the more a region's induced exports, the greater can be its marginal propensity to import consistent with achieving a given share of the income increase.

Expenditure programs not involving imports

In order to examine the maximum possible efficiency of government expenditures in meeting regional targets, similar comparisons can be made for a different set of government expenditure programs. In the previous comparisons the marginal propensity to import from government expenditures was the same as the import propensity from all other expenditures. As one limiting case, we can analyze an expenditure program so designed that all of the initial expenditure will give rise to income only in the region in which expenditures are made, and where imports will occur only in the second round via induced consumption. Such a program could involve either creation of employment through government hiring of additional labor, or expenditures specifically designed to utilize only locally produced goods and services. While these cases are hypothetical, they permit a comparison with policies in which the import share of the government expenditures does not differ from that of the private consumption sector.

The first ratio. The first ratio is now:

$$\frac{\frac{dY}{dG_a}}{\frac{dY}{dG_b}} = \frac{1 - c_b(1 - m_b) - m_a m_b + (1 - m_b)m_a c_a}{1 - c_a(1 - m_a) - m_a m_b + (1 - m_a)m_b c_b}.$$

This ratio will again differ from 1 only if the marginal propensities to consume in the two regions differ. If $c_a = c_b$ the effect on national income of an expenditure increase in either region would be the same; otherwise the effect would be greatest if the expenditure were made in the region with the larger propensity to consume. In the case of equal consumption propensities, the increases in national income from these 'local-intensive' expenditures will be the same as in the previous case. If they differ, there will be a greater increase in national income from an expenditure in the region with the higher propensity to consume.

The second ratio. The second ratio is now:

$$\frac{\frac{dY_a}{dG_a}}{\frac{dY_a}{dG_b}} = \frac{1 - c_b(1 - m_b) - m_a m_b}{(1 - m_a)m_b c_b}.$$

Unlike the ratio in the case of an expenditure involving imports, this ratio now depends upon the marginal import content of expenditures in a, although not upon its propensity to consume. This ratio will be higher the lower are m_b and c_b and the higher is m_a. It will be greater than 1 if $(1 - c_b)(1 - m_a m_b) > 0$. If m_b and c_b are less than 1 the income increase in a from an expenditure in a is larger, and the income increase in a from an expenditure in b is smaller, than in the previous case. Thus the 'local-intensive' expenditures make it more desirable that expenditures be increased in the region where the income increase is needed. This can be seen by comparing the values of this ratio for hypothetical values c_b, m_b, and m_a, shown below, with those for government expenditures involving imports:

| $c_b = 0.7$ | | | | | $c_b = 0.5$ | | | | |
| $m_a =$ | | | | | $m_a =$ | | | | |
0	0.2	0.4	0.6	0.8	0	0.2	0.4	0.6	0.8
$m_b =$					$m_b =$				
0 ∞	∞	∞	∞	∞	0 ∞	∞	∞	∞	∞
0.2 3.14	3.57	4.29	5.71	10.00	0.2 6.00	7.00	8.67	12.00	22.00
0.4 2.07	2.23	2.50	3.04	4.64	0.4 3.50	3.88	4.50	5.75	9.50
0.6 1.71	1.79	1.90	2.14	2.86	0.6 2.67	2.83	3.11	3.67	5.33
0.8 1.54	1.56	1.61	1.70	1.96	0.8 2.25	2.31	2.42	2.63	3.25

The third ratio. The third ratio is now:

$$\frac{\dfrac{dY_a}{dG_a}}{\dfrac{dY_b}{dG_a}} = \frac{1 - c_b(1 - m_b) - m_a m_b}{(1 - m_b)m_a c_a}.$$

Unlike the previous cases, the comparison now depends upon the marginal propensities to consume in both regions, as well as upon their marginal propensities to import out of expenditures. The ratio will be higher (the spillover less) the smaller are m_a, c_a, and c_b, and the larger is m_b. If m_b and c_b are less than 1, the spillover will be less than from the government expenditure involving imports. As shown by the values of this ratio for hypothetical values of c_a, c_b, n_a, and m_b, the introduction of a 'local-intensive' policy widens the range in which the achievement of desired employment changes in both regions can be attained:

| $c_a = 0.7, c_b = 0.7$ | | | | | $c_a = 0.5, c_b = 0.7$ | | | | |
| $m_a =$ | | | | | $m_a =$ | | | | |
0	0.2	0.4	0.6	0.8	0	0.2	0.4	0.6	0.8
$m_b =$					$m_b =$				
0 ∞	2.14	1.07	0.71	0.54	0 ∞	3.00	1.50	1.00	0.75
0.2 ∞	3.57	1.61	0.95	0.63	0.2 ∞	5.00	2.25	1.33	0.88
0.4 ∞	5.95	2.50	1.35	0.77	0.4 ∞	8.33	3.50	1.89	1.08
0.6 ∞	10.71	4.29	2.14	1.07	0.6 ∞	15.00	6.00	3.00	1.50
0.8 ∞	25.00	9.64	4.52	1.96	0.8 ∞	35.00	13.50	6.33	2.75

$c_a = 0.7, c_b = 0.5$					$c_a = 0.5, c_b = 0.5$				
$m_a =$					$m_a =$				
0	0.2	0.4	0.6	0.8	0	0.2	0.4	0.6	0.8
$m_b =$					$m_b =$				
0 ∞	3.57	1.79	1.19	0.89	0 ∞	5.00	2.50	1.67	1.25
0.2 ∞	5.00	2.32	1.43	0.98	0.2 ∞	7.00	3.25	2.00	1.38
0.4 ∞	7.38	3.21	1.83	1.13	0.4 ∞	10.33	4.50	2.56	1.58
0.6 ∞	12.14	5.00	2.62	1.43	0.6 ∞	17.00	7.00	3.67	2.00
0.8 ∞	26.43	10.36	5.00	2.32	0.8 ∞	37.00	14.50	7.00	3.25

Such policies will also have the effect of raising the level of the marginal propensity to import in a region, consistent with any distribution of income increases among regions. For an equal distribution, m_a must equal $\dfrac{1 - c_b(1 - m_b)}{c_a(1 - m_b) + m_b}$. This value of m_a for hypothetical values of m_b, c_a, and c_b, is shown below:

	$c_b = 0.7,$ $c_a = 0.7$	$c_b = 0.7,$ $c_a = 0.5$	$c_b = 0.5,$ $c_a = 0.7$	$c_b = 0.5,$ $c_a = 0.5$
$m_b =$				
0	0.429	0.600	0.714	1.000
0.2	0.579	0.733	0.789	1.000
0.4	0.707	0.829	0.854	1.000
0.6	0.818	0.900	0.909	1.000
0.8	0.915	0.956	0.957	1.000

It is interesting to note that these magnitudes of m_a makes it probable, for all but the smallest regions, that more than 50 per cent of the national income increase from any 'local-intensive' expenditure program will occur within the region in which the expenditure is made.

Tax and transfer programs

Similar comparisons for regional changes in taxes and transfers will depend upon the parameters previously discussed in the comparisons for government expenditures. While regional tax policies are generally considered difficult to administer and unacceptable on constitutional grounds, such comparisons are still significant, especially since programs may take the more feasible form of differential transfer payments.[20] The specific manner in which such taxes (or transfers, considered as negative taxes) are treated within the model will affect the nature of the comparisons. In the simplest case, that of lump-sum tax changes, the ratios will be similar to those discussed in the case of government expenditures involving imports, except for the introduction of additional terms representing the marginal propensities to consume of the two regions. These propensities, multiplied by the changes in taxes, will produce the initial expenditure arising from tax changes. The remainder of the terms compared will be the same as in the previous cases. If the marginal propensities to consume are the same in both regions, all three ratios will be the same as above.[21] If marginal propensities to consume differ, the first two ratios will be those shown multiplied by a factor (c_a/c_b). The effects of differences in the parameters will increase, as compared with effects in the expenditure cases.

If tax changes are introduced via variations in tax rates rather than lump-sum taxes, then all ratios will depend not only upon the regional parameters, but also upon the income levels in the two regions. For equal incomes, the ratios will be determined by the parameters, as discussed in the preceding paragraph. If incomes are unequal, equal tax rate changes in either region would not provide a valid comparison since they would result in different absolute changes in the government budget. The first two ratios will thus vary with differences in regional income levels. Since the more realistic case entails nationwide tax changes, it suggests that the regional distribution of income changes may be harder to control through tax measures than through government expenditures.

The fiscal responses of lower-level governments

An additional factor which will be important is the effect of federal policies upon the revenues and expenditures of the lower levels

20. For suggestions concerning regionally differentiated unemployment compensation benefits, see Galbraith (1958) p. 301; and Senate Special Committee on Unemployment Problems (1960) pp. 170–1 – the report of the Republican minority.

21. If the marginal propensities to consume are less than 1, while the ratios are the same, the absolute amounts of the income changes will be less than in the expenditure cases.

of government. To the extent that these governments pursue a balanced budget policy, increased income in response to federal policies will, at constant tax rates, permit an increase in their expenditures. As long as the marginal propensities to consume in the private sector are less than 1, these expenditures would provide an additional supporting effect on changes in national income resulting from federal stabilization policies (Somers, 1949). For equal marginal propensities to consume, the gain in national income would then be higher if expenditures were made in the region with the higher tax and expenditure patterns.

If the import content of public (sub-federal) expenditures is the same as that of private expenditures, the second and third ratios will be reduced. Although absolute increases in income would be higher, it would be less important to place the federal expenditure in the region in which the increase is desired, and the regional distribution of the effects of any federal expenditure would be more even. These results would hold also in the case of federal expenditures with zero import content. If the lower-level governments had lower marginal propensities to import than did the private sector, both ratios would be higher, for it becomes more efficient to increase expenditures in the region in which the increase is desired, and the spillover between regions is reduced.

Thus, if the import patterns of the public and private sectors are the same, induced expenditures of lower-level governments increase spillover and reduce the importance of the region where expenditures are initiated. If the public import propensities are lower, spillovers are reduced, and a greater concern with the regional pattern of federal expenditures is needed.

Qualifications

Lags. The policymaker may be interested not only in the distribution of the total income change arising from a given policy change, but also in the time path of these changes within the various regions. Thus, he may desire not only that a greater income increase occur in one region, but also that it occur more rapidly there than in other regions. The use of the undated multipliers in this section precludes any comparisons of this nature, but the introduction of a lag between expenditures and income permits them. If consumption (and induced government or other private expenditures) occurs one period after the receipt of income, then 'the time in which a certain proportion of a straight multiplier effect is realized is shorter than that which is required to realize the same proportion of any cross multiplier effect' (Morishima and Kaneko, 1962). That is, during any moment of time a larger percentage of the final income change will have occurred in the region in which the expenditure was made than in any other. Thus not only will the total regional income increases be greater for an expenditure made within a region, but the increases will also occur more rapidly.

Bottlenecks. The multiplier discussion thus far has been in terms of income and output expansion at constant prices in both regions. But, as already noted, differences in the initial levels of unemployment within regions may cause the expenditure increase to lead to bottlenecks and price rise in one region before these occur in other regions. To the extent both that this leads to increased import demands in the region with price rise and that these demands can be met from production in regions which are still below full capacity output, such regions will enjoy a larger output effect for the given expenditure change. The marginal suppliers in these regions will increase exports in the short run, thus moderating inflationary pressure in the bottleneck region and reducing unemployment in the others.

This is the argument underlying the position that, even in the absence of labor mobility, sufficiently large increases in aggregate demand will eliminate concentrations of unemployment by raising (through internal price increases) the marginal propensity to import in regions which reach full employment. The more similar the range of goods produced in these regions, and the lower the transport costs, the smaller will be the increase in prices required to raise the regional marginal propensity to import. However, if the demand for the output of localized industries is price inelastic, interregional spillover from price increases would be lessened, and some spread between regional price levels would be possible without necessarily leading to more imports from other regions.

If such a situation persists, the longer-run effect of regional differences in unemployment should be to accelerate the movement of capital and labor to the region of higher employment. If labor responded to wage differentials, mobility would narrow cyclical differentials over time. Thus, short-term and long-term effects of changes in the regional terms of trade should occur in a manner which reduces unemployment differentials over time.[22]

If there exist differences in regional industrial structures, the expected effects of price changes upon the compatibility of high employment and price stability could be positive or negative, depending upon the relationship between the patterns of demand change and the respective regional industrial structures. If the region of full employment were to increase its demands for the imports of final and intermediate goods from the other region, the pressure upon prices in the former would be reduced. To the extent that intermediate products could be obtained at constant prices, the possibility of cost-induced price increases would be reduced.

If, however, the production in the region of higher unemployment required imports from the fully employed region, or there existed final demands for products which could not be satisfied within the region, the attempt to increase employment in the former, even with the use of pinpointed regional programs, would be precluded. Any increased demands would bring about higher prices for intermediate inputs and final demand products, thus diluting the employment effects of the increase in expenditures. In this case full employment nationally could not be achieved unless some inflation were tolerated, since the effect of price increases works against full employment in the short run.

22. However, an argument has been made that the short-run effects can outweigh the long-run effects, and maintain differentials. If the creation of employment opportunities due to spillover into regions of high unemployment will deter mobility (since workers respond to wage differentials only if employment is not available where currently located) in the upswing, no readjustment can occur since labor will not move when unemployment exists in all regions. Thus booms which get too large, combined with nationwide recessions, would reduce pressures toward labor mobility. If this is true, the short-run reduction in unemployment in all regions may preclude the longer-run adjustments. See Duesenberry (1962). More empirical information is required, however, before anything definitive can be said concerning the relationship between labor mobility and cyclical stability.

An Input–Output Analysis of Alternative Fiscal Programs

The preceding multiplier analysis suggests possible regional impacts of alternative stabilization measures, but it also raises several questions which require empirical estimation and a consideration of the existing characteristics of regional industrial structures. Unfortunately, the information necessary for empirical evaluation of the regional effects of alternative stabilization measures is not readily available. A complete study would require input–output tables for each region (however defined) which allow for imports from other regions as well as for the effects of demand increases in other regions upon each region in question. Besides the customary information on technological production coefficients for each industry, such a study would require data on trade flows among regions for each industry.[23] This information would be necessary for the construction of a series of regional–output tables suitable for the present discussion. Since it is not readily available, an existing interregional input–output table has been used instead for illustrative purposes. This table is conceptually useful, but it is somwhat imperfect for present purposes, owing to its over-aggregation on both the regional and industrial levels (Moses, 1955). Nevertheless, calculations obtained from this table provide some measure of the orders of magnitudes involved.

Procedure

The Moses input–output table divides the nation into three regions: the New England, Middle Atlantic, and South Atlantic census regions are region I, the Pacific and Mountain states are region III, and the remaining states are region II. There are ten industries, and an endogenous household sector. The table allows for interregional trade, and has built a pattern of trade transactions into the matrix of production for each region. This permits the computation of the regional distribution of income changes resulting from an expenditure in any one region. Given the recent geographic distribution of unemployment, the regional breakdown of the table is not especially useful for contrasting actual

23. For discussions of interregional and regional input–output techniques, see Isard and others (1960), pp. 309–74, and Meyer (1963).

with hypothetical policies, but it shows the importance of considering the regional factor in the design of stabilization policies.

The assumptions underlying input–output analysis, and more particularly, those underlying interregional input–output analysis, make caution necessary when these analyses are applied to problems of stabilization policy. These assumptions – perfect elasticity of supply in all industries, fixed production coefficients implying proportionality between labor income and product output, constant prices, and unchanging trade patterns – quite obviously reduce the strength of the particular conclusions obtained. This is even truer in the present case, because it includes an endogenous household sector with an average pattern of consumption expenditures, rather than the marginal pattern which would be desirable in a discussion of stabilization policy.[24] All of these difficulties could no doubt be eliminated, given sufficient data, and the resultant more refined measures would permit more nearly accurate quantitative solutions to the problem. But such refinements would almost certainly not alter the qualitative nature of the present findings.

The trade coefficients in the interregional table are low, thus unevenness in the regional distribution of the policy-induced income changes is to be expected (Moses, 1955, p. 818, Table VI). Only eight of the sixty-six coefficients are above 0.2. These were in the following industries: agriculture, animal and products, forest products, manufactures, and petroleum and gas. For six of these, region II was the exporter. The trade coefficients in the electric power, transportation and communications, trade and finance, and service sectors were all zero, or very close to zero, which accords with what the definition of local industries would suggest. Another point of interest is the falling off of the trade coefficients with distance, the east and west having less direct trade with each other than each has with region II.

Computations of the income changes and their regional distributions were made for several alterntive policy measures. The fiscal policy measures considered were personal tax reductions and various expenditure programs of federal, state, and local governments which are frequently suggested as useful for contra-

24. The average propensity to consume for the household sector (net of foreign transactions) is approximately 0.7. See Appendix B, page 331.

cyclical purposes. For comparative purposes, several private construction projects which could be affected by monetary policy were included, as was a projected increase in the demand for manufactures. The method used in estimating the effects of various measures was to introduce the expenditure increase in each of the three regions separately, and then to compare the three results. This simplifies matters even though it does not reflect a very realistic set of expenditure measures.[25]

Results

Table 7 shows the increases in household income arising from an additional $1,000 expenditure of various types and from a $1,000 reduction in personal income taxes.[26] Essentially this table demonstrates the relationship between the region in which an expenditure is made and the regional distribution of the income changes to which these expenditures give rise. In all cases except manufacturing, the percentage of the income increase occurring in the region in which the expenditure was made is above 60 per cent of the total increase for the nation. Because of the importance of on-site construction employment, the expenditures considered appear to have greater local effects than does the tax reduction. Similarly, the spillover from increasing expenditures in manufacturing appears to be greater than that from the construction expenditures considered. The differences in spillover from the alternative construction expenditure programs appear small, and the orders of magnitude of the results are similar. This result is in accord with the values estimated from the ratios of the second section, above, for low values of the marginal propensities to

25. More realistically, the pattern for government expenditures would depend upon the nature of the initial expenditures, or upon the pattern in which grants to sub-federal governments are allocated, while the distribution of changes in disposable income from tax reductions (or transfer payment increases) would depend upon the levels of personal income (or the method of distributing the transfers). To determine the regional responses to changes in monetary policy it would be necessary to evaluate the regional effects of the policy change upon investment in the several regions. For any regional pattern of expenditure changes, the total effects would be the weighted average of the regional distributions shown by treating expenditures in each individual region separately.

26. See Appendix B, page 331, for a description of the methods employed in making these computations.

Table 7

Increases in Income and Their Distribution by Regions,
Alternative Stabilization Measures

Stabilization measure	Region I	Region II	Region III	Total
I. Type of private expenditure increase ($1,000)				
a. All residential construction, initial increase in expenditures in:				
I	$1,215.37	$488.40	$91.32	$1,795.09
	(67.7)[1]	(27.2)	(5.1)	
II	295.98	1,426.97	135.27	1,858.22
	(15.9)	(76.8)	(7.3)	
III	177.38	456.71	1,211.45	1,845.54
	(9.6)	(24.7)	(65.6)	
b. Industrial construction, initial increase in expenditures in:				
I	1,237.44	521.02	84.23	1,842.69
	(67.2)	(28.3)	(4.6)	
II	325.32	1,461.59	121.34	1,908.25
	(17.0)	(76.6)	(6.4)	
III	196.78	497.65	1,189.02	1,883.45
	(10.4)	(26.4)	(63.1)	
c. Manufacturing, initial increase in expenditures in:				
I	1,044.41	695.47	105.41	1,845.29
	(56.6)	(37.7)	(5.7)	
II	461.70	1,327.35	145.47	1,934.52
	(23.9)	(68.6)	(7.5)	
III	287.41	689.88	918.57	1,895.86
	(15.2)	(36.4)	(48.5)	

Stabilization measure	Region I	Region II	Region III	Total

II. Type of Government expenditure increase ($1,000)

a. Educational, hospital and institutional construction, initial increase in expenditures in:

	Region I	Region II	Region III	Total
I	1,247.55	525.16	84.72	1,857.43
	(67.2)	*(28.3)*	*(4.6)*	
II	327.89	1,473.64	122.08	1,923.61
	(17.1)	*(76.6)*	*(6.4)*	
III	198.12	500.78	1,195.38	1,894.28
	(10.5)	*(26.4)*	*(63.1)*	

b. Army corps of engineer projects, initial increase in expenditures in:

	Region I	Region II	Region III	Total
I	1,336.40	459.83	75.23	1,871.46
	(71.4)	*(24.6)*	*(4.0)*	
II	282.08	1,530.66	110.76	1,923.50
	(14.7)	*(79.6)*	*(5.8)*	
III	160.99	422.65	1,331.37	1,915.01
	(8.4)	*(22.1)*	*(69.5)*	

All new highway construction, initial increase in expenditures in:

	Region I	Region II	Region III	Total
I	1,264.32	442.28	70.68	1,777.28
	(71.1)	*(24.9)*	*(4.0)*	
II	272.80	1,450.41	104.30	1,827.51
	(14.9)	*(79.4)*	*(5.7)*	
III	155.70	407.94	1,253.44	1,817.08
	(8.6)	*(22.5)*	*(69.0)*	

Table 7 *Continued*

Stabilization measure	Region I	Region II	Region III	Total
d. All highway maintenance, initial increase in expenditures in:				
I	1,461.39	438.68	70.66	1,970.73
	(74.2)	*(22.3)*	*(3.6)*	
II	260.38	1,657.28	104.41	2,022.07
	(12.9)	*(82.0)*	*(5.2)*	
III	149.91	401.32	1,455.56	2,006.79
	(7.5)	*(20.0)*	*(72.5)*	
III. Tax reduction Tax reduction of $1,000 in:				
I	838.49	436.20	71.12	1,345.81
	(62.3)	*(32.4)*	*(5.3)*	
II	239.09	1,057.28	103.94	1,400.31
	(17.1)	*(75.5)*	*(7.4)*	
III	142.14	395.01	837.80	1,374.95
	(10.3)	*(28.7)*	*(60.9)*	
(National)[2]	468.85	693.36	211.57	1,373.78
	(34.1)	*(50.5)*	*(15.4)*	

Source: See text and Appendix B page 331.

Note: Regions are defined on page 319. Percentages may not add to 100.0 because of rounding.

1. The numbers in parentheses refer to percentages of the national income increase resulting from each expenditure increase or tax reduction.

2. 41 per cent in I, 42.5 per cent in II, and 16.5 per cent in III. See Appendix B.

import in two regions. Thus Table 7 again demonstrates the importance of pinpointing stabilization measures when the regional pattern of income increases is a policy target. The advantages of such a policy are made clear when the income increases in any region from internally made expenditures are compared with the increases resulting from expenditures in other regions (ratio 2). Also to be noted is the fall-off of the increase in income as the distance from the source of the initial expenditure increases.

In summary, the calculations based on the interregional input–output table emphasize the regional concentration of a large proportion of income increases in the region in which expenditure is made (ratio 3). While political and administrative problems may make it difficult to apply regionally-oriented stabilization policy in a flexible fashion selectivity clearly increases the efficiency of stabilization policy in the achievement of specific targets.

Conclusion: Regional Orientation with Central Responsibility

The major conclusions of this essay have been that employment fluctuations vary regionally, and that regionally pinpointed stabilization measures increase the efficiency of stabilization policy. But this emphasis on regional aspects does not imply as a corollary that the responsibility for stabilization should be left to regional governments. Federally directed policy is called for because the origins of differential rates of regional unemployment are largely national in character, as are effective solutions to problems of regional unemployment. Moreover, financial constraints and the possibilities of interstate mobility of individuals and businesses place major limitations on any contracyclical policies of subfederal governments. While these governments have an important role in influencing the industrial structures of their jurisdictions in such a way as to reduce cyclical problems in the longer run, they are in an inferior position to promote policies which affect unemployment in the short run.

Interdependence among regions in the national economy is an important factor in accounting for the unemployment of a state, and forces outside the political boundaries of a state have a major influence upon the magnitude of its internal movements. Because of the spillover of demand, an attempt by any one state in isolation to reduce its own unemployment may lead to unpaid-for benefits in other states, while attempts by all the states acting independently may lead to an excessive increase in demand from the national point of view. Thus, as long as stabilization measures are left to particular states, there can be no expectation of an optimal national policy, for there may be either smaller or larger changes in demand than would be considered desirable.[27] In the contemporary situation, given both financial constraints and interstate strategy, the presumption that stabilization measures will be in-

27. See Tinbergen (1956), pp. 172–8, for a discussion of the implications of centralized vs. decentralized policy administration.

sufficient if they are left to lower-level governments appears most reasonable.

Nevertheless, the fact that the federal government is the most efficient unit for undertaking stabilization measures and for bearing their costs does not eliminate a concern with regional factors, nor does it follow that state (and local) governments have no role to play in stabilization policy. Indeed, through proper inter-level cooperation, a more efficient regional orientation can be secured than would be possible by reliance on purely federal policies, such as the letting of contracts on the basis of regional criteria (as distinguished from cost alone), the use of regionally selected public works programs, or regionally oriented variation in excise tax rates. State and local governments can function as administrative and planning units in the implementation of federally financed policies. Perhaps the most efficient policy would establish federal grants to state (or local) governments yet leave these governments considerable discretion in the choice of specific programs.[28]

28. See Dahl, and Lindblom (1953), for a more detailed discussion of the desirability and usefulness of this inter-governmental division of labor in stabilization policy.

Appendix A: **Tables**

This appendix contains three tables which, with Tables 3 and 4 in the text, were used to compute the rank correlations presented in Tables 5 and 6. All three appendix tables were computed from state employment data compiled by the Bureau of Labor Statistics.

Table 8

Ratios of Growth, by States, 1949–58

State	Growth By Cycle Bases[1]		Peak to Peak[2]	
Alabama	(17)	110.03	(19)	119.87
Arizona	(3)	134.55	(1)	174.69
Arkansas	(35)	105.02	(36)	113.47
California	(5)	119.77	(5)	141.68
Colorado	(6)	115.64	(6)	136.79
Connecticut	(23.5)	107.77	(24)	117.26[3]
Delaware	(7)	114.46	(7)	135.75[3]
District of Columbia	(47)	98.29	(45)	106.30
Florida	(1)	135.09	(2)	174.61
Georgia	(12)	111.64	(12)	127.51[3]
Idaho	(33)	105.91	(21)	117.82
Illinois	(36)	105.00	(41)	109.88[3]
Indiana	(39)	104.33	(29)	116.31[3]
Iowa	(43)	103.39	(39)	110.23[3]
Kansas	(23.5)	107.77	(13)	126.65[3]
Kentucky	(29)	106.52	(25)	117.13
Louisiana	(9)	113.41	(10)	129.83
Maine	(44)	102.73	(46)	105.48[3]
Maryland	(13)	111.45	(14)	126.59
Massachusetts	(45)	102.17	(43)	106.68[3]
Michigan	(34)	105.05	(28)	116.43[3]
Minnesota	(25)	107.46	(30)	116.09
Mississippi	(16)	110.42	(17)	122.39[3]
Missouri	(40)	104.17	(37)	113.43[3]
Montana	(18)	108.29	(27)	116.67
Nebraska	(31)	105.97	(32)	115.31[3]
Nevada	(2)	134.88	(3)	166.10
New Hampshire	(32)	105.95	(42)	108.46
New Jersey	(21)	108.03	(20)	118.18
New Mexico	(4)	119.85	(4)	156.71
New York	(38)	104.52	(40)	109.93
North Carolina	(14)	110.63	(16)	123.64
North Dakota	(27)	106.67	(22)	117.67
Ohio	(26)	106.91	(31)	116.05
Oklahoma	(15)	110.50	(15)	124.40[3]
Oregon	(37)	104.95	(35)	113.51[3]
Pennsylvania	(46)	100.17	(47)	103.26
Rhode Island	(48)	96.45	(48)	99.09[3]
South Carolina	(28)	106.53	(18)	120.28
South Dakota	(22)	107.81	(33)	115.15[3]
Tennessee	(19)	108.23	(26)	117.07[3]
Texas	(8)	113.69	(8)	134.21
Utah	(10)	112.51	(9)	130.72
Vermont	(42)	103.52	(44)	106.40[3]
Virginia	(11)	111.89	(11)	127.96
Washington	(20)	108.11	(23)	117.63
West Virginia	(49)	94.70	(49)	92.83
Wisconsin	(30)	106.23	(34)	113.85
Wyoming	(41)	103.82	(38)	111.46
National[4]		107.80		117.36
National[5]		107.78		117.75

Source: Bureau of Labor Statistics.
Note: Numbers in parentheses indicate rank.
1. Ratio of 1954–8 Cycle Base to 1949–54 Cycle Base.
2. Ratio of 1956 or 1957 peak to 1948 peak.
3. 1956 peak.
4. National total given by the Bureau of Labor Statistics.
5. Total of state figures.

Table 9

Percentage of Manufacturing and Mining Employment to Total Employment, by States, 1953 and 1956

State	1953		1956	
Alabama	(18)	37.24	(19)	35.41
Arizona	(39)	20.21	(39)	21.02
Arkansas	(29)	28.41	(27)	29.47
California	(30)	28.32	(28)	28.53
Colorado	(41)	19.53	(41)	18.94
Connecticut	(1)	52.09	(1)	47.88
Delaware	(11)	43.75	(14)	39.08
District of Columbia	(49)	3.42	(49)	3.21
Florida	(45)	15.50	(45)	14.95
Georgia	(20)	35.60	(20)	35.08
Idaho	(38)	21.16	(37)	22.04
Illinois	(17)	39.82	(17)	37.78
Indiana	(3)	48.00	(4)	44.01
Iowa	(32)	27.76	(31)	26.55
Kansas	(28)	28.62	(33)	25.72
Kentucky	(23)	33.34	(21)	33.77
Louisiana	(33)	27.71	(34)	25.65
Maine	(14)	41.79	(13)	39.61
Maryland	(22)	33.69	(23)	31.58
Massachusetts	(15)	40.68	(15)	38.50
Michigan	(2)	50.49	(3)	45.03
Minnesota	(31)	28.25	(32)	26.53
Mississippi	(27)	29.77	(25)	30.45
Missouri	(24)	32.91	(24)	30.68
Montana	(42)	19.39	(40)	20.16
Nebraska	(43)	17.98	(44)	17.01
Nevada	(46)	12.99	(46)	12.79
New Hampshire	(5)	46.99	(2)	45.37
New Jersey	(8)	45.99	(10)	42.87
New Mexico	(44)	17.69	(42)	18.68
New York	(21)	34.14	(22)	31.93
North Carolina	(10)	44.80	(6)	43.70
North Dakota	(48)	7.54	(48)	7.25
Ohio	(6)	46.53	(5)	43.82
Oklahoma	(36)	24.71	(35.5)	25.04
Oregon	(25)	31.06	(26)	29.88
Pennsylvania	(9)	45.51	(11)	42.23
Rhode Island	(4)	47.98	(8)	43.37
South Carolina	(13)	42.61	(7)	43.55
South Dakota	(47)	11.98	(47)	11.30
Tennessee	(19)	36.09	(18)	35.98
Texas	(35)	25.07	(35.5)	25.04
Utah	(37)	21.25	(38)	21.72
Vermont	(16)	40.25	(16)	38.17
Virginia	(26)	30.50	(29)	28.46
Washington	(34)	26.98	(30)	27.21
West Virginia	(7)	46.19	(9)	43.08
Wisconsin	(12)	43.56	(12)	40.85
Wyoming	(40)	19.54	(43)	17.54
National		36.41		34.21

Source: Bureau of Labor Statistics.

Note: Numbers in parentheses indicate rank.

Table 10

Percentage of Durable Manufacturing Employment
to Total Employment, by States, 1953 and 1956

State	1953		1956	
Alabama	(14)	17.88	(17)	16.57
Arizona	(33)	9.98	(33)	10.59
Arkansas	(22)	14.43	(19)	14.93
California	(13)	17.89	(13)	18.53
Colorado	(38)	7.40	(39)	7.40
Connecticut	(2)	38.91	(2)	35.93
Delaware	(25)	13.81	(29)	11.83
District of Columbia	(49)	0.20	(49)	0.18
Florida	(43)	6.22	(43)	6.01
Georgia	(30)	11.39	(30)	11.64
Idaho	(32)	10.91	(31)	11.50
Illinois	(6)	25.73	(6)	24.65
Indiana	(3)	36.32	(3)	32.90
Iowa	(23)	14.08	(25)	13.17
Kansas	(21)	14.82	(23)	13.30
Kentucky	(29)	12.61	(21)	14.05
Louisiana	(36)	8.99	(40)	7.05
Maine	(28)	13.03	(28)	12.54
Maryland	(12)	19.56	(12)	18.70
Massachusetts	(16)	17.70	(16)	16.78
Michigan	(1)	42.28	(1)	36.80
Minnesota	(24)	13.99	(26)	12.88
Mississippi	(26)	13.16	(27)	12.79
Missouri	(19)	15.91	(20)	14.10
Montana	(40)	6.87	(38)	8.16
Nebraska	(42)	6.46	(44)·	5.14
Nevada	(45)	3.07	(45)	2.71
New Hampshire	(18)	16.55	(15)	17.32
New Jersey	(7)	25.50	(7)	23.68
New Mexico	(44)	5.73	(41)	6.62
New York	(20)	15.09	(22)	13.97
North Carolina	(31)	11.08	(32)	11.42
North Dakota	(48)	0.98	(48)	0.94
Ohio	(4)	33.86	(4)	31.63
Oklahoma	(37)	8.39	(36)	8.91
Oregon	(11)	22.69	(10)	21.78
Pennsylvania	(8)	25.45	(8)	23.66
Rhode Island	(10)	23.21	(11)	21.48
South Carolina	(41)	6.57	(42)	6.28
South Dakota	(46)	2.40	(46)	1.93
Tennessee	(27)	13.08	(24)	13.23
Texas	(35)	9.38	(35)	9.48
Utah	(39)	6.93	(37)	8.25
Vermont	(9)	25.39	(9)	23.28
Virginia	(34)	9.84	(34)	9.68
Washington	(15)	17.85	(14)	18.21
West Virginia	(17)	16.66	(18)	16.00
Wisconsin	(5)	27.61	(5)	26.06
Wyoming	(47)	1.49	(47)	1.59
National		20.34		19.00

Source: Bureau of Labor Statistics.
Note: Numbers in parentheses indicate rank.

Appendix B: Data and Methods Used in the Input–Output Analysis

This appendix is a discussion of the data and methods used in the input–output analysis. The source of the construction estimates was the study prepared by the Bureau of Labor Statistics for use in the 1947 input–output study – *New and Maintenance Construction: Construction in the 1947 Inter-Industry Study* (August 1952). The estimates for the bill-of-goods for manufacturing expenditures and for tax reductions are discussed below. The domestic propensities to consume for regions I, II, and III are approximately 0.704, 0.714, and 0.710, respectively. Because of imports from abroad, the increases in national income for expenditures differ among the regions but the differences are minor.

Construction expenditures

The construction cost data on bills-of-goods for various construction projects were prepared on the basis of the four-digit S.I.C. classifications. The information necessary to allocate these bills-of-goods in a manner consistent with the ten-industry breakdown used in the input–output table was obtain at the Harvard Economic Research Project. Certain items of expenditures were omitted in deriving the bills-of-goods, either because of difficulties in assigning the location of recipients or of applying a consumption pattern to these expenditures, and they are omitted from the measures of the increases in national income. They are: pensions, profits after tax, interest paid, depreciation, travel expenses, and all federal, state, and local taxes.

Since data for the construction projects (except for all residential construction) are given at purchasers' cost it was necessary to divide this amount into producers' value and margin (the share going to the trade and the transportation and communication sectors). This division (except for all residential construction) was made by use of the separate margins for each industry derived from the relationship between producers' value and purchasers' value for all new construction for all projects except highway maintenance, for which the relationship for all maintenance construction was used. The margins on materials were 23.6 and 28.6 per cent, respectively. The margin was then divided between the

331

trade and transportation sectors in accordance with the ratio for all new or all maintenance construction. Half of transportation was allocated in the region of expenditure and half in the region of production. Each bill was then distributed among the regions on the basis of the trade coefficients presented by Moses (1955), p. 818, Table VI. Because of the manner in which the household sector is treated, it was necessary to compute a set of final demands for the initial wage-earners on the project. This was done by multiplying wage payments by the consumption pattern shown in the matrix. The bills-of-goods applied were therefore the initial demands from each industrial sector, except households, plus the final demands from the initial incomes of the on-site construction workers.

Since the important question was the effect on household incomes, not output by industries, it was necessary to multiply the increases in output for each industry by its household income coefficient in the production matrix. These totals were then added to the initial labor income to obtain the total household income arising from each project.

Manufacturing expenditures

To approximate the manner in which the construction estimates were made, the $1,000 expenditure increase was divided between increased demand at producers' value and the margin components, in the same ratio as manufacturers purchased in all new construction. The bill was then distributed among regions in accord with the trade coefficients in Moses (1955).

Tax reduction

The final bill of goods introduced was taken from the average household consumption pattern for each region, which is distributed regionally within the matrix. The bill-of-goods for the national tax reduction was based upon the distribution of personal income by states in 1958: 41 per cent in region I, 42.5 per cent in II, and 16.5 per cent in region III. Graham (1959).

References

BORTS, G. H. (March 1960) 'Regional cycles of manufacturing employment in the United States, 1914–1953', *Journal of the American Statistical Association*, vol. 55, pp. 151–211. Reprinted as *National Bureau of Economic Research Occasional Paper*, 73 (1960).

BRECHER, I., and REISHMAN, S. S. (1957) *Canada–United States economic relations*, pp. 69–71, Royal Commission on Canada's Economic Prospects.

DAHL, R. A., and LINDBLOM, C. E. (1953) 'Variations in public expenditure', in M. F. Millikan (ed.), *Income stabilization for a developing democracy*, pp. 347–96, Yale University Press.

DUESENBERRY, J. S. (1962) 'The co-ordination of policies for full employment and price stability', in D. C. Hague (ed.), *Inflation*, pp. 129–46, Macmillan.

ENGERMAN, S. (1962) *Postwar regional cycles and their implications for fiscal policy* (Dissertation: University of Rochester, Johns Hopkins).

GALBRAITH, J. K. (1958) *The Affluent Society*, Houghton Mifflin, p. 301.

GRAHAM, R. E. (August 1959) 'Regional markets in 1958', *Survey of current business*, vol. 39, pp. 9–24.

HANNA, F. (1959) *State income differentials*, 1919–1954, ch. 3, Duke University Press.

HOOVER, E. M. (1948) *The location of economic activity*, p. 287, McGraw-Hill.

ISARD, W. (1957) 'The value of the regional approach in economic analysis', *Regional income: Studies in income and wealth*, vol. 21, pp. 69–78, Princeton University Press.

ISARD, W., and OTHERS (1960) *Methods of regional analysis: an introduction to regional science*, Technology Press of MIT and Wiley.

KREININ, M. E. (August 1959) 'Use of the excise tax as a counter-cyclical measure', *Review of economics and statistics*, vol. 41, pp. 319–20.

LEE, E. S., and OTHERS (1957) *Population redistribution and economic growth, United States, 1870–1950*, vol. 1, *Methodological considerations and reference tables*, pp. 623–31, American Philosophical Association.

LICHTENBERG, R. M. (1960) *One-tenth of a nation*, pp. 21–24, apps. B and G, Harvard University Press.

MEYER, J. R. (March 1963) 'Regional economics: a survey', *American Economic Review*, vol. 53, pp. 19–54, esp. pp. 32–6.

MORISHIMA, M., and KANEKO, Y. (October 1962) 'On the speed of establishing multi-sector equilibrium', *Econometrica*, vol. 30, pp. 818–22.

MOSES, L. N. (December 1955) 'The stability of interregional trading patterns and input–output analysis', *American Economic Review*, vol. 45, pp. 803–32.

MOSES, L. N. (November 1960) 'A general equilibrium model of production, interregional trade and location of industry', *Review of Economics and Statistics*, vol. 42, pp. 373–97.

SCHELLING, T. C. (1951) *National income behaviour*, p. 202, McGraw-Hill.

SCHULTZE, C. L. (1959) *Recent inflation in the United States*, Study Paper 1, Joint Economic Committee, 86 Cong. 1 sess. (1959).

SENATE SPECIAL COMMITTEE ON UNEMPLOYMENT PROBLEMS (1960) *Report of the Special Committee on Unemployment Problems*, 86 Cong. 2 sess., pp. 170–71.

SOMERS, H. M. (May 1949) 'The multiplier in a trifiscal economy', *Quarterly Journal of Economics*, vol. 63, pp. 258–72.

STROUT, A. M. (November 1958) 'Primary employment effects of alternative spendings programs', *Review of Economics and Statistics*, vol. 40, pp. 319–28.

SUITS, D. B. (March 1962) 'Forecasting and analysis with an econometric model', *American Economic Review*, vol. 52, pp. 104–32.

TINBERGEN, J. (1956) *Economic policy: principles and design*, North Holland Publishing Co.

U.S. BUREAU OF LABOR STATISTICS (1960) *The structure of unemployment in areas of substantial labor surplus*, Study Paper 23, Joint Economic Committee, 86 Cong. 2 sess., p. 25.

U.S. BUREAU OF LABOR STATISTICS (1961) *Employment and earnings statistics for the United States, 1909–1960*.

U.S. DEPARTMENT OF COMMERCE (1956) *Personal income by states since 1929*, pp. 146–203.

VINING, R. (July 1945) 'Regional variation in cyclical fluctuation viewed as a frequency distribution', *Econometrica*, vol. 13, pp. 182–213.

VINING, R. (January 1946) 'Location of industry and regional patterns of business cycle behavior', *Econometrica*, vol. 14, pp. 37–68.

VINING, R. (July 1946) 'The region as a concept in business cycle analysis', *Econometrica*, vol. 14, pp. 201–18.

VINING, R. (March 1953) 'Delimitation of economic areas: statistical conceptions in the study of spatial structure of an economic system', *Journal of the American Statistical Association*, vol. 48, pp. 44–64.

Part Five **Location Theory**

The formal part of the normative theory of the location of firms is simple. Given the objective function of the firm – say, for simplicity, that it is a function only of profits, then *if* the firm can forecast how its profits will vary with different locations, the choice of the profit-maximizing location is straightforward. The problem is one of maximization subject to constraints and is conveniently handled using programming techniques. The major difficulty in practice is in forecasting, in any particular instance, how profits are likely to be affected by different locations, and on this, very little that is generally applicable can be said.

Alonso, in his non-mathematical introduction to the subject does touch on some of the informal aspects of location theory, but the greater part of his paper is concerned with how transport costs may vary with location.

10 W. Alonso

Location Theory

W. Alonso, 'Location theory', in J. Friedmann, and W. Alonso (eds.), *Regional development and planning: a reader*, M.I.T. Press, 1964, pp. 78–106.

Introduction

This article tries to acquaint the reader with the theory of the location of the firm. The formal theory originated in the work of Alfred Weber and, through the contributions of later writers, developed rapidly until the 1950s, when further additions to its elegant structure seemed to bring increasing costs in terms of complexity of form and decreasing marginal returns in terms of new insights. At this time Walter Isard demonstrated its unity with the classical economics of substitution analysis, and an awareness developed of other problems of location and regions beyond the scope of this theory. Consequently scholars have turned elsewhere, and significant contributions to location theory have become rare.

In these pages are presented some of the principal insights of this branch of economic theory as it stands today. The first part of the article tries to synthesize the work of many scholars. To trace the intellectual ancestry of the various parts would be a laborious exercise; rather, a brief bibliographic note has been appended pointing to seminal and representative works. The second part seeks to clarify some of the deficiencies and limitations of this type of theory, and in doing this it points to some areas where further work would be fruitful. In particular, the theory of market areas seems to be the key to future developments. It was, in a sense, the culmination of the theory of the firm. But it was also the beginning of the theory of August Lösch, as represented by his article in this volume [Friedmann and Alonso (1964)], and, in the form of central place theory, it constitutes the principal tool for understanding the empirical regularities that concern Brian Berry, among others. The theory of market areas is implicit too in the modern theories of regional development such as Perroux's growth poles. Thus, in a way as yet unrealized, it may be said to be the fulcrum on which turn the various spokes of the under-standing of regional structure and development.

The theory of the location of the firm has been developed in the context of a free market. In recent years, however, concern has turned to national regional development. Increasingly the ques-tion of the location of a factory is being considered as a 'project' by a government agency rather than as a profit-making venture by a private corporation. It is clear that, as long as the decision turns on the project maximizing its own returns, there is little difference whether those making the decision serve a public or a private body. But the theory has little force in considering the costs and benefits accruing outside the books of the particular enterprise. Regional economics is concerned with these external or multiplicative effects within the region, and national regional planning with these effects among regions. In this sense, the theory of the location of the firm extends to project planning but ante-cedes regional and national spatial planning.

Because of the variety of backgrounds of those interested in regional development, and at the risk of irritating the knowledge-able, I have explained the technical terms in this article. Moreover to avoid awkwardness of language, I have based most of the analysis on the businessman as protagonist rather than the pro-ject planner.

In essence, the firm wishes to maximize its profits. If the busi-nessman can state clearly what factors are involved and what relations bind them, his problem is one of manipulating these variables to get the largest profits. In reality these variables are many, and some cannot be quantified. Here we shall begin with very simple problems, paring the problem down to a few essentials, and introducing complications gradually to make the theory more realistic; but some considerations will remain outside the formal theory. We shall call attention to some of these, but they are po-tentially infinite. For instance, a study of the New England region found a manufacturing firm in Worcester which would clearly have been better off in Boston. The reason for its location, it was discovered, was that the manufacturer's mother-in-law lived in Worcester, and his wife insisted on living in the same city. No amount of formal theory would have unearthed this reason, but formal theory could tell the manufacturer how much this cost him.

The Principle of Median Location

Let us begin by considering the location of a firm which, let us say, makes and delivers bakery products. Neither the cost of making these products nor the volume of business will vary with the location of the firm. The only variable in this case is the delivery costs, so that maximizing profits is identical with minimizing delivery costs. The customers, $A, B, \ldots, G$, each take one delivery a day, and are distributed along a road as shown in Figure 1. The bakery sends out a boy who can carry only one customer's order at a

blocks

Figure 1   Distribution of the bakery's customers

time, so that he has to make one trip per customer. Where then to locate the bakery to minimize the boy's trips? The almost automatic answer would be the 'average', center of gravity, or mean location. This is easily found by summing the distances from either end and dividing by the number of customers. In this case, summing from A, it would be $0 + 1 + 2 + 4 + 6 + 14 + 15 = 42$; dividing by the number of customers or trips (7), the mean is 6 blocks to the right of A, at the same location as E. *But this is the wrong solution.* Examine Table 1. The total distance is less if the bakery locates at D than if it locates at E. If we had gone about the problem in a systematic fashion, we should have asked: Which location minimizes the sum of the distances from the bakery to its customers? This can readily be solved by elementary calculus. In fact, however, we might have recognized that the point on a distribution along a line at which the total distance to all other points is minimized is the median (that is to say, the point at which there are as many points to one side as to the other). The median in this case is D. The mean or center of gravity, on the other hand, minimizes the sum of the squares of the distances, and therefore is irrelevant for our purposes.

Table 1

Total Trips According to Location of the Bakery at E or D in Figure 1

Customer	Distance from location at E	Distance from location at D
A	6	4
B	5	3
C	4	2
D	2	0
E	0	2
F	8	10
G	9	11
Total distance	34	32

This simple example is a very enlightening one. We would not often meet a bakery in these precise conditions, but the logic often applies to other enterprises. For instance, a factory which has shipping costs proportional to the weight of the shipments and the distance shipped would benefit from locating at the median location unless there were strong reasons to the contrary. Thus, a firm selling 200 units in one city, 300 in a second, and 550 in a third would have its median location in the third city. Since the median of the distribution of customers will tend to be in large cities, this is one of the reasons why big cities tend to grow bigger.

Competition Along a Line

It is a truism that what may be good for someone may be disadvantageous for another, but this is often forgotten. It is important, therefore, to make clear whose point of view we are considering when we say that a location is optimal.

Imagine a long beach, with people evenly distributed along its length. Each person on the beach buys one ice-cream cone, and will walk as far as necessary to get it, though he will naturally prefer to walk the shortest possible distance. If there is a single vendor of ice-cream, he will not care where he locates since every customer on the beach will walk as far as necessary to buy his cone. Every customer, however, would prefer to minimize his walk by having the vendor as near to him as possible. A third point of view might be that of a public official who wants to minimize the total amount of walking for the general benefit. As shown in our first example, this total will be minimized at the median location, in this case the midpoint of the beach.

Consider now the same problem with two vendors, A and B, who are at two locations as in the first stage of Figure 2. Vendor A will sell to all the customers to his left, and Vendor B to all those to his own right; of the customers between the two, the left half

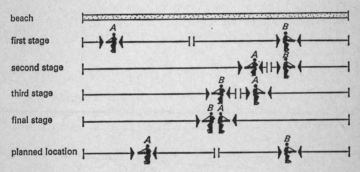

Figure 2 Locations of vendors on the beach

will go to A and the right to B. But A, after examining the situation, decides that by moving to the right he can take away many of B's customers without losing any of his own (second stage). Vendor B then decides to hop over to the left of A (third stage). It can easily be seen that the final stage will have both A and B together at the center of the beach, each selling to half the customers. Neither A nor B will then be able to increase the number of his customers by moving, and the situation will be stable.

Free competition in this case will result in both vendors joining at the middle of the beach. Since people are evenly distributed along the length of the beach, the average distance walked will be one fourth of the length. A public official might point out, however, that this average distance is unnecessarily high. If the two vendors were located at the quarter points, as in the 'planned location' of Figure 2, the average distance walked would be reduced by half, while both vendors would still enjoy the same sales.

To obtain the benefits of this solution it is only necessary to assure each vendor that the other will not start moving in on him.

There are two lessons to be learned from this. On the one hand, we have seen once again a tendency toward concentration, which may be interpreted as another indication of the reasons for the development of centers of human activity. On the other, we have seen that the solution of free competition may differ from that of the public interest. This is not to say that the results of private initiative need be in conflict with the interests of the community. In fact, it will be seen that theory indicates they usually coincide. But this coincidence of interests is something to be proved in each case, rather than something to be taken for granted.

The Firm with One Market and One Raw Material

Let us consider an activity that uses only one material and sells all of its product at one market. Such a firm might use sheets of steel from a steel plant at M in Figure 3 as its raw material, and

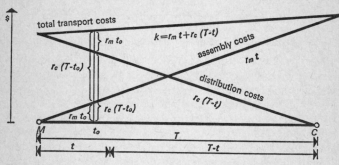

Figure 3   Transport costs of a firm with a single market and a single material; transport costs proportional to distance

bend them into boxes which it sells in a city at C. For simplicity say that the costs of production are the same everywhere, so that the firm's only consideration will be to minimize its *total transport costs*. These consist of *assembly costs* of bringing the steel from M to the factory, and *distribution costs* of sending the boxes from the factory to C. Let T be the distance from M to C, and t the distance from M to the box factory. The distance from the factory to

C is the remainder of T, or $(T - t)$. Now, if the cost per mile of carrying enough steel to build one box is r_m, assembly costs per unit will be $r_m t$; and if the cost of carrying one box is r_c per mile, distribution costs per unit will be $r_c(T - t)$. The total transport costs, which we represent by k, are the sum of these:

$$(1) \qquad k = r_m t + r_c (T - t)$$

The firm will locate at that value of t that minimizes k.

Examine Figure 3, where assembly, distribution, and transport costs are shown for one case. The curve of total transport costs is the sum of the other two, as illustrated for location t_0. In the case illustrated it can be seen that transport costs will be least when the box factory is at M, where $t = 0$. As the diagram is drawn, the curve of assembly costs is steeper than that of distribution costs, meaning that it is more expensive to move steel than boxes; or, to put it another way, that the transport rate for steel (r_m) is greater than that for boxes (r_c). We may rewrite Equation 1 as $k = (r_m - r_c)t + r_c T$ without changing its meaning. From this form of the equation it can be seen that when r_m is greater than r_c, as in Figure 3, the firm will want to keep t as small as possible (that is, locate at M, where $t = 0$). But when r_c is greater, the coefficient of t will be negative, and the firm will want to locate at the maximum t (that is, at C, where $t = T$). Finally, if the costs of moving boxes or steel are equal, so that $r_m = r_c$, the coefficient of t will be zero and transport costs will be $r_c T$ wherever the plant locates. The plant may then locate at M, at C, or at any point in between.

The Structure of Transport Costs

Although the costs of transportation do increase with distance, it is not accurate to say, as we have been saying, that they increase in direct proportion. In the first place, there are terminal costs: the costs of putting things on a truck or train, and of taking them off, the costs of packaging and certain paper work. These in general will not vary with distance. Therefore, transport costs are better represented by an expression such as $s_m + r_m t$, where s_m are the terminal costs, r_m is the rate per mile, and t the number of miles. Thus, above, we used the expression $r_m t$, which results in a

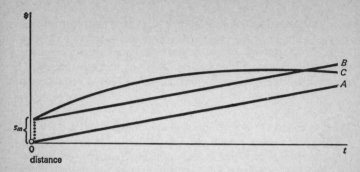

Figure 4 Transport costs: (*A*) proportional to distance, (*B*) considering terminal costs, (*C*) considering decreasing marginal costs

straight line passing through the origin, such as *A* in Figure 4. Introducing terminal costs will add s_m all along to line *A*, resulting in line *B*. Of course, at $t = 0$ nothing has been moved and costs will be zero. This is indicated by the dot at the origin in Figure 4.

Another realistic refinement considers that the rate per mile is lower for longer hauls. This is common practice in the transportation industry as in most others: costs are lower when buying in bulk, it is cheaper to rent by month than by the week, and so on. This results in a flattening of the slope of the curve of transport costs with increasing distance, reflecting the lower rates. In practical terms, it is cheaper to make one 1,000-mile shipment than

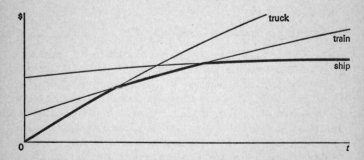

Figure 5 Transport costs considering alternative carriers

344

two 500-mile ones. The curvature of the curve of transport costs is increased by the variety of carriers: ship, train, truck, pipe, and so on. Usually trucks have lower terminal costs but higher per-mile costs than trains, as do trains with respect to ships. Figure 5 shows the relation of transport costs to distance when alternative carriers are considered. The skipper will choose the carrier with the lowest costs for a particular distance, so that his effective curve of transport costs will be the heavy line in Figure 5, which is more curved than that of any one carrier.

Terminal costs and the curvature of transport costs reinforce the attractiveness of end-point locations, such as M or C in the example of Figure 3. In Figure 6 the case of identical transport costs for steel and boxes is re-examined under this more realistic structure of transport costs. When we considered the case without

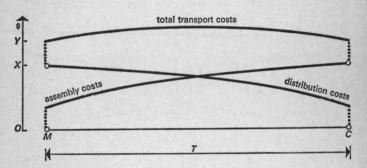

Figure 6   Transport costs of a firm with a single market and a single material, considering terminal costs and decreasing marginal costs

regard for terminal costs or the economies of longer hauls, we concluded that when the rates are the same for assembly and distribution costs the firm would locate at M or C or at any intermediate point. But now, the curvature of the curves of assembly and distribution costs leads to a curvature of the curve of total transport costs, with the midway point the costliest although assembly and distribution costs are symmetrical. The economy of long hauls points to location at either end since the continuous curve of total costs reaches as low as OY. But by locating at either M or C the firm can save the terminal costs on either steel or boxes, and have only OX transport costs. Even without considering the curvature, the elimination of one set of terminal costs would lead to location either at the source of the material or at the market. Although the conclusion requires some reservations, this is part of the explanation for the spatial concentration as opposed to the dispersion of industry.

Trans-shipment Points: the Importance of Ports

One special case deserves attention since it accounts in large measure for the existence of many great cities of the world such as New York, London, and Buenos Aires. This is the case of points of trans-shipment, of which a seaport is a prime example. At these points things brought in by water must be taken off ships and put on trucks or railroads, and vice versa. This provides an excellent

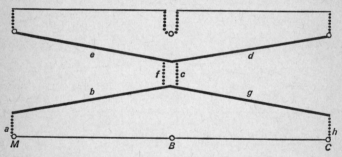

Figure 7   Transport costs involving a trans-shipment point

opportunity to process materials as they are being taken off one carrier and before they are put onto another. For instance, the American Midwest ships wheat to Buffalo by water. There it is taken off the ships, milled into flour, and the flour shipped by train to the bakeries of the Eastern markets. Or petroleum is brought by ship to New York, there refined, and the petroleum products are sent to other cities. Or cattle is brought from the interior by rail to Buenos Aires, there slaughtered, tinned or frozen, and shipped to foreign markets.

A diagrammatic analysis of the advantages of a trans-shipment point is presented in Figure 7 for a one-material, one-market concern such as our steel-box manufacturer. Let us say that steel is produced at M, which is separated by a sea from B, from which there is rail connection to the market at C. The curve of assembly costs is $a - b - c - d$, where a indicates the costs of putting the steel on a ship and taking it off, b the costs of moving the steel across the sea from M to B, c the costs of putting it on and taking it off the train, and d the costs of moving it from B to C. The curve of distribution costs is $e - f - g - h$, where e are the costs of moving the boxes from M to B across the sea, f are the costs of putting them on and taking them off the ship, g are the costs of moving them from B to C, and h the costs of putting them on and taking them off the train. The top curve represents the total costs of transportation, and is the sum of the other two curves. Because of terminal and trans-shipment costs it has three low points: if the plant is located at M, the costs will be $e + f + g + h$; if it is located at B, the costs will be $a + b + g + h$; and if it is located at C, they will be $a + b + c + d$. In Figure 7 all three are shown as having the same total transport costs, but which will be best will depend on the particular values of the components in each case. Ports owe their growth to the fact that they often turn out to be the best location.

The existence of a trans-shipment point clearly depends on the technology and development of transportation. Thus, some believe that the development of the St Lawrence Seaway, which permits direct shipment by water from the Midwest to world markets, may affect adversely cities such as Buffalo and Montreal, which have been trans-shipment points. There have been instructive instances of artificial trans-shipment points at locations where railroads of different gauges meet, or where two railroad networks serving a city have purposely refused to interconnect. Even such trivial breaks in transportation can bring about local development. Within cities, commuter railroad and subway stations represent trans-shipment points for those who use them, and generally foster development of local centers of activity. Looking into the future, one may well speculate the possible effects of the development of craft that travel on a cushion of air, able to move indifferently over land or water. It would seem that should such craft prove to be economical, they would seriously threaten the age-old pre-eminence of ports.

Location Theory

Location of Industry with Many Raw Materials

In the analysis of the location of firms with one market and one source of raw material we used diagrams (such as that in Figure 3) of only two dimensions: the horizontal for the distance, and the vertical for the costs of transportation. But when we consider distances between three or more locations, a one-dimensional straight line is not enough and we need a map, which uses up the

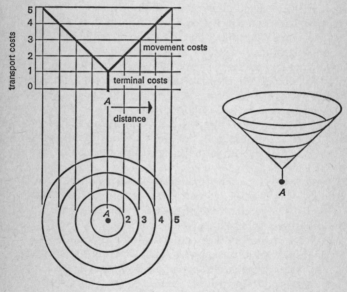

Figure 8 Transport costs: three diagrammatic representations

two dimensions available on a page. Now the costs of transportation require a third dimension. Although difficult, it would be possible to work with three-dimensional models to analyze these cases: there is, however, a simpler way of handling them. In the upper part of Figure 8 the transport costs from some point A are shown much as in Figure 6, except that we are considering the possibility of movement in both directions from A. In reality we have in mind movement in every direction from A, so that the

348

transport costs would look like a windblown umbrella as shown in the side-diagram, where the stem represents the terminal costs, and the umbrella itself the movement costs. The lower part of Figure 8 shows the costs seen from above as in a map. The $2 level of transport costs would be a circle around A, the $3 level a larger concentric circle, and so forth. The meaning of each circle is that one unit of whatever is being shipped from A can be carried

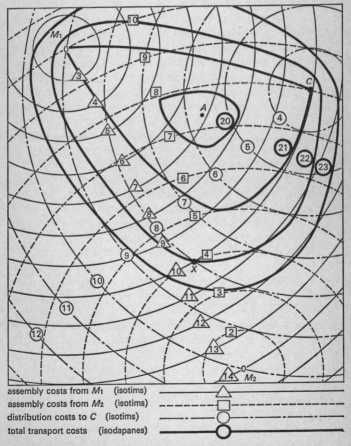

assembly costs from M_1	(isotims)	——————△——————
assembly costs from M_2	(isotims)	------□------
distribution costs to C	(isotims)	— · —○— · —
total transport costs	(isodapanes)	——————◎——————

Figure 9 Isotims and isodapanes for a firm with two materials and one market

to any point in the circle at that cost. At A itself, of course, the transport cost are zero.

Consider now the location of a firm which uses two raw materials, M_1 and M_2, and sells its products at a city C. It is necessary to standardize the quantities per unit of product; let us say that for one unit of product we need two tons of M_1 and one of M_2. We find that terminal costs per ton are $1.00 for M_1 and for M_2, so that terminal costs *per unit of product* are $2 for M_1 and $1 for M_2. Movement costs per ton are $0.67 per hundred miles for M_1 and $1 for M_2. Movement costs per unit of product, therefore, will be $1.34 for M_1 and $1 for M_2. The terminal costs for the product are $3, and the movement costs $1 per hundred miles.

We may now carry out the analysis as in Figure 9. We draw around M_1 the transport costs for the two tons needed per unit of product, shown by the thin continuous lines in Figure 9. These curves are called *isotims*. Similarly, we draw the transport costs of moving the necessary quantity of M_2, shown by the dashed circles. And finally, we draw the isotims for the product, centered around the market at C, shown by the dot-and-dash lines. The total transport costs at any point will be the sum of the isotims; for instance, at point X the costs of bringing two tons of M_1 are $10, the cost of bringing one ton of M_2 are $4, and the cost of delivering the product to C is $8. Total transport costs, then, are $10 + 4 + 8 = 22$. As total transport costs are calculated over the map, points with the same total costs may be joined. The resulting lines, shown by the heavy solid curves in Figure 9 are called *isodapanes*, and constitute a mapping of total transport costs.

To locate the plant, we want to find the point of least transport costs. The isodapanes in Figure 9 show a low point in transport costs at point A within the $20 isodapane. In many cases the true minimum may be at such an intermediate point; that is to say, at a point which is neither one of the sources of materials nor the market. In this case, however, the intermediate location A is only a relative minimum. Location at M_1 results in only $19 transport costs ($10 from M_2 and $9 to C); and location at C in $18 total costs ($10 from M_1 and $8 from M_2). The best location, therefore, would be at C. The minimum found by isodapane mapping should be checked against location at the sources of materials or at the markets to insure that the true minimum is found.

By this method we may consider a problem involving any number of points. Figures 10, 11, and 12 deal with an industry with three markets, C_1, C_2, and C_3, and three sources of materials, M_1, M_2, and M_3. For simplicity, let us say that terminal costs are insignificant, although they could be considered just as they were in the discussion of Figures 4, 6, and 7.

The firm sells 20 per cent of its products at C_1, 30 per cent at C_2, and 50 per cent at C_3. In this case we may observe in advance, from the rule of median location, that the minimum of these distribution costs must be at C_3. However, a full mapping of the isotims of distribution costs will be necessary to combine with the assembly costs to find total transport costs. Since the proportions shipped to each market are known, we may draw a set of isotims for each market. If the transport rate per unit of product is $4 per

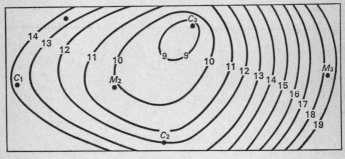

Figure 10   Isotims of combined distribution costs

hundred miles, we may consider that 0.20 of that unit will be shipped to C_1, at a cost of $0.80 per hundred miles; that 0.30 units will be shipped to C_2 at a cost of $1.20 per hundred miles, and 0.50 units to C_3 at a cost of $2.00 per hundred miles. If we were considering terminal costs, they too would be divided proportionally. On this basis a set of isotims may be drawn around each of the markets, and they may be summed (in the same way as in Figure 9) to obtain a set of distribution costs isotims. The resulting distribution costs isotims are shown in Figure 10. Note that the lowest point is indeed at C_3, where distribution costs are $8.65 per unit.

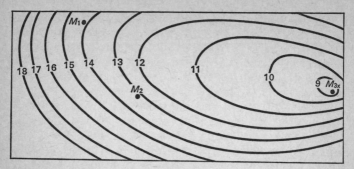

Figure 11 Isotims of combined assembly costs

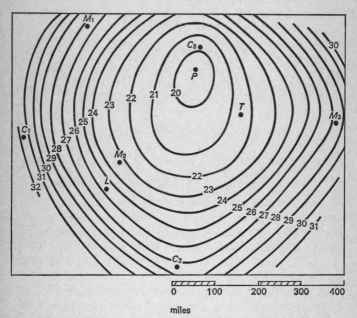

miles

Figure 12 Isodapanes: sum of isotims in Figures 10 and 11

Similarly, we may draw the isotims for each of the raw materials and sum them to obtain an isotim mapping of assembly costs, as has been done in Figure 11. The basis of this mapping is as follows:

	M_1	M_2	M_3
Units of material per unit of product	2	1	1
Rate per unit of materials per 100 miles	$0.50	0.50	2.00
Rate per units of material necessary per unit of product	$1.00	0.50	2.00

Now, total transport costs (isodapane mapping) may be obtained by summing the isotims of distribution costs (Figure 10) to the isotims of assembly costs (Figure 11). The result is Figure 12. Minimum total transport costs will be at point P, where they will be $19.70 per unit of product, and the firm would locate there. Clearly, this minimum must always be within the polygon whose vertices are the locations of the markets and materials.

It would have been possible, of course, to have added the six sets of isotims (from M_1, M_2, M_3, to C_1, C_2, C_3) at the same time, but having so many lines in one map is confusing, and it is easier to do it by parts.

Production Cost Differentials

Suppose that at point L in Figure 12 there is a city with surplus labor, so that wages are lower than elsewhere. The manufacturer wants to know if he should locate there rather than at P. He would calculate the savings per unit of product that cheaper labor would imply, considering both the wage rates and the efficiency of that labor. If the saving is, let us say, $10, L would be the best location, since total transport costs at L are shown in the isodapane mapping as $25.50, as compared with $19.70 at P. The extra transport costs, then, are $5.80, leaving a net savings of $4.20. We could consider, similarly, another point such as T, where there is a tax saving of $1 per unit of product (would T be better than P?, better than L?), or any other point at which special conditions obtain, such as special climatic conditions, association with other activities, and so on.

Market Areas

If a firm needs a certain raw material that may come from either of two sources, the choice of one source or the other will depend on the location of the firm. But to decide the location of the firm we must know which of the two sets of isotims to consider. To do

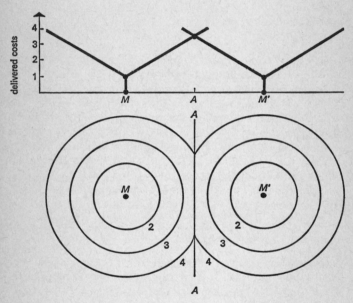

Figure 13   Market areas: identical production and transport costs

this we delimit the areas best supplied by each of the alternative sources, and consider only the isotims of the preferred source within its market area. In other words, we construct an isotim mapping for the material, rather than for the sources as such.

In Figure 13 two alternative sources M and M' of one material are considered. In the upper part of the figure are shown the delivered costs from each of the two sources. The stems are the pro-

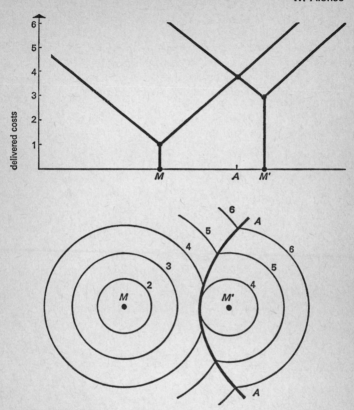

Figure 14   Market areas: different production costs and identical transport rates

duction costs for the material plus the terminal costs, while the gradients are the costs of moving the material over space. It can be seen that to the left of A, M can deliver more cheaply, while to the right of A, M' has the advantage. In the bottom part of the figure, the analysis is carried out by curves similar to isotims except that the cost of production as well as that of transportation is considered at every point. The line $A–A$ (the perpendicular bisector of the line $M–M'$) is the market boundary between M and M'. In constructing the isodapane mapping we would use isotims

355

centered about M to the left of A–A, and isotims centered about M' to the right of it.

In Figure 14 another case is considered, where production costs are greater at M' than at M, but transport rates are the same. The resulting market boundary is an open hypercircle A–A (similar to a hyperbola), as shown in the figure. In Figure 15 a case is

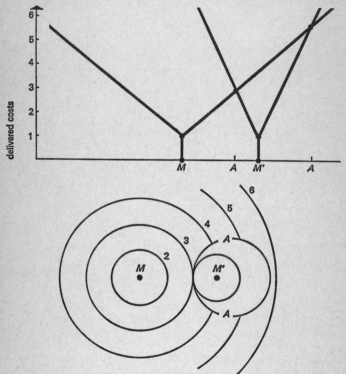

Figure 15 Market areas: different transport rates

shown for which transport rates are higher for M' than for M. The market area of M' will be that bounded by the closed hypercircle A–A. This situation might arise, for instance, if we were considering coal mines, and the coal produced at M' were of inferior quality, so that greater quantities per unit of product are necessary.

356

This analysis holds as well for determination of the market of firms of known location if their pricing policy is such that the customer bears the transport costs. However, if the producers charge the same 'list' price everywhere, their markets could not be determined in this way. It would depend on the policy of the producer with respect to how far he would be willing to ship his products when he himself absorbs the transport costs. Moreover, in some

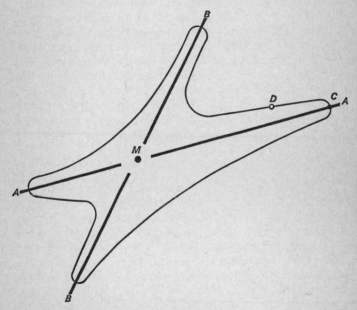

Figure 16   Isotim considering transport network

cases firms may engage in quite elaborate price wars to capture certain markets, or may be able to sell in certain areas even at higher prices because of advertising.

Some Realistic Complications

In the preceding illustrations isotims have been shown as evenly spaced concentric circles. The economies of longer hauls, which were reflected in a curvature of the transport gradient in Figure 4, will be reflected in increasingly wider spacing of isotims with increasing distance from the source.

There are other realistic features that may be considered by the use of isotims. We have been assuming that transportation is equally possible in all directions. But if we realize that there exist roads and railroads only in some directions, we see that, rather than perfect circles, isotims will take forms more similar to starfish, with arms extending along the transport routes, as in Figure 16, where A–A and B–B are highways or railroads and a single isotim is shown. Although point D is nearer than C to M, it is as expensive to reach, since part of the travel must be over routes inferior to A–A. Similarly, we could consider the effects of intervening seas or lakes, mountains, or tariff barriers, routes with fixed stops that may require some backtracking to reach certain points, and so on. All of these will complicate the geometry of the isotims, but not their logic: an isotim is a curve over a map that joins points of equal transport costs.

Some Terms and Shortcuts

The analysis thus far could to some extent be paralleled by a device of strings, pulleys, and weights where, disregarding terminal costs, the weight at each material or market point is proportional to the weight per unit of product times the relevant transport rate, and all the strings are tied together at one knot. This knot will come to rest at the optimal transport location. More formally, the pull at each point is $w_i r_i$, where w_i is the amount of i necessary per unit of product, and r_i is the cost of moving one unit of i a given distance. For the product itself, w_i is unity if there is only one market, and the proper fraction if there is more than one market. The quantity $w_i r_i$ is called the *ideal weight*. Clearly, if one of the ideal weights is greater than the sum of all the others, it will pull the knot right to its pulley. Such an ideal weight is called a *dominant weight*; represented formally, $w_j r_j$ is the dominant weight when $w_j r_j \geq \sum_i w_i r_i, i \neq j$. The significance of the dominant weight is that if there is a location with the least transport costs, it will be at the source of the dominant material (or at the destination, in the case of the product). Therefore, it is not necessary to do the isotimisodopane analysis, since we know the answer. It will be noted, of course, that this is no more than the principle of median location in another form.

But what if there is no dominant weight? If we disregard terminal costs, this means that the point with least transport costs will be within the polygon formed by drawing the lines between the various sources of materials and markets, but not at either a source or a market. In other words, the full analysis must be carried out, and because of terminal costs the low point of transport costs within the polygon must be compared with the costs at the various sources and markets. Thus, the best location may, after all, be at one of the terminal points.

In the production of some goods, much of the materials is wasted or expended: dirt is washed from ore, material is cut into shape, chemicals are used up. In such cases, of course, the product will weigh less than the materials that go into it. Such industries are called *weight-losing* and are often *material-oriented*. The classical example of this type was the iron and steel industry, which burned great quantities of coal per ton of product, and therefore was usually found in coal-producing regions. Modern technology, however, has greatly reduced the quantities of coal used, and reduced the material-orientation of the industry.

Conversely, there are cases in which the product weighs more than the materials that go into it. This strange-seeming phenomenon is quite frequent, and may stem from either of two sources. The freight rate of the product may be very high, because of refrigeration, fragility, great bulk, or other reasons, so that the ideal weight of the product is very high. This is the case with some glass products and precision machinery. The other common reason is the use of an ubiquitous material, such as water or air, which is available everywhere and thus does not need to be transported. Such ubiquitous materials do not enter into the calculations of dominant weights, and this type of industry is called weight-gaining and often is market-orientated. A prime example of this type of industry is beer production, which locates its plants at the major markets. But calling an industry material-orientated or market-orientated only tells us of a tendency. These terms are verbal shortcuts, similar to the concept of dominant weight, but less precise. For any particular firm, it is necessary to do a full analysis to be certain of its best location.

We have been considering industries which find transportation costs of paramount importance in selecting a location, that is, *transport-orientated industries*. Typically these are industries with a high bulk-to-value ratio for materials or products; or to be more precise, with high ideal weight-to-value ratios. For other industries, especially those with a high value-to-bulk ratio, other considerations may be more important. Thus, textiles are usually attracted to places with abundant cheap labor and are called *labor-oriented*, and aluminium is attracted to cheap electricity and is called *power-oriented*. Another type of orientation is emerging that might be called *amenity-orientation*. Research industries, such as electronics, have small transport costs but need very specialized scientists and engineers. To attract them these firms often locate where there are climatic or cultural advantages. The Worcester manufacturer mentioned at the beginning of this chapter, was, in a sense, amenity-oriented. It will be noted, however, that these various orientations are really instances of the production cost differentials, and that they can be integrated with the analysis of transport costs.

Industries that have no strong locational preferences, and particularly industries that are not transport-oriented, are often called *foot-loose*, and there is good reason to believe that technical developments are making more industries foot-loose. In the first place, in the long run, transportation tends to become cheaper, quicker, and more efficient, lessening transport-orientation. Second, production processes tend to become more efficient, requiring less materials per unit of product, thus reducing total transport costs, and, incidentally, increasing market orientation. Finally products themselves are improved and made more efficient, so that they do more of a job per unit of weight.

Concentration and Dispersion of Industry

Does increasing foot-looseness mean that industrial activities will become increasingly dispersed? Probably not. Foot-looseness simply means that transport costs are relatively less important, not that one place is as good as any other. Industries may now be attracted to areas of good weather, either because it is important to their operations (as in the case of the aircraft industry), or because it will be attractive to their workers (as in the case of some research industries). Or they may be attracted to special site advantages, or to cheap labor, or, perhaps most important, to contacts. These contacts are infinitely varied in their forms. They may be managerial exchanges, where vital information is exchanged casually over lunch, or close supplier–customer coordination, or the chance remark that discloses an unsuspected opportunity, or the shoptalk of technical people that stimulates new ideas. The importance of contacts will probably increase the attraction of large urban centers for many industries, and lead to further concentration.

Concentration in cities does not necessarily mean concentration in downtown. We are using the word city in its technical sense of the geographic extent of the area of homes and work places of an urban concentration. Thus, by 'city' we may mean a metropolitan area, central city and suburbs. Since World War II, much of the industry in metropolitan areas in the United States has moved to the suburbs. The principal reason for this movement is that plants need more land because one-story buildings are better suited to today's production processes and because vast areas are needed for workers' parking. Since much more land is needed, plants go to the suburbs, where it is cheaper. The increasing shift from railroads to trucks has helped to make this possible, since trucks are more versatile and can better service industry dispersed over a metropolitan area. This dispersion or decentralization *within* metropolitan areas has sometimes been confused with a national dispersion.

Although it is hard to generalize about industrial location patterns within cities (both because we know little about it and because much of what we know requires very cumbersome technical description), one frequent pattern or life cycle of industries has become relatively recognizable. It is similar to the cycle of residential migration for American families: young couples or those recently arrived from rural areas live at first in small apartments near the center of the city. As the families grow or the rural immigrants become adapted, they tend to move to newer houses in the suburbs. Similarly, many new industries get their start in the old buildings near the center of the city, where they can rent space relatively inexpensively. When the firm becomes successful and needs more space, it frequently builds its new plant in the suburbs. In our sense of the word, this is a move to another part of the city, but not a movement out of the city.

How is it Done in Practice?

We have been discussing the logic of the location of industries. But the question may be raised whether businessmen or project planners do in fact follow the methods outlined here. Many, of course, do not. In many cases the decision is made almost by whim: the businessman may simply operate his business in the town in which he was born and raised, or in a city that has persuaded him with a clever promotional campaign. However, irrational decisions in a competitive economy usually pay a heavy penalty. The 'survival of the fittest' will mean that, however the decision is made, it will be those industries which are well located that will survive and become important. A planned economy would suffer similarly from inefficient locations, although the cost of the inefficiency may be dispersed throughout the economic system. The reader is reminded, however, that here we are considering the point of view of the firm or, in the planned case, that of the project. As discussed in the introduction to this volume, regional considerations may in some cases justify higher costs from the point of view of the project in pursuing such goals as the development of a depressed region.

The majority of businessmen do not consciously go through the analysis in the form presented here. They are familiar with the operations of their industry, they know where their markets are and where their raw materials come from, and from this general knowledge can pick the likeliest spots and investigate them further. The businessman will then, if he is prudent, do a careful comparative examination of these alternatives. He will check transport costs, frequency of schedules, labor availability, rates, quality, and organization, power costs, local taxes and prospects, available sites, climate, the housing situation, educational opportunities, availability of finance and cost of borrowing, local regulations, and any other factors of importance to his operation. This type of analysis is quite difficult, however, and most businessmen do not have within their staffs people with the training and experience to do such investigations. Consequently, businessmen are increasingly turning to location consultants to help them make a decision. These consultants do follow the logic that has been outlined, although often with differences of style.

Limitations of this Analysis

We have been examining the underlying logic of the location decision from the point of view of the firm or of the project, but, of course, only in outline. We have concentrated on transport costs because these vary in a patterned way over space, and only touched on such things as labor costs and taxes, which vary in no regular way. For these, all that is necessary is to compare the savings per unit among alternatives, setting off a savings here against an extra expense there to arrive at the total localization economies. Certainly there is no theoretical difficulty here. But the theory has little to say on some important topics which remain matters of judgment rather than of scientific analysis. I shall briefly discuss some of these.

Demand has been taken for granted: we have been saying that we know where the markets are and how many units they want. This, of course, is not always a cut and-dried matter. The demand may vary for many reasons, price often being the most important. Therefore, when a producer may sell in several markets, the delivered price of the product and the quantities sold at each of these markets may depend on the location of the plant. At the same time, the scale of operations of the plant affects the unit costs of production. Thus, it is quite possible that a plant may choose a location where transport costs are somewhat higher per unit than the minimum possible, so that it may sell its products to a city that would otherwise be outside its market area, and thus obtain a volume of production sufficient to reduce the unit production costs. And, of course, very often decisions are made in the face of competition. There may already be a firm producing the same thing at the point of minimum transports costs, so that if the new plant located there, it would be fighting for the same customers. It may be better to locate at some point with higher transport costs, but where the firm can have to itself some customers that are now distant from the existing plants. Further, when a firm makes a decision it must keep in mind how its competitors are likely to react. And finally, many firms do not make just one product. A shoe factory makes many sizes and styles, and perhaps wallets and luggage. A chemical plant can turn out thousands of different combinations of products by slight changes in the processes it uses. Therefore when the firm considers alternative locations, it must also consider variations of its 'product mix'. The combination that may be best at one location may not be best at another.

All of these are in essence complications of the basic theory, and although the analysis may be long and difficult, fairly good answers should be possible. But there are problems of another type, involving things that are hard to quantify. Perhaps the principal one is that of *external economies*. These are the advantages or disadvantages that arise from the close proximity of the plant to other activities. For instance, a group of plants may use a machine-repair shop jointly, rather than each having its own. Among the disadvantages, higher rents and insurance rates are often mentioned. However, many of these advantages and disadvantages are very hard to measure. How much is it worth to have access to a good tax lawyer, or to be able to visit a supplier or a customer in person, or to have a first-rate printer to do a report, or to be able to receive some supplies within minutes of ordering? On the other hand, how much does it cost to fight congested traffic? It is not only hard to measure these advantages and disadvantages, it is often difficult to identify them. For instance, one large office that moved out of the city into the country was forced to return when it discovered that it could not get girls to work so far away from marriageable men. On the other hand, one research concern moved from a big city to a small town in order to keep competitors from raiding its technical personnel.

Further, and most difficult of all, are the problems of uncertainty and of time. The future is usually uncertain: tastes may change, there may be a technological revolution, tax laws and customs duties may be revised. In short, when decisions are made, it is only rarely that one can be sure of the exact results. Some interesting new work is being done in location theory to take uncertainty into account in the location decision, but so far only a small beginning has been made. In general terms, the new theory tries to estimate the costs and benefits of alternative decisions in the light of the probabilities of different things happening. This, of course, is what businessmen themselves try to do. For instance, an American businessman will be attracted by a 10 per cent return on investment in the United States, but he will not be interested in a similar investment in an unstable foreign country unless it pays 30 per cent or more because of the danger of revolution, expropriation, severe restrictions, and so on. Thus far one of the most interesting conclusions of these investigations is that there often is no single best strategy for the businessman. He may choose to act boldly for big gains or losses, or conservatively for smaller ones, both being rational possibilities with the choice depending on the goals and attitudes of the businessman.

Uncertainty aside, the question of time itself is not sufficiently considered in the existing location theory. The decision that is best in the light of today's situation may not be best at some future time: production methods will change, and transport routes and costs, as well as the tastes, location, and resources of customers and the nature of the competition. Even when these changes can be predicted with certainty, we do not have a fully spelled-out method of making a decision that will be best over a period of time rather than at a moment in time. Such a theory would seem to be possible – in fact, not particularly difficult to develop – if we are willing to grant that all the relevant changes can be predicted with some accuracy. To combine time and uncertainty in a meaningful method of analysis will be much more difficult, but may be possible. It is clear, however, that there may be no single best answer, but that the choice would depend to a large degree on 'time preference': whether to try for early profits or for larger later ones. Both may be rational choices.

Bibliographic Note

The seminal book in this field is Alfred Weber's *Theory of the location of industries*, first published in German in 1909, and edited and translated into English by C. J. Friedrich in 1928 (Chicago, University of Chicago Press). Edgar M. Hoover, in *The location of economic activity* (New York, McGraw-Hill Book Co., Inc., 1948), improved on many aspects of the analysis and introduced a greater measure of reality. Walter Isard in *Location and space-economy* (New York: The Technology Press and

John Wiley & Sons, Inc., 1956), generalized and extended the theory. The works of Melvin Greenhut, such as *Microeconomics and the space economy* (Chicago, Scott Foresman and Co., 1963) and *Plant location in theory and practice* (Chapel Hill, University of North Carolina Press, 1956) continue to explore this topic.

The reader interested in the practitioner's views may refer to L. C. Yaseen, *Plant location* (New York, American Research Council, 1960) for the private firm; and for government projects, to the *Manual on economic development projects* (New York, United Nations, 1958).

The example of the ice-cream vendors on the beach is based on H. Hotelling, 'Stability in competition' *Economic Journal*, vol. 39 (March 1929), pp. 41–57. For an attempt to consider probabilities in the location decision, see W. Isard and T. A. Reiner, 'Aspects of decision-making theory and regional science', *Papers and Proceedings of the Regional Science Association*, vol. 9 (1962).

Part Six Some Statistical Techniques

A frequently recurring problem in regional analysis is to decide
whether observed values of variables such as unemployment, income
per head, etc., are significantly different between different regions.
The problem, though almost entirely a statistical one, is not simple,
and the student of regional economics whose statistical background
is shaky may welcome an introduction to some of the relevant
techniques. Such an introduction is provided in the article by Gordon
Fisher reprinted here, in which only a little previous knowledge of
statistics is assumed and which combines sophistication of treatment
with exceptional clarity of exposition.

11 G. Fisher

Further Calculations on Regional Differences in Profitability and Growth

G. Fisher, 'Further calculations on regional differences in profitability and growth', *Scottish Journal of Political Economy*, vol. 9 (1962), pp. 147–58.

A. Introduction

In a recent paper Hart and MacBean (1961) presented an analysis of data from company accounts collected from a sample of 50 Scottish and a sample of 50 English companies in order to throw some light on the relative advantages of being located in Scotland and England. Their approach and results have been criticized by Smyth (1961). The object of this paper is to amplify and extend the work of Hart and MacBean.

The outline of the paper is as follows: In section B the joint effect of mean of growth and mean of profitability is used in an attempt to explain differences between the Scottish and English companies analysed by Hart and MacBean. In sections C and D the analysis is extended to other characteristics of the regional distributions of growth and profitability. Section C compares the regional distributions of each variable separately. Section D attempts to explain differences between the samples in terms of the variation over time of growth and profitability. Two analyses of variance of the measurements made by Hart and MacBean are discussed in section E and the conclusions are summarised in the final section.

B. Mean Profitability and Mean Growth

Hart and MacBean calculated regional means of measurements of growth and profitability for their samples of Scottish and English companies. Tests showed that there were no statistically significant differences between the regions.

Smyth was not surprised that mean profitability in Scottish industry was much the same as in English industry because he expected 'profit rates to be much the same for comparable industries in all regions as they both determine and reflect regional allocations of industrial and commercial capital' (Smyth, 1961, p. 246).[1] Furthermore, because they were stratified by company size and industry according to the Scottish pattern, the two samples were not chosen independently of one another. The Scottish sample was a random sample of Scottish business units, but the probability of selection in the English sample depended directly on what companies were selected in the Scottish sample. To compare like with like was the admitted purpose, but the methodology of doing so precluded observations in one region from being statistically independent of observations in the other. In these circumstances the tests used by Hart and MacBean do not strictly apply because the necessary assumption of independence is not satisfied (Fisher, 1941, pp. 115–16 and 125–6; Hoel, 1960, p. 114).

One method of handling matched observations is to examine the mean of differences between paired companies rather than the differences between regional means (Fisher, 1941, pp. 115–16). Such a test has been performed on Hart's and MacBean's observations for profitability and growth. For profitability the calculated value of $t = 0.20$ and for growth $t = 1.09$ neither of which is significant at the 5 per cent level. This perhaps, is not a surprising result. It illustrates a much emphasized point that the t test can be relied upon to give substantially correct results even when the requirements of the test are not strictly maintained.[2]

Another criticism of Hart's and MacBean's methodology is that although location was made to depend on profitability *and*

1. Others have undoubtedly held the view that some cost factors were higher in Scotland. For example, Edwards and Townsend (1958) have emphasized that transport costs may be important even where these are a small proportion of turnover. It has also been claimed that Scottish managerial ability is inferior compared with that in England. If these cost factors were significant, profit rates should be lower in Scotland unless there were compensating advantages. Thus, observed similarities in profit rates reflect either that cost differences were unimportant or that compensating advantages existed in Scotland. Furthermore, Smyth's point that profit rates should not differ by region only applies in equilibrium and in the real world the equilibrium situation need not exist.

2. This is not to say that the requirement of statistical tests should be disregarded or that different results have never been obtained from tests using differences of means and tests on the mean of differences. See Fisher (1941), pp. 125–6.

growth, the mean of each variable was tested as if dependence were univariate and not bivariate.

If regional variances were equal a t test was used; if the variances were not equal, a Welch–Aspin test was used. The multivariate analogue of the square of t is the T^2 statistic, originally proposed by Hotelling (1931). A simple transformation of T^2 is distributed as F. If the regional variance–covariance matrices of growth and profitability are equal, the F distribution based on the T^2 statistic, can be used to test if a linear combination of growth and profitability can significantly distinguish Scottish from English industry on the basis of the measurements in the selected samples. A linear combination of this kind is known as a discriminant function, which was suggested but not considered by Hart and MacBean, and the test for significant discrimination is equivalent to testing for significant differences between two dimensional column vectors composed of the regional means of growth and profitability. The discriminant function and the test are due to Fisher (1936).

The discriminant function Z can be written

$$(1) \qquad Z = \lambda_1 g + \lambda_2 p$$

in which λ_1 and λ_2 are constants to be determined and g represents growth and p profitability. The measurements g and p for each company are used to calculate λ_1 and λ_2 so as to optimally distinguish the Scottish from the English observations. Z can then be calculated for each company. A critical value of Z, say Z^*, is chosen so that if $Z \leqslant Z^*$ the company is assigned to the Scottish sample; if $Z > Z^*$, it is assigned to the English sample. If a high proportion of companies are correctly assigned, the function is said to be able to significantly differentiate Scottish from English companies on the basis of the measurements used, and the F test would then show as significant at a chosen level of probability.

The calculated discriminant function is

$$(2) \qquad Z = 7.90\,g + 3.09\,p.$$

The calculated value of F is 0.726, which is not significant at the 5 per cent level.

Clearly, without the discrimination function, it would always be possible to correctly place 50 companies out of the total of 100 (50 Scottish; 50 English) simply by assigning all companies to the

Scottish, or all to the English sample. Fifty would then be correctly assigned and 50 incorrectly. By computing equation (2) only 52 companies (30 Scottish; 22 English) can be correctly assigned, so that there is only a 2 percentage point gain over the simple method of assigning all companies to one region.

If it is not assumed that the regional variance–covariance matrices are equal, a different test must be used which is the multivariate analogue of the t test for paired differences described above and an extension of Scheffe's test (1943) outlined by Anderson (1958).[3] Let $\bar{g}(i)$ and $\bar{p}(i)$ represent respectively mean growth and mean profitability, over time and companies, in the ith region, $i = 1, 2$, If $i = 1$, the mean refers to the English sample and if $i = 2$, it refers to the Scottish sample. The null hypothesis is that

$$
\begin{bmatrix} \bar{g}(1) \\ \bar{p}(1) \end{bmatrix} - \begin{bmatrix} \bar{g}(2) \\ \bar{p}(2) \end{bmatrix} = \begin{bmatrix} 0 \\ 0 \end{bmatrix}
$$

The observed value of $T^2 = 1.97$ which is not significant at the 5 per cent level.

C. Distributions

The mean is only one moment of a given distribution. Other moments may serve to distinguish two distributions and these may have an economic interpretation which is relevant in determining relative locational advantages. For example, if past performance has any bearing on future performance, mean profitability now has some influence on what future profitability will be. Thus, if there are regional differences in mean profitability, a firm located in the region with the higher mean would be expected to do better, on average, than in the region with the lower mean, other things being equal. But if regional variances were different, the distribution symmetrical and regional means equal, although, on average, future profitability would be the same in each region, a firm located in the region with smaller variance would have, on average, a smaller chance of exceeding or falling short of the average expected future profitability than the region with larger variance. There is a lower chance of doing very well, but also a lower

3. See the third paragraph of this section.

chance of doing very badly. If an entrepreneur has a high aversion to the risk of doing badly he would prefer the region with smaller variance, given that the regional means are equal. If he is sure of his own ability to do well, wherever he is, he will choose the region with the larger variance because the chances of doing extremely well are higher and he does not entertain the prospect of being a worse-than-average entreprenuer. Thus charactcristics other than the means of the regional distributions of profitability and growth

Table 1
Distribution of Companies by Mean Profitability, 1950–58

Profitability %	Number of observations	
	Scotland	England
8·7 and less	5	7
8·8–10·9	5	7
11·0–13·6	7	5
13·7–16·2	9	5
16·3–19·0	10	3
19·1–21·4	7	6
21·5–24·5	3	9
24·6 and over	4	8
Total	50	50

might have some bearing on the decision to operate in a particular region.

The χ^2 test may be used to test whether two distributions are statistically different. Unfortunately, as Cochran (1952) has pointed out, the power of the test varies considerably with the size of sample. With a small sample, although an alternative hypothesis may depart violently from the null, it may still have a small chance of yielding a significant value of χ^2. In a very large sample, however, minor departures from the null hypothesis are virtually certain to be detected. Consequently when χ^2 is not significant, the amount by which the null hypothesis is strengthened depends, to a large extent, on the sample size. Furthermore, the text is not unique (Gumbel, 1943) because there is freedom of choice of the number of class intervals. Therefore, a non-significant value of χ^2 should not be regarded as conclusive evidence to support the null hypothesis.

Table 1 gives the distribution of companies by mean profitability per company for the period 1950–1958. Table 2 gives corresponding figures for growth.

For Table 1, the calculated value of χ^2 is 10.32, which is not significant at the 5 per cent level for seven degrees of freedom. However, if four classes are used instead of the eight used in Table 1, a significant value of χ^2 is obtained at the 5 per cent level for three degrees of freedom, and, although more importance should be attached to the test on Table 1, there is some evidence that there exists differences between the two regional distributions.

Table 2
Distribution of Companies by Mean Growth, 1950–58

Growth %	Number of Observations	
	Scotland	England
2·0 and less	4	4
2·1– 4·0	6	8
4·1– 6·0	11	4
6·1– 8·0	9	6
8·1– 9·5	9	8
9·6–12·0	7	9
12·1–16·0	2	8
16·1 and over	2	3
Total	50	50

Table 2 gives a non-significant value of χ^2. The calculated $\chi^2 = 8.26$ and to be significant at the 5 per cent level, for seven degrees of freedom, the calculated value must be greater than 14.07.

So far, the results obtained seem to support those of Hart and MacBean. There are no significant differences between regional bivariate means of growth and profitability and the χ^2 tests show, in a general way, that there are similarities between the regional distributions. However, it has been pointed out that the power of the χ^2 test depends on sample size and there is the possibility that, in truth, differences exist between the English and Scottish samples which cannot be detected by the test with the relatively few observations available. Furthermore, the tests have been performed on pairs of univariate regional distributions whereas, as was stressed earlier, it is the joint or bivariate effect of profitability and growth which is important, not the separate individual effects taken in isolation. In these circumstances it seems reasonable to follow Cochran's suggestion (1952, p. 340) and supplement the χ^2 test with further tests on lower order moments. Since the means have already been intensively tested, the next section describes an analysis which focuses on observed intra-company variation over time.

D. Range of Growth and Range of Profitability

It was suggested at the beginning of section C that the variance of a distribution might provide a measure of the future prospect of doing better or worse than average. It might also serve to illustrate a point made by Smyth with respect to growth and discussed by Stone (1960): namely, that within region variation is greater in England than in Scotland because England should rightly be regarded as a group of regions, some of which are similar to Scotland but others which are markedly different. The North and North-East of England are much more similar in economic characteristics to Scotland than, say, London, the South-West and the South of England.

For computational convenience the range of company growth and profitability over time have been used in place of the corresponding variances.[4] Let $r(g)$ be the range of growth over time, that is the difference between the largest annual percentage increase in growth and the smallest. Let $r(p)$ represent the corresponding range of profitability. A discriminant function D may then be defined similar to that used in Section 2:

$$(3) \qquad D = \gamma_1 r(g) + \gamma_2 r(p).$$

The observations $r(g)$ and $r(p)$ for each company are used to find γ_1 and γ_2 and to calculate the F statistic as described in Section B.

---

4. It may be objected that calculations based on the range are unreliable because the range is heavily influenced by extreme observations. This is not a serious objection, however, first because most measures of variability are influenced by extreme observations and, secondly, because it can be shown that for small samples from a normal population the range is nearly as efficient for estimating the population standard deviation as is the usual sample estimator. See Hoel (1955), pp. 237–8.

The calculated function D is

(4) $$D = 2.93r(g) - 3.18r(p)$$

and the calculated value of $F = 3.38$ which, for 2 and 97 degrees of freedom, is significant at the 5 per cent level of F.[5]

On average the range of growth in the English sample is very much larger than that in the Scottish sample. The difference in the average ranges of profitability is much smaller, the range of the Scottish sample being the larger.[6]

The discriminant function may be interpreted as a linear probability function (Suits, 1957). The larger the calculated value of D, the greater is the chance of belonging to the English sample; the smaller D, the greater is the chance of belonging to the Scottish sample. Since γ_1 is positive and γ_2 negative, the larger the value of $r(g)$ and the smaller the value of $r(p)$, the greater is the chance of coming from the English sample. The chances of coming from the Scottish sample increase as $r(g)$ decreases and as $r(p)$ increases. Since the average regional difference in the range of growth is about six times as large as the corresponding difference for profitability, the effect of growth is, on average, more important to discrimination than the range of profitability.

The range of growth measures the spread between the highest and lowest annual growth rates over time for a given firm. A large value of $r(g)$ represents a large rate of change in annual growth rate; a low value indicates the maintenance of a steady annual growth rate. In general the achievement of a very high growth rate in one year is likely to prevent the maintenance of that rate for a few years later partly because large-scale investment in one year may make large-scale investment unnecessary in the next few years and partly because later growth rates are computed on a substantially increased level of capital which tends to reduce subsequent annual growth rates. Thus, when large-scale re-equipment has taken place, the value of $r(g)$ is likely to fluctuate more than when small-scale re-equipment takes place regularly. One explanation of $r(g)$ being larger on average for the English than

---

5. This test should be regarded as approximate since the distribution of range is treated as if it were comparable to the distribution of the corresponding mean. See Hoel (1955), pp. 238–40.

6. See the opening paragraph to this section.

for the Scottish sample is that more large-scale re-equipment has taken place with the English companies. Also, because the discriminant function tests the average values over companies in one region against the average values in the other, value of $r(g)$ in England partly reflects the regional differences in growth rates within England suggested by Smyth. In summary, therefore, the higher average value of $r(g)$ in the English sample indicates that growth has been relatively more spasmodic in England so that the chances of growing very fast in certain periods are higher in England than in Scotland, but that this characteristic depends to some extent on the region in which the firm is located within England. Given a free choice, therefore, an entrepreneur would prefer to locate in one of the more advantageous regions of England; but would still prefer Scotland to one of the less advantageous regions of England.

Although profitability is more uniform between the regions, it is less variable in England than in Scotland. Thus the English companies were able to maintain a steadier rate of profit on capital than the Scottish companies, in spite of the former's more variable annual rates of growth. This might be because Scotland is more strongly influenced by changes in general economic conditions than England. In good times, the Scottish firms do better than the English firms; in bad times, they do worse. If this is the case, large-scale expansion by a given firm is a more risky business in Scotland than in England because the rate of return on capital is, on average, more variable and presumably more vulnerable to changes in the general economic climate. Thus, in Scotland, growth is likely to be more cautious and large-scale re-equipment and development less common.

E. Analysis of Variance

Any test of the average differences in profitability and growth between firms in Scotland and England should allow for variation in the data used. Variation arises from many sources. The tests used above and by Hart and MacBean consider the aggregative influence of all sources of variation in each region. A more powerful procedure is to resolve total variation into its components and consider each source of variation separately. Thus, to take an agricultural analogy, a firm may be considered as a seed of given variety, i.e. industry. The seeds (firms) are planted (located) in different plots of land (regions). The attribute of a region is that the treatment (regional economic environment) applied influences the yield of the seeds (profitability or growth of the companies). But the yield varies over time because as time proceeds a seed grows. Consequently the yield is assumed to vary from seed to seed depending on three main factors: the variety of seed, the treatment applied and time.

In the case of the Scottish and English companies considered in this paper, total variation can be resolved into three components: industry, region (i.e. regional environment) and time. In addition, the main effects may interact one with another; industry as a whole may have a higher 'yield' in one region than in the other, yet at the same time, a particular industry may flourish more than average in a given region because that region is particularly suited to its needs. The variation that remains after extracting the main effects and the interactions may be used to test their significance. By splitting up total variation in this way the research worker may be able to sort out the causes of observed variation in his data. The technique used is known as the analysis of variance (Hoel, 1955, pp. 248–64; 1960, pp. 182–93; Fisher, 1941, pp. 204–92).

The firms studied by Hart and MacBean have been classified into eight industry groups: chemicals (3 pairs of firms); metals (3 pairs of firms); shipbuilding and engineering (9 pairs of firms); textiles (6 pairs of firms); brewing and distilling (5 pairs of firms); paper and printing (9 pairs of firms); rubber and timber (7 pairs of firms) and a miscellaneous group consisting of 8 pairs of firms. The group means of profitability and growth were calculated for each year 1950–58, for each of the two regions. These aggregations provided eight groups of observations over nine years for two regions. An analysis of variance table was then constructed for profitability and for growth, the results of which are given in Tables 3 and 4.

The analysis of variance calculations for profitability reveal that the time–region interaction is not significant; as time has proceeded, the regions have not become more different. But individual industries have become more different through time when the regions are considered together because the industry–time

Table 3
Profitability

Source of variation	Degrees of freedom	Sum of squares	Mean squares	F
Regions (R)	1	13·26	13·26	0·14
Industries (I)	7	2700·64	385·81	†
Time (T)	8	583·00	72·88	5·20*
R×I	7	685·99	98·00	19·68*
T×I	56	784·87	14·02	2·82*
T×R	8	29·31	3·66	0·71
Residual	56	289·54	5·17	
Total	143	5086·61	—	—

* Significant at the 5 per cent level of F.

† Because the R × I and T × I interactions are significant, it is not possible to demonstrate the existence of the I main effect. See Brownlee (1949), p. 89.

Table 4
Growth

Source of variation	Degrees of freedom	Sum of squares	Mean squares	F
Regions (R)	1	5·40	5·40	0·14
Industries (I)	7	978·11	139·73	3·69
Time (T)	8	495·44	61·93	3·53*
R×I	7	265·29	37·90	2·16*
T×I	56	1204·60	21·51	1·53
T×R	8	152·75	19·09	1·44
Residual	56	744·89	13·03	—
Total	143	3846·48	—	—

* Significant at the 5 per cent level of F.

interaction is significant. So is the region–industry interaction. This means that the average performance of each industry through time has been affected by the region in which the industry is located. This is an important result especially when compared with the main region effect for there are no significant differences between the regions considered as a whole. Thus, although the regions as a whole do not differ from each other, individual industries do differ and the differences depend on the region in which these industries are located.

A similar result follows from the analysis of variance for growth given in Table 4. Again the time–region interaction is not significant. The industry–time interaction is not significant.[6] The industry–region interaction is significant. Thus the average growth of each industry over time is shown to depend on the region in which it is located even though, taking all industries together, there is not a significant difference between the regions.

The important conclusion, therefore, from Tables 3 and 4 is that it is not possible to distinguish between Scotland and England on the basis of profitability and growth if the influence of time and the differences between industries are averaged out in making comparisons. This is so (*inter alia*) because although the growth and profitability of an industry depends on the region in which it is located, so that some industries are more suited to Scotland and others to England, the better than average industries in each region more or less balance with the worse than average so that, considered as a whole, the regions appear similar.

F. Summary and Conclusions

In this paper calculations on Hart's and MacBean's data (Hart and MacBean, 1961) have been presented in order to throw further light on the relative advantages of operating in Scotland and England. In general, the conclusions do not conflict with those obtained by Hart and MacBean. There are apparently no differences between the average rate of profit earned on capital and no differences in average growth rates for the English and Scottish companies examined if these are compared in regional groups. This is true whether the variables are considered individually or

6. The calculated F value lies very close to the significance margin and it is difficult to tell on which side. In these circumstances the usual procedure is to favour the null hypothesis (that the observed differences are not significant). In doing so it is possible to test all of the main effects which would not be possible if the industry–time interaction was significant. Also, the tests of main effects are weighted in favour of accepting the null hypothesis of no differences and the industry–region interaction is significant irrespective of whether or not the industry–time interaction is significant.

jointly and whether dependence between the samples is allowed for or not.

From a methodological point of view the similarities between the two sets of results help illustrate the robustness of the tests used by Hart and MacBean. That is, the ability of the univariate t test and the univariate Welch–Aspin test to give substantially correct results even when dependence is multivariate and the assumptions of the tests are not strictly upheld. In many applications of statistical theory to economic problems, econometricians are often criticized for using the results of a body of theory in situations where the assumptions of the theory are not strictly valid. Fortunately the results of much theory remain substantially true even when assumptions fail to hold. This is not to suggest that applied economists should always adopt simple procedures or that assumptions do not matter. But it is to suggest that the results of some econometric work are not as susceptible to underlying assumptions as is often suggested and that very useful information can often be gained from simple procedures.

In section C and D the analysis was extended to consider other characteristics of the regional distributions of profitability and growth. The χ^2 tests showed that the distributions were similar though doubt was raised as to the power of the χ^2 test to detect differences when these were small and the samples were not large.

The discriminant analysis of section D showed the differences between the English and Scottish samples could be explained by a linear combination of a measure of variability of growth and variability of profitability. The conclusions of this analysis support some of the points made by Smyth (1961) but the results have been given a wider economic interpretation which is relevant in determining the relative advantages of locating in England and Scotland.

Finally, the analysis of section E revealed that although on average there are no differences in growth and no differences in profitability between Scottish and English firms if these are compared in regional groups, there are regional differences in profitability and in growth to the extent that individual industries have been more profitable and have grown faster in one region than in the other.

Some Statistical Techniques

References

ANDERSON, T. W. (1958) *Introduction to multivariate analysis*, Wiley.

BROWNLEE, K. A. (1949) *Industrial experimentation*, 4th edn., H.M.S.O.

COCHRAN, W. (1952) 'The x^2 test of goodness of fit', *Ann. Math. Statist.*, vol. 23, pp. 315–43.

EDWARDS, R. S., and TOWNSEND, H. (1958) *Business enterprise*, Macmillan.

FISHER, R. A. (1936) 'The use of multiple measurements in taxonomic problems', *Ann. Eugen., Lond.*, vol. 7, pp. 179–88.

FISHER, R. A. (1941), *Statistical methods for research workers*, 8th edn., Oliver and Boyd.

GUMBEL, E. J. (1943) 'On the reliability of the classical chi-square test', *Ann. Math. Statist.*, vol. 14, pp. 253–63.

HART, P. E., and MACBEAN, A. I. (1961) 'Regional differences in productivity, profitability and growth: a pilot study', *Scottish Journal of Political Economy*, vol. 8, pp. 1-11.

HOEL, P. G. (1955) *Introduction to mathematical statistics*, 2nd edn., Wiley.

HOEL, P. G. (1960) *Elementary Statistics*, Wiley.

HOTELLING, H. (1931) 'The generalization of student's ratio', *Ann. Math. Statist.*, vol. 2, pp. 360–78.

SCHEFFÉ, H. (1943) 'On solutions of the Behrens–Fisher problem based on the *t* distribution', *Ann. Math. Statist.*, vol. 14, pp. 35–44.

SMYTH, R. L. (1961) 'A note on regional differences in productivity, profitability and growth', *Scottish Journal of Political Economy*, vol. VIII, pp. 246–50.

STONE, R. (1960) 'A comparison of the economic structure of regions based on the concept of distance', *Journal of Regional Science*, vol. 2, pp. 1–20.

SUITS, D. B. (1957), 'Linear probability functions and discrimination' Discussion Paper, Research Seminar in Quantitative Economics, University of Michigan (mimeographed).

Further Reading

1 General works

The three best-known and probably most useful comprehensive introductions to regional economics are:

ISARD, W., *et al.* (1960) *Methods of regional analysis: an introduction to regional science*, M.I.T. Press.

PERLOFF, H. S., DUNN, E. S., LAMPARD, E. E., and MUTH, R. F. (1960) *Regions, resources, and economic growth*, Johns Hopkins Press.

FRIEDMANN, J., and ALONSO, W. (eds.) (1964) *Regional development and planning: a reader*, M.I.T. Press.

The first work discusses most of the major techniques used in regional analysis and has a magnificent bibliography on each technique or topic discussed. The second book is complementary to the first, in that, though some fifty pages are devoted to a summary of the theory of regional development, the greater part of the book is concerned with the application of the theory to explain regional development in the United States. The third work is a collection of some thirty-five papers on regional development many of them modern classics. There is also a useful guide to the literature.

The two major academic journals specializing in regional studies are:

Papers and Proceedings of the Regional Science Association and the *Journal of Regional Science*.

2 Regional accounting
Two surveys of regional accounting, both concentrating on the techniques used are:

STONE, R. (1966) 'Social accounts at the regional level: a survey', *Mathematics in the social sciences and other essays*, Chapman and Hall, pp. 118–51.

ISARD, (1960), ch. 4.

Most other aspects of regional accounting are discussed in papers in the following four collections of essays on regional accounting:

Regional income, National Bureau of Economic Research, Studies in Income and Wealth, vol. 21, Princeton University Press, 1957.

HOCHWALD, W. (ed.) (1961) *Design of regional accounts*, Johns Hopkins University Press.

HIRSCH, W. Z. (ed.) (1964) *Elements of regional accounts*, Johns Hopkins University Press.

HIRSCH, W. Z. (ed) (1966) *Regional accounts for policy decisions*, Johns Hopkins University Press.

Further Reading

3 Regional input–output analysis

Once more a survey of the topic is to be found in ISARD (1960), ch. 8.
An early classic in the field is:

LEONTIEF, W 'Interregional theory', in Leontief, W., *et al.* (1953) *Studies in the structure of the American economy*, Oxford University Press, pp. 93–115.

There have been a number of applications of the theory, three of the best of the empirical studies are:

MOSES, L. N. (1955) 'The stability of interregional trading patterns and input–output analysis', *American Economic Review*, vol. 45, pp. 803–32.

MOORE, F. T., and PETERSON, J. W. (1955) 'Regional analysis: an inter-industry model of Utah', *Review of Economics and Statistics*, vol. 37, pp. 368–83.

HANSEN, W. L., and TIEBOUT, C. M. (1963) 'An intersectoral flows analysis of the California economy', *Review of economics and statistics*, vol. 45, pp. 409–18.

4 Country studies

A useful comparative study of regional development in European countries is:

'Problems of regional development and industrial location in Europe' in *Economic survey of Europe in 1954*, United Nations, Department of Economic and Social Affairs, 1955, pp. 136–71.

References to a selection of the numerous case studies on individual countries are given in Friedmann and Alonso, op. cit. pp. 716–18.

A useful collection of such studies appearing after the publication of Friedmann and Alonso is:

Area Redevelopment Policies in Britain and the Countries of the Common Market, Area Redevelopment Administration, U.S. Department of Commerce, 1965.

5 Inter-regional trade and payments

For a survey of the analysis of trade and payments between regions, see Isard (1960), ch. 5. Much of the chapter is concerned with regional balance of payments adjustments. An interesting early article omitted from the bibliography in Isard (1960) is:

GILBERT, J. C. (1938) 'The mechanism of interregional redistributions of money', *Review of Economic Studies*, vol. 5, pp. 187–94.

Of the studies published after the compilation of the bibliography in Isard (1960) see:

MUNDELL, R. A. (1961) 'A theory of optimum currency areas', *American Economic Review*, vol. 51, pp. 657–65.

There are some areas which though virtually economic regions of another country are yet sufficiently separate politically so as to have their own international trade statistics. A good example of such a territory is Puerto Rico considered as a region of the United States.

INGRAM, J. C. (1962) *Regional payments mechanisms: the case of Puerto Rico*, University of North Carolina Press.

On the non-monetary aspects of inter-regional trade, a major development has been the attempt to synthesize trade and location theory.

ISARD, W., and PECK, M. J. (1954) 'Location theory and international and inter-regional trade theory', *Quarterly Journal of Economics*, vol. 68, pp. 97–114.

MOSES, L. N. (1960) 'A general equilibrium model of production inter-regional trade and location of industry', *Review of Economics and Statistics*, vol. 42, pp. 373–97.

6 Regional cycles and stabilization policy

Isard (1960), ch. 6 provides a survey of the field. A classical article on the subject is:

VINING, R. (1946) 'The region as a concept in business cycle analysis', *Econometrica*, vol. 14, pp. 201–18.

A good empirical study on the situation in the United States is:

BORTS, G. H. (1960) 'Regional cycles of manufacturing employment in the United States, 1914–1953', *Journal of the American Statistical Association*, vol. 55, pp. 151–211, reprinted as National Bureau of Economic Research Occasional Paper 73, 1960.

Two recent British studies of interest are:

THIRLWALL, A. P. (1966) 'Regional unemployment as a cyclical phenomenon', *Scottish Journal of Political Economy*, vol. 13, pp. 205–19.
BRECHLING, F. (1967) 'Trends and cycles in British regional employment', *Oxford Economic Papers*, vol. 19, pp. 1–21.

The paper by Thirlwall contains an account of an attempt to explain the relative fluctuations in regional employment compared with national levels in terms of the industrial structure of the regions. Only about half of the variation could be explained by the industrial composition of the region. See Thirlwall (1966), pp. 213–15.

7 Location theory

The bibliographic note by Alonso at the end of his article (p. 365 above) refers to most of the major works on location. An additional topic of importance, the application of linear programming to location decisions, is surveyed in Isard (1960), ch. 10. See also:

BECKMAN, M., and MARSHAK, T. (1955) 'An activity analysis approach to location theory', *Kyklos*, vol. 8, pp. 125–41.

The most thorough empirical study of location in Britain is:

LUTTRELL, W. F. (1961) *Factory location and industrial movement*, National Institute of Economic and Social Research, London, 2 vols.

8 Statistical techniques

The boundaries of regional analysis are too ill-defined for there to be any single book explaining all the statistical techniques that a regional economist might wish to use. Nor is there any agreement even on the minimum statistical knowledge required for professional competence. In these circumstances, suggestions for further reading must be of a fairly general nature.

Most introductory texts that assume no previous knowledge of statistics cover such topics as: summarizing data, sampling, testing hypotheses, simple regression, occasionally reaching the fringes of analysing relationships between many variables. Three out of the many good books at this level are:

HOEL, P. G. *Elementary Statistics*, Wiley, 1960

SUITS, D. B. (1963) *Statistics: an introduction to quantitative economic research*, Rand McNally and Co.

WALLIS, W. A., and ROBERTS, H. V. (1956) *Statistics: a new approach*, Free Press of Glencoe.

Beyond this level come the more specialist works that assume that their readers have some previous statistical knowledge. Most of the works referred to by Fisher in his article (pp. 369–82 above) fall into this category.

Three broad topics of particular interest to social scientists are multiple regression analysis, multivariate analysis and the analysis of variance and covariance. An introduction to multiple regression analysis in which the mathematics is kept to a minimum is:

EZEKIEL, M., and FOX, K. A. (1959) *Methods of correlation and regression analysis*, Wiley, 3rd edn.

Two more advanced works dealing with mutiple regression but containing much more besides on the economic applications of statistical techniques are:

JOHNSTON, J. (1963) *Econometric methods*, McGraw-Hill.

CHRIST, C. (1966) *Econometric models and methods*, Wiley.

On multivariate analysis, a concise introduction is given in:

KENDALL, M. G. (1961) *A course in multivariate analysis*, Griffin.

An elementary non-mathematical treatment of the analysis of variance and covariance can be found in:

SNEDECOR, G. W. (1946) *Statistical methods*, Collegiate Press, 4th edn., ch. 10–13.

A more advanced treatment is:

SCHEFFE, H. (1961) *The analysis of variance*, Wiley.

Finally, a comprehensive work of statistical reference is:

KENDALL, M. G., and STUART, A. (1958–66) *The advanced theory o statistics*, Griffin, 3 vols.

Acknowledgements

Permission to reprint the readings published in this volume is acknowledged from the following sources:

Reading 1   John Meyer and the American Economic Association
Reading 2   Charles L. Leven and the Regional Science Association
Reading 3   Charles M. Tiebout and the *Southern Economic Journal*
Reading 4   The University of Chicago Press
Reading 5   *Scheizerische Zeitschrift für Volkswirtschaft und Statistik*
Reading 6   The *Quarterly Journal of Economics* and Harvard University Press
Reading 7   James C. Ingram, the *Quarterly Journal of Economics* and Harvard University Press
Reading 8   John R. Moroney and the University of Chicago Press
Reading 9   The Brookings Institution
Reading 10 The M.I.T. Press
Reading 11 Oliver & Boyd Ltd

Author Index

389

Author Index

Subject Index

Penguin Modern Economics

Other titles available in this series are:

Economics of Education 1
Ed. M. Blaug

The quality of the labour force and the methods of training it have
recently attracted the attention of economists. The education system
is an important factor in economic growth, the degree of mobility of
labour and the distribution of income. These important issues are
considered in this volume of articles. A second volume, also edited by
Professor Blaug, will examine the internal efficiency of schools and the
relations between the costs of education and methods of financing these
costs. These Readings will be widely welcomed by educationists,
sociologists and political scientists as well as economists. X56

The Labour Market
Ed. B. J. McCormick and E. Owen Smith

'Workers cannot be bought and sold, and people cannot be
disassociated from their services.' This is the starting point for an
analysis of the workings of the labour market. Wages are a means of
allocating labour and a source of income, and considerations of
efficiency frequently clash with equity criteria. This volume of Readings
throws light on the efficiency of the wage system as an allocator of
labour, the effects of trade unions and the role of the labour market in
the problem of inflation. X55

Managerial Economics
Ed. G. P. E. Clarkson

The growth, range and complexity of problems facing the modern
corporation mean that many managers must acquire new skills.
Managerial Economics deals with the process of decision making within
the firm. It uses the economist's concepts of utility and maximizing of
profit to analyse with mathematical and statistical techniques a wide
range of problems of finance, marketing and production. X57

Public Enterprise
Ed. R. Turvey

The public sector as a consumer of resources and a producer of goods and services is apparent. But the methods of ensuring efficiency in public corporations are not obvious. Public enterprises may aim at social as well as commercial ends in conjunction with a private sector which is all too often imperfect in structure and behaviour. This volume of Readings is deliberately selective and provocative in an area where there is much confusion and disagreement. X59

Transport
Ed. Denys Munby

'There is no escape from transport.' 'Almost every transport decision is a public issue.' These two challenging statements form the prelude to a collection of articles devoted to the economics of transport. The quality of the analysis and prescriptions is dictated by Dupuit's article and proceeds through Lewis, Vickrey, Walters, Meyer and Foster. All demonstrate the important contribution economists can make to the analysis of transport problems and the formulation of appropriate policies. X58